The
COUNTRY
MUSIC
Book

The COUNTRY MUSIC Book

Edited by
MICHAEL MASON

CHARLES SCRIBNER'S SONS

NEW YORK

Copyright © 1985 Michael Mason

Library of Congress Cataloging in Publication Data
Main entry under title:
The Country music book.
    Includes record reviews and index.
    "Country music books, magazines, and movies /Robert K. Oermann": p.
    1. Country music—History and criticism.   2. Country musicians.   3. Country music—Vocational guidance.   4. Music trade.   5. Sound recordings—Reviews.
I. Mason, Michael, 1939–
ML3524.C69 1985   784.5'2'009   85-1880
ISBN 0-684-18013-8
ISBN 0-684-18046-4 (pbk.)

This book published simultaneously in the United States of America and in Canada—Copyright under the Berne Convention.

1 3 5 7 9 11 13 15 17 19 V/C 20 18 16 14 12 10 8 6 4 2

Printed in the United States of America.

CONTENTS

ACKNOWLEDGMENTS

The editor and authors would like to thank Richard Harbert, former editor and publisher of the *Nashville Gazette*; Carolyn Lloyd, whose idea initiated this project; Ronnie Pugh and all the staff of the Country Music Foundation Library and Media Center; the staff of the Jimmie Rodgers Museum in Meridian, Mississippi; John Groomer and Capitol Records; John Morris of Old Homestead Records; Charles Wolfe; Jeff Richardson; Keith Kolby; Russ Bernard and *Country Music* magazine; Tom Wheeler of *Guitar Player* magazine; Ebie Ensign of the Northern Westchester Bluegrass Society and Woodchuck Productions; Beth Kirshner; Tom and Patricia Eaton of Eaton Productions; John Keil; France Menk; Ludwig Lanko; the helpful staffs of Rutledge and Scribners; devoted archivists Rees and Jerry Mason; Patti Lynn Glenn; and Jemima James Mason. Some of the information contained in the brief biographies in the "Listening" section was supplied by record companies and the artists themselves. However, most was drawn from books listed in the "Reading" section; any errors of transcription or interpretation are the editor's.

CONTRIBUTORS

MICHAEL MASON plays guitar, bass, banjo, keyboards, and bagpipes. He has worked as a staff songwriter for Leeds Music/MCA, done independent record production, and has worked in clubs throughout the country as a singer and instrumentalist. He continues to write songs, is the author of children's books and short stories, and works as an editor and writer.

ROBERT K. OERMANN is the daily popular music reporter for *The Tennessean* and the weekly entertainment writer in Nashville for *U.S.A. Today*. He has written for many other publications, including *Billboard, Esquire, Bluegrass Unlimited, Frets, Country Song Roundup*, and *The Journal of Country Music*.

RICH KIENZLE has worked as a music critic, historian, and journalist since 1975. A longtime contributing editor to *Country Music Magazine* and author of that magazine's "Buried Treasures" column, his articles have appeared in numerous other music publications. He served as a consultant for the Time-Life Country Classics series of historical reissue record albums. He is the author of *Great Guitarists* and *Rockabilly*.

JOHN LOMAX III has worked in Nashville since 1973 as a publicist, promotion man, journalist, and manager. He is currently the Nashville editor of *Country Rhythms* magazine and he has written for such publications as *Esquire, The Record, Texas Monthly*, and *Billboard*.

BOB MILLARD is currently the Nashville correspondent for *Variety* and for *Pro Sound News*. His work is published frequently in leading country music periodicals, including *Country Music, Country Rhythms, Country Song Roundup*, and *Tune-In*.

PREFACE

The Country Music Book is intended as a guide for listeners, players, and those hoping for a professional career in this field. The book traces the development of country music through some seventy years to the present. The authors and editor have tried to create a compact but complete history of the major song and instrumental styles of country music, one that is useful and interesting in itself, and that also functions as a structure into which the recommended recordings and publications listed here—and the many others available from sources listed here—may be fitted. This book is not intended to be encyclopedic; well over a thousand different artists have had records on the national country charts in the last thirty-five years, and many others—including some fine musicians and writers—have released records that never sold enough copies to make those charts.

Therefore, in trying to indicate the lines of development within country music, we have had to limit the number of specific performers included. The artists and albums included were chosen not necessarily because they are "the best" (though a great many of them are considered to be), but because we felt that they best represent a certain period, style, or essential influence in country music. There are some wonderful performers and many wonderful albums (by performers listed and unlisted here) that readers will have the opportunity of discovering for themselves—the histories, reference books, and discographies described in the "Reading" section of this book will prove useful guides in that effort. Also useful will be the Phonolog listing of records in print (available for use in most record stores and many public libraries) and, for new material, the charts published in Billboard and Cashbox magazines, and the reviews in specialized country and bluegrass publications listed in the "Reading" appendix.

Readers should keep in mind that virtually all of the artists included here to some degree transcend categories of period or style. Jerry Lee Lewis, for example, listed here under "Mainstream Country," is viewed by many as the supreme master of rockabilly. Others whose work is listed in earlier categories in the "Listening" section continue to be major hit-making artists in the 1980s.

There are a few areas of country music that, regrettably, we couldn't fit into the scale of this volume, but that can be further researched with the help of the reference books and other publications listed here. The work of the great trucking triumvirate, Dick Curless, Dave Dudley, and Red Sovine, is an example. Similarly, we had to make the hard decision to leave out—on the grounds that their identification was less with country than with rhythm-and-blues or rock—geniuses Chuck Berry and Ray Charles, and such other gifted performers and writers as Tracy Nelson, Jesse Winchester, and The Band. Bluegrass is another area where making selections was particularly difficult. This form of country, with its own record labels, concert and festival circuits, and devoted audiences, is coming to include an increasingly wide range of American acoustic music. Stellar performers ranging (in closeness to traditional styles) from the Seldom Scene to Peter Rowan have created artistic space for themselves between the old and the new in this field. Readers may note other areas of omission, and we would be very happy to hear from them, with an eye toward future editions of this book.

M.M.

INTRODUCTION: A BRIEF HISTORY OF COUNTRY MUSIC

Robert K. Oermann

Of the three American musical traditions that came together to form modern country music, the oldest is folk music, a heritage that reaches deep into the past of American culture and its roots. In southern mountain areas, such traditional British ballads as "Barbara Allen," "Pretty Polly," "Greensleeves," and "Black Jack Davy" were part of the rural musician's repertoire. The occupational songs of working men such as cowboys, coal miners, train men, soldiers, and farmers, form another American folk idiom that provided significant additions to early country music. Topical folk songs, usually composed to moralize on a noteworthy event or tragedy, included such classics as "Tom Dooley," "Casey Jones," and "The Wreck of the Old 97." Blues music from the Afro-American tradition was also tremendously influential on early country styles.

Traditional fiddle tunes like "The Eighth of January" and "Sallie Gooden" were other contributions from country's folk roots. The tunings of the fiddle and the mournful, minor tones of the dulcimer—both traditional instruments brought to this country by early settlers—formed a melodic basis for early country music. These instruments gave country music tunes the minor-key quality that is prevalent to this day, while the ballad tradition gave them a respect for lyrics and words they have never lost.

The conventions of nineteenth-century American show business also were a major influence on commercial country music. The sentimental lyrics of the so-called "parlor" or "heart" songs produced by Tin Pan Alley in massive numbers from the 1880s to the beginning of the Jazz Age were certainly one of the strongest of these conventions. The Victorian songs of dying mothers, tragic love affairs, orphaned (or crippled or blind) children, pitiful tramps, and broken hearts were kept alive in rural areas long after urbanites had moved on to the Charleston, flappers, and more modern lyric topics. These formed the literal basis for early country songs as well as the spiritual basis for later country material. Numbers like "Maple on the Hill," "The Letter Edged in Black," "Molly Darlin'," and "Wildwood Flower" are generally thought of as country music standards, but they all originated in nineteenth-century sheet music.

Performance styles from nineteenth-century stage entertainment were also kept alive in country music. From the minstrel show tradition came up-tempo country novelty tunes like "Old Dan Tucker," "Turkey in the Straw," and "Buffalo Gals." Early country

1

The cast of Chicago's WLS radio broadcast, "National Barn Dance."

performances incorporated humor from the South's traveling minstrel shows and some of vaudeville's old jokes and comedy situations. Vaudeville also provided the stage "hayseed" conventions that early country performers adopted; this rube image and its costumes can still be seen today on the TV show "Hee Haw." Medicine shows, which toured widely throughout the nineteenth-century South, left their mark on early country music, too. The way country shows were staged, the touring and promotion methods they used, and frequently the medicine show performers themselves, greatly influenced country music's development.

Instruments from show business were selectively adopted by country performers. The popularity of the banjo, mandolin, and guitar with country musicians can be traced in part to their use by entertainment professionals who toured the South in the late nineteenth and early twentieth centuries. Later, the nationwide popularity of Hawaiian music and musicians contributed the distinctive sounds of the Dobro and steel guitar to country music.

The existence of a theatrical shouting banjo song like "Are You from Dixie?" alongside a traditional ballad like "Streets of Laredo" encapsulates the mixing of two musical traditions that form country music. Early commercial hillbilly music was certainly folk-derived and close to an amateur music-making tradition, but it was also part of American show business and drew from the sounds and styles of professional entertainment.

The third major tradition involved in country music is that of old-time religion. From nineteenth-century gospel music came many of country's melodies and harmonies, as well as a certain vocal fervor. Besides touring minstrel, tent, and medicine shows, the only music from outside the rural community came with the traveling evangelists and singing-school teachers. These folks taught isolated families how to sing harmonies at large gatherings such as camp meetings and popularized hundreds of standards like "Amazing Grace" and "Can the Circle Be Unbroken?" by selling their hymnals and tunebooks. There is hardly a country musician, living or dead, who does not trace his or her musical experience back to religious singing. The pounding gospel piano and wheezing church pump organ have been extremely influential.

Exuberant revival singing, fiddle and string band music at square dances, hokum comedy and novelty performances, blues moaning, mournful ballad singing, and living-room harmonizing of sentimental old songs might have continued to exist on a purely local level had it not been for the coming of radio and records. The mass media made it possible for country music to become an industry.

Radio technology had been around for a few years by 1920, but it was the inauguration of commercial radio broadcasting in Pittsburgh in that year that opened the doors for local entertainers to reach wider audiences. By 1922 both Fort Worth's station WBAP and Atlanta's WSB were featuring programs by favorite local fiddlers and gospel singers. In 1924 Chicago's WLS began its hugely popular "National Barn Dance," which spread the fame of country musicians far and wide. A year later WSM in Nashville began broadcasting what became known as "The Grand Ole Opry," now the longest-running, continuously aired radio show in America.

The crowd outside the Eighth Street Theatre in Chicago, from which the "National Barn Dance" originated. This photo was taken on July 22, 1933. (Country Music Foundation)

Phonograph records had been produced since 1877, but the business only really began to thrive around World War I. At first only the affluent could afford record players, but as prices came down the machines were increasingly found in working-class homes as well. Vaudevillians had recorded hicks-in-the-sticks comedy sketches, and some violinists had recorded rural standards like "Arkansas Traveler" prior to the 1920s, but it was not until 1922 that authentically rural musicians were recorded. To their surprise, record company officials discovered that there was a good-sized market for records made by poor blacks and whites. They began recording blues and country musicians with regularity in the mid-1920s. This, coupled with radio broadcasting, began the country music business.

The first "star" in the hillbilly field was an Atlanta musician named Fiddlin' John Carson, who performed on that city's WSB radio station, won many Southern fiddle contests, and sold thousands of records in the Southeast for the Okeh and Bluebird labels. His recording of "The Little Old Log Cabin in the Lane" and "The Old Hen Cackled and the Rooster's Going to Crow" is sometimes cited as country music's first hit. Carson was not the only early fiddling country star; throughout the 1920s the fiddle, not the guitar, was the central country instrument. Clayton McMichen, Earl Johnson, Uncle

Fiddlin' John Carson (Country Music Foundation)

Jimmy Thompson, Eck Robertson, Gid Tanner, Fiddling Powers, and Bob Larkin were all popular country fiddlers of this era.

In 1924 "The Prisoner's Song" and "The Wreck of the Old 97" were recorded by a Texas operetta tenor who called himself Vernon Dalhart. They were issued back-to-back on what became country music's first million-selling record. Under this name and a bewildering number of pseudonyms, Dalhart recorded a prodigious quantity of folk songs, ballads, sentimental parlor songs, and comic ditties over the next few years, virtually defining the early country singer's repertoire.

Another early milestone was Victor Records' discovery of Jimmie Rodgers and the Carter Family in 1927. Their nationwide popularity assured record executives, once and for all, that authentic country music would constitute a significant disc market. Rodgers—billed as "The Singing Brakeman" and "America's Blue Yodeler"—became the single most influential singer in country music history, despite his short, tubercular life. Rodgers's style is a perfect illustration of the way country music absorbed elements of black music. Several of his most black-derived songs like "Muleskinner Blues," "T for Texas," and "In the Jailhouse Now" are still widely performed today. The Carter Family (A.P., Sara, and Maybelle) can lay claim to being the most important song preservers in country music history. Their "Wabash Cannonball," "Can the Circle Be Unbroken?," "Wildwood Flower," "Worried Man Blues," and hundreds of other songs are immortal pieces of Americana. In addition, Maybelle's guitar playing was largely responsible for transforming the instrument from background rhythm to lead status in popular music.

Ballad singers and string bands coexisted on radio and records just as they had in the folk tradition and on the commercial stage. Popular string bands of the 1920s included the Skillet Lickers, Charlie Poole's North Carolina Ramblers, the Leake County Revelers, the Stoneman Family, Al Hopkins's Original Hill Billies, the East Texas Serenaders, and Otto Gray's Oklahoma Cowboys. Besides Dalhart and Rodgers, some of the influential early singers were Henry Whitter, Carl T. Sprague, Kelly Harrell, Clarence Ashley, Riley Puckett, and, most important, Bradley Kincaid.

Kincaid recorded a great deal, but his greatest impact was probably as a radio star. With the coming of the Depression in the 1930s record sales fell drastically. Country music thrived, however, for this became a golden era for the radio barn dance programs. And Bradley Kincaid was a star on the most powerful of them, WLS's "National Barn Dance." Later, he became one of the first radio entertainers to take country music into the Northeast, but it was at WLS that he first made his mark.

Chicago's "National Barn Dance" was so popular that one of its stars, Lulu Belle, was voted the most popular female radio entertainer in America in the mid-1930s. Others the show brought to prominence included Mac and Bob, Louise Massey and the Westerners, Red Foley, Arkie the Arkansas Woodchopper, the Girls of the Golden West, Grace Wilson, the Hoosier Hot Shots, and the Cumberland Ridge Runners. It also featured the first woman in country music to have a million-selling record, Patsy Montana (and her excellent Prairie Ramblers band). Not the least of the show's accomplishments was the launching of singing cowboy Gene Autry.

Autry was at the forefront of country's singing cowboys, and this put him at the

Bradley Kincaid (Country Music Foundation)

Patsy Montana (Country Music Foundation)

The Ryman Auditorium in Nashville, former home of the "Grand Ole Opry" (Bob Millard)

forefront of country music, for the cowboy image took hold in the 1930s and 1940s to the virtual exclusion of all others. The dominant figures were the Sons of the Pioneers, Roy Rogers, Tex Ritter, Eddie Dean, Ray Whitley, Foy Willing and the Riders of the Purple Sage, Red River Dave, Wilf Carter, and Rex Allen, but even performers of non-western material adopted the cowboy look. For a time, the image was so popular that the entire field became known as "country and western music."

Gene Autry was also notable as one of the few country performers who continued to record all through the lean Depression years. Others who did included some of WSM's Grand Ole Opry acts. Although not as popular as WLS's "National Barn Dance," the Opry was heard by millions each week and several of its early stars achieved wide acclaim. Boisterous, banjo-whacking Uncle Dave Macon was first and foremost of these. The Pickard Family, and Asher and Little Jimmie Sizemore, were two sometime Opry acts who nearly equaled Bradley Kincaid as national popularizers of mountain and old-time songs. Fiddling Arthur Smith, the Delmore Brothers, Sam and Kirk McGee, the Vagabonds, DeFord Bailey, Sarie and Sally, Zeke Clements, and Texas Ruby also made their reputations on Nashville's radio barn dance.

The third major Depression-era country radio show was in Wheeling, West Virginia, where WWVA began broadcasting its "Jamboree" in 1933. There, the talents of such stars as Grandpa Jones, Wilma Lee and Stoney Cooper, and Doc Williams were developed.

The 1930 cast of the "Grand Ole Opry" (Country Music Foundation)

WLS, WSM, and WWVA were all tremendously successful with their radio country music programs. As a result, by the 1940s the "barn dance" shows were everywhere in America. They thrived in Cincinnati (WLW), Shreveport (KWKH), Des Moines (WHO), Richmond (WRVA), Springfield (KWTO), Kansas City (KMBC), Fort Wayne (WOWO), Tulsa (KVOO), St. Louis (KMOX), Minneapolis/St. Paul (KSTP), Dallas (KRLD), and dozens of smaller cities. Even radio stations in New England, Canada, Philadelphia, and New York City had radio barn dances during the 1940s. The country craze was tied to the fad for movie "shoot-em-ups," cowboys, and all things Western during this period. Besides the radio barn dance shows, dude ranches, rodeos, John Ford movies, country music parks, and Western clothes were extremely popular. Country music boomed.

In addition, the cultural activities of the Library of Congress and WPA (Works Progress Administration) had enlivened an interest in American folk culture. Country musicians naturally benefited from this.

It was not only a movement of people coming around to liking country music, however. Country reached out to them as well. Commercial country music had changed a great deal during the first two decades of its existence, and many of the changes attracted a broader audience.

First of all, highly professional songwriters had come to the hillbilly field and many of their products soon attracted a mass audience. Country performers who at first had recycled old-time tunes and folk songs were creating a good deal of their own material by the mid-1930s. One of the earliest song professionals was Blind Andy Jenkins, who wrote many popular religious and topical songs such as "The Death of Floyd Collins" and "God Put a Rainbow in the Clouds." Even more significant were the hits produced by the prolific Carson Robison ("My Blue Ridge Mountain Home," "Barnacle Bill the

Sailor," "Left My Gal in the Mountains") and Bob Miller ("21 Years," "Rocking Alone in an Old Rocking Chair," "There's a Star-Spangled Banner Waving Somewhere"). These men were followed in the 1940s by a host of gifted country writers, including Stuart Hamblen, Fred Rose, Bob Nolan, and Cindy Walker.

A second important trend that broadened country music's popularity was the development of several major stars whose songs and styles had mass appeal. Jimmie Davis, who had huge hits with "Nobody's Darling But Mine" and "You Are My Sunshine," was one of these. Roy Acuff became known as the "King of Country Music" because of the wide popularity of numbers like "Wreck on the Highway" and "Great Speckled Bird." Comedienne/singer Judy Canova parlayed country success into a major film and radio career, and the Opry's humorous Minnie Pearl also became widely loved. The gospel-singing Chuck Wagon Gang built a career of astounding longevity and popularity. The beautiful harmonies of many brother acts delighted the ears of radio listeners during the 1930s and 1940s. The Blue Sky Boys, the Shelton Brothers, the Mainers, the Callahan Brothers, the Morris Brothers, and dozens of others gave country music some of its most lasting songs.

A meshing of pop and country styles also contributed to country's increasing popularity. The music of Hollywood's singing cowboys like Gene Autry ("Back in the Saddle

Minnie Pearl (Country Music Foundation)

The Chuck Wagon Gang (Country Music Foundation)

Again," "That Silver-Haired Daddy of Mine") and the Sons of the Pioneers ("Tumbling Tumbleweeds," "Cool Water") is a perfect example of this process. Another is the amalgam of country and jazz. Called Western swing, this genre was country music's answer to the big-band swing music of the day. It was spawned in Texas and Oklahoma by groups like Bill Boyd's Cowboy Ramblers, the Light Crust Doughboys, and Milton Brown's Musical Brownies. But the exemplary Western swing unit was unquestionably Bob Wills's Texas Playboys, whose "Faded Love" and "San Antonio Rose" are timeless.

Bill Monroe's construction of a band featuring Lester Flatt and Earl Scruggs in the 1940s brought old-timey songs and the string band concept to a wider audience. It also began one of country music's most universally loved genres, bluegrass music. Bluegrass is essentially acoustic old-time music with added urgency, flash, and drive—Alan Lomax called it "folk music in overdrive." Through popular acts like Reno and Smiley, Mac Wiseman, Jim and Jesse, the Stanley Brothers, Jimmy Martin, and the Osborne Brothers, bluegrass has brought old-fashioned country sounds to millions of new fans.

Besides developing gifted songwriters and stars and new styles such as Western swing and bluegrass, country music broadened its popularity by absorbing and incorporating music from America's diverse ethnic groups. The German/Slavic polka tradition entered the country mainstream in bands like that of Adolph Hofner, and for a time in the 1940s its lead instrument, the accordion, was ever-present in country bands. Cajun music from

Louisiana had been popular with country audiences since the late 1920s, but national hits in the 1940s like "Jole Blon" solidified this and resulted in performers like Moon Mullican, Jimmy C. Newman, and Doug Kershaw becoming strongly identified as "country" in decades to come. Mexican songs like "Cielito Lindo" became country standards, too, and English-Spanish bilingual singing by Tex-Mex bands came to be considered country music as well. Diverse folk material from the likes of Burl Ives, Woody Guthrie, Pete Seeger, Cisco Houston, Jean Ritchie, Leadbelly, and the Weavers was easily absorbed. Indeed, there was a period in the late 1940s and early 1950s when record companies lumped all their country-related products under the heading "folk music."

World War II thrust America fully and unalterably into the modern world. Country music, like nearly every other aspect of American society, was never the same again. Social upheaval and disruption deeply changed the content and style of the country song. As the music of everyday life, country began to focus increasingly on problems of divorce, job, infidelity, and disillusionment. "Born to Lose" (1943), "Pistol Packin' Mama" (1943), "Divorce Me C.O.D." (1946), and "Smoke! Smoke! Smoke! (That Cigarette)" (1947) typify the big hits of the immediate postwar era.

Increased social mobility had transplanted large populations of working people to the labor camps of California and the oil fields of Texas. There, drinking and rough bar life forged the dominant postwar country style—honky-tonk music. Besides adult, hard-

Woody Guthrie (Country Music Foundation)

hitting lyrics, honky-tonk music featured the wail of the electric guitar, the thump of drums, and the whine of the pedal steel guitar.

No performer better illustrates the style and content of classic honky-tonk music than Hank Williams. After Jimmie Rodgers, Williams is surely the most influential of country's singer-songwriters. The sounds of "Lovesick Blues," "Cold, Cold Heart," "I'm So Lonesome I Could Cry," "Your Cheatin' Heart," "I Saw the Light," "Jambalaya," and "Hey, Good Lookin' " influence country music to this day.

The other major honky-tonk stars were Ernest Tubb, Al Dexter, Ray Price, Lefty Frizzell, Ted Daffan, and Floyd Tillman. Latter-day practitioners of this emotional, note-bending style include George Jones and Moe Bandy. All of these men came from Texas, the state that can justifiably claim preeminence in the development of postwar talent and trends.

Nevertheless, it was Nashville, Tennessee, that became the world's country music capital during this era. In the late 1940s and early 1950s the Grand Ole Opry began to gather talent on a scale that lifted it to the front ranks of the barn dance shows. For duets it acquired the Wilburn Brothers, Johnnie and Jack, and the Louvin Brothers. For female performers it signed Kitty Wells, Jean Shepard, Mother Maybelle and the Carter Sisters, and Del Wood. The emotion-packed voices of Webb Pierce, Hank Snow, the Bailes Brothers, Ernest Tubb, George Morgan, Little Jimmy Dickens, Carl Smith, Porter Wagoner, and Faron Young soon filled its broadcasts. These talents in turn attracted others to Nashville: Marty Robbins, Ferlin Husky, Sonny James, Hank Locklin. Most significant

"Grand Ole Opry" founder George D. Hay, whose voice announced the start of Opry broadcasts for decades (Country Music Foundation)

of all the immigrants were Eddy Arnold and Pee Wee King. Arnold was to become the most successful and wealthy country singer of all time and a leader in popularizing Nashville music nationally.

Pee Wee King and songwriter Redd Stewart co-wrote the songs that put Nashville on the map as a song publishing center: "Slow Poke," "You Belong to Me," "Bonaparte's Retreat," and "Tennessee Waltz." The last-named became the biggest hit in popular music history. In hopes of emulating its spectacular success, songwriters and song publishers set up shop in Tennessee's capital all through the 1950s. Acuff-Rose, a Nashville publishing outfit founded in 1942, was soon joined by many similar firms trying to duplicate the golden touch it had with the tunes of King and Stewart, Hank Williams, and its founders Roy Acuff and Fred Rose ("Blue Eyes Crying in the Rain," "Low and Lonely").

Shortly after Acuff-Rose started making Nashville a song publishing center, RCA Records initiated the process that soon made the city a recording center as well. In December 1944 the company recorded Eddy Arnold in Nashville at WSM. In 1946 Decca Records recorded Red Foley and Ernest Tubb in the city, and within a few years all of the major record labels were recording their country acts in Nashville as well. In time, the city was to become a record-making mecca for all kinds of American popular music.

The centralizing of country talent in Nashville, the development of a lucrative songwriting and song publishing scene there, and the decision of all the major record labels to make it a center for recording studios combined to give the city the label "Music City U.S.A." by the mid-1950s. All kinds of southern talent sang into its studios' microphones. Thus it was that teenage rockabilly stars like Elvis Presley, the Everly Brothers, and Brenda Lee came to town to sing.

The up-tempo, beat-heavy rockabilly style had been developed largely in Memphis by country-reared performers like Elvis, Carl Perkins, Jerry Lee Lewis, Roy Orbison, and Conway Twitty. But the breakthrough rockabilly artist, Bill Haley, was East Coast–based; and the form was also developed in California (Eddie Cochran, Gene Vincent) and in the Southwest (Buddy Holly, Wanda Jackson). Rockabilly was country's essential contribution to the musical revolution of the mid-1950s.

While the massive sales figures of Elvis Presley and Brenda Lee certainly helped the Nashville recording industry, the overall radio trend to teen-oriented music hurt the average adult-oriented country artist. In response, Nashville's record producers developed an appealing, country-pop music style known as the "Nashville Sound." The "heart" in the country singer's voice and the skill of the country songwriter were retained, but backing the singer and the song were violin sections (not fiddles), piano filigrees, and smooth-sounding background voices. Only the strumming rhythm guitar sound was kept from earlier country records' instrumentation. The Nashville Sound was largely created by producer-executive Chet Atkins (at RCA), a former country guitarist; Owen Bradley (at Decca), an ex-WSM pianist and bandleader; producer Don Law (at Columbia); and Anita Kerr, a Memphis-raised vocal arranger. Their talents were combined with a small, close-knit group of professional studio musicians, often led by guitarist Grady Martin, who worked together to create this easy-going, efficient recording style.

By the early 1960s records by Nashville Sound artists like Patsy Cline, Jim Reeves, Bobby Bare, the Browns, Don Gibson, and Eddy Arnold were appearing regularly on the big-money pop music charts as well as on country listings.

A second folk revival helped country music, too. Acts like the Kingston Trio, Joan Baez, Peter, Paul and Mary, Ian and Sylvia, Buffy Saint Marie, Gordon Lightfoot, and Judy Collins redirected national attention to America's folk roots. From the ranks of these late 1950s and early 1960s folk revivalists came later country stars like John Denver, Don Williams, and Emmylou Harris. Equally important, the movement aided the saga-song successes of Johnny Horton ("The Battle of New Orleans"), Claude King ("Wolverton Mountain"), Jimmy Dean ("Big Bad John"), Stonewall Jackson ("Waterloo"), and Marty Robbins ("El Paso"), and revitalized the careers of many bluegrass and old-time country performers.

The Nashville Sound and folk revival forces were met by the energies of the Country Music Association (CMA), a promotion organization formed to bring radio stations back to country music. In 1961 there were only 81 full-time country radio stations in the United States. Twenty years later, there were more than 1,800, and largely through their influence country now sells more records than any other musical genre except the vast, amorphous pop/rock category. Country also has its own nationally televised awards show, museum, songwriters organization, Hall of Fame, library, and archive. No other form of American popular music can say that.

In addition to all this Nashville-based activity, country music thrived elsewhere. Elton Britt recorded in New York City. Slim Whitman was based at "The Louisiana Hayride" in Shreveport. The West Coast had long been an important country center. Performers such as Spade Cooley ("Shame on You"), Hank Thompson ("Wild Side of Life"), Tennessee Ernie Ford ("Sixteen Tons"), and Merle Travis ("So Round, So Firm, So Fully Packed") already had enjoyed considerable success there. Then, in the 1960s Bakersfield, a small city in hot central California, became the new country locus. The most successful of its performers was Buck Owens, who ruled the roost with an incredible streak of country hits. Another, Merle Haggard, became one of America's popular music giants with his mastery of virtually all styles and aspects of country music.

The 1960s also saw the elevation of several country stars to TV-star status. Red Foley ("The Ozark Jubilee") and Jimmy Dean ("Town and Country Time") were pioneers in this area in the 1950s, but neither ever got the level of media attention accorded Glen Campbell and Johnny Cash. Roy Clark and Buck Owens headlined the most durable country television venture of all, "Hee Haw." Roger Miller, Charley Pride, Tammy Wynette, Lynn Anderson, and several other country personalities enjoyed national media attention as well during this decade. Next, country musicians like Kris Kristofferson, Jerry Reed, Willie Nelson, and Dolly Parton made the transition to movie stardom.

One of the major trends of recent years has been the ascendance of country music women. Despite breakthroughs by Patsy Montana (1935: "I Wanna Be a Cowboy's Sweetheart"), Kitty Wells (1952: "It Wasn't God Who Made Honky Tonk Angels"), and Patsy Cline (1961: "I Fall to Pieces"), no decade prior to the 1970s saw many female country artists in the top rank of popularity. And as always, country music reflected the

Elton Britt (Country Music Foundation)

spirit of the times, for all three of the leaders—Loretta Lynn, Tammy Wynette, and Dolly Parton—made their reputations singing strongly female-oriented material.

Another major trend has been the discovery of country music by rock performers, resulting in country-rock, a form exemplified by acts like the late Gram Parsons, Poco, the Eagles, Linda Ronstadt, and the Burrito Brothers. Asleep at the Wheel, Commander Cody and His Lost Planet Airmen, Jimmy Buffett, the Grateful Dead, the Marshall Tucker Band, and the Amazing Rhythm Aces also contributed stylistic elements to this genre. Groups like Alabama and the Charlie Daniels Band demonstrated that the musical cross-pollination could go from country to rock as well.

This was also a feature of country's so-called Outlaw movement. Spearheaded by Willie Nelson and Waylon Jennings's renegade wishes to make country music their own way rather than by Nashville methods, a loose-knit group of performers conducted rock-flavored musical experimentation around Austin, Texas. Ultimately, several became commercially highly successful.

Today, country music is as diverse as it has ever been. The pop-country of Anne Murray, Razzy Bailey, Crystal Gayle, and Ronnie Milsap is played alongside the gutbucket sounds of George Jones, Gene Watson, Jeanne Pruett, and Loretta Lynn. Folkie Doc Watson draws crowds and so does torchy Sammi Smith. Foreigners like Tom Jones and

Olivia Newton-John are as prominent as Nashville veterans Dottie West and Jack Greene. Dave Dudley still sings working-men's anthems. Margo Smith still yodels. The Statler Brothers, Oak Ridge Boys, and Kendalls have kept country harmony singing as popular as ever. Songwriting geniuses like Bill Anderson, Mel Tillis, Harlan Howard, Dallas Frazier, Shel Silverstein, Boudleaux and Felice Bryant, John D. Loudermilk, Tom T. Hall, Sonny Throckmorton, Curly Putman, Bobby Braddock, and Billy Sherrill are still deeply respected. New musical stylings from Larry Gatlin, Rosanne Cash, Lacy J. Dalton, and Karen Brooks are played, but Gail Davies and Emmylou Harris still sing the oldies, too. Barbara Mandrell and Charlie Rich continue their blues-tinged stylings; and Hank Williams, Jr., pounds out electrifying, snarling redneck rock. Connie Smith sings gospel music with as much feeling as anyone ever has. Billie Jo Spears dabbles in country-disco. Freddy Fender and Johnny Rodriguez have maintained country's Mexican heritage. Bluegrass festivals are booming. Country's old-style string-band music is being revived. Eddie Rabbitt and Tanya Tucker flavor their country music with rock to appeal to the youngsters, and Conway Twitty has racked up more number-one records than anyone in history by emphasizing "adult" themes and lyrics. Kenny Rogers, still going strong, is one of the best-selling popular artists of all time. More than forty years after Acuff-Rose started Nashville's ascendancy as country music's center, the city remains one of the few boom towns left in America. Country has made a long journey from mountain music to international industry. And it's traveling on.

part one

LISTENING TO COUNTRY MUSIC

Robert K. Oermann

Hundreds of country records are released each month. Choosing essential performances from this bewildering amount of product has not been easy, but certain criteria have been applied toward the task. Availability has been a primary consideration. Only American releases have been chosen, and only records currently available made the list. This is somewhat unfortunate since many country music greats had to be excluded for lack of any currently available record. This approach also excluded the products of several superb European, Japanese, and British labels. Several of these have been noted, however, in the notes to the discs chosen. Only albums have been cited; collectors interested in 45s and 78s will have to look elsewhere. Only one release per artist was allowed, which also eliminated many fine records.

The albums cover the whole spectrum of country styles. They are presented within each chapter in roughly chronological order, so that they provide a history of a musical genre as well as a guide to recordings. A great many of the albums were in a sense preselected by the fact that they are universally recognized classics that have stood the test of time. Others are personal favorites. The titles marked with an asterisk (*) are the indispensable items for a beginning country record collection. The musical explorer will, however, find delight wherever the finger lands in these pages.

OLD-TIME MUSIC

Country music has come a long way since the first records of rural musicians appeared in the mid-1920s. Those scratchy, thin-sounding, tinny, faint performances now sound as if they might have come from another planet, so far removed are they in time and style from what we are used to hearing. Consequently, of all country music's categories, old-time music sounds the most "foreign" to modern ears.

Nonetheless, the diligent and open-minded listener will discover a tremendous legacy in these discs. Once you've adjusted to the sounds and styles of old-time records, you'll become hooked, for they evoke a past America more eloquently than any history book.

The songs are among country music's most timeless. The performances have charm, simplicity, enthusiasm, and immediacy that have all but vanished in the technology and sophistication of today's Nashville industry. The entertainers themselves were about the grandest collection of southern kooks and characters show business has ever seen.

Getting to know old-time music may be a labor of love, but it's a love that frequently blossoms into a passion. As the number of reissue albums in this section indicates, enthusiasm for old-time music has never been higher. And these selections represent just a few of those available.

Various Artists
Anthology of American Folk Music, Vols. 1–3 1926–1932
Folkways 2951, 2952, 2953

These record sets were the single most important influence on the boom of interest in old-time music. Compiled by Harry Smith in the early 1950s, they virtually introduced the modern world to the 78s made by early country musicians. Nearly all of the great names of old-time music are represented in this collection. Buell Kazee, Frank Hutchison, the Carolina Tarheels, Kelly Harrell, Charlie Poole, the Carter Family, Uncle Dave Macon, Dock Boggs, the Stonemans, and Bascom Lamar Lunsford are just a sampling of the pioneers included. Dance tunes, blues, ballads, and comic ditties are included in the wide range of old-time styles covered.

Buying the whole set is an expensive proposition, but if you want to learn about country's roots, you won't find a more comprehensive package or a better investment.

If the *Anthology* really whets your appetite, the next step is Richard Spottswood's Library of Congress fifteen-album Bicentennial record set. Called the *Folk Music in America* series, this massive set is bound to grow in prestige, popularity, and influence for years to come.

Various Artists
Smokey Mountain Ballads 1930–1938
RCA Camden ACL–1-7022

The Victor Talking Machine Company was arguably the single most important recording firm in country music's formative years. Many corporate mergers later, that company is now RCA, a firm that over the years has provided old-time music collectors with many fine reissue albums.

This collection is the last available disc from what was once a fine series of records RCA called its "Vintage Series." Among the excellent, now out-of-print companions to this album were repackagings of Leadbelly (*The Midnight Special*), Woody Guthrie (*Dust Bowl Ballads*), railroad songs, bluegrass music, and Western folk songs. All were superb; they may sometimes be found in used record shops or at garage sales.

Smokey Mountain Ballads collects the works of several of Victor's best old-time acts, including the Monroe Brothers, the Carter Family, Uncle Dave Macon, the Mainers, and the Dixon Brothers. If you want to start with a single-record anthology of old-time music, this budget LP is the disc to get.

Various Artists
Old Time Fiddle Classics, Vol. 1 1925–1935
County 507

Originally, country music was dominated by the fiddle. Before the advent of the guitar as a lead instrument and before the rise of the solo singer, fiddle jigs, reels, hornpipes, and hoedowns comprised the most popular country records.

This album brings together the works of most of the major early country fiddlers. Such highly influential stylists as Eck Robertson (the man who made the first country record, for Victor in 1922), Clayton McMichen (widely regarded as the most important of the early recorded fiddlers), Arthur Smith (often considered the best of the lot), Charlie Bowman, Lowe Stokes, and Earl Johnson are represented on this record. The only major figure missing is Atlanta's Fiddlin' John Carson, the first country "star" (whom Ralph Peer first recorded for Okeh in 1923).

Vernon Dalhart (Country Music Foundation)

Vernon Dalhart
Old Time Songs 1925–1930
Davis Unlimited Du–33030

Fiddle records notwithstanding, the country music industry virtually began with Vernon Dalhart. Dalhart was born Marion Try Slaughter in 1883 in northeastern Texas, where his father ranched and farmed until knifed to death by his brother-in-law. Dalhart herded cattle for a summer in his early teens and studied at the Dallas Conservatory of Music. He moved to the Bronx in 1910 with his wife and children and made his professional operatic debut in New York in 1912. Around 1915, out of work, he answered an Edison Company ad and cut "Can't Yo' Heah Me Callin', Caroline?," which was billed as a black dialect song. Recordings of operatic material followed. In 1924 he recorded the first million-selling country hit. Indeed, "The Prisoner's Song" coupled with "Wreck of the Old 97" was the biggest-selling record of *any* kind up to that point in recording history and has had few challengers since to its reputed 25 million sales. Dalhart's reign as a country star was brief, but he still places near the top of the most prolific recording artists of all time with his 5,000 releases.

Listening to this compilation of his work, it is easy to understand the man's phenomenal popularity. Dalhart was an extremely pleasant singer, full of sincerity, tone, and relaxation. Carson Robison's backup guitar playing is the perfect foil for Dalhart's Texas drawl. (Robison worked with Dalhart for four years and wrote many of his hits.) The songs are nearly all jewels of the period's sentiments and opinions. In addition to being historically significant, as music they have survived the test of time well.

The Carter Family
'Mid the Green Fields of Virginia 1927–1934[*]
RCA ANL–1107

It would be hard to overstate the Carter Family's importance to popular music history. Their role in preserving and popularizing American folk songs and nineteenth-century parlor songs was greater than that of any other act. An extraordinary number of songs that have become essential parts of American musical culture were originated or first popularized by this group. "Wildwood Flower," "Are You Lonesome Tonight," "Can the Circle Be Unbroken?," "Keep on the Sunny Side," "Worried Man Blues," "I'm

The Carter Family—Sara, A.P. and Maybelle (Country Music Foundation)

Thinking Tonight of My Blue Eyes," "I Never Will Marry," "Hello Stranger," "Gold Watch and Chain," "Lonesome Valley," and "Foggy Mountain Top" form just a partial listing. Maybelle Carter's guitar playing helped to transform that instrument's role from rhythm background to prominence as a lead instrument.

The Carter Family act was made up of A. P., born in Virginia in 1891; his wife Sara Dougherty, born in Virginia in 1898; and her cousin Maybelle Addington, born in Virginia in 1909, who married A. P.'s brother Ezra in 1926. The trio first recorded for Victor, under Ralph Peer's direction, in Bristol, Tennessee in 1927. (Jimmie Rodgers also recorded for the first time for Peer in Bristol that week.) All three sang, with Maybelle playing lead guitar (sometimes acoustic steel) and Sara playing second guitar or Autoharp. Sara specialized in the vocal leads; A. P. specialized in collecting, sometimes composing, and arranging songs for the group.

The Carters and Jimmie Rodgers were the first rural acts to have nationally distributed and widely popular records. This record contains many of the family's homespun masterpieces, performed with quiet dignity and sincerity.

Jimmie Rodgers
This is Jimmie Rodgers 1927–1933[*]
RCA VPS–6091

Among the work of old-time musicians, Jimmie Rodgers's recordings have a uniquely familiar quality for modern country audiences. His influence is so all-pervasive that echoes of his voice can still be heard in many country singers of today. His songs and style transcend the barrier of time.

Rodgers was born in Mississippi in 1897 and went to work on the Mississippi-and-Ohio railroad in 1911 (his dad was a foreman) as a water carrier for the black railroad workers. According to his wife, Carrie, it was those workers who taught him how to play banjo and guitar. His songs and singing style were also clearly shaped there. In 1927, two years after tuberculosis forced him to look for alternatives to railroading (and after some work with his sister-in-law, composer Elsie McWilliams, who co-wrote or wrote many of the songs he sang), he auditioned for Victor's Ralph Peer in Bristol, Tennessee.

Known as "America's Blue Yodeler," "The Singing Brakeman," and sometimes "The Father of Country Music," Rodgers recorded for Victor between 1927 and 1933, the year he died of TB. A superb, original composer, he wrote "Waiting for a Train," "T for Texas," "Muleskinner Blues," and many other country classics. Many of the best are collected in this fine double-album introduction to his music.

Jimmie Rodgers (Country Music Foundation)

Jimmie Rodgers's wonderful blend of blues, jazz, hillbilly, crooner, and vaudeville musical styles formed one prototype of a new kind of American music. His records are probably the most popular and effective introduction to the pleasures of old-time music.

Various Artists
Nashville: The Early String Bands 1925–1934
County 541, 542

These two discs document music from the early years of the Grand Ole Opry. In those days, the radio show's acts were drawn from the ranks of middle Tennessee's traditional music performers. These albums have also preserved the fruits of the first recording sessions ever held in Nashville, in 1928.

Uncle Jimmy Thompson was the program's very first performer. This old-time fiddler's style is presented here, along with the music of Nashville's first radio string band, Dr. Humphrey Bate and His Possum Hunters. The show's first black star, harmonica wizard DeFord Bailey, is showcased, as are such Opry old-timers as the Crook Brothers Band, Sid Harkreader, and Kirk McGee.

Besides being a valuable document of the Grand Ole Opry's history, this set is a fine introduction to old-time string band styles.

Riley Puckett
Waitin' for the Evening Mail 1925–1940
County 411

Riley Puckett was the lead singer and guitarist for one of the most successful old-time string bands, the Skillet Lickers, formed by fiddler Gid Tanner. Born in Georgia in 1894, Puckett had an eye infection that left him almost blind soon after his birth. He began making his living as a musician at an early age, at venues ranging from street corners to dances and parties. In 1922 he appeared with Clayton McMichen on WSB and in 1924 he accompanied Gid Tanner to New York to record for Columbia. He was one of the most influential country musicians around in the 1920s and 1930s, but for many years his recordings have been unavailable and his reputation has slipped.

This reissue should help to restore Riley Puckett's renown. He remains an engaging singer, even to modern ears, and his always excellent tune choices were based on a wide-ranging repertoire.

Those interested in investigating the string band side of Puckett's recorded work are encouraged to try County's two volumes of the Skillet Lickers best 78s (County 506 and 526), Vetco's Gid Tanner and His Skillet Lickers (Vetco 107), Rounder's compilation of Tanner-Puckett collaborations Hear These New Southern Fiddle and Guitar Records (Rounder 1005), and Voyager's collection of the fourteen Corn Licker Still in Georgia musical skits the band recorded (Voyager 303). In these records you'll discover the music of such prime Puckett partners as fiddler McMichen, Lowe Stokes, Gid Tanner, and banjoist and harmonicist Fate Norris.

Uncle Dave Macon
The Early Years 1925–1935
County 521

The charming, rollicking, eccentric Uncle Dave Macon was for many the brightest of the Grand Ole Opry's early stars. Born in a Tennessee hamlet in 1870, he was raised in Nashville (where his father bought a hotel) from the age of thirteen. He started farming near Murfreesboro, Tennessee, when he was nineteen and founded the Macon Midway Mule and Transportation Company around 1900. He drove freight wagons for some twenty years, until a rival company using trucks turned his thoughts elsewhere. He had met touring vaudevillians and other performers around his father's hotel and had begun playing banjo when he was fifteen. Marcus Loew heard him playing for the Shriners in Nashville in 1923 and arranged for him to play on a show in a Loew's theater in Alabama.

Uncle Dave Macon
(Country Music
Foundation)

He soon began touring the Loew's vaudeville circuit and recorded for Vocalion in New York in 1924. He began appearing on the Opry broadcasts in 1925 or 1926.

A beloved entertainer and natural-born showman if there ever was one, the Uncle Dave we hear on records probably only hints at the delight he must have been to watch. Regardless of the missing visual element, these sides are delightful listening experiences. No appreciator of American humor can fail to find pleasure in this record and no lover of banjo playing will want to be without it either.

Various Artists
Mountain Blues 1925–1932
County 511

Country music has always incorporated sounds and styles from many different kinds of American music. This great flexibility has allowed it to continually absorb influences from jazz, pop music, Cajun music, cowboy songs, rock 'n' roll, Tex-Mex, folk tunes, gospel, boogie-woogie, Latin music, and other forms while retaining its essential character.

From its very beginnings, country music has included a strong strain of the blues. This album documents the deep relationship between black and white rural music. It includes such hillbilly pioneers as Doc Roberts, Frank Hutchison, Jimmie Tarlton, Sam McGee, Dock Boggs, Narmour and Smith, the Leake County Revelers, and the Carolina Tarheels all translating Southern blues into the country idiom.

Charlie Poole
Charlie Poole and the North Carolina Ramblers 1925–1930
County 505

Charlie Poole is one of the handful of old-time music performers whose work is so consistently good that it impresses discerning and sophisticated musical ears of today. Born in North Carolina in 1892, Poole went to work early in the textile mills and learned to play banjo. In West Virginia in 1917 he teamed up with Posey Rorer, a crippled coal miner who played fiddle. In 1925, joined by North Carolina guitarist Norman Woodlief, they auditioned for Columbia, cut four tunes (including "Don't Let Your Deal Go Down Blues"), and soon were able to make a living playing music full time.

Possessed of a brilliant and crazed genius, Poole drank himself into an early grave at age thirty-nine. Happily for us, he left behind a superb recording legacy that includes such classics as "If the River Was Whiskey" and "Take a Drink on Me." Along with the Blue Sky Boys and the Mainers, Charlie Poole defines the old-time music played in the state of North Carolina.

This record, along with its companion volumes (County 509, 516, and 540), fully demonstrates Poole's greatness. He was part bluesman, part jokester, part sentimental balladeer, and all musician. Almost all of Poole's recorded output was created in the 1920s, but his performances remain timeless and fresh on these delightful reissue albums.

Various Artists
Steel Guitar Classics 1927–1949
Old Timey 113

This record is a reissue that deals with a specific aspect of old-time music. The steel guitar didn't assume a very important role in country music until much later, but as this LP demonstrates, its sound has colored country discs since the early years. (For other albums, see the "Steel Guitar" chapter in Part Two.)

Jimmy Tarlton was an early steel guitar artist who, along with such popular 1920s Hawaiian bands as Kanui and Lula, and Sol Hoopii's Trio, laid the groundwork for the distinctive sound. Jenks "Tex" Carmen, Cliff Carlisle, Jimmie Davis, and Roy Acuff were later pioneers. All of these artists are represented in this album, which is a listening joy from start to finish.

Various Artists
Songs of the Railroad 1924–1934
Vetco 103

Unlike the *Mountain Blues, Old Time Fiddle Classics,* and *Steel Guitar Classics* albums, which isolate musical aspects of old-time music, *Songs of the Railroad* focuses on a theme.

The country musician's fascination with the train is a deep and abiding one. The railroad has often been said to have represented the technology, speed, excitement, and escape of the outside world to the rural mountain-dweller. The sounds and sights of the monstrous steam machines must have been powerful images indeed, and the electrifying news of train disasters captured songwriters' imaginations for decades. Such classic railroad songs as "Orange Blossom Special," "Wabash Cannonball," and "Casey Jones" are still frequently performed favorites.

The songs presented on this album are fascinating, but the record is also worthwhile as an introduction to several significant country pioneers. Al Hopkins and His Buckle Busters, favorites in the early days of Grand Ole Opry, are represented by two songs. Vernon Dalhart, country music's first million-selling artist, has three selections. Fiddlin' John Carson, the Atlanta man whose work first convinced New York record executives that there was a market for country music, is featured on one selection. The Pickard Family, important early popularizers of American folk music, also have a tune on the album. Henry Whitter, one of the first hillbillies to record, is here, as are eight other pioneer artists on this sixteen-song collection.

BLUEGRASS MUSIC

Despite its acoustic sound, bluegrass is not an old country style. It is a product of the mid-1940s and not of an earlier era as is commonly thought. But country music's early songs have been kept alive in bluegrass music, and those who find the distant sounds and styles of true old-time music difficult to enjoy can appreciate a charged form of early country music in bluegrass.

The name comes from Bill Monroe's Blue Grass Boys, for the style was created by Monroe and the many gifted pickers he gathered around him. Bluegrass music's intense heartfelt singing, virtuoso playing, beautiful vocal harmonies, and flashy fast instrumentals were all the products of Monroe's vision. No other form of country music owes so much to one man.

Bluegrass constitutes almost a second world of country music, with its own fans, record labels, and national concert and outdoor festival circuit that often outdraws Nashville-style music in some parts of the country. The albums listed in this section offer only a taste of bluegrass; many additional albums are listed in Part Two, *Country Music Instruments and Players*.

Wilma Lee and Stoney Cooper
Early Recordings 1949–1953
County CCS–103

The act that best illustrates the transition between old-time music and the more modern, high-powered bluegrass style is Wilma Lee and Stoney Cooper. Their songs range from ancient ballads to postwar heartache laments. Stoney's exuberant fiddling and Wilma Lee's impassioned, exhortative singing have the quality of true bluegrass, yet their hard-driving style also owes something to the honky-tonk tradition, and there's a sizable element of hand-clapping gospel enthusiasm here as well.

Stoney Cooper, born in West Virginia in 1918, met Wilma Leary, born in West Virginia in 1921, when he added his fiddle to the Leary Family, a religious singing group. Wilma was a guitarist, organist, and singer-songwriter. Married in 1939, they left the Family in the 1940s and started appearing regularly on the WWVA "Jamboree" in Wheeling, West Virginia, in 1947. They were stars at WWVA when these recordings were made in the early 1950s, and at the peak of their musical powers. They were later honored by the Smithsonian Institution, the Library of Congress, and a national audience for their performance and repertoire on such records as these. In the mid-1950s their style was modified in Nashville studios when they made the transitions to being Grand Ole Opry stars, but toward the end of Stoney's life they returned to the simpler style heard on this album.

After Stoney's death, Wilma Lee completely revitalized her career with an excellent band of young pickers, and continued on Rounder Records, on the bluegrass festival circuit, and on the Opry stage with her timeless, classic sound. Only Roy Acuff is more revered as an exponent of this mountain style.

Bill Monroe
16 All-Time Greatest Hits 1945–1949[*]
Columbia CS–1065

Bill Monroe is an American musical titan. His mandolin playing alone would qualify him for membership in the Country Music Hall of Fame, but on top of that, he is simply

Bill Monroe (Country Music Foundation)

(CBS Records)

one of the greatest singers in the history of country music. He has also written dozens of songs that will live forever, as demonstrated on this album.

Monroe was born in Kentucky in 1911, and practiced his singing style in the fields of his father's farm. He started playing mandolin and guitar when he was ten, and began playing guitar behind his fiddling Uncle Pen at dances when he was twelve or thirteen. Around the same time, he began backing black fiddler Arnold Schultz at dances. Schultz's guitar and fiddle playing—including his blues playing—were an important influence on him (as, via Schultz's pupil Mose Rager, they were on Merle Travis and Ike Everly). Bill Monroe began performing with his brothers Birch and Charlie at parties and square dances in Indiana in 1929. In 1934 Bill and Charlie began working full time on radio and made their first recording in 1936, in Charlotte, North Carolina. In 1938 the Monroe Brothers split up. In Atlanta, Bill placed a newspaper ad for musicians and formed the first Blue Grass Boys lineup. In 1939, the Grand Ole Opry enthusiastically signed him up.

The recordings compiled here are the ones that brought Monroe immortality. The original versions of "Molly and Tenbrooks," "Blue Moon of Kentucky," "Footprints in the Snow," "Will You Be Loving Another Man?", and other standards are present. There are many albums of Bill Monroe's "greatest hits," but his work with his band of Blue Grass Boys—Chubby Wise on fiddle, Howard Watts ("Cedric Rainwater") on bass, Lester

Flatt on guitar, and Earl Scruggs on banjo—for Columbia in the 1940s is often considered his finest. His later work on MCA is also important, but this record defines bluegrass.

Flatt and Scruggs
Golden Era 1950–1955
Rounder SS-05

Lester Flatt and Earl Scruggs are the most famous of Bill Monroe's many Blue Grass Boys alumni. Indeed, Earl's revolutionary banjo style was very nearly as important as Monroe's musical vision in creating the bluegrass sound. Compare his finger-picking with the earlier frailing style of Uncle Dave Macon and Grandpa Jones to see just how dramatically he transformed the instrument. Lester's singing and songwriting were among the greatest contributions to bluegrass made by a single musician.

Flatt was born in 1914 in Tennessee, and Scruggs in 1924 in North Carolina. Both came from musical families and both performed in bands on Carolina radio in the late 1930s. They both played with the Blue Grass Boys in the mid-1940s, and both left in

Lester Flatt (right) and Earl Scruggs (Country Music Foundation)

1948, soon forming The Foggy Mountain Boys. They recorded for Mercury and Columbia, joined the Grand Ole Opry in 1955, and toured widely under the sponsorship
of the Martha White Flour Mills. They eventually brought bluegrass to such new frontiers
as the college circuit, the Ash Grove in Los Angeles, and Carnegie Hall.

Among the many Flatt and Scruggs albums, this one stands out as definitive. It
collects the performances that brought them fame long before the days of "The Ballad
of Jed Clampett" and *Bonnie and Clyde*.

The Stanley Brothers
16 Greatest Hits 1958–1964
Starday 3033

The Stanley Brothers were born in Virginia, Carter in 1925 and Ralph in 1927.
With Carter on guitar and vocals and Ralph on banjo and vocals, they assembled the
Stanley Brothers and the Clinch Mountain Boys in 1946. They began appearing on
Virginia radio, and recorded for Rich-R-Tone in 1948. Ralph and Carter were signed

The Stanley Brothers (Country Music Foundation)

by Columbia in 1949 and began a career of touring and recording together that lasted until Carter's death in 1966. Ralph continues to record and perform.

The Stanley Brothers are often cited as the most moving musicians in bluegrass history. This reputation seems to grow each year. Like Wilma Lee and Stoney Cooper, Carter and Ralph Stanley mined a rich vein of American folk songs, emotional gospel standards, and tragic mountain songs, and they sang these tunes in angelic hillbilly harmony.

Reno and Smiley
The Best of Reno and Smiley 1952–1960[*]
Starday SLP–961

"I Know You're Married But I Love You Still," "I Wouldn't Change You If I Could," "Freight Train Boogie," and "Money, Marbles and Chalk" are among the titles popularized by this fine bluegrass duo. These and the eight others presented on this Starday album make this an essential bluegrass collection.

Don Reno, born in 1927, and Red Smiley, born in North Carolina in 1925, were a banjo-guitar combination like Lester Flatt and Earl Scruggs. They teamed up in 1949, after Reno left the Blue Grass Boys (he was replaced by Earl Scruggs on banjo in that group), to form a group called Don Reno and Red Smiley and the Tennessee Cut-ups. Unlike their predecessors, the Reno-Smiley team tackled songs from outside the strict bluegrass repertoire. In 1961 they had two country chart hits on King—"Don't Let Your Sweet Love Die" and "Love Oh Love, Oh Please Come Home." The duo broke up in 1964, but this record documents their finest musical moments together.

The Osborne Brothers
The Best of the Osborne Brothers 1963–1970
MCA 2-4086

Even if they had done nothing but popularize "Ruby, Are You Mad at Your Man?" and "Rocky Top," the Osborne Brothers' place in country music history would be assured. The Osborne Brothers also helped to initiate the so-called Newgrass movement, moving bluegrass from its grounding in old-time music into the modern music world of contemporary songwriting, electrified instruments, and flashy performance style.

The Osbornes were born in Kentucky, Bob in 1931 and Sonny in 1937. They performed on radio in Tennessee in the early 1950s, and recorded first for RCA and then for MGM. They performed on the Wheeling "Jamboree" in the 1950s, on the Opry, and in nightclubs, and were important in introducing bluegrass to the college circuit in the late 1950s. Their use of electrification when needed, and sometimes of pianos, drums, and steel guitar, represented quite a break with bluegrass as established by Bill Monroe.

The traditional bluegrass elements of mandolin, banjo, and piercing tenor vocals are present on these sides, but the Osbornes also knew how to transform bluegrass music's appeal into wider commercial terms, and achieved that great rarity for bluegrass bands, hit singles (mostly in the late 1960s). This double-album set contains them all.

The Lewis Family
16 Greatest Hits 1965–1975
Starday SD–3019

The manic, unbridled enthusiasm of Lincolnton, Georgia's, Lewis Family is irresistible. The way this group tears into gospel music, you have *got* to be moved. If their rip-roaring shout-style harmony singing, breakneck instrumental licks, and tambourine pounding don't quicken your pulse, you're dead.

Pauline and Roy Lewis were married in 1925; by 1949 four of their sons were performing together around their Lincolnton, Georgia, hometown as "The Lewis Brothers." Soon Roy and Miggie, the oldest daughter, began performing with the brothers, and they began to play gospel exclusively, rather than the old-time and bluegrass repertoire the brothers had started out performing. Two more sisters were added to the group, and eventually two of the four brothers were replaced by grandsons of Roy and Pauline. In 1954 the Lewis Family began a long-running weekly TV show over WJBF-TV in Augusta, Georgia, and soon began cutting a long series of albums for Starday.

The premier act of bluegrass gospel, the recorded family consists of Roy "Pop" Lewis; his sons Wallace and Little Roy; three daughters, Miggie, Polly, and Janis; Janis's son Lewis; and Wallace's son Travis. Little Roy's banjo abilities are so highly developed that he could have made a small fortune playing in Nashville sessions or in some high-dollar country star's band. His showmanship, sense of comedy, and unflagging salesmanship are so overwhelming that he might have easily become a solo star on his own. Instead, he's stayed with his music-making family.

Singling out individual tracks or even individual albums by this act is irrelevant. Lay your hands on the first Lewis Family album you run into and be healed at once. They're that stone-guaranteed good.

Doyle Lawson and Quicksilver
Rock My Soul 1981
Sugar Hill SH–3717

Doyle Lawson formed Quicksilver in 1979. A singer and mandolin player, he had worked over a period of twenty years with such outstanding performers as J. D. Crowe, Jimmy Martin, and the Country Gentlemen. With Terry Baucom (formerly of Ricky Skaggs's early 1970s group Boone Creek) on banjo, Jimmy Haley on guitar, and Lou Reed on bass, Doyle Lawson and Quicksilver had an established reputation as a straight-ahead bluegrass act when they recorded this all-gospel effort for Sugar Hill. The move surprised many in the bluegrass community, but paid off handsomely for the group in terms of critical acclaim and spawned a sequel two years later (*Heavenly Treasures*).

What makes *Rock My Soul* so special is the spine-tingling ensemble singing of the quartet. The tenor of Lou Reed (who later left to join Ricky Skaggs's band) is an astonishing vocal instrument that soars and wails above the others on "I'll Have a New Life," "On the Sea of Life," "Rock My Soul," "A Beautiful Life," and the nine other gems heard here. Besides being one of the best bluegrass albums of its year, *Rock My Soul* is downright inspirational.

The Bluegrass Cardinals
Where Rainbows Touch Down 1981
CMH 6259

The Bluegrass Cardinals have one of the most complex and unique vocal sounds in bluegrass today. The group's personnel has changed several times since it was founded in 1974, but the core of the band is and always has been banjo-playing Don Parmley and son David, who plays rhythm guitar and sings. The Cardinals were organized in Los Angeles by Kentuckian Don Parmley, who for nine years did the backup banjo work for the "Beverly Hillbillies" TV series, and David, who was then fifteen. In 1976 the group moved to Virginia and released their first album, *The Bluegrass Cardinals*, on Briar Records.

Unlike many lead bluegrass singers, David Parmley sings low lead. He is more comparable to Lester Flatt than to Bill Monroe. Papa Don sings low harmony beneath him and mandolinist Norman Wright sings tenor on this recording. *Where Rainbows Touch Down* is an important record, not just because it is a showcase for one of the most exciting young bluegrass bands around. It is also an aural snapshot of what is going on in contemporary bluegrass songwriting. In a genre of country music that often seems imprisoned by its devotion to the past, it is heartening to discover that eleven new bluegrass songs this fine are to be found. The Bluegrass Cardinals' superb style and taste in finding this material are to be applauded.

STARS OF
DEPRESSION RADIO

The long years of the Great Depression in the 1930s came between the first recording of old-time music and the rise of the more modern styles of bluegrass, Western swing, and honky-tonk. Record sales generally dropped off dramatically during this period and the record industry suffered badly. It was the Golden Era of radio, however, and millions listened at home even when they couldn't afford to go out or buy records.

Thanks to radio broadcasting, country music did not die in the 1930s. On the contrary, it entered the period of its greatest growth and diversity. During this era, country music became truly professionalized as a part of the entertainment business. The honey-voiced country radio stars may have performed in many different styles, but they were united in the tremendous progress they made for nationally popular country entertainment. It was a time of great hardship, but country music has historically done well during such years. Indeed, to many country buffs, this was country music's finest hour.

The records in this section include country blues, old-time tunes, gospel music, and cowboy melodies. Brother duets were especially popular and several of country music's classic pairs of this type are represented here.

Lulu Belle and Scotty Wiseman
Sweethearts of Country Music 1963
Starday SD–206

The biggest radio barn dance show of the 1920s, 1930s, and most of the 1940s was WLS's "National Barn Dance" from Chicago. The biggest star on that show was the irrepressible singer and comedienne Lulu Belle, twice voted the most popular female radio entertainer in the United States.

Lulu Belle was born in North Carolina in 1913 and joined the Barn Dance when she was nineteen; the next year Scotty Wiseman joined the show. Also born in North Carolina, in 1909, Scotty played guitar and banjo, sang, and wrote fine songs, among

Lulu Belle and Scotty Wiseman
(Country Music Foundation)

them "Mountain Dew" (in collaboration with Bascom Lamar Lumsford), "Remember Me," and "Have I Told You Lately That I Love You?"

In addition to twenty-five years of WLS Barn Dance broadcasts and road show tours, and three years at WLW in Cincinnati, Lulu Belle and Scotty starred in movies and, for eight years, on a daily TV show. They also recorded for a number of labels. Although no reissue album of their old 78s has yet appeared, this album the couple made for Starday in the 1960s recaptures what was best about their simple, affecting style, and contains fine versions of the above-mentioned standards they introduced.

The Blue Sky Boys
The Sunny Side of Life 1936–1949
Rounder 1006

The Bolick Brothers, known as the Blue Sky Boys to country music fans of the 1930s and 1940s, were perhaps the outstanding example of the special perfection members of the same family bring to singing together. Their twin-like voices harmonized eloquently, weaving in and out in alternating phrases, creating an effect of sublime poetry.

Both born in North Carolina, Bill Bolick was seventeen and Earl was fifteen in 1935 when they started singing on radio, calling themselves the Blue Sky Boys. Bill played mandolin and Earl guitar.

The Bolicks' voices recall an era long past, with music that sounds as though it was practiced and perfected on back porches in North Carolina summer evenings. It is plain-spoken, melodic, evocative music that looks back to the Carter Family and ahead to the Louvins, Wilburns, and Everlys. All the Blue Sky Boys reissues are worth listening to; this album is the one that has remained in print most steadily. It is titled for the first song they released, written by Bill and recorded for Victor in 1936, and now a standard.

Once you've become a fan, you'll probably also want to purchase the JEMF reissue of the Blue Sky Boys' work for Capitol and seek out the out-of-print discs on Starday, RCA Camden, and Bluebird. If you're an aspiring country harmony singer, you'll find yourself wanting them all.

The Delmore Brothers
Brown's Ferry Blues 1933–1941[*]
County 402

The Grand Ole Opry's Delmore Brothers were as creative as instrumentalists as they were as harmony singers—their warm soft voices were beautifully complemented by their rippling guitar work.

The Delmore Brothers—Rabon (left) and Alton (Country Music Foundation)

Born in Alabama in 1908 and 1910, respectively, Alton and Rabon were raised on the farm and learned fiddle playing from their mother. They added guitar to their musical skills and played locally in their teens. They made their first appearance on the Opry in 1932 and stayed with the show until 1938. Through the 1940s and into the 1950s they were heard on a number of radio stations through the South and Midwest and made numerous records for King. They were prolific songwriters and were responsible for some country classics, among them "Beautiful Brown Eyes" (which Alton co-wrote with Arthur Smith) and "Blues Stay Away from Me," composed by Alton and Rabon, which went to number two on the country charts in 1949 in their version. They were also influential guitarists and key members of the Brown's Ferry Four gospel quartet.

The Delmores' music may sound simple, even unexciting on first hearing, but the simplicity is deceptive. Beneath their quiet, somewhat dignified presentation is a soulfulness that becomes mesmerizing on repeated listenings.

The Delmore Brothers' music divides roughly into two periods: their country-blues period during the 1930s and their successful boogie-woogie phase in the 1950s. Both periods produced excellent black-influenced country music. This LP summarizes the earlier period; the second is anthologized on the album *Best of the Delmore Brothers* (Starday SLP–962).

The Bailes Brothers
Early Radio Favorites, Vol. 1 1945–1947
Old Homestead OCHS–109

Old Homestead is one of the smaller old-time country music labels, but it has put out consistently worthwhile records, such as this one.

The Bailes Brothers have been somewhat overlooked by country historians. They are seldom mentioned as first-rank performers of their time, despite the fact that they wrote and popularized such standards as "Dust on the Bible," "I Want To Be Loved (But Only by You)," and "Oh So Many Years." There were four Bailes brothers in the act at various times—Johnnie, Walter, Kyle, and Homer. Johnnie, born in West Virginia in 1918, and Walter were the mainstays of the group. The Bailes Brothers appeared on the Grand Ole Opry in Nashville from 1942 to 1948, and then moved to the "Louisiana Hayride" in Shreveport. Although they attained mass radio popularity in the 1940s, their outlook and repertoire belong essentially to the previous decade.

The Bailes Brothers, and acts like them, demonstrate the immense importance of gospel music to country traditions. In the cases of nearly all brother acts, the vocal harmonies came right out of the South's Holiness churches.

Carson Robison
The Immortal Carson Robison 1930–1939
Glendale GL–6009

Robison's career spanned the entire early history of country music. Born in Kansas in 1890, he started working professionally when he was fifteen. After performing for a time in Kansas City and Chicago in the early twenties, he moved to New York in 1924. There he recorded for Victor as a whistler and guitarist, worked with Vernon Dalhart as guitar accompanist and duet partner, and wrote many of Dalhart's hits. When he became a solo act in the 1930s, he turned toward cowboy imagery and continued as one of country music's major songwriters. He became a nationally broadcast NBC radio star during this period, the time of the recordings on this album.

In the 1940s Robison became known as "The Grand-daddy of the Hillbillies" and scored the biggest hit of his career with the novelty talking-blues "Life Gets Tee-Jus, Don't It." He wrote a number of standards, and his work shows the connections between vaudeville, hillbilly, country, and western—he wrote "Barnacle Bill the Sailor," "Take Me Back to My Boots and Saddle," "Bury Me Not On the Lone Prairie," and "1942 Turkey in the Straw." In 1957 he cut "Rockin' and Rollin' with Grandpa."

Carson took the version of his Buckeroos group heard here across the nation and to England. Of all the records in this section, this one comes closest to capturing the ambiance of Depression-era radio.

The Girls of the Golden West
The Girls of the Golden West 1933–1938
Sonyatone STR–202

Dolly and Millie Good—the Girls of the Golden West—were Midwesterners, born in 1915 and 1913. Vocalists and guitarists, they debuted on radio in St. Louis in 1930 and joined WLS's "National Barn Dance" in 1933. They stayed there until 1937, when they settled in for a long run on WLW in Cincinnati.

The Barn Dance, which began broadcasting in Chicago in 1924, had a homey warmth established by the pleasant, dulcet quality of its biggest stars. Unlike the rustic string bands of WSM in Nashville and WWVA in Wheeling, the WLS acts dispensed a smooth, lovingly burnished version of country music that sometimes included pop-type material. This had a truly national appeal.

The Girls of the Golden West illustrate the special quality of the Barn Dance acts on this reissue of some of their work. Their projection of a gentle, rosy, fireside ambiance made them the most popular female duo in country music history.

COWBOYS

The cowboy craze that dominated American popular culture for most of the first half of this century was a boon to country music. Amercians' fascination with all things Western was one of the most significant developments in our cultural history, and country musicians learned to capitalize on it effectively. In the 1930s, the cowboy replaced the hillbilly as the dominant performing image in country music. Vaudeville-style hayseeds, bumpkins, and rubes were transformed into dashing, dramatic, dazzlingly dressed cowboys and cowgirls singing songs in praise of the American West. This change in imagery was to stamp country music indelibly for decades afterward. It brought such unprecedented popularity to country music that the Western genre of country was for a long time given equal billing with its parent in the phrase "country and western."

The charisma and romance that the singing cowboys brought to country music added significantly to its dignity and respectability. As a result, country came of age as a commercial music form.

Gene Autry
Gene Autry's Country Music Hall of Fame Album 1940–1950
Columbia CS–1035

Unquestionably the single most important figure in the Western movement was Gene Autry. Born in Texas in 1907, he parlayed his Western background, good looks, songwriting talent, and pleasant singing into a career that eventually made him a multimillionaire. Autry began performing in the late 1920s as a Jimmie Rodgers imitator. After serving an apprenticeship at WLS and releasing the hit "That Silver Haired Daddy of Mine" (which he co-wrote and sang with Jimmie Long in 1931), he arrived in Hollywood with his own singing cowboy style, which became the model for all who followed him.

The songs collected on this album, from "Back in the Saddle Again" and "Mexicali Rose" to "Take Me Back to My Boots and Saddle," are planks in the cultural bridge that carried Americans from the 1930s to the post–World War II era. Autry's relaxed, crooning tenor sounds as wholesome as ever.

Gene Autry (Country Music Foundation)

The Sons of the Pioneers
The Sons of the Pioneers 1940*
JEMF 102

This record, one of the nicest in the superb John Edwards Memorial Foundation series of releases, captures the work of country music's premiere Western harmony group. There is probably no other act in country history that succeeded so brilliantly on so many levels as the Sons of the Pioneers. Vocally, these men perfected a breathtakingly beautiful blend. Instrumentally, they could play as hot as any small jazz combo of the day. Best of all, in Bob Nolan and Tim Spencer the Sons of the Pioneers had two of the most eloquent and sophisticated songwriters country music has ever seen. "Cool Water" and "Tumbling Tumbleweeds" alone would have assured Nolan's considerable reputation in this department, and Spencer's "Room Full of Roses" and "Cigareets, Whiskey, and Wild, Wild Women" also come under the heading of classics.

The founding Sons—Roy Rogers, born in Ohio in 1911; Bob Nolan, born in New Brunswick, Canada, in 1908; and Tim Spencer, born in Missouri in 1908—met and joined forces in Hollywood in the early 1930s, where they found each other through newspaper ads. They first appeared on KFWB in Los Angeles in 1934 as the Pioneer Trio. Over the next two years they became the Sons of the Pioneers and added Hugh

The original Sons of the Pioneers in 1936 (Country Music Foundation)

and Karl Farr, born in Texas in 1903 and 1909, respectively, and Lloyd Perryman, born in Arkansas in 1917. They made their first recording in 1934 for Decca, then moved to the American Record Company in the late 1930s, eventually going to Columbia and then to RCA. Roy Rogers (then Leonard Slye) was signed by Republic Pictures in 1937 and left the group. He was replaced by Pat Brady. The Pioneers were also signed by Republic in 1940 and appeared with Rogers in many pictures.

Roy Rogers
The Best of Roy Rogers 1945–1947
RCA Camden ACL–1-0953(e)

The most famous graduate of the Sons of the Pioneers was Roy Rogers, a good-looking, well-mannered, kind, affable fellow from Ohio who succeeded Gene Autry as a singing cowboy matinee idol. Roy also possessed the most beautiful singing voice and yodeling ability of all the major singing cowboys. His charisma was so strong that he was able to supplant Gene Autry as King of the Cowboys and install his wife, Dale Evans, as the Queen of the West.

Roy Rogers was born Leonard Slye in Cincinnati in 1911. From the age of seven until his teens he lived with his family on a farm in Duck Run, Ohio, where he first learned to ride. With an ambition to work in movies he learned to play guitar and he

Roy Rogers (center) and a non-Pioneers group, the Cactus Cowboys (from left): Joe Caliente, Jake Watts, Windy Bill McKay, and Bobby Gregory (Country Music Foundation)

sang and called at square dances. In 1930 he moved to Los Angeles and worked at various jobs while trying to join or organize the right singing group. The Sons of the Pioneers proved to be the answer. As the success of that group grew, various members, separately and together, appeared in movie roles. In 1938 Republic Pictures auditioned Roy and signed him for the lead in *Under Western Skies*. It was the first of close to a hundred Western pictures he made before starting a TV series with Dale Evans that stayed in production through the 1950s.

This record serves as a reminder of Rogers's considerable musical abilities. Many of the performances were heard in his Republic pictures, some of which communicated a uniquely poetic vision of the West. The Sons of the Pioneers sing with him on two cuts on this album.

Tex Ritter
American Legend 1942–1966
Capitol SKC–11241

Although he was never as widely popular as a TV and movie actor as Gene Autry or Roy Rogers, Tex Ritter was certainly one of the best-loved entertainers in show business—one of the first country artists to popularize country music in New York City,

Tex Ritter (Country Music Foundation)

and among the few Western stars to have a widely diversified career on Broadway, in movies, over radio, at rodeos, and in academic recital.

Born in East Texas in 1905, Ritter dropped out of law school and began singing on Houston radio in 1929 with a repertoire based on the Western songs he had collected when he was young. After a financially unrewarding year of one-nighters in the South and Midwest, he moved to New York, appearing on Broadway in 1931 in "Green Grow the Lilacs," on which "Oklahoma" was based. After more appearances on stage, at the Madison Square Garden rodeo, on New York radio, and on the college lecture circuit, he moved to Hollywood in 1936. He eventually starred in more than fifty Westerns and made numerous hit records from the 1940s into the 1970s. He moved to Nashville in 1965 and appeared on the Grand Ole Opry.

This album set is a loving tribute to a unique Western singer, a pioneer on the trail Willie Nelson and Waylon Jennings later followed. Ritter's voice will evoke fond memories of Saturday matinee shoot-em-ups, but also of the great Southwestern reality behind them.

WESTERN SWING

Western swing music is a particularly complex and sophisticated subgenre of country music.

Created in the dance halls of the Southwest, this product of the late 1930s was a combination of country music and the swing jazz of the day. Western swing was part hep jive, part beer parlor stomp, part polka, part blues, part old-time fiddle virtuosity, part Mexican-American, and part Hollywood singing cowboy. This unlikely mix made one of the most distinctive of all country styles, one that became wildly popular.

Small bands initiated the Western swing sound, but the size of the groups increased dramatically as the music grew in popularity. At the height of its popularity in the mid-1940s, Western swing units were nearly the size of small orchestras. Country music's big band sound nearly died out (as did many other classic swing dance bands of the period) when small combo honky-tonk and rock 'n' roll groups took over in the 1950s. But in the 1970s, Western swing enjoyed a revival and it is now on its way to being as timelessly popular as country's other styles.

Bob Wills
The Bob Wills Anthology 1935–1947[*]
Columbia PG–32416

The name Bob Wills has become synonymous with Western swing. His Texas Playboys were the greatest practitioners of this country-jazz amalgam, and there are still passionate partisans who maintain that they were the greatest country band that ever existed.

Wills was born in Texas in 1905 and fiddled at a ranch dance when he was ten years old. His father and grandfather were fiddlers; their folk and frontier tunes, and those of his mother's family, formed the basis of Wills's repertoire. But Wills attributed equal influence to the blues and jazz of black neighbors he played, worked, and danced with while growing up in the ranch country. He moved to Fort Worth in 1929 and, after a

Bob Wills (Country Music Foundation)

(CBS Records)

stint in a medicine show, formed a duo that eventually grew into the Light Crust Dough-boys. When he was fired from the Doughboys radio show in 1933, he moved to Waco, taking many of the original Doughboys with him to form the original five-piece Texas Playboys. In 1934 the band moved to Tulsa, where it remained until World War II, broadcasting on KVOO. In 1935, with thirteen pieces, including horns, the band cut its first records for Brunswick, in Dallas. Wills and the Playboys toured until 1964.

This anthology is an easy record to recommend, for it is likely to appear on most lists of the all-time ten best country records. As is the case with Bill Monroe, there are many other albums of Bob Wills hits, but make this Columbia two-disc set your first Wills acquisition. It contains the original material that created a musical legend.

Milton Brown
Country and Western Dance-O-Rama, Vol. 1 1935–1936
Western 1001

Milton Brown gets credit from many country historians as the pioneer of Western swing. His Musical Brownies showed strong jazz influences and their repertoire was based far more on pop than on folk or country material. They were the inspiration for a number of jazz-influenced Western groups, and Milton Brown's reputation might have soared very high had his career not been cut short.

Born in Texas in 1903, Brown began his professional career in 1930 in Fort Worth, when he became the vocalist for the Wills Fiddle Band, which thereby became a trio. In 1932 he was with the Light Crust Doughboys when they had trouble with their sponsor over the issue of whether they could play dances. Brown left that group and soon formed his own, the Musical Brownies. The Brownies recorded in 1934 for Bluebird, then moved to Decca. The group recorded more than a hundred sides, some very successful, before Brown's death in a car crash in 1936.

This record is in a recently revived LP format, the ten-inch mini-album (like many of the early 33⅓ rpm releases). It is a faithful reproduction of the Brown album Decca released in the early 1950s and could prove to be nearly as sought-after a collector's item as the original record itself.

Spade Cooley
Spade Cooley 1945–1946
Columbia Historic Edition FC-37467

The self-proclaimed "King of Western Swing," Spade Cooley had good reason to boast, although he never achieved the popularity or renown of Bob Wills.

Born in Oklahoma in 1910, Cooley was mostly raised in Oregon. He began taking violin lessons at an early age and later played fiddle at local square dances. He was twenty when he moved with his family to a California farm. He started playing in local clubs until, on a second try at Los Angeles in 1934, he was hired as a movie stand-in for Roy Rogers in Republic westerns. He also worked as a fiddler, formed a band, got a recording deal, and released the war-time hit "Shame, Shame on You." He and his band became a major draw in live performances in the Los Angeles area, had more nationally successful record releases, and appeared in movies. In 1947 Cooley began heading up his own very successful show on L.A.'s first commercial TV station, KTLA.

In the 1950s Cooley recorded a great deal of overblown pop orchestral music at RCA. Later, as his drinking problem worsened his performing career faltered; an argument with his estranged wife led to her death and his imprisonment. All these factors combined to dim the memory of the great music he had made at his peak.

This LP is the first major-label attempt to dust off Spade Cooley's reputation. It is a thing of beauty, containing both his best-known hits ("Detour," "Shame, Shame on You") and previously unreleased treasures "Troubled Over You," "I Can't Help the Way You Feel"). Tex Williams's vocals in Cooley's best band were a standout, but the versions of "Steel Guitar Rag," "Oklahoma Stomp," and "Swinging the Devil's Dream" contained here will keep swing instrumentalists busy for a good while copying licks.

Various Artists
Western Swing, Vol. 2 1936–1944
Old Timey LP–116

Only a few of the top Western swing units have had entire reissue albums devoted to them. Besides Bob Wills, Milton Brown, and Spade Cooley albums from various labels, RCA's Bluebird division marketed a superb two-record set on Bill Boyd until recently. There are several excellent compilation albums, however. In England the String label distributed by Topic has some fine Western swing reissues called *Beer Parlor Jive*. In the United States there are the compilation volumes available from Old Timey.

Of the Old Timey sets, Volume 2 contains the least Wills and Brown material and the most representation of other bands. This disc contains fine efforts by such significant Western swing bands as those of Adolph Hofner, Cliff Bruner, and Jimmie Revard. The Tune Wranglers and the famous Light Crust Doughboys are also represented here. The other Old Timey Western swing albums, LP–105 and LP–117, are fine records as well.

Asleep at the Wheel
Wheelin' and Dealin' 1976
Capitol ST–11546

Ray Benson, Chris O'Connell, and a rotating cast of redneck hippies undertook the task of reviving Western swing in the 1970s. Collectively known as Asleep at the Wheel, the group made a series of uniformly great albums from 1973 on that drew on the music of Bob Wills, Moon Mullican, and other experimenters of the 1940s. These records reacquainted young audiences with this form of country music, but also presented innovative blends of country, Western, blues, rock, jazz, and Cajun that made this group a trend-setting contemporary country band.

Asleep at the Wheel first took shape on a West Virginia farm in 1970, working first in local clubs and then in Washington, D.C., and eventually opening for such nationally known acts as Poco. The founding members were Ray Benson and Lucky Oceans (Reuben Gosfield), both born in Philadelphia in 1951; Vermonter LeRoy Preston; and Danny Levin, also born in Philadelphia. Maryland-born Chris O'Connell was added to the group on rhythm guitar and backup vocals. The group relocated in 1971 to San Francisco (minus Danny Levin, who rejoined in 1974), where they added pianist Floyd Domino. They put out a first album for United Artists, which was not notably successful. They moved to Austin, Texas, in 1974 and put out a second album, on Epic. Meanwhile the group had grown to eight members. In 1975, having shifted to Capitol, the group released a third album, *Texas Gold*, which made the country top ten, appeared on the pop charts, and was nominated for a Grammy award.

There is no such thing as a bad Asleep at the Wheel album. The group's first, on United Artists, contained the most Western swing material, but it is out of print. Of the several Capitol albums, the best are probably *Wheelin' and Dealin'*, *Texas Gold*, and *Served Live*. *Framed*, on MCA, is Asleep at the Wheel's least country LP, but is also a fine effort.

The 1940s

The decade of the 1940s marked country music's emergence as a truly national phenomenon. Radio barn dances were everywhere. Even the usually resistant Northeast was not immune, as stations in Philadelphia, Boston, and Cleveland inaugurated regular country broadcasts. Bluegrass was born, Western swing was thriving, and gritty honky-tonk, soon to become the dominant country style, was forged during World War II and the postwar years. Most of the old-time music acts were still thriving in the 1940s, too. Singing cowboy films played to packed houses, there were country music parks scattered throughout such populous states as Pennsylvania, and large casts were maintained on dozens of successful Saturday-night barn dance stage shows. It was a highly diverse and creative decade for country music, and many of its greatest stars were at their peak.

Various Artists
Country Hits of the 1940s 1944–1949
Capitol SM–884

Capitol Records was organized in the early 1940s and quickly moved successfully into the country field. Nashville attracted country musicians from the South and Southeast, but Capitol's location on the West Coast made Los Angeles an important mecca for performers from the West and Southwest. For many years California rivaled Nashville as a country recording center partly because of Capitol's activities.

The young company signed up many of the new honky-tonk stylists, some of the singing cowboys, several fine instrumentalists, and many Oklahoma and Texas talents. By the end of the 1940s, Capitol had achieved the status of a major record label and country had played a major role in its success.

This record collects many of the hits that brought the company greatness. Tex Williams's "Smoke! Smoke! Smoke! (That Cigarette)," Al Dexter's "Pistol Packin' Mama," Leon Payne's "I Love You Because," Jack Guthrie's "Oklahoma Hills," and Margaret Whiting and Jimmy Wakely's "Slippin' Around" were all smash successes that make this album a treasure to own.

The Brown's Ferry Four
16 Greatest Hits 1945–1952
Starday SD–3017

The gospel male quartet is one of the most enduring forms of country music. The Oak Ridge Boys are currently the most visible graduates of this school of music. Gospel quartet conventions are still annual events in the Bible Belt, and the style can also still be seen on television's "Hee Haw."

But few quartets of today come close to the matchless singing of the Brown's Ferry Four, which first recorded in 1945. Small wonder, for this group was composed of immortals Grandpa Jones, Merle Travis, and Rabon and Alton Delmore. When Travis was unavailable, another future Hall of Famer, Red Foley, sang bass. All that is fine about rural gospel harmony singing and songwriting is in the grooves of this record. Since no reissue of the classic Columbia Chuck Wagon Gang records of the 1930s exists, this album is the single best introduction to country's gospel tradition.

Grandpa Jones
The Grandpa Jones Story 1976
CMH 9007

Born in Kentucky in 1913, Louis Marshall Jones has played an extremely important role in the preservation of old-time styles and repertoire, along with his contributions as a first-class banjoist, singer, and comedian. He became "Grandpa" in his early twenties, while working with Kentucky performer and folklorist Bradley Kincaid. He formed a band called Grandpa Jones and His Grandchildren, which performed on WWVA in Wheeling, West Virginia, and WLW in Cincinnati, where he began recording for King.

There is an excellent reissue of Grandpa's original hits of the 1940s, such as "Ol' Rattler" and "Eight More Miles to Louisville," on Starday 3008. *The Grandpa Jones Story*, however, demonstrates his continuing role as a reservoir of old-time tunes and his contemporary musical vitality. (CMH Records has rerecorded many legendary country performers like Joe Maphis, Mac Wiseman, Lester Flatt, Carl and Pearl Butler, Merle Travis, Johnny Gimble, and Jim and Jesse, and given their music to new audiences in attractive packages.)

This album, along with *Grandpa Jones Family Album* (also for CMH), tries to encompass part of the huge Jones repertoire and capture his exuberant, expansive style. Many historically significant Grandpa Jones numbers are reprised with the benefits of modern recording technology. Lovers of good old-timey country songs will find a wealth of material here, as the double-album set also contains many lesser-known titles. The fine liner notes by Doug Green effectively summarize and explain Grandpa's career and importance as far more than a brash banjo clown.

Grandpa Jones (Country Music Foundation)

Merle Travis
Best of Merle Travis 1946–1947
Capitol SM–2662

Merle Travis was born in Kentucky in 1917. He acquired the fundamentals of his unique finger-picking guitar style from Mose Rager (who also instructed Ike Everly and had himself been taught by black fiddler and guitarist Arnold Schultz, whom Bill Monroe worked with). In turn, "Travis-picking" was to greatly influence the playing of Chet Atkins and many other musicians. In his early twenties Travis played with the Georgia Wildcats on Cincinnati's WLW. After World War II he settled in California and soon began writing and recording hits for Capitol. He played an important part in the development of the new, more cosmopolitan country styles and in the development of the kind of folk-based songwriting that blossomed in the 1960s.

Perhaps most famous today as the composer of the huge Tennessee Ernie Ford hit "Sixteen Tons," Merle Travis produced many other excellent songs: "Divorce Me C.O.D.," "No Vacancy," and "Dark as a Dungeon," among others. Along with Chet Atkins, Maybelle Carter, Les Paul, and Joe Maphis, Travis had the exalted status of a "musician's musician." Whether you enjoy him as one of America's finest songwriters, as one of the great instrumentalists, or as a singer of great charm, you'll come to understand why he's a member of the Country Music Hall of Fame.

Moon Mullican
Greatest Hits 1946–1962
Starday 398

Moon Mullican was arguably the greatest hillbilly piano player who ever lived and recorded. More than that, as a pianist, vocalist, and songwriter he was a crucial figure in the melting pot of country styles of the 1940s. Part honky-tonk, part boogie-woogie, part swing, part Cajun, part old-timey, and maybe just a bit of a rockabilly, Moon's careening, freewheeling style was a synthesis of just about everything around him.

Born in Texas in 1909, Mullican learned guitar from a black farmhand, then started playing blues on a family pump-organ bought for religious purposes. He started playing professionally in dance halls and clubs in Texas and Louisiana in the late 1930s, with his own and other groups. In 1947 he had a major hit on King with his reworking of the Cajun folk standard "Jole Blon."

"Sweeter than the Flowers," "Jole Blon," "I'll Sail My Ship Alone," and "Cherokee Boogie" all came tumbling out during his creative peak in the late 1940s and early 1950s. His reputation has dimmed somewhat in recent years, but new generations of fans will discover him in years to come.

Molly O'Day
A *Sacred Collection* 1945–1951
Old Homestead 101

Molly O'Day has been frequently called the best female country singer of her day. Like her contemporary Wilma Lee Cooper, she has a repertoire laced with holiness numbers and Acuff-like mournful old-time songs. This LP brings together some of her classic sides of the late 1940s.

Born Laverne Williamson in Kentucky in 1923, Molly O'Day started working professionally in her teens under the name "Mountain Fern." In the early 1940s she worked in Western style as "Dixie Lee," with her husband, Lynn Davis. She first recorded for Columbia Records in 1946, and was an early performer of Hank Williams's compositions. In 1950, at the height of her success on Columbia, O'Day, who had always emphasized religious numbers, refused to sing anything else at all. Soon thereafter she gave up her music career and secluded herself in the Appalachian coal country, working in poverty as a dedicated evangelist and minister for years, out of the public eye. An occasional religious album has surfaced during the past thirty years, but this LP is all that remains of her promise as country's first postwar female superstar—a role that was filled by Kitty Wells a few years after O'Day's retirement.

Pee Wee King
Best of Pee Wee King and Redd Stewart 1964
Starday 965

Surprising as it seems, the singer-composer-bandleader who in the late 1940s and early 1950s co-wrote and performed "You Belong to Me," "Bonaparte's Retreat," and "Slow Poke," not to mention the phenomenally successful "Tennessee Waltz," does not have a reissue album available of his original work. Pee Wee King and his cowriter Redd Stewart are perhaps the most shockingly overlooked country performers of the late 1940s. Together, they wrote and recorded an amazing string of country classics. In addition, King's band, the Golden West Cowboys, served as a launching pad for such notable stars as Eddy Arnold and Minnie Pearl.

Pee Wee King was born in 1914 in Wisconsin, where his father led a polka band. Pee Wee learned to play fiddle, harmonica, and accordion. In the early 1930s he worked on WLS in Chicago, and in 1934, when Gene Autry gave up his WLS show to go to Hollywood, Pee Wee took over Autry's band, which became the Golden West Cowboys. The band moved to the Grand Ole Opry in 1938, and after some movie work in Hollywood, toured with the Opry's wartime "Camel Caravan."

Until RCA puts together a Pew Wee King collection of original versions of the hits, this batch of rerecordings from Starday will have to suffice, but try to find the old RCA Camden LP that is out of print.

The Maddox Brothers and Rose
The Maddox Brothers and Rose, Vol. 1 1946–1951
Arhoolie 5016

These spangled crazies formed their family band in California, where they moved during the Depression from Alabama (where Rose was born in 1925). They began performing in the 1940s. Once billed as "the most colorful hillbilly band in the land," a reference to the group's showmanship and Western costumes, this record indicates that their performances were pretty colorful as well. Instantly identifiable by the boys' wild cackling laughter, by their speed-freak honky-tonky playing style, and by Rose's bouncy, whoop-it-up hillbilly singing, the Maddox Brothers and Rose were like no other act before or since.

There are two volumes of the Maddoxes' finest performances available from Arhoolie, and either or both of them is worth having. The first contains the bigger hits, such as "Philadelphia Lawyer," but both illustrate perfectly country music at the moment of its raucous transition between innocence and cold, modern reality, between rural and urban experience, and between pent-up honky-tonk and the explosion of rockabilly.

Rose Maddox continues to record and perform today. Her recent recordings on Takoma Records, a fine West Coast country/folk label, reveal a still-strong, blustery, husky delivery that harkens back to these early efforts, applied to the material of the present.

HONKY-TONK

The history of country music in the late 1940s and early 1950s is the history of the social transformation from a rural lifestyle to an urban existence. During World War II people became considerably more mobile. Social relationships became unstable. The divorce rate soared.

Country music reflected these changes. A sound and style emerged from rough Texas bars that dealt with drinking, marital infidelity, work problems, anxiety, sex, and other painfully real circumstances. Musically, this honky-tonk style was loud with whining pedal steel, twanging electric guitars, thumping drums, and a wailing lead singer.

Born in the oilfield roadhouses where beer and blood flowed freely, honky-tonk music came to be the dominant country style in the decades to come. Even today, most people think of country music as the gutbucket cheatin'-and-drinkin' songs of the honky-tonkers. Contemporary performers like George Jones, Merle Haggard, Moe Bandy, and John Anderson bring this tradition up to date.

Ernest Tubb
The Ernest Tubb Story 1958*
MCA 2-4040

"E.T.," as he was known far and wide, was one of country music's true originals. His Texas drawl, humble sincerity, and endless road work are legendary. Most important, Tubb has the special gifts of a master song stylist and he is the very embodiment of honky-tonk music—a living relic of the genre who seems forever preserved in postwar Texas. Willie Nelson, Jack Greene, Merle Haggard, and Ray Price will say that the singer who has forever stamped himself on their styles is Ernest Tubb.

Born in Texas in 1914, E.T. first performed on radio in San Antonio when he was twenty, not long after he had learned to play guitar. An early deal with RCA, arranged by Carrie Rodgers (widow of his hero, Jimmie Rodgers) proved to be a false start, but three years later—again with her help—he recorded in Houston for Decca at a session supervised by famous New York country music man Dave Kapp. A year later, in 1941, his stardom was confirmed when "Walking the Floor Over You" was released.

A Rounder album now available presents less well known Tubb songs in the original, beautifully simple, tight-and-tasty shitkicker style of his 1940s 78s. When Decca/MCA decided to put his classic material together for this double-album set, it added extra

Ernest Tubb (Country Music Foundation)

instrumentation, background voices, and smooth strings to the original Tubb vocals and backing. This, of course, was completely wrongheaded and a contradiction to everything essential to great honky-tonk music. Although the technique often swamps the sound of his Texas Troubadours band, it's hard to completely break the magic Tubb spell.

Floyd Tillman
The Best of Floyd Tillman 1947–1954
Columbia KC–34384

When it comes to off-the-beat singing, jazz vocal phrasing, blue notes, and slurred tones, Floyd Tillman could write the book. If Willie Nelson's eccentric, expressive singing fascinates you, you owe it to yourself to hear the original country master of the style.

Tillman was born in Oklahoma in 1914 and grew up in Texas. He first worked professionally in San Antonio with Adolf Hofner, playing a mixture of Western swing and European styles directed at the large Texas community with roots in Germany and central Europe. While a member of the Blue Ridge Playboys in Houston, he wrote "It Makes No Difference Now," a song that became a national crossover hit when Bing Crosby cut it in 1941. In 1946 Tillman moved from Decca to Columbia and began developing as a song stylist, while continuing to write fine songs. In 1949 "Slippin' Around" went to number five on the country charts in his version, and number one in the version cut by Margaret Whiting and Jimmy Wakely.

Tillman is a honky-tonk pioneer and a unique singer, one of country music's best songwriters, and a lead guitar innovator. This well-done Columbia reissue LP includes such Tillman compositions as "Slippin' Around," "I Love You So Much It Hurts," "I Gotta Have My Baby Back," and "This Cold War with You."

Hank Williams
24 of Hank Williams Greatest Hits 1947–1952[*]
MGM SE–4755-2

If you're unsure what is meant by honky-tonk music, then the name Hank Williams should instantly clarify the matter. His tremendous success with this form was greatly responsible for honky-tonk remaining the dominant country style for more than twenty-five years. Only Jimmie Rodgers could claim a similarly lasting and all-pervasive influence.

Born in Alabama in 1923, Hank's major early influences included his church-organist mother, Lilly; Tee-Tot (Rufus Payne), a black street-singer bluesman who taught him guitar; and the singing of Roy Acuff and Ernest Tubb. Williams won an amateur contest singing his own composition, "The WPA Blues," at age twelve, formed his first Drifting Cowboys band, and began playing on Montgomery radio when he was fourteen.

Hank Williams (Country Music Foundation)

After ten years of playing with various bands in local honky-tonks, medicine shows, and the like, he auditioned in 1946 for the Acuff-Rose publishing company in Nashville, and Fred Rose began publishing his songs and managing his career. With Fred's help, Hank was signed to MGM records. The success of his 1947 release of his own song "Move It on Over" helped to get him on the Louisiana Hayride, and in 1949, after "Lovesick Blues" went to number one on the country charts, he debuted on the Opry.

In a few brief years he developed a vast following. Then, on a cold January day in 1953, 25,000 people stood in front of the Montgomery Municipal Auditorium during Hank's funeral service.

Several tracks on this album have been "modernized," thanks to the kind of continual self-doubt that surfaces each year on national TV with an overblown orchestra for the Country Music Association awards. Fortunately, the majority of these great Hank Williams numbers have been kept in their original forms. "Your Cheatin' Heart," "I'm So Lonesome I Could Cry," "Kaw-Liga," "Cold, Cold Heart," "Lovesick Blues," "Jambalaya," "Hey Good Lookin'," "I Can't Help It (If I'm Still in Love with You)," "Half as Much," "You Win Again," "Why Don't You Love Me (Like Ya Used to Do)?," and "Take These Chains from My Heart" just scratch the surface of the man's genius. The follow-up two-record set *Hank Williams, 24 Greatest Hits, Vol. 2* (MGM 2-5401) has nearly as many jewels, including the gospel standards "I Saw the Light" and "House of Gold." Be extremely cautious in buying other Hank Williams albums. Most of them are mutilations of what was once great honky-tonk.

Lefty Frizzell
Remembering . . . the Greatest Hits of Lefty Frizzell 1950–1964*
Columbia KC–33882

For many years Columbia's *Greatest Hits* package for the titanically gifted Lefty Frizzell was a slicked-up, voices-and-strings monstrosity. That record is still around. In the 1970s, however, the company put together this compilation of Lefty's original recordings. Take note: the tricked-up album has a white jacket; this lovely one comes in a black-colored package.

Born in Texas in 1928, Lefty began performing as a teenager in the Texas bars where honky-tonk was being created. In 1950 he cut his first hit for Columbia, "If You've Got the Money, Honey, I've Got the Time." The next year he reached the number one chart spot with "I Want to Be with You Always" and "Always Late." The flip side of "Always Late," Lefty's "Mom and Dad's Waltz," went to number two on the chart.

One of the very finest of honky-tonk singers and writers—past or present—Lefty has inspired tribute albums by both Willie Nelson and Merle Haggard. George Jones and his generation of stylists also owe a tremendous debt to this man. For an all-too-brief time in the early 1950s, Frizzell rivaled even Hank Williams in popularity.

Lefty Frizzell (Country Music Foundation)

Ray Price
Ray Price's Greatest Hits 1956–1961
Columbia PC–8866

Ray Price was born on an East Texas farm in 1926. Despite his present image as a tuxedoed country crooner, in the mid-1950s Price was one of country music's superior honky-tonk performers. With his fine Cherokee Cowboys band, Price paid his dues in sleazy redneck dives like many other country acts of the time. During the same period he released a series of smooth solid-country singles, such as "I'll Be There," "Crazy Arms," "Release Me," "City Lights," and "Heartaches by the Number." The Cherokee Cowboys included former members of Hank Williams's Drifting Cowboys and, at various times in Ray's career, Buddy Emmons, Roger Miller, and Willie Nelson.

Bear in mind when shopping that there are two Ray Prices—the same man, but different styles. If you're looking for the fellow who sang "Danny Boy" and "For the Good Times," find his later Columbia *Greatest Hits* albums. If you're looking for wailing honky-tonk soul, though, make an effort to find this collection. The album cover has a greenish-background photo of Ray in a winter coat.

Webb Pierce
Best of Webb Pierce 1958–1968
MCA 2-4087

Webb Pierce, born in Louisiana in 1926, is the embodiment of the 1950s country singer, one of the "rhinestone wonders" who recorded some of the greatest country songs in history. "Slowly," "I Ain't Never," "In the Jailhouse Now," and "Missing You" only partially comprise his long string of 1950s successes, which began in 1952 with "Wondering" and the number one "Back Street Affair." He then moved along to "The Last Waltz" and "There Stands the Glass" in 1953, and kept on going into the 1970s. With his nasal, sharp-edged delivery and hauntingly pure country voice, Webb Pierce is one of the outstanding honky-tonk heroes.

As with all the other MCA collections, you'll have to put up with the violins and ooohing background singers that have been added to the original recordings. Nevertheless, this is a superb reminder of one of country's greatest decades and of Pierce's importance in it.

Webb Pierce (Country Music Foundation)

Hank Thompson
The Best of Hank Thompson 1957–1959
Capitol DT–1878

Born in Texas in 1925, Hank Thompson began his career on local radio, sponsored by one of the flour companies that did so much for country music (and vice versa). After his discharge from the navy in 1946, and a stretch at Princeton University, he returned to station WACO in Waco and formed his famous and influential band, the Brazos Valley Boys. Tex Ritter brought him to the attention of Capitol Records, and he soon had a hit with "Humpty Dumpty Heart." In 1952 his recording of "The Wild Side of Life" went to number one.

Thompson straddles honky-tonk and Western swing. His mixture of the two styles was hugely popular with country fans of the late 1940s and early 1950s, and he racked up some twenty top-ten hits in a row. Still a major figure in country recording and performing, Hank Thompson has tried other styles over the years, but he always seems to return to the classic sound of these early hits.

George Jones
Greatest Hits 1958–1962*
Mercury ML–8014

How do you choose a George Jones album from among the dozens of great ones he's released? His Starday records, cut from 1954 to 1957, show him during the raw Texas beginnings of his career. Many of his biggest Nashville hits are on United Artists albums. Musicor Records had him during his longest sustained hit streak, and some of that material also appeared later on RCA reissues. The contemporary George Jones has produced an immensely satisfying string of LPs for Epic. To put it simply, there's no such thing as a bad George Jones record. Even when he's mediocre, he's head-and-shoulders above most others, which is why he's been called "the Rolls Royce of Country Singers."

George Jones was born in Texas in 1931, and although his family's background was rural, his music owes much to the culture of East Texas industrial workers. When he got his first guitar, at age nine, it was in time to plug his ears into the great current of hillbilly music that was flowing from stages and loudspeakers in cities like Beaumont and Houston to soothe the souls of country people who had come to escape the Depression in the defense plants. After service with the marines in Korea, Jones gigged locally part-time, until he began recording first for Starday, then for Mercury in Beaumont and Nashville.

This Mercury album, out of print for many years, is available again, and it is a good place to begin a Jones collection. It's George during the years 1958–1962, when he ranged from rockabilly ("White Lightning") to ballads ("Tender Years") to whiskey-soaked honky-tonk ("Color of the Blues," "Window Up Above"). There were times during this period when his musical accompaniment wasn't always the most sympathetic, but he seldom found a better collection of songs to showcase his remarkable voice.

CLASSIC OPRY STARS

During the late 1940s and early 1950s, Nashville's Grand Ole Opry made an unprecedented talent drive, bringing together the most impressive roster of country stars ever assembled in one place. The move brought the Opry to the top of barn dance shows; although it had been on the air since 1925, the program was never so clearly dominant as during these years. At the same time, Nashville became the national center for country recording and song publishing, a position it has never relinquished.

Many of these singers continue on the show, reminders of the days when a WSM Opry broadcast consisted of one giant hit after another. They're the acts that made Nashville what it is today; a collection of their records alone would make a fine country music library.

Roy Acuff
Greatest Hits 1936–1947
Columbia CS–1034

Roy Acuff was the Opry's first true solo singing star. When he joined the show in 1938 it was still dominated by old-time string bands. His excellent, toe-tapping band, the Smoky Mountain Boys, and his own moaning, yearning vocal style electrified audiences at once. The release of a few dynamic Columbia 78s in the early 1940s catapulted him to stardom on records as well. He has reigned ever since as the King of Country Music.

Acuff was born in Tennessee in 1903 to musical parents. After some years spent trying to develop a career in professional baseball, illness confined him to bed for most of 1930. During that year he listened to his father's collection of fiddle records and practiced fiddle and voice. In 1932 a neighbor invited Roy to tour with his medicine show for the summer; the next year Roy began to play with a group of Knoxville part-time musicians. In 1935 the group began performing on WROL in Knoxville and became the Crazy Tennesseans. In 1936 they recorded their first session for ARC, soon to become Columbia Records.

Roy Acuff (Country Music Foundation)

It is sad and unfitting that there is no in-print album containing *all* the great original Acuff singles, such as "Wabash Cannonball," "Low and Lonely," "Great Speckled Bird," "Pins and Needles," "Wreck on the Highway," "Precious Jewel," "Night Train to Memphis," "Fire Ball Mail," and "My Tears Don't Show." Listening to these again would inspire many country lovers to crown him king once more. The two Harmony albums *Great Speckled Bird* and *Night Train to Memphis* used to do the job, but now all we're left with is this one-disc Columbia collection of a few of the originals. ("Wabash Cannonball" is not in the original version on this record.) The Capitol and Elektra so-called *Greatest Hits* sets are worse. Stick with this one.

Red Foley
Red Foley Memories 1947–1954
Vocalion 73920

Red Foley is another Opry legend whose best performances are mostly out of print. There is an MCA package of slicked-up, overlaid-with-strings performances, but Foley's original singles—mostly cut during the 1940s and 1950s—suffer more than most of his contemporaries' under that kind of treatment, which can be heard on Decca's *Red Foley Story*. This budget-priced LP might be a better starting place for those unfamiliar with Foley's work. Although it doesn't contain any of the really big hits, at least it's composed of his songs as they were originally heard in his heyday.

Foley was born in Kentucky in 1910. When he was seventeen he won a talent contest sponsored by the Atwater Kent radio company, and in 1930 he went to Chicago to appear on WLS with fellow Kentuckians the Cumberland Ridge Runners. In 1937 with his brother Cotton, John Lair, and Whitey Ford—the "Duke of Paducah"—he started the "Renfro Valley Barn Dance," which eventually drew thousands to the small Kentucky village on Saturday nights. The show began broadcasting over WLW in 1938. He also joined Red Skelton as the costar of "Avalon Time" on network radio. Along with Eddy Arnold and Ernest Tubb, he was one of the earliest country stars to record regularly in Nashville. In 1947 he was signed to the Opry. He charted such up-tempo numbers as "Tennessee Saturday Night" (1948), but became perhaps best known for gospel tunes like "Peace in the Valley" and "Just a Closer Walk with Thee." He toured steadily until his death in 1968.

In addition to this record, the other available collection of Foley's original sides is the duet package, *Kitty Wells' and Red Foley's Golden Favorites* on MCA (MCA 83). It's a coupling of two of the most expressive country singers of their era.

Kitty Wells
The Kitty Wells Story 1958–1963*
MCA 2-4031

Kitty Wells, known as the Queen of Country Music, was the first woman to achieve modern country music stardom, borne to such heights by her unmistakable high, keening delivery that brings out the "country" in country tunes.

1952   1954

1959   1960

Kitty Wells (Country Music Foundation)

Born in Nashville in 1918, Kitty sang gospel as a child and started playing guitar in her early teens. She began appearing on radio, and around 1936 began touring with her husband-to-be, Jack Wright, as part of the Johnny and Jack (Anglin) show. In 1947 they joined the Opry. They moved to the "Louisiana Hayride," rejoining the Opry in 1952, the year that Kitty's recording of an answer song to Hank Thompson's "The Wild Side of Life" became the first record by a woman to reach number one on the country charts. That record, "It Wasn't God Who Made Honky Tonk Angels," started it all. But there are many equally fine performances on this reissue that paved the way for a wholesale invasion of gifted female singers in Kitty Wells's wake. This unassuming Nashville house-wife may seem like an unlikely standard-bearer for the women of country music, but listening to these songs, it's easy to understand why she was. For a smaller, excellent sampling of Wells's music, try *The Golden Years* on Rounder (SS 13).

Jean Shepard
The Best of Jean Shepard 1935–1955
Capitol SM–11888

An Oklahoman born in 1933 who started out playing Western swing, Jean Shepard shared chart space with Kitty Wells in the 1950s and helped define country music in that period. Her successes continued through the 1960s and 1970s—she has had more than forty hit singles over twenty-five years—and she still performs regularly on the Opry.

Shepard cut fine singles in the 1960s for Capitol and more in the 1970s for United Artists, but none of these are currently in print on reissue albums. This record contains the earliest Shepard hits.

The Louvin Brothers
The Louvin Brothers 1951–1952*
Rounder SS-07

Ira and Charlie Louvin are arguably the best brother duet ever, for hardly any others in country music have matched their combination of expert songwriting and spine-tingling singing. If you have never yet heard them, you may already know their songs from Emmylou Harris records. Imagine the Everly Brothers singing more country, a bit harsher, somewhat higher-voiced, and a lot less teenaged, and you'll have an idea of the Louvin sound.

The Louvin Brothers (Country Music Foundation)

Born in Alabama, Ira in 1924 and Charlie in 1927, the Louvin (originally Loud-ermilk) brothers began with a repertoire of older country and gospel music played on mandolin and guitar. In time their repertoire included country music of all kinds, and their Nashville recordings featured the electric guitar. In 1951 they signed with MGM Records, then moved to Capitol and began appearing on the Opry. In 1955 a string of hits began with their composition, "When I Stop Dreaming." Their last hit as a duo came in 1962 ("Must You Throw Dirt in My Face?"), then they split up to work as soloists. Ira died in a car crash in 1965. Charlie continues to perform on the Opry.

As with several of country music's authentic geniuses, any Louvin Brothers record is a good one to get. Capitol has some gospel songs of theirs in print; Pickwick/Hilltop has a budget-priced hits compilation. Rounder records stay in print almost permanently, and their Louvin Brothers records are both excellent and easily available.

Cowboy Copas
Best of Cowboy Copas 1946–1960
Starday SLP–958

Cowboy Copas was born in Oklahoma in 1913 and was killed in the March 5, 1963, plane crash that also took the lives of Patsy Cline and Hawkshaw Hawkins. Before his death he had accumulated an impressive string of hits on King and Starday, including "Alabam," "Filipino Baby," "Signed, Sealed and Delivered," and "Tragic Romance."

Raised on a ranch and instructed in Western music and folklore by his grandfather, Copas formed a duo with Natchee, an Indian fiddler; they toured together in the late 1930s. After they split up Cowboy began performing regularly in Knoxville and recording in Cincinnati. In 1946 he became an Opry regular, singing with Pee Wee King's Golden West Cowboys. He had a top ten hit in 1951, then his career slowed until 1960, when "Alabam" went to number one.

Since Starday Records now has the rights to the King recordings, it's possible to get the hits Copas recorded for both companies together on this one record.

Hank Snow
Best of Hank Snow 1950–1963 *
RCA ANL1–3470

Born in Nova Scotia in 1914, Hank Snow was the first Canadian artist elected into the Country Music Hall of Fame. His north-of-the-border nasality, distinctive accent, and wide-open-spaces subject matter clearly mark him as an individualist. Snow's fascination with trains, ships, and rambling in general, are mirrored in the restless quality

Hank Snow (Country Music Foundation)

of his finest records. His clipped enunciation of lyrics followed by a vocal slide at key words make listening to him a continually intriguing experience. Frequently overlooked is the fact that he's nearly as great a country guitar picker as he is a singer.

Snow began working in Nova Scotia clubs in his mid-teens, after four years as a cabin boy. Jimmie Rodgers was an early influence. In 1934 Snow got his own radio show in Halifax; he started recording for RCA in 1936. His record of "I'm Moving On," his own composition, went to number one in 1950, and his hits didn't slow down for the next two decades.

This, the first volume of RCA's packages of Snow's biggest hits, contains mainly cuts from the early 1950s, including "I'm Movin' On," "Rhumba Boogie," "Let Me Go, Lover," and "I Don't Hurt Anymore," plus a few 1960s sides like the famous tongue-twisting "I've Been Everywhere" and the saga song "Miller's Cave." This sampling of a singer who stayed on the same record label longer than anyone in history will probably make you hungry for many more Hank Snow discs.

Marty Robbins
More Greatest Hits 1959–1962*
Columbia CS–8435

Marty Robbins was born in Arizona in 1925 and received his early training in the tall-tale tradition of the West from his grandfather, Texas Bob Heckle. He began working in clubs and on radio and TV in Arizona; in 1952 Little Jimmy Dickens brought him to the attention of Columbia Records. His third release for Columbia, "I'll Go on Alone," went to number ten, and three years later "Singing the Blues" went to number one. Less than a year later he was back at the number one spot with the country/pop hit "A White Sport Coat." The rockabilly, teenage-oriented phase of his career continued until 1959. The next phase, represented by this album, was Robbins singing his immortal cowboy songs, "El Paso" and its successors, and heartache laments ("Don't Worry," for instance). That period was followed by Robbins's transformation into a smooth balladeer ("My Woman, My Woman, My Wife," "You Gave Me a Mountain"), followed by his service as a contemporary Nashville star with lush arrangements and sometimes superior material ("Among My Souvenirs," "El Paso City"). Through all these changes he proved himself to be a top-rank, versatile singer, a great composer, a fine humorist, and perhaps the Opry's best showman.

(CBS Records)

Various Artists
Country Hits of the 1950s 1951–1957
Capitol SM–885

Country Hits of the 1950s contains hits by some of the Nashville acts of that day who are not Opry entertainers now. "Don't Let the Stars Get in Your Eyes" made Skeets McDonald a star. "You Better Not Do That" by Tommy Collins was one of the top ten records of 1954. Faron Young began his long career with such records as "If You Ain't Lovin' (You Ain't Livin')." Ferlin Husky scored early in his musical life with the throbbing "Gone." Like its companion Capitol packages of 1940s and 1960s hits, this record is an excellent introduction to the music of its era.

ROCKABILLY

Rock 'n' roll, the most popular music of all time, was born in the 1950s from the mating of country music and rhythm-and-blues; one of the very first sounds to come from this mating was rockabilly. In its purest form, rockabilly music is only lightly amplified and electrified, retaining the little yodels, vocal cries, and hiccoughs of country music. It is a style that was created by a combination of the repertoire and personnel of mainstream country music with the liberated singing feeling, blues directness, rhythmic intensity, and stage mannerisms of the R&B music of the time.

Rockabilly instrumentation is unusually spare, often featuring staccato guitar playing and slapped stand-up bass. The boogie-woogie piano style was an important influence, as was the syncopated finger-picking playing style of ragtime and country boogie guitar.

This music is very closely identified with the Memphis label, Sun Records, but it was also recorded and developed in Nashville (at RCA), Los Angeles (at Liberty Records), Texas (at Starday), Louisiana, New Mexico, and elsewhere. It burst upon the national music scene along with the teenage culture revolution of the mid-1950s.

As with its other substyles, country music retained rockabilly and its influence long after the nation at large went on to the highly produced and more complicated rock music of the 1960s. The influence of rockabilly can still be heard in songs on today's country charts, as in the works of Waylon Jennings, Mac Davis, and Jerry Lee Lewis.

Elvis Presley
The Sun Sessions 1954–1955[*]
RCA AYM–1-3893

Bill Haley and the Comets made the first big rockabilly breakthrough with "Rock Around the Clock," and their *Golden Hits* album on MCA (MCA 2-4010) is certainly worth having as a souvenir of some of the finest toe-tappers of the mid-1950s. But it was Elvis Presley steaming out of Memphis a little later who ignited the rockabilly fire.

Born in Mississippi in 1935, Elvis moved to Memphis with his family when he was thirteen. He sang with his family in church and at revival meetings. In Memphis he played with local groups, appeared on radio shows, and found the label—Sam Phillips's Sun Records—able to recognize and channel his special talent and unique melting-pot musical sensibility.

Presley's later work as a mainstream rock and ballad singer has obscured the raw intensity of his first recordings on Sun Records. It is easy to forget just how sizzling those records were. When RCA brought out this collection of "The Hillbilly Cat's" early material, it was an astounding revelation to many.

Johnny Burnette
Listen to Johnny Burnette 1956–1957
MCA 1513

Johnny Burnette's music is a reminder of the wonderful simplicity of rockabilly. It sounds like a gang of crazy country teenagers bouncing around with their instruments

Elvis Presley (Country Music Foundation)

in Dad's garage, having the time of their lives and cooking up hot music. Burnette and his brother, Dorsey, were Memphis teenagers inventing music that expressed both their country soul and their near-violent teenage frustrations. Perhaps more than any other single album, this MCA release captures the true spirit and meaning of rockabilly. Even though most of the songs on it may be unfamiliar, it will get you dancing and send you after more Burnette music.

Carl Perkins
Original Golden Hits 1956–1958
Sun 111

An amazing array of talent was collected at the Sun Records studios on Union Avenue in Memphis during the mid-1950s. Jerry Lee Lewis, Roy Orbison, Johnny Cash, Dickey Lee, Elvis Presley, Harold Dorman, Conway Twitty, Narvel Felts, Bill Black, Jack Clement, and Charlie Rich were all affiliated with Sun and helped forge the rockabilly sound. Among the label's hottest rockabillies were Billy Lee Riley, Charlie Feathers, Sonny Burgess, Carl Mann, and the archetype, Carl Perkins.

Perkins was born a poor Tennessee farm boy and performed as a youth in a family string band with his brothers before moving to Memphis to make his fortune. He auditioned for Sam Phillips, and in 1955 Flip, a Sun affiliate, released "Movie Maggs," a composition by Carl, along with his country composition "Turn Around." After his single of his own composition "Blue Suede Shoes" became a hit in 1956, Perkins rivaled even Elvis in popularity, but a car accident called a temporary halt to his career and he never again reached the top of the charts. He did continue to release fine singles, including "Honey Don't," "Boppin' the Blues," "Dixie Fried," "Match Box," "Everybody's Trying to Be My Baby," and "Pink Pedal Pushers." Several of these became famous songs to a new generation of listeners when the Beatles recorded new versions of them in the 1960s.

The Everly Brothers
24 Golden Hits of the Everly Brothers 1957–1964
Arista Records AL 9-8207

The Everly Brothers were born in Kentucky, Don in 1937 and Phil in 1939. Their parents, Ike and Margaret, were well-known country performers who toured and performed on radio. At the ages of eight and six respectively, Don and Phil began working regularly with their parents on summer tours. After Ike and Margaret Everly retired, the brothers kept working together, soon moving to Nashville. They signed with Cadence in 1957 and began cutting a wonderful series of records. Their inspired, soulful harmonizing was matched with astonishing songs written by another family team, Felice and Boudleaux Bryant, as well as with some outstanding compositions by the Everlys themselves. Production was supervised by Chet Atkins (who also contributed guitar work), and it was extraordinary in its balance of simplicity and power. At the end of the 1950s, the Everlys moved to the Warner Brothers label.

The Everly Brothers—Don and Phil (Country Music Foundation)

The Cadence Records singles everyone remembers ("Bye Bye Love," "Wake Up Little Susie," "Poor Jenny," "When Will I Be Loved?", "Bird Dog," "All I Have to Do Is Dream"), were packaged and repackaged on a number of labels, and then became unavailable for a long time. The rerecordings of these songs that they made for Warner lacked the punch and drive of the originals. This recently released set now offers twelve of the great Cadence original singles, plus twelve of the later hits, such as "Cathy's Clown," "Walk Right Back," and "Crying in the Rain" which, while not as rockabilly as the Cadence cuts, are great records all the same. Start your Everlys collection here, then go hunting for the rest of the great oldies—those Cadence albums just didn't quit.

Eddie Cochran
Legendary Masters 1957–1959
United Artists UA UAR-LWB-9959

Cochran is the best example of West Coast rockabilly. Like another rockabilly hero, Gene Vincent, he has always been much more popular in England than in his U.S. homeland. In fact, probably as many people know Cochran's "Summertime Blues" from the 1970 recording by the English rock band the Who as from the original 1958 hit.

Born in Oklahoma in 1938, Cochran was raised in Minnesota until he was eleven, when his family moved to California. In 1954 he started working as a guitar player, backing up country singer Hank Cochran. When they began touring as a duo they called themselves "The Cochran Brothers," although they weren't related. They cut a couple of country singles for the Hollywood-based Ekko label and then, after watching Elvis perform in 1955, started cutting rock material. They split up in 1956, Hank Cochran eventually going to Nashville to compose such standards as "I Fall to Pieces" and "Make the World Go Away," and Eddie Cochran starting with Liberty Records. In 1958 Eddie's smash hit "Summertime Blues" was released. He spent a lot of time with musician friends in the studio, where he displayed great potential as a producer and arranger, as well as a singer and songwriter. It was in England, at the end of a 1960 tour, headed for the airport, that Eddie Cochran was killed in a taxicab crash.

This is highly exciting music that fairly sizzles and tingles. It combines hot guitar playing, good songwriting, and an inspiring heavy beat.

Buddy Holly
A Rock 'n' Roll Collection 1957–1964*
MCA 2-4009

Of the most widely heard rockabilly performers, the Everly Brothers might be said to represent the southern Appalachian element of rockabilly; the early Elvis and Jerry

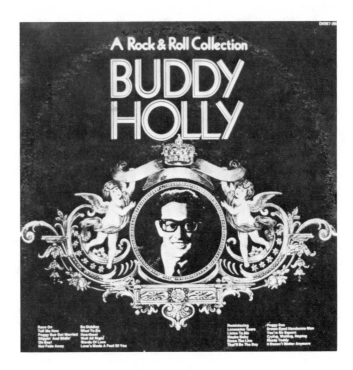

Lee Lewis the Deep South element; and Buddy Holly—along with Roy Orbison—might be seen as the Southwestern representative of rockabilly.

Born in Lubbock, Texas, Holly grew up listening to the rich mix of country, blues, jazz, Mexican, German, and other influences that made up Texan musical culture. After several years of local work around Lubbock, Buddy recorded in Nashville in 1956 for Decca. After five unsuccessful singles, he and the Crickets retreated to record in Clovis, New Mexico, and in 1957 "Peggy Sue" became a hit.

Buddy Holly's recording career was barely three years long—he was killed in a plane crash in 1959—but he seems to grow in stature and influence as time goes by. The Crickets, who backed him up, still tour singing his songs; his last bass player, Waylon Jennings, is a country music superstar; his first partner, Bob Montgomery, is now a successful music publisher and producer in Nashville. Several of Buddy's hits have been revived on the country charts in recent years, and his records still sell. British MCA's boxed set of albums containing all the material Holly recorded is the package for the true devotee. However, this two-record set available from MCA in America is the single best introduction to Buddy Holly and the Crickets' most memorable performances.

THE NASHVILLE SOUND

The advent of rock 'n' roll in the mid-1950s sent country music reeling. It dropped drastically in popularity as more and more radio stations switched over to playing the new teenage music. In response, several Nashville producers began to produce country records for the adult buyers of easy-listening pop music: they developed what became known as the Nashville Sound.

The architects of and most significant contributors to this new approach to recording country songs were producer/guitarist Chet Atkins, vocal arranger Anita Kerr, and producer Owen Bradley. The procedure was to smooth over the roughness of the country style of a singer with violin sections, soft background voices, sophisticated arrangements, and studio technology. A typical Nashville Sound record features a high jangling rhythm guitar strum, country instruments overlaid with a soaring violin section, vocal background "oooohs" from either the Jordanaires or the Anita Kerr Singers, and a slight echo effect on the lead singer's voice.

The Nashville Sound was a phenomenal success. Many of the classic records ("I Fall to Pieces," "He'll Have to Go," "The End of the World," "The Three Bells") became huge pop music hits, and Nashville rose to being one of the world's largest recording centers.

Chet Atkins
A Legendary Performer Vol. 1 1947–1970
RCA CPL–1-2503

Eddy Arnold
Best of Eddy Arnold 1949–1965
RCA AYS1-3675

Eddy Arnold (seated) and Chet Atkins (Country Music Foundation)

Jim Reeves
Best of Jim Reeves 1957–1963
RCA AYL-1-3678

Chet Atkins and RCA were prime movers behind the Nashville Sound. Atkins's records showcase his ability as a guitarist of high technical proficiency. As a production executive his two greatest Nashville Sound artists were Eddy Arnold and Jim Reeves.

Chet Atkins was born on a farm in Tennessee in 1924. His older half-brother, Jim, was a fine jazz and pop guitarist who eventually worked as a member of the Fred Waring Orchestra and the Les Paul Trio. He helped influence Chet to start playing guitar early in a difficult childhood which included serious bouts with asthma. Chet started working young: he played fiddle on WNOX in Knoxville when he was eighteen, eventually becoming staff guitarist for that station. In the second half of the 1940s, Chet worked as a sideman for Red Foley, Homer and Jethro, and the Carter Family, and tried recording as a vocalist and instrumentalist. In the early 1950s, as Nashville began to become an important recording center for country music, his talent, wide experience, and connections formed during his years in the industry led to an increasingly important role as a sideman, artist-and-repertoire (A&R) man, producer, instrumental recording artist, and record executive. He was made RCA Nashville A&R manager in 1960, and a vice-president of RCA Records in 1968.

Eddy Arnold was born on a Tennessee farm in 1918. His father fiddled, his mother taught him to play guitar. Leaving high school to help on the farm, he performed locally part-time, moving on to jobs on radio and in clubs, and performing for six years on

Jim Reeves (Country Music Foundation)

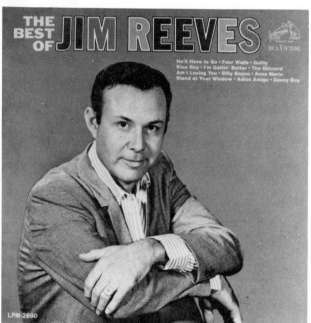

WTJS in Jackson, Tennessee. He signed with RCA in 1944 and within just a few years was demonstrating his ability to reach an uncommonly broad audience. With the help of the Nashville Sound he became the most successful and wealthy crooner in Music City history.

Many people feel that Jim Reeves was the ultimate country-pop Nashville Sound singer, for his velvet voice was perfectly married to Atkins's rich orchestrations. He was born in Texas in 1924 and moved into the music business after a leg injury ended his career as a professional ballplayer. While working as an announcer for KWKH in Shreveport, Louisiana, he recorded "Mexican Joe" for Abbot Records; this led to Nashville and RCA, where his subtle country balladeer style was developed and encouraged. Tight and controlled, yet warm and expressive, the voice of Jim Reeves perfectly illustrated the coming together of pop and country music.

Patsy Cline
The Patsy Cline Story 1960–1963*
MCA 2-4038

Dottie West
Would You Hold It Against Me? 1966
RCA Camden ACL–1–0125

Decca Records (now MCA) dressed most of its country acts in the new Nashville Sound clothes. Even Kitty Wells and Webb Pierce were given the treatment. Most successful of all the label's acts with this type of production was Patsy Cline. Like Jim

Patsy Cline (Country Music Foundation)

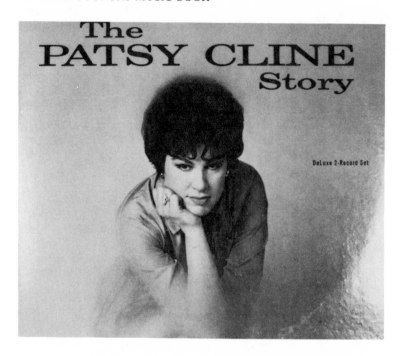

Reeves, Patsy had the ability to keep the "heart" in her voice while blending perfectly with the elegant, cool orchestral setting.

Patsy was born in Virginia in 1932 and displayed talent at an early age. She got a guest spot on the bill of a Grand Old Opry traveling unit when she was sixteen and was encouraged to try Nashville, without success. She returned home, but in 1957 she won an Arthur Godfrey Talent Scouts show, singing "Walking After Midnight." She recorded the song for Decca and the record soon reached both the pop and country charts. In 1961 her recording of "I Fall to Pieces" went to number one, "Crazy" went to number two, and in 1962 "She's Got You" went to number one. Her hits continued until her death in a plane crash in 1963.

Dorothy Marie March, who became Dottie West, was born in Tennessee in 1932. Her father gave her beginning guitar lessons, and she continued her music studies, working part-time to pay for them. Eventually she attended Tennessee Technological University as a music major. There she met and married Bill West, a steel guitar player and electronics engineering student. For some years after graduation they performed professionally together part-time. In 1959 Dottie was signed to Starday, and they moved to Nashville. After switching to RCA in the early 1960s, she recorded "Here Comes My Baby," which she co-wrote with her husband; it went to number ten in 1964 and won her a Grammy Award.

Long before her 1980s success as Kenny Rogers's duet partner, Dottie West was making fine records in Nashville and writing fine songs. Although she was overshadowed at the time by the bigger hits of RCA's Skeeter Davis, in retrospect it appears that Dottie West was RCA's finest female representative of its Nashville Sound. This budget-priced album is a good introduction to West's work during this period, but her out-of-print *Best of* RCA album is a better sampling of what she was capable of.

The Browns
Best of the Browns 1956–1964
RCA AYL1-3861

If there had been vocal group honors back in the 1950s, the Browns would have won as many awards as the Statler Brothers later did. Maxine, born in Louisiana in 1932; Jim Edward, born in Arkansas in 1934; and Bonnie, born in Arkansas in 1937, formed the Brown family trio in 1955. (Jim and Maxine had worked together as a duet earlier and had appeared regularly on the Louisiana Hayride.) Signed to RCA, the Browns had their first hit on that label in 1956, "I Take the Chance." In 1959 they had a number one country hit with an English-language version of the Compagnons de la Chanson's "Three Bells." The lovely close-harmony sound of the Browns remains one of the nicest discoveries a novice country fan can make.

Bobby Bare
This Is Bobby Bare 1963–1969
RCA VPS–6090

Bobby Bare's contribution to the Nashville Sound era was his unerring good taste in songs. More than any other individual of the time, he collected the best Nashville had to offer. Bare's easy-going sophistication and "modernity" are particularly striking in view of the classic "hard country" elements in his background. Born in Ohio in 1935, he lost his mother when he was five and was a farm worker at fifteen. The youngster's first hit was in the pop field, the talking blues "The All-American Boy," recorded under the name Bill Parsons. He began his hit-making country career in 1962 with "Shame on Me." "Detroit City," "The Streets of Baltimore," "Four Strong Winds," "500 Miles Away from Home," and "(Margie's at) The Lincoln Park Inn" are just a few of the fine songs compiled on this album.

Bare continues to get top hits with excellent, unusual material. For samplings of his more recent work try *Bobby Bare, Greatest Hits* (RCA AYL1–4118), which includes "The Winner," and *Bobby Bare, Biggest Hits* (Columbia FC–38311), which includes "Tequila, Sheila" and "The Winner."

NASHVILLE POP

During the Nashville Sound era, the national music community also began to look toward Nashville as a pop music publishing and recording center. The tremendous success of Elvis Presley and his Nashville-recorded products focused attention on the young and small Music Row, site of Nashville's record and song publishing companies, as never before. Brenda Lee's incredible string of hit ballads from Nashville confirmed the town's reputation.

Pop music had been a part of the Nashville music scene from the start. The town's first million-selling record was "Near You," a ballad by the Francis Craig Orchestra, released by Bullet in 1947. During the 1950s and 1960s Nashville singers and songwriters proved that it was no fluke by turning out consistently excellent and highly commercial pop music smashes. Nearly all of Nashville's leading pop music figures, however, began as country music acts.

Patti Page
Golden Hits 1949–1957
Mercury 60495

Brenda Lee
The Brenda Lee Story 1959–1964*
MCA 2-4012

Roy Orbison
The Very Best of Roy Orbison 1960–1965
Monument MC–6622

Bobby Goldsboro
10th Anniversary Album 1964–1974
United Artists UAR–LWB–311

THE BRENDA LEE STORY
HER GREATEST HITS

Patti Page started out as a country singer in Oklahoma, where she was born in 1927. Her multimillion-selling recording of "Tennessee Waltz," composed by Pee Wee King, topped the pop charts and made the country top five; it marked the beginning of Nashville Pop. Her finely controlled vocal phrasing was frequently applied to country songs in pop arrangements.

Brenda Lee, born in Georgia in 1944, started out singing Hank Williams's gospel tunes when she was a child. Her first hits were on the country charts. Then her huge pop hits recorded in Nashville studios made her a teenage rage. Then she became a country star again. This MCA album set spans all these changes.

Roy Orbison, born in Texas in 1936, began his career at Sun Records in Memphis, with rockabilly. He placed only a few hits on the country charts, but his pop chart hits were among the most powerful ever produced in Nashville and his unique, emotional songs are now regularly recorded by mainstream country acts.

Bobby Goldsboro, born in Florida in 1941, began performing while in high school in Dothan, Alabama. He began his Nashville career playing in Roy Orbison's band. His mid-1960s pop hits range from melodic ballads to big-beat rhythm-and-blues–flavored tunes. Later he became an even bigger star with "Honey," which went to number one in 1968 on the country charts. He has since become a regular country hit-maker.

THE 1960s

Country music staged a comeback of major proportions in the 1960s. By the end of the decade a thousand American radio stations were broadcasting country music, the Country Music Association Awards show was among the highest-rated TV yearly specials, and Nashville had become a tourist mecca. Glen Campbell, Johnny Cash, "Hee Haw," and folk music were all over national television. Numerous stars inaugurated successful syndicated country TV variety shows. The first trickle of what was to become a flood of country-oriented movies began to appear. And several of Nashville's finest country talents achieved international stardom.

It was a decade marked by several different musical trends. In California, Buck Owens's Bakersfield empire for a while rivaled Nashville as a country recording center. Roger Miller achieved unprecedented national stardom with a string of straight-ahead country novelty tunes. Johnny Cash likewise became a celebrity with honest, plain country records. Jimmy Dean, Johnny Horton, Claude King, Stonewall Jackson, Don Gibson, Dave Dudley, Bobby Helms, Wanda Jackson, Jody Miller, Jeannie C. Riley, and Sue Thompson all enjoyed attention with hits that went way beyond the country charts during the decade. No one style predominated in the 1960s, but all of the older ones—especially honky-tonk—thrived with new vigor.

Johnny Horton
Greatest Hits 1959–1960
Columbia CS–8396

Johnny Horton, born in Texas in 1929, made his first appearances on KLTV in his home town of Tyler. In 1948 he starred on KWKH in Shreveport, along with Hank Williams and Jim Reeves. His first big hit, "Honky-tonk Man," went to number fourteen in 1956, but his greatest success came in 1959 and 1960 with records that were pop-chart hits as well as number-one country hits: "When It's Springtime in Alaska," "The Battle of New Orleans," "North to Alaska," and "Sink the Bismarck." He was killed in an automobile accident in 1960.

Until recently Horton had been largely forgotten and ignored, despite the fact that his *Greatest Hits* album has sold steadily throughout the years. Now a Horton revival seems to be under way, especially in Europe, where several compilations of his work are available once more. This is good news, for Johnny Horton possessed one of the most electrifying voices ever heard. Listening to this collection of his greatest hits is a revelation of white-hot country soul.

Various Artists
Country Hits of the 1960s 1960–1969
Capitol SM–886

Capitol Records' success in the 1960s is usually associated with the rise of its Bakersfield, California, artists Buck Owens, Merle Haggard, Buddy Alan, Wynn Stewart, Susan Raye, and Bonnie Owens. This album conclusively demonstrates that the company had a lot of other artists going for it as well. Roy Clark's "The Tip of My Fingers," Glen Campbell's "By the Time I Get to Phoenix," Tex Ritter's "I Dreamed of a Hillbilly Heaven," and Wanda Jackson's "Right or Wrong" are strong reminders of the diversity Capitol had. Ferlin Husky, Faron Young, and Sonny James were strong Nashville hit-makers for the label as well. All are represented on this album with excellent songs.

Buck Owens
The Best of Buck Owens 1961–1964
Capitol ST–2105

Buck Owens was born in Texas in 1929, and grew up in Arizona. His parents gave him a mandolin when he turned thirteen—he left school that same year. He made his radio debut when he was seventeen. He moved to Bakersfield in 1951, formed a band and worked as a guitar session-player. He had his first hit in 1959, "Second Fiddle," and every year of the 1960s brought more Buck Owens hits—usually number ones on the charts. There was a time when Owens rivaled even George Jones as Country King.

In all, Capitol released six volumes of Buck Owens's classic songs. All are worth having, because if you really want to understand country music in the 1960s decade, hearing Buck Owens may be the quickest way.

Buck Owens's success was so overwhelming that it spawned, for a time, a whole sub-genre of country music known as the California Sound. Buck had built and staffed an empire in his base of Bakersfield, California. Capitol had always been oriented toward the West Coast, and Buck, with his stable of artists, songwriters, and studios, attracted most of the label's talent into his orbit. Wynn Stewart, Bonnie Owens, Merle Haggard, Susan Raye, Buddy Alan, and others all enjoyed lucrative 1960s careers in country thanks to Owens's tremendous success and business sense.

Roger Miller
Golden Hits 1964–1966
Smash 67073

Roger Miller was born in Texas in 1936 and raised in Oklahoma. When he came to Nashville after three years in Korea, he began selling his songs—among them his classic, "Invitation to the Blues," recorded by Ray Price in 1958. His first recording success came in 1960 when "You Don't Want My Love," recorded for RCA, reached number fifteen on the country charts. Miller moved to Mercury Records' Smash label, and in 1964 "Dang Me" reached number one on the country charts. He quickly followed it up with "Chug-a-Lug," "King of the Road," "England Swings," and "You Can't Roller Skate in a Buffalo Herd." Unlike that of another Nashville singing-songwriting genius, Don Gibson ("Oh, Lonesome Me," "I Can't Stop Loving You," "Sweet Dreams," "Sea of Heartbreak"), Miller's greatest hits album has remained in print.

His work represents an unparalleled synthesis of pure country-vaudeville hokum with faint, clear, light overtones and commercially brilliant and moving pop music. Because of his relatively low profile in subsequent decades, Miller's importance to country music's development has been somewhat obscured. But no one except Johnny Cash was so essential to the 1960s boom in country's popularity.

Roger Miller (Country Music Foundation)

CAJUN MUSIC

In 1755 and 1758, the British expelled thousands of French colonists from Acadia, a region taking in Nova Scotia, New Brunswick, Prince Edward Island, and part of present-day Maine. They were deported south to many places; a hardy group eventually reached the bayous and backwoods of Louisiana, where they settled in virtual isolation. In the course of time their language developed a unique form in which the French word "Acadien" became "Cajun." Their music also developed a form of its own. Like mountain music it was fiddle-based and developed within a close-knit local culture. Instead of old Anglo-Irish dance tunes, the basis was French folk fiddle music.

On and off through country music's history, Cajun music intersected and interacted with the string bands, singers, and hillbilly songwriters. The fiddle and concertina sounds of Cajun have proved to be as durable as the banjos and steel guitars of country. Sometimes the two forms combined. Even more often, they shared the same barn dance stages, package shows, honky-tonks, and small town auditoriums that are country music's bread and butter.

Harry Choates
Jole Blon: The Original Cajun Fiddle of Harry Choates 1946–1951
D Records 7000

Jimmy C. Newman
Happy Cajun 1979
Plantation 544

Doug Kershaw
Cajun Way 1970
Warner Brothers 1820

Jo-El Sonnier
Cajun Life 1980
Rounder 3049

Jimmy C. Newman (Country Music Foundation)

Although groups such as the Hackberry Ramblers were popular regionally earlier, Harry Choates was the first Cajun musician to gain mass attention in the country market. Born in Louisiana, he died in 1951 at the age of twenty-eight. His compositions, such as "Jole Blon," helped to popularize Cajun culture in the late 1940s and early 1950s.

Doug Kershaw is perhaps the best known of contemporary Cajun musicians. *Cajun Way* includes most of his best-known songs, such as "Louisiana Man" and "Diggy Diggy Lo." Born in Louisiana in 1936, Kershaw began appearing on local TV with his brothers when he was seventeen. The "Ragin' Cajun's" exuberant style has proved nearly as popular with rock and folk audiences as it has with fans of traditional country music.

Jimmy C. Newman, born in Big Mamou, Louisiana, in 1927, keeps the Cajun spirit alive on the Grand Ole Opry. He began working around Lake Charles and appeared regularly on the Louisiana Hayride. His "Cry, Cry Darling" reached number nine on the country charts in 1954. In the 1960s he recorded mainly standard Nashville country tunes, but in recent years he has reclaimed his Louisiana heritage and now sports the hottest of all contemporary Cajun bands.

Of the young, up-and-coming Cajun musicians, none shows more ability than Jo-El Sonnier, who is widely known in Nashville as a session musician and songwriter. The excellent *Cajun Life* LP was his first real chance to shine as a solo recording artist.

THE FOLKIES

Folk song revivalists have always played an important part in country music. In the 1940s such artists as Woody Guthrie, Pete Seeger, Jean Ritchie, and Burl Ives attracted both country and pop fans with fresh renditions of country music's oldest songs. Before that, Bradley Kincaid had done much the same thing with authentic material becoming one of the major popularizers of country music in the Northeast.

The revival phenomenon appeared again in the late 1950s and early 1960s. Peter, Paul, and Mary, the Kingston Trio, and Joan Baez reacquainted audiences with folk songs, with old-time Carter Family tunes, and with the joys of acoustic music—music made with non-electrified instruments. Country musicians followed suit, and began calling themselves "folk artists."

Several graduates of this second wave of revivalists went on to create new songs with an acoustic orientation in the spirit of folk music. Bob Dylan, Gordon Lightfoot, Tom Paxton, and others thus continued to be referred to as "folk" musicians, and continued to provide popular country songs.

In the 1970s many young people became interested in reviving other old-time styles that mainstream country music had left behind. The New Lost City Ramblers, Hazel and Alice, the Hotmud Family, the Red Clay Ramblers, and dozens of local groups have taken part in this. Instead of traditional folk songs, these groups have rediscovered early country artists like the Blue Sky Boys, Uncle Dave Macon, and Charlie Poole, but the folk revival spirit still reigns.

The folkies' songs and styles have frequently influenced commercial country music. Such acts as George Hamilton IV, Burl Ives, Don Williams, Hoyt Axton, Emmylou Harris, John Denver, and Kenny Rogers have come from folk-revival backgrounds to success on the country charts, and songs from many others (John Hartford, Billy Edd Wheeler, Tom Paxton, for instance) have become country standards.

Jean Ritchie
None But One 1977
Sire SA–7530

When this album won *Rolling Stone* magazine's Best Folk Album of the Year award in 1978, it marked a career triumph for the woman who was the mother of the first American folk music revival. Jean Ritchie was born in 1922 and grew up in the Cumberland Mountains of Kentucky. Her family was well known as preservers of folk music originating in the British Isles. Folk-song collector Cecil Sharp had visited them in 1917 to gather songs that had been handed down through five generations, and John and Alan Lomax later recorded them for the Library of Congress collection. Jean learned to play dulcimer from her father. At college she pursued her interest in traditional music as a scholar, winning a Fulbright scholarship to do research in Great Britain. After college she began giving concerts of traditional music. Eventually she performed widely on the folk music circuit, gradually adding her own compositions to her repertoire. She released albums on both major and specialty labels and published several song collections in book form.

The release of this album showed her in a new light. With middle age, her voice became more naturalistic and "country." Her accompanying musicians on the album were a virtual Who's Who of the country/folk scene. And her songwriting was superb. This is a beautifully produced and performed record that brings together the best of a traditional mountain singer, the finest aspects of the folk revivalists, and the tops in country/folk songwriting.

John Denver
Greatest Hits 1970–1974
RCA CPL–1-0374

John Denver is one of the best known of all the musicians from the folk-revival fold. He was born in New Mexico in 1943 but, as the son of a career air force pilot, he spent his childhood in a number of locations around the United States. He began his performing career on the West Coast and eventually replaced Chad Mitchell in the Mitchell Trio, one of the premier college campus folk revival groups of the 1960s. After some success as a songwriter ("Leaving on a Jet Plane"), he embarked on a highly successful solo career on RCA in the mid-1970s.

Most of the songs collected here were hits on both the country and pop charts. In fact, the Country Music Association named John Denver its Entertainer of the Year in 1974, demonstrating that clear simple songwriting, gentle guitar-based musical accompaniment, and pure unaffected tenor singing can reach country audiences as effectively as the more elaborate Nashville recording styles.

Buffy Sainte-Marie
I'm Gonna Be a Country Girl Again 1971
Vanguard VSD–79280

Buffy Sainte-Marie was born in Maine in 1941 and raised in Massachusetts. She was part of the Greenwich Village folk scene in the early 1960s, had a hit as a songwriter when Donovan recorded her "Universal Soldier," appeared at the Newport Folk Festivals, and recorded her first album in 1964.

I'm Gonna Be a Country Girl Again is perhaps the greatest yet most overlooked country album to come out of the folk revival. Sainte-Marie's American Indian heritage and social conscience had made her well known to college students in the 1960s. Her songs "Universal Soldier" and "Until It's Time for You to Go" had made her familiar to pop and rock audiences as well. However, at the time of her arrival in Nashville in 1968 to record this album, she was largely unknown to country fans. She assembled the greatest session musicians in town, recruited the Jordanaires to sing backup, and chose thirteen of the most beautiful songs imaginable. Her own compositions for the album were firmly within the country mainstream, and the remainder were age-old traditionals. *I'm Gonna Be a Country Girl Again* is a near-perfect country disc that deserves to be far better known.

Emmylou Harris
Roses in the Snow 1980
Warner Brothers BSK–3422

Along with Don Williams, Emmylou Harris is probably the most famous of today's country musicians with a folk-revival background. She was born in Alabama in 1949, the daughter of a military man. She was part of the folk-club scene in New York and Washington, D.C., in the 1960s. In 1971 the Flying Burrito Brothers heard her in Washington, and she performed on two albums with group leader Gram Parsons before his death. In 1975 she released her first album, *Pieces of the Sky*, which included a wide range of country material. On that and other early albums, Emmylou successfully applied her skills as a song revivalist to old Louvin Brothers, Buck Owens, and Loretta Lynn material. On this one, she reached even further back into country music's past to produce a collection of bluegrass songs, sacred numbers, and traditional folk songs.

As a result of her various band members' influences, Emmylou Harris has demonstrated that she is equally at home with folk, country-rock, honky-tonk, and rockabilly music. This particular album was heavily influenced by Ricky Skaggs, a multi-instrumental wizard who was a member of her Hot Band at the time. Skaggs's knowledge of and feel for traditional and bluegrass music combined brilliantly with Harris's folk background and instincts.

The Red Clay Ramblers
Twisted Laurel 1977
Flying Fish FF–030

One of the most striking developments in country music of the late 1970s was the emergence of bands that revived the old-timey sounds of country's earliest decades. Whereas in the 1960s folk revivalists had brought back mainly the old folk melodies, in the 1970s such musicians turned their attention to the forgotten songs and styles of country's old-time era. This material was so removed in style and content from contemporary popular music that it seemed as exotic as any authentic traditional material.

Another remarkable difference between present-day country music folkies and their earlier counterparts is that many of today's groups strive for an authenticity of sound that groups like the Kingston Trio and Peter, Paul and Mary never attempted. The best of them, like the Red Clay Ramblers, are much more than academic song revivalists. The members of this group have so much rollicking enthusiasm and feeling for old-time music that they sometimes perform it better than the original musicians did.

The Red Clay Ramblers began in 1972 as a trio formed by Tommy Thompson, Jim Watson, and Bill Hicks, all veterans of traditional North Carolina string bands. Mike Craver joined the group in 1973, and in 1974 they made their first album, *The Red Clay Ramblers with Fiddlin' Al McCanless*, for Folkways. They spent 1975 singing and acting in *Diamond Studs*, a successful off-Broadway dinner-theater musical written and performed (and table-waited) by a company of North Carolina–based talent. They also released the first of their series of albums on Flying Fish that year.

When you buy a Red Clay Ramblers album be prepared for one of the most delightful musical experiences of your life. If you find their kind of music to your taste, you might also enjoy bands like the Any Old Time String Band (Arhoolie), the Hotmud Family (Flying Fish), the Backwoods Band (Rounder), and the New Lost City Ramblers (Folkways).

Ian and Sylvia
Greatest Hits! 1962–1969
Vanguard VSD–5/6

These two Canadians owe as much stylistically to country music as they do to the folk revival. Ian, in particular, has country music credentials as authentic as any of Nashville's best. Nevertheless, it was as folkies that the duo first gained fame.

Ian Tyson and Sylvia Fricker were both born in farm country—Ian in British Columbia in 1933, Sylvia in Chatham, Ontario, in 1940. Ian had collected folk music since his teens and worked in clubs and coffeehouses, along with farming, rodeoing, lumberjacking, and working as a commercial artist. Sylvia had taken piano lessons from her mother and learned to accompany herself on guitar. She met Ian in 1959 in Toronto, where she had moved in search of a career in music. In 1961 they decided to work together full time. Their first album, *Ian and Sylvia*, was released in 1962.

This duo's repertoire ranges from straight country music ("Come in Stranger") to Dylan tunes ("This Wheel's on Fire," "Tomorrow Is a Long Time"), folk-revival classics ("Circle Game," "Early Morning Rain"), and superb original material ("You Were on My Mind," "Four Strong Winds," "Some Day Soon"), all performed with fine acoustic instrumentation and striking harmony. Individually, they possess two of the most expressive country-folk voices ever; together, they are dynamite.

An Ampex Records album called *Great Speckled Bird* was perhaps their finest effort, but it is long out of print, as is *Full Circle* on MGM Records, another excellent album. But you can't go wrong with their classic Vanguard records—the ones that made Ian and Sylvia's reputation.

Various Artists with the Nitty Gritty Dirt Band
Will the Circle Be Unbroken 1971[*]
Capitol LKCL–9801

In 1966 six young men in Long Beach, California formed the Nitty Gritty Dirt Band to play American music of many kinds, but mainly along the folk-country-blues axis. They had a big hit in 1970 with Jerry Jeff Walker's "Mr. Bojangles." In 1973 they initiated this unique album project—unique both because it unites members of the sixties generation with people who originally created country music, and because it brings so many of the latter together in a single set of productions. The Nitty Gritty Dirt Band accompanies on this album such great country artists as Roy Acuff, Merle Travis, Doc Watson, Mother Maybelle Carter, Earl Scruggs, and a host of others. This three-record set was very successful and it remains essential to any country music lover's record collection.

Perhaps more than any other album, *Will the Circle Be Unbroken* demonstrated just how much folk-oriented performers and country artists have in common. The playing and singing here illustrates just how well folkies like the Dirt Band can absorb, understand, and perform mainline country music.

COUNTRY-ROCK

After decades of being alternately ignored and despised by pop and rock musicians, country music began to make strong inroads into the rock world in the 1970s. Combining the basic instrumentation and chord structure of country music with a rock beat and sensibility, groups like the Eagles, Poco, the Flying Burrito Brothers, and the Byrds created an amalgam of the two styles that became known among music critics and fans as country-rock.

Generally speaking, country-rock is characterized by smoother vocals than hard country, and a smoother rhythmic pulse than hard rock. The characteristic close-harmony group singing on choruses is as reminiscent of the Beach Boys as of Nashville—but it should be remembered that country has been migrating to California for years.

Country-rock was largely a West Coast movement, although important developments also occurred in Nashville and Memphis. At first, mainstream country radio ignored the trend, but by the beginning of the 1980s, country-rock releases appeared regularly on the country charts. A few, such as Linda Ronstadt's "Silver Threads and Golden Needles," the Amazing Rhythm Aces' "Third Rate Romance," the Eagles' "Lyin' Eyes," and the Burrito Brothers' "Does She Wish She Was Single Again?" were even substantial country hits. Such superstar country acts as the Charlie Daniels Band and Alabama have now brought country-rock mainstream acceptance.

Gram Parsons (with Emmylou Harris)
Grievous Angel 1974
Reprise MS–2171

Unquestionably the single most influential musician in the country-rock movement was Gram Parsons. He was born in Florida in 1946 of well-to-do but emotionally unstable parents. After time in Greenwich Village and at Harvard and in several folk-oriented bands, he brought his knowledge of the country music he'd heard and loved as a youth in the South to the West Coast in the early 1960s. His membership in the Byrds and then the Flying Burrito Brothers pulled these groups in a country music direction, which in turn affected the whole California rock community. He discovered Emmylou Harris and recorded both of his solo albums with her, helping to shape and form her style. Every country-rocker owes a debt to the late Gram Parsons for blazing the trail.

Grievous Angel was released after Parsons's untimely death, following his first Reprise album GP. Both are great records, but this one contains versions of Gram's classics "Las Vegas," "Brass Buttons," "Hickory Wind," and "In My Hour of Darkness," as well as oldies like the Louvin Brothers' "Cash on the Barrelhead," Tom T. Hall's "I Can't Dance," and the Everly Brothers' hit "Love Hurts."

The Byrds
Sweetheart of the Rodeo 1968
Columbia CS–9670

To the Byrds goes the credit for giving Gram Parsons's country-rock ideas their first big national exposure. The group was an established star rock act when it made this radical change-of-direction album with Parsons as a member of the band on guitar and vocals. Critics and music lovers sat up and took notice, and country-rock was launched.

The Byrds—Gene Clark and David Crosby, both born in 1941, and Jim McGuinn and Chris Hillman, both born in 1942—all had extensive backgrounds in commercial folk music (Hillman had also played bluegrass professionally). In 1964, with Michael Clarke (born in 1944) on drums, they started rehearsing and recording demo tapes at a Los Angeles studio. They put out one record as the Beefeaters for Elektra ("Please Let Me Love You"), which was not a success. Renamed the Byrds, they switched to Columbia and released their very successful version of Bob Dylan's "Mr. Tambourine Man." Having cut five albums, the Byrds (minus Gene Clark, David Crosby, and Mike Clarke) added Gram Parsons and Kevin Kelley on drums and recorded this album in Nashville, where they also appeared on the Grand Ole Opry.

In addition to showcasing Parsons's songwriting, *Sweetheart of the Rodeo* introduced rock audiences to country song masterpieces like Haggard's "Life in Prison," Guthrie's "Pretty Boy Floyd," the Louvins' "The Christian Life," and Cindy Walker's timeless "Blue Canadian Rockies."

Linda Ronstadt
Hand Sown . . . Home Grown 1969
Capitol ST–208

Linda Ronstadt was born in Arizona in 1946 and moved to Los Angeles when she was eighteen. She formed the Stone Poneys there and in 1967 they cut the first of several albums with her. In 1969 she left the group and made a solo album, "Hand Sown . . .

Home Grown." Most of Ronstadt's albums have been mixtures of styles, containing some country-rock, some country, some soul, some rock, and some reggae. What she really does best is reveal the soul of country music to rock audiences.

There are three albums that show her in her best country-rock light. *Silk Purse*, made in Nashville, contains the hit "Long, Long Time" as well as Ronstadt versions of "Lovesick Blues," "Mental Revenge," and "Life Is Like a Mountain Railway." *Prisoner in Disguise* (1975–76) features "Love Is a Rose," "I Will Always Love You," "The Sweetest Gift," and "Hey Mister That's Me Up On the Jukebox." (*Heart Like a Wheel* and *Simple Dreams*, although two of her most popular albums, contain little of interest to pure country or country-rock fans.) *Hand Sown . . . Home Grown* was the singer's first real exploration of country-rock and remains one of her most satisfying records. It contained the first version she did of "Silver Threads and Golden Needles"—much superior to the version she later released as a single—and a collection of similarly strong country-rock numbers.

The Amazing Rhythm Aces
How the Hell Do You Spell Rythum? 1980
Warner Brothers BSK-3476

The six original Amazing Rhythm Aces—Russell Smith, Butch McDade, Jeff Davis, Billy Earhart III, Barry Burton, and James Hooker—assembled between 1972 and 1974. Based in Memphis, the group's members combined country and rock and rhythm-and-blues influences. In 1975 the group cut its album *Stacked Deck*, featuring "Third Rate Romance," which became a major country and pop hit for them. That album is unfortunately out of print. After several other albums on ABC, and one each for Columbia and MCA, this one was released. Despite its excellence, the group disbanded. The group's lead singer and songwriter, Russell Smith, has cut his own first album, *Russell Smith*, distributed by Capitol. Search out an Amazing Rhythm Aces record for a taste of Memphis's contribution to country-rock.

Charlie Daniels Band
Million Mile Reflections 1979

SINGER-SONGWRITERS

Songwriting and song publishing are the center of the Nashville music scene. As the Nashville Songwriters' Association keeps reminding us, "It all begins with a song." Interest in the country songwriter now seems to be at an all-time high as more and more people discover that there is a whole group of hard-working men and women creating such personal and moving poetry behind the scenes. On a 1981 awards show, Conway Twitty stated that the country singer puts the heart into a song, but that the country songwriter puts the soul there.

There are many who contend that no one can sing the songs better than the writers themselves. Whether or not that is true, Nashville's songwriters have made many albums over the years that are very fine listening experiences. In most cases, the writers have gotten the very best from Music City's session musicians, studios, and producers.

One hundred and fifty songwriter albums could have been listed here, and a basic library of great music would have resulted. Unfortunately, wonderful writers like Harlan Howard, Linda Hargrove, John D. Loudermilk, Ava Aldridge, Sonny Curtis, Bobby Braddock, Cindy Walker, Boudleaux and Felice Bryant, Ed Bruce, Dallas Frazier, Liz Anderson, Troy Seals, Bill Anderson, and Bob McDill were omitted either for reasons of space or more often because there are no currently available records of their songs.

Hank Cochran
Make the World Go Away 1980
Elektra 6E-277

Along with Harlan Howard, John D. Loudermilk, the Bryants, Bill Anderson, Dallas Frazier, and other writers of that calibre, Hank Cochran virtually defined modern country songwriting in the 1960s. Throughout his long and illustrious career he has recorded

Hank Cochran
(Jim Shea, Elektra)

albums sporadically. Liberty, RCA, and Capitol have all recorded him in the past; this album is on Elektra, his most recent major label.

Born in Mississippi in 1935, Cochran worked in the Southwest oil fields in the fifties, then moved to California where he worked clubs and local TV and radio, and did some recording with Eddie Cochran (not his brother) as the Cochran Brothers (see the earlier chapter on rockabilly). In 1960 he moved to Nashville and soon began placing his songs.

Cochran has a reedy, thin voice not unlike that of his close friend Willie Nelson. Nelson, in fact, sings harmony with Hank on some songs on this album and the blend of their voices is quite good. To Hank Cochran's credit, the songs of his presented on this LP—"A Little Bitty Tear," "Make the World Go Away," "I Fall to Pieces," "You Comb Her Hair," "He's Got You"—sound fresh. While Cochran may not be the world's greatest singer, he is certainly an expressive one.

Sonny Throckmorton (Mercury)

of friends who had preceded him there, he moved to Nashville, where he worked for several publishing companies. Bobby Lewis's record of his "How Long Has It Been?" went to number six on the country charts in 1966, and he had a few other songs on the charts, but not enough. In 1975 he moved his family to Texas, but didn't find any quick alternatives to songwriting for making a living. He soon returned to Nashville to sign a new contract with Tree International, his former publishers. Beginning in 1977 his songs began charting with amazing regularity, with Dave and Sugar's cut of "Knee Deep in Loving You," giving him his first number one record that year. The steady stream of hits on contemporary loving, losing, and cheating themes was joined by such thought-provoking numbers as "Middle Age Crazy" and the beautiful "The Way I Am."

Throckmorton spent many years as a background harmony singer on other people's records, and his love of harmonies and gospel singing are evident on this, his debut LP. Some find his solo singing laughably bad, but others have always loved his wheezy, whining, and soulful way with a melody.

Several of his most famous songs are sung here by their composer. Among them are "Knee Deep in Loving You," "Middle Age Crazy," which Jerry Lee Lewis popularized, the T. G. Sheppard numbers "Last Cheater's Waltz" and "I Feel Like Loving You Again," Merle Haggard's hit "If We're Not Back in Love by Monday," and a song Connie Smith popularized called "Smooth Sailin'." They're a tiny fraction of the fine songs Throckmorton has written.

Guy Clark
Old No. 1 1976
RCA APL–1-1303

The Houston area has produced several of country music's finest young writers. Mickey Newbury, Townes Van Zandt, Rodney Crowell, and Guy Clark all made their way to Music City from that east Texas urban sprawl. Guy and Susanna Clark have been Nashville godparents of sorts to this large, ever-changing crew of songwriters, pickers, and music junkies of all types.

Guy Clark began playing guitar as a boy growing up in Texas, where he was born in 1941. He moved to Los Angeles in the 1960s to pursue a musical career, and worked for a time in the Dobro guitar factory there. With his wife, Susanna, also a fine songwriter ("I'll Be Your San Antone Rose"), he moved to Nashville in 1971 and his songs soon

Guy Clark (Warner Brothers Records)

began to be recorded by Jerry Jeff Walker, Johnny Cash, Rita Coolidge, and many others. RCA signed him as a recording artist and eventually released this, his first album.

The quiet humanity Clark displays is perhaps most evident in his songwriting. His images are of Texas countryside, down-and-out losers, southwestern culture, and lost love. Tunes like "Texas-1947," "Desperados Waiting for the Train," and "L.A. Freeway" reveal an acute observer of the human scene. After years as a cult favorite, Clark finally got a number-one hit with Ricky Skaggs's version of his "Heartbroke."

Rodney Crowell
Ain't Living Long Like This 1978
Warner Brothers BSK–3228

Although Rodney Crowell took his early inspiration from Guy Clark's songwriting, and while they both come from Houston, their writing styles are quite different. Whereas most of Clark's material seems to be deeply personal, Crowell has the song craftsman's skill of inventing characters and placing himself into new situations.

Rodney Crowell was born in Texas to a musical family and started learning drums when he was eleven. In his teens he was a member of his father's country band. His interest in country music and in songwriting took him to Nashville in the early 1970s, where he got a songwriting job with Jerry Reed's publishing company. In the mid-1970s Emmylou Harris began recording Rodney's songs; he joined her band as a guitarist in 1975. He signed with Warner's as a recording artist in 1977, and this record was released in 1978.

This astoundingly excellent first album from Crowell yielded three massive hits almost immediately upon its release. Waylon Jennings topped the charts with the title tune. Shortly thereafter the Oak Ridge Boys took "Leaving Louisiana in the Broad Daylight" to country's number-one slot. Meanwhile, on the pop music charts, the Dirt Band, with some help from Linda Ronstadt, scored with Crowell's "Voila, an American Dream." Suddenly Rodney Crowell was one of the hottest young writers in country music, and now he's on his way to becoming known as a singing star as well.

MAINSTREAM COUNTRY TODAY: THE MEN

The archetypal male country voice is deep, soulful, and bruised. It's tender yet masculine. Like a great many country songs, it must convey both weakness and strength.

Most of the hard-country performers of today draw their inspiration from the honky-tonk stylists of the late 1940s and early 1950s. Their success has come from their varying abilities to translate the honky-tonk ethos into the contemporary world. All have miraculously survived the 1970s rush to convert country music into bland, easy-listening mush. Several have, in fact, benefited from the pop music attention by promoting themselves, as examples of pure country soul, just as Loretta Lynn among the female performers has.

Merle Haggard
Songs I'll Always Sing 1976*
Capitol SABB 11531

Bluntly put, Merle Haggard is one of the greatest musicians in any form of American popular music. As an instrumentalist, he has consistently challenged himself and his band members to ever-greater involvement with music. As a writer, he has maintained his commitment to the concerns of the working class and has raised country songwriting to new plateaus of eloquence. As a singer, he is without peer in drawing emotion from lyrics. *Songs I'll Always Sing* collects the best material from his early years on Capitol, but the Mighty Merle is one artist from whom *any* album he's ever released would be a good buy.

(Courtesy of Capitol Records)

Conway Twitty
The Very Best of Conway Twitty 1967–1977
MCA 3043

Conway Twitty has had more number one records than any individual in any field of music. His astounding popularity stems from the brilliant mix of sensuality and reverence conveyed in his trembling, growling vocals and his slice-of-life contemporary honky-tonk songwriting. Conway is the essence of the male country persona. Alone among country men singers, he seems to have found a direct pipeline into the hearts of women country fans. They have remained loyal to him despite his virtual exclusion from industry awards and critical acclaim. His *The Very Best of Conway Twitty* collects several of his most potent, throbbing single hits.

Waylon Jennings
Dreaming My Dreams 1975
RCA AYL1-4072

Like Conway, Waylon Jennings has been relatively ignored by award-givers. Nevertheless, he is one of the most effective and distinctive singers, songwriters, and instrumentalists now active. His public image is a mean-tempered outlaw, but both his music and his private life reveal a tender, sensitive, compassionate soul. *Dreaming My Dreams*

Willie Nelson (Columbia Records)

is easily his masterpiece. Among his many excellent releases, it shines brightest because of its uniformly excellent songs and its brilliant, spare, clean production by fellow-maverick Jack Clement.

Hank Williams, Jr.
Habits Old and New 1980
Elektra 6E-278

Closest in spirit to Jennings on today's scene is renegade Hank Williams, Jr. *Habits Old and New* was his breakthrough record, winning praise and sales. Williams threw off the mantle of being a clone of his famous father, and blazed a new musical trail for himself as the pounding, snarling, redneck rocker presented here. With this album he also demonstrated extraordinary depth as a songwriter and remarkable sensitivity as a singer.

Willie Nelson
Red Headed Stranger 1975
Columbia KC–33482

Willie Nelson's *Red Headed Stranger* album is perhaps the record most familiar to non-country audiences of those listed in this chapter. Justifiably popular as a concept-western record, this album was Willie's first to display his mass appeal. "Blue Eyes Crying in the Rain," its hit single, is just one of many delightful performances on the disc.

Jerry Lee Lewis
The Best of Jerry Lee Lewis, Vol. II 1970–1976
Mercury SRM–1-5006

Jerry Lee Lewis is a true American original. This flamboyant mixture of barrel-house rocker, gospel testifier, honky-tonker, and all-around raging bull of country music has enjoyed a twenty-five-year career that spans the spectrum of popular song. This particular *Best of* album has some of his rock 'n' roll, some of his cry-in-your-beer honky-tonk style, and some of his readings of great Nashville lyrics. It's a potpourri of Lewis at his tempestuous best.

Jerry Lee Lewis (Ethan Russell, Elektra)

Moe Bandy
Best Of, Vol. 1 1974–1976
Columbia KC–34715

Among interpreters of straight modern honky-tonk music, Moe Bandy holds a high position. He has reinterpreted all the classic themes of cheating, drinking, and carousing that characterized the works of Hank Williams, Webb Pierce, and Lefty Frizzell, and brought them up to date. His first *Best of* album on Columbia wisely reprised the shitkickers he put out on the little GRC label before he became a country superstar. These cuts, and the big-label hits that immediately followed them, defined Moe's uncompromising style and made him a hero to lovers of hard-country music.

The Statler Brothers
Best of the Statler Brothers 1970–1975
Mercury SRM–1-1037

The Statler Brothers quartet is widely admired by devotees of solid country sound. The group's gospel-derived harmonies, sense of humor, showmanship, and clever, down-home songwriting style have combined to make them the most awarded group in country music history. Both volumes of their greatest hits (*Best of*) albums are essential. The first one, listed here, is one of the biggest-selling country records of all time and thus warrants inclusion in any basic country library.

Charlie Rich
Behind Closed Doors 1973
Epic KE–32247

Charlie Rich's million-selling *Behind Closed Doors* album is another of country music's all-time biggest hit LPs. It demonstrated that the much-vaunted Nashville Sound of the 1960s was still alive and well in the 1970s, for Rich's hits like "The Most Beautiful Girl," "Behind Closed Doors," and "I Take It on Home" were excellent combinations of sophisticated strings-and-voices production, heartfelt singing, and fine country-oriented songwriting.

Charley Pride
The Best of Charley Pride 1966–1969
RCA LSP–4223

Mel Tillis
24 Greatest Hits 1970–1976
MGM 2-5402

Charley Pride (RCA Records)

Mickey Gilley
Greatest Hits, *Vol. 1* 1974–1978
(Epic) Playboy KZ–34743

Mel Tillis, Charley Pride, and Mickey Gilley are three country vocalists who have enjoyed considerable success in like manner. All make consistently fine records by variously adapting Nashville Sound techniques to their individual styles. Each is an established hitmaker who has had his best works collected in numerous greatest-hits packages. The three cited here are the most concise introductions to their styles and songs.

MAINSTREAM COUNTRY TODAY: THE WOMEN

    Although very few of the women on today's scene have produced hard-country recordings, those few have done some of the finest work of recent years. Several of the women listed here also have contributed notable compositions to the country repertoire. Each is unique, so there is no particular order of achievement, interest, or quality in the following list.

Loretta Lynn
Greatest Hits, Vol. II 1968–1973[*]
MCA 420

Dolly Parton
Best of Dolly Parton
1967–1970
AYL1-4077

Tammy Wynette
Tammy's Greatest Hits
   1966–1970
Epic BN–26486

Tanya Tucker
Greatest Hits 1972–1975
Columbia KC–33355

Jeanne Pruett
Encore! 1979
IBC 1001

Dolly Parton (RCA Records)

Coal Miner's Daughter
I Wanna Be Free
Wings Upon Your Horns
Fist City
You're Lookin' At Country
Ain't It Funny
One's On The Way
Your Squaw Is On The Warpath
What Sundown Does To You
Hey Loretta
Love Is The Foundation

The Dolly Parton record chosen is her first *Best of* LP, but her *Coat of Many Colors,* *My Tennessee Mountain Home,* and *Touch Your Woman* albums would also be good solid country choices. Loretta Lynn's second *Greatest Hits* album and Tammy Wynette's first one were selected because they contain the performances these stars are most famous for. Tanya Tucker actually has two excellent *Greatest Hits* packages available, one on MCA ("San Antonio Stroll," "It's a Cowboy Lovin' Night," "Here's Some Love") and one on Columbia ("Delta Dawn," "Would You Lay With Me," "Blood Red and Goin' Down"). The choice between them is a tough one. Jeanne Pruett has been making perhaps the most consistently excellent country music of nearly any woman in Nashville. *Encore!* is the finest work of her career to date and should not be overlooked just because it is on a small, independent label.

TODAY'S GREAT DUETS

The male-female duet so common today is actually a fairly recent phenomenon in country music. Although scattered examples flourished earlier, duet teams didn't achieve big success in country music until after World War II. And it was not until the 1960s that they became commonplace.

In addition to being great listening experiences for lovers of harmony, male-female duets frequently perform the function of airing men's and women's points of view in country songs. Whether you listen for singing styles or lyric content, however, these duet records are four great albums in country music history.

The Kendalls
The Best of The Kendalls 1977–1980
Ovation OV–1756

Porter Wagoner and Dolly Parton
The Best of Porter Wagoner and Dolly Parton 1968–1971
RCA AHL–1–4556

George Jones and Tammy Wynette
Greatest Hits 1972–1977*
Epic KE–34716

Loretta Lynn and Conway Twitty
The Very Best of Loretta and Conway 1973–1980
MCA 3164

COUNTRY-POP SUPERSTARS

The dramatic increase in the popularity of country music in the 1980s was helped along by a host of performers who made music specifically designed to attract pop music listeners to country radio stations. These acts perform an amalgam of pop and country music, most often centered on the adult love ballad. The music is generally referred to as "crossover" music, meaning that it's intended to cross from the country music charts into the pop charts. On the list below, Kenny Rogers, Glen Campbell, Anne Murray, Crystal Gayle, and Larry Gatlin fit this definition of country-pop best. Barbara Mandrell (and sometimes Crystal and Anne) frequently performs soul songs for the white audience in her crossover attempts. Eddie Rabbitt and the Oak Ridge Boys play in a modified pop-rock style with vaguely country overtones. Only Jerry Reed and Don Williams on this list play in more countrified modes. Reed is in this section because of his notoriety on film and TV; Williams's folkie/country singles sometimes show up on the pop charts both here and abroad. Thus these two men also qualify as country-pop superstars although their music makes little concession to pop radio or easy-listening tastes.

Kenny Rogers
Greatest Hits 1976–1980
Liberty LOO–1072

Anne Murray
Country 1970–1974
Capitol ST–11324

Glen Campbell
The Best of Glen Campbell 1967–1975
Capitol ST–11577

Crystal Gayle
Classic Crystal 1974–1979
United Artists UA UAR–LOO–982

Larry Gatlin
Greatest Hits 1973–1978
Monument MG–7628

Barbara Mandrell
Best of Barbara Mandrell 1975–1978
MCA AY–1119

Eddie Rabbitt
Best of Eddie Rabbitt 1976–1978
Elektra 6E-235

The Oak Ridge Boys
Greatest Hits 1976–1980
MCA 5150

Don Williams
Best of Don Williams, Vol. 2 1975–1978*
MCA 3096

Jerry Reed
Best of Jerry Reed 1967–1971
RCA AYL 1-4109

PROGRESSIVE COUNTRY: THE FUTURE

Country music is a constantly changing and evolving art form. Although widely regarded as the most change-resistant American popular music because of its respect for its own past, country has in fact undergone a great many stylistic shifts. Alone among American popular music forms, country has managed to honor its traditions while creating new ones.

The rustic string band music of 1925 is a far cry from the smooth radio cowboys of 1935. The musical styles of the Depression radio stars are very distinct from the hot, jazzy western swing units of the 1940s. These, in turn, are worlds away from their contemporary bluegrass and Cajun bands. Hank Williams's honky-tonk music has been supercharged into redneck rock by his son Hank Williams, Jr. And who would recognize the 1960s solid country sound of Loretta Lynn as being the forerunner of her sister Crystal Gayle's 1980s torch-singing style? Over the years, the definition of what's "country" has changed considerably.

No music critic or record collector can resist the opportunity to spot and predict trends, to turn folks on to gifted new artists, to plug favorites, and to encourage exciting new musical developments. The performers and groups listed in this chapter are the contemporary acts who have perhaps the best understanding of what country music is all about, yet are taking it into new territory.

Alabama
My Home's in Alabama 1980
RCA AHL–1-3644

The first members of Alabama to perform together were bassist Teddy Gentry and lead singer and rhythm guitarist Randy Owens, cousins who grew up in the same northeast Alabama town; sang gospel together in church from an early age; and in the 1960s performed (separately) in various local top-forty, soul, gospel country, and bluegrass groups. In 1968 they started working with a third hometown cousin, lead guitarist and keyboardist Jeff Cook, who at age fourteen in the early sixties had started working as a rock 'n' roll DJ. In 1972 they added the first of several drummers who preceded Mark Herndon, and in 1973 they began playing music for a living full-time in a South Carolina nightclub. In 1979, not long after Herndon (an Easterner raised on air force bases) joined the group, they cut "I Want to Come Over" and it was released on the tiny Dallas-based MDJ label. They followed it with "My Home's in Alabama," also on MDJ. That record got an astonishing amount of air-play for a small-label single, and RCA bought their tapes. With a little promotion, a little luck, and a lot of talent, Alabama soon had a string of top country hits on one of country music's strongest and biggest labels.

Alabama plays a mixture of straight country, Southern-boogie rock, and Austin-type outlaw music. Randy Owen is a lead singer in the best country-soul tradition; the group's harmony vocals are as strong as anything the Eagles have produced. The groups' members are fine songwriters as well, as both this album and its follow-up, *Feels So Right*, demonstrated.

Alabama plays a tight small-combo country-rock/honky-tonk type of music that defies precise labels, which is perhaps the key to their remarkable success.

John Anderson
John Anderson 1980
Warner Brothers BSK–3459

Despite his youth, John Anderson is one of the most exciting new honky-tonk singers country music has seen in years. This first album collected a string of powerful singles Anderson had been releasing on Warner's for several years. "Low Dog Blues," "Your Lyin' Blue Eyes," and "She Just Started Liking Cheatin' Songs" had already demonstrated to country fans just how good this newcomer was, while "If There Were No Memories" and "1959" soon confirmed his mastery of country emotion.

Anderson grew up in a town in central Florida, began playing guitar at seven, and joined a local rock band around the age of ten. In his mid-teens he began to give up rock for acoustic music, partly inspired by his older sister Donna, also a musician. At eighteen he followed Donna to Nashville, and put in eight years of odd jobs and performing in small clubs.

After a single on a small Nashville label failed to move his career along, he tried his luck in Texas, Colorado, and Los Angeles before a single on a new label, CSI, "What Did I Promise Her Last Night?", brought him to the attention of publisher Al Gallico. Gallico brought him to Warners Records, which released this album, his first, in 1980.

Fans of hard country rejoiced when John Anderson arrived on the scene. His rapid rise to popularity indicates that in the midst of change a purist can shine through if he interprets down-to-earth country with fresh ideas, intelligence, and imagination.

Karen Brooks
Walk On 1982
Warner Brothers 23676-1

If there's a spirit hovering over this record, it is that of Roy Orbison. Two of Brooks's songs, "Every Beat of My Heart" and "Walk On," are pounding wailers that build to dramatic crescendos—unmistakable Orbison song structures. And as an overt homage, Brooks revives his "Candy Man" on this, her debut LP.

There are ballads as well as rockers here, for the singer-songwriter is an independent Texan who goes her own way, heedless of musical categories. The sound of *Walk On* is a dense, guitar-dominated mixture with plenty of rock bottom in the mix. Karen Brooks's liquid alto rides above this, occasionally soaring upward effortlessly into soprano range.

Brooks was raised in Texas by her mother, a successful film makeup artist, and taught to play guitar by her brother. After leaving high school she worked as a commercial layout artist and on a quarter-horse ranch before deciding to try the music business. She moved to Austin, worked as an opening act for some of the well-known Texas performers playing there, and began to get her songs recorded. She next moved to Nashville, where Rodney Crowell heard her songs and suggested a move to California. There she worked as a backup singer with Crowell, Bee Spears, Hank Divito, and Donivan Cowart. Mean-

Karen Brooks (Warner Brothers Records)

time her composition "Couldn't Do Nothing Right" had been cut by Jerry Jeff Walker, Tracy Nelson, and Rosanne Cash (who had a major country hit with it), and her "Tennessee Rose" was recorded by Emmylou Harris. In 1980 she moved back to Nashville and finally got a chance to present her own unique, warm, expressive vocal sound on disc.

This immensely appealing country-rock album is all the more impressive because it sounded like nothing else on the market when it was released. Critics instantly praised Karen Brooks's excellence and liberated, new-Nashville, country-girl qualities; the Academy of Country Music followed suit by giving her its Most Promising Female award, based on this disc.

Carlene Carter
Musical Shapes 1980
Warner Brothers BSK–3465

Musical Shapes is a head-on collision between new wave and country-rock. Carlene Carter is exploring frontier territory with this Nashville-meets-Anglopop record.

Carlene Carter was born in Nashville, the daughter of June Carter and Carl Smith. She began playing piano when she was five, and went on to study classical piano for

Carlene Carter (Warner Brothers Records)

thirteen years. She began writing when she was nineteen, pitching songs in Nashville. Emmylou Harris's recording of one of her songs brought her to the attention of Warners, and she released her first album, *Carlene Carter* (recorded in England with the help of The Rumour), in 1978.

Carlene's country-punk rockers are infectious compositions. Especially engaging here are the hook-filled "Bandit of Love," "Cry," and "That Very First Kiss." Her singing is spotlighted best on the most country-flavored tracks. She wails on her mother June Carter's song "Ring of Fire," and essays the Carter Family standard "Foggy Mountain Top" with ham-fisted vigor. The LP's best song, and arguably Carlene's best vocal, is Richard Dobson's "Baby, Ride Easy." This is sung as a prickly and piercing duet with British rocker Dave Edmunds, and the result is one of the most fresh-sounding country performances of the 1980s.

Musical Shapes is the most unusual and adventurous country music experiment of its year, and possibly its decade. It solidified Carter's reputation as a songwriter of considerable ability, but failed to garner big sales because of its odd mixture of British rock and American country traditions. Only time will tell if it was a pioneering country music effort or musical dead end.

Rosanne Cash
Seven Year Ache 1981
Columbia JC–36965

Like her step-sister Carlene Carter, Rosanne Cash cut her teeth in music as a member of the Carter-Cash clan. Carlene is June's daughter; Rosanne is Johnny's. Like Carlene, Rosanne is way out on the edge of country music. There's something inescapably "country" about Rosanne's music, while it also reaches far over into pop-rock territory. The country style it is closest to is rockabilly, but even that label doesn't quite fit exactly.

Born in Tennessee in 1955, Rosanne was raised mostly in California. She joined her father's tour show after high school, working first backstage and then as a performer. She started her own independent career in Europe, recording an album in Germany for Ariola Records, for foreign release. In 1979 she signed with Columbia and recorded her first album for them, *Right or Wrong*; it was produced by Rodney Crowell, whom she had recently married.

All things considered, *Seven Year Ache*, her second release, is a masterpiece of an album. On it, Cash draws on her own fine compositions as well as those of Merle Haggard, Steve Forbert, Sonny Curtis, newcomer Keith Sykes, and husband/producer Rodney Crowell. It's an eclectic mix of tunes, but she handles them all exceptionally well. This strikingly innovative album managed to please pop and country fans equally. It earned Cash her first gold record.

David Allan Coe
Greatest Hits 1974–1978
Columbia KC–35627

David Allan Coe has tattoos and long hair, pierced ears, and outrageous jewelry, plus a following of bikers and real outlaws. He's been a convict, believes in having more than one wife, is a wild self-promoter, self-costumer, and self-revealing songwriter. He's also a fine country musician.

Born in Ohio in 1939, David Allan Coe is reported to have spent most of the years of his life between ages nine and twenty-seven in reform schools and prisons. He learned to play guitar along the way and began writing songs. During his last years in the Marion (Ohio) Correctional Institute he was warmly received as a performer in prison shows; when he was paroled he moved to Nashville and began pitching his songs. He recorded his first LP for SSS, *Penitentiary Blues*, but his career really took off in 1973 when Tanya Tucker's recording of his "Would You Lay with Me (In a Field of Stone)?" became a number-one country hit. The next year his first Columbia album, *The Mysterious Rhinestone Cowboy*, was released.

Coe is outspoken, outrageous, and out-of-bounds—truly deserving of the country music "outlaw" brand. "Longhaired Redneck" and "Willie, Waylon, and Me" sum up his outlaw image; "A Sad Country Song" and "Would You Lay with Me . . ." reveal his sensitivity; Steve Goodman's "You Never Even Called Me by My Name" shows his sense of humor. They're all worthy of inclusion in a basic country music library.

Gail Davies
I'll Be There 1980
Warner Brothers BSK–3509

Like most "new country" acts today, Gail Davies's musical background is a varied one. Born in Oklahoma in 1948, she was raised in the state of Washington from the age of five. Her parents, who separated that year, were both country fans—her father played guitar and her mother sang—and Gail was raised on a musical diet of 1950s honky-tonk tunes. Gail began singing country duets with her brother Ron, now also a successful songwriter, but they switched to folk-rock in their teens. She started touring with a rock band before she was twenty, continuing to perform mostly rock for nine years. She moved to Los Angeles and eventually began performing country again, but couldn't get a country music career off the ground there. She tried Nashville in 1975, but was judged not country enough. Back in L.A., she continued to write and do backup vocals on recording sessions. In 1978 she returned to Nashville, where her writing and singing talents were finally recognized and her first album was released.

That first LP, *Gail Davies* (on the defunct CBS Lifesong label), contained the trio of songs that made her reputation as a writer—"Bucket to the South," "Someone Is Looking for Someone Like You," and "Grandma's Song." It is arguably her clearest

Gail Davies (Warner Brothers Records)

musical statement. Subsequent records repeated its pattern of mixing Davies originals with terrific remakes of country oldies.

By the time of *I'll Be There*, Gail had polished her art to diamond purity. On this album she revived the songs of Ray Price ("I'll Be There") and Carl Smith ("It's a Lovely, Lovely World"); dipped into old-time country music ("Kentucky," "No One To Welcome Me Home"); and provided lovely original songs ("I'm Hungry, I'm Tired," "Mama's Gonna Give You Sweet Things," a remake of "Grandma's Song," and others).

Following this album, she reintroduced her rock roots by mixing some L.A. pop-rock with her country oldies and originals. Whatever combination she tries, her musical taste ensures that the elements work well together. This silver-voiced singer has never made a bad album.

Ricky Skaggs
Sweet Temptation 1979
Sugar Hill SH–3706

Multi-instrumental wizard Ricky Skaggs was born in Kentucky in 1954. His father started teaching him mandolin when Ricky was five; less than two years later he played with Flatt and Scruggs on their Nashville TV show. He was influenced early on by the music of the Stanley Brothers and when he was fifteen Ralph Stanley invited him to join his group. After several years on the road with Stanley, Skaggs moved to Washington, D.C. and joined the newgrass group the Country Gentlemen. From that band he moved to J. D. Crowe and the New South, then started his own group, Boone Creek. In 1977 Emmylou Harris asked him to take over as leader of her Hot Band, where he began to be very visible to a much wider audience.

Sweet Temptation, Skaggs's first album of his own, bowled over lovers of acoustic music when it appeared. The album revives songs of A. P. Carter, Lester Flatt, Merle Travis, Carter Stanley, and Dolly Parton, among others; the result is a country music lover's delight. If you love the old songs and if you care for country music the way it was meant to be played without strings, horns, and background ooooohs, buy this wonderful record at once. Ricky Skaggs's records are a gust of fresh air into a country music marketplace glutted with overproduced and undercreative products. Although his albums are old-fashioned, honest country, they don't smack of narrow-minded purism; they're solidly classy records of good acoustic music performed with verve, professionalism, and love.

Joe Sun
Old Flames (Can't Hold a Candle to You) 1978
Ovation OV–1734

Year after year, the familiar jangle of rhythm guitars and the predictable ooze of strings and background voices along about the second verse still mark the typical country record as surely as they did in the heyday of Jim Reeves and Patsy Cline. But there are always a few in Music City who make records that buck and challenge the Nashville Sound method. Waylon Jennings and Willie Nelson of course come to mind; and Hank Williams, Jr., and Merle Haggard always make great records by doing pretty much whatever they want. With this album, Joe Sun joined their ranks.

Born in Minnesota, Sun worked as a rock DJ in Minneapolis until, in 1972, he decided to move to Nashville with the idea of working at something connected with country. After time as a cartoonist, magazine writer, handyman, and successful record promotion executive (for Ovation), he cut several sides himself. One of them, the title tune of this album, soon made the upper levels of the country charts and launched his new career.

This album is an invigorating mixture of classic honky-tonk, blues-rock, gospel, atmospheric pop, and country-rock. Tying it all together is a remarkable, haunting voice. Joe Sun is extremely innovative, but derives great onstage sustenance from the grand honky-tonk tradition. In both style and content he's solidly country, yet he's also creating something that pushes at country's boundaries. His fine albums are progressive in the best sense of the word.

Buck White and the Down Home Folks
Poor Folks' Pleasure 1978
Sugar Hill SH–3705

Buck White and his daughters Sharon and Cheryl plugged away in Nashville for years, releasing their albums on small labels as they honed their skills. When they broke through to mass acceptance by recording and touring with Emmylou Harris in 1978–79, the promise they'd shown to local residents was finally fulfilled. The home-town folks had made good.

Buck White, born in 1931, grew up in north-central Texas. He listened to broadcasts coming from several different directions—Mexican border radio, the Opry, the WLS (Chicago) "Barn Dance"—and his own music reflects that variety of influences. He started playing accordion when he was fourteen, then moved on to piano, and played dancehalls in a Western band as a teenager (meanwhile learning to play mandolin as well). For four-and-a-half years, starting in 1953, he played in a five-piece band that did a daily live Wichita Falls TV show. In 1962 he moved his family to Arkansas and soon put together an early edition of the Down Home Folks, with his wife, Pat, and three friends. In the late 1960s, teenage daughters Sharon and Cheryl began working with their parents and the family began performing at bluegrass festivals. In 1971 they moved to Nashville and began performing in Music City's clubs. The group now consists of Buck, Sharon, Cheryl, and dobroist Jerry Douglas. Ricky Skaggs, Sharon's husband, produces the act's Warner Bros. releases. Thus, the Whites' Warners LP *Old Familiar Feeling* is also highly recommended.

This Sugar Hill album was the first that really showed the Whites to their best advantage. It succeeds brilliantly as a demonstration of their talents as country and country-pop performers solidly grounded in bluegrass virtuosity. Nowhere will you hear lovelier family harmony singing than here.

part two

COUNTRY MUSIC INSTRUMENTS AND PLAYERS

Rich Kienzle

When we look at country music in its instrumental form, we are actually going back to its roots. That may seem odd in an age when vocalists dominate matters (as they have, in fact, for a half-century), but in fact the earliest country recordings were primarily instrumental; the essence of the music was old-time fiddling, later expanded to the instrumental string bands, which augmented the fiddle with banjo, mandolin, and, later, guitar.

For years, the fiddle dominated; the other stringed instruments were primarily used to provide a more defined sense of rhythm, highly important for square dances. There were variations, of course: pianos, where available, were popular. Still, bowing, plucking, and picking string instrumentalists dominated the easy stages of early commercial, meaning recorded, country music.

The popularity of vocalists, beginning in the late 1920s with Jimmie Rodgers, forever changed the instrumentalist's place in country music. Certainly the old-time string bands continued in popularity, but now a new type of country instrumentalist was emerging, one who had been prevalent in pop music for many years: the sideman, an instrumentalist dedicated to backing the vocalist and enhancing his singing. It started slowly, and a decade passed before a truly significant group of such players appeared.

As the thirties ended, a few singers began to organize their own backup bands, groups of instrumentalists who performed and recorded with a particular singer. Roy Acuff's Crazy Tennesseeans (later known as the Smoky Mountain Boys) were one notable example. In the Southwest, Milton Brown and His Musical Brownies, and Bob Wills and His Texas Playboys were groups dominated by instrumentalists, including strong soloists like steel guitarists Bob Dunn (with the Brownies) and Leon McAuliffe (with the Playboys), fiddler Jesse Ashlock (with both bands at different times), Playboy guitarist Eldon Shamblin, and Brownies pianist Fred Calhoun. Like the best jazz and pop instrumentalists, these musicians and others created music of sufficient substance to sustain a listener's interest.

Until the mid-1930s, the instruments of country music hadn't changed much. The average hillbilly string band consisted of fiddle, acoustic guitar, banjo, and bass, or some variation on that lineup. Some groups used harmonicas, pianos, or even the odd cello or two. However, cultural and technological trends gradually and permanently expanded the lineup. Hawaiian music's popularity in the 1920s helped to introduce the slide guitar to country music. The development of the resonator guitar, particularly the Dopyera Brothers' "Dobro" guitar, which provided greater volume through the use of acoustic resonators, moved the voicelike sound of steel guitar even further into country music.

Although amplified instruments were being developed in the late 1920s and first became commercially available in the early to mid-1930s, the more conservative southeastern musicians were loathe to use them. Things were different in Texas, however, where Western swing steel guitar virtuoso Bob Dunn began playing a homemade amplified steel in 1934. The next step was the introduction of specially made, commercially available electric Spanish guitars, and the proliferation of electric pickups that could be attached to acoustic instruments made an even more profound difference. However, as the following chapters show, the inherent conservatism of country peformers made amplified instruments controversial for the better part of a decade. Likewise, the introduction of drums into country music, something Bob Wills had done in the 1930s, was fiercely fought. Only in the mid-1970s were full drum sets permitted on the Grand Ole Opry stage, nearly two decades after they were accepted by the majority of country performers.

By the 1940s, the country music instrumental lineup we know today was beginning to coalesce. First a novelty, amplified instuments became integral to the musical identities of performers. The sparse, melodic electric guitar leads on the late Ernest Tubb's hits of the period became as much a part of his sound as his own raw, slightly off-pitch singing. Amplified steel guitars were becoming more sophisticated as well. In bluegrass, acoustic instruments were still predominant. Yet even there a new type of instrumentalist, exemplified by banjoist Earl Scruggs, was raising acoustic country music to new levels of proficiency, creating a revolution in acoustic music that has yet to cease.

Although backup bands became increasingly popular during that period, many singers didn't have their own groups. As the recording industry moved from the field recording setups of the twenties and thirties to more formal recording operations in Cincinnati, Chicago, Dallas, and Nashville, things began to change. Groups of instrumentalists used for accompaniment in recording sessions—the same sort of studio musicians long ensconced in the studios of New York, Chicago, and Los Angeles—began to proliferate in these country music centers. Their musicianship and new stylings brought guitar, steel, and fiddle to new heights. Though names like Jabbo Arrington, Zeke Turner, Hank Garland, Bob Foster, Bob Moore, and Tommy Jackson never became household words, these men were among the first in this new group of instrumentalists oriented to providing fresh accompaniment on recordings. More important, their work was copied by amateur musicians across the country, as was the work of better-known virtuoso players like steel guitarist Jerry Byrd and guitarist Merle Travis.

The early 1950s brought still more changes. Country instrumental recordings, which had progressed considerably from the days of fiddle tunes like "Sallie Gooden," were again popular. Jerry Byrd's "Steelin' the Blues" had been a favorite, but even more important were the recordings of Chet Atkins, who had begun as a disciple of Les Paul and Merle Travis, and went on to create a durable, vibrant guitar sound of his own. Atkins was of immense importance in developing credibility for country players, who were suffering from being stereotyped as shallow, sloppy players. The stereotype was never really correct after the 1940s, and probably wasn't accurate even in the 1920s, either. But Atkins was the first player whose interest in other kinds of music was visible, proving the depth of the best players.

The conservative barriers gradually wore down by the 1960s as country musicians continued to become more sophisticated. The lineup of instruments had expanded considerably by then. Fiddle, guitar, mandolin, banjo, bass, harmonica, and piano were joined by electric guitar, pedal steel guitar, drums. Even horns were not unusual additions to country recordings; in fact, they'd been used intermittently since the 1930s.

Today, synthesizers are gaining acceptance, although it is doubtful that veteran hard-country singers like George Jones or Merle Haggard and such 1980s neoconservatives as Ricky Skaggs, John Anderson, Reba McEntire, and George Strait will ever totally accept them. That is the pattern of initiation of new instruments: a period of trepidation and/or hostility, followed by grudging acceptance, and ending with the instrument in the mainstream.

Each chapter in this section looks at a single instrument and details its history and development within country music in a list of LPs featuring the finest recordings of that instrument. There is a list of instruction books, as well as another list of periodicals that cover instruments used in country music. Addresses can be found in the Appendix.

Standard histories of musical instruments rarely note the fact that American folk, country, and blues music were greatly responsible for the creation of an entire family of new or redesigned string instruments. In the italicized inserts in each of the following sections, the editor has described the most widely used of these instruments. Descriptions of the fiddle and piano, which have changed less to meet the needs of country music, have been included so that the entire country string lineup can be compared.

M.M.

BANJO

Earl Scruggs's Vega banjo (Country Music Foundation)

The roots of the banjo are undeniably African, yet the evolution occurred in North America. The earliest mentions of the forerunners of the banjo as we know it date from the 1600s, when Jamaican slaves were reported playing unusual gourdlike instruments strung with horse hair. The instrument's names, *banju, bana,* or *banjar* (and other variants) were of African origin. Thomas Jefferson, in his *Notes on Virginia,* noted seeing a "banjar" being played by his slaves, and other accounts of the Colonial period describe similar instruments played by slaves.

Music undoubtedly had a particularly deep significance for people involuntarily deprived of so many other elements of their own culture. The early forms of the banjo were used to accompany singing and dancing. The instrument evolved slowly toward its present form.

One individual believed by some to have played a significant role in the banjo's evolution in America was Joel Sweeney, a white Virginian born in 1813. Sweeney, who had frequently heard the banjo while he was growing up, built one of his own, adding a fifth string to what had been a four-string instrument. However, pre-1800 five-string banjos have been identified, so he cannot be considered the inventor. Sweeney and his brothers subsequently became entertainers, featuring the banjo prominently in shows that were forerunners of the minstrel show. While white theater audiences initially were hostile to black minstrels, they did accept whites in blackface. Banjo music was an integral part of such productions, and minstrel shows enjoyed enormous popularity among white audiences. Not surprisingly, banjos became popular with white musicians in the South. (Joel Sweeney died in 1860. His younger brother Sam became an aide to Confederate cavalry commander Jeb Stuart, and often rode with Stuart, his banjo slung over his shoulder, entertaining the troops between battles with topical songs about the war.)

In the post–Civil War period the banjo remained popular throughout the South. It gradually became an accompanying instrument for the fiddle among rural white musicians, and provided a rhythmic, ringing accompaniment for dancers. It remained important in black culture as well. However, by the turn of the century the emergence of the blues form found many black musicians switching to the guitar, in part because strings could be "bent" more easily to create "blue" notes, and those notes sustained better on the guitar. By the 1920s only a handful of black musicians, such as Papa Charlie Jackson and the Memphis Jug Band's Gus Cannon, were still using the banjo. But as blacks turned to other instruments, it became a staple in many white southern string bands.

During the World War I years the four-string tenor banjo was often used in popular music orchestras as well as in Dixieland bands, where it was used as a rhythm instrument. It was seldom used in country music. The Gibson company of Kalamazoo, Michigan, already known for its fine mandolins (mandolin orchestras were popular around the country), made its first tenor banjo in 1918. By the early 1920s banjos were popular enough for Gibson to market a number of models. Aside from tenor and five-string instruments, they made the banjo-mandolin (a scaled-down banjo body with a mandolin neck), ukelele banjos, banjo guitars, and other models.

Five-string banjos were first played by country performers in a style that became known by a number of terms, among them "drop-thumb," "clawhammer," and "frailing." What this amounted to was using the thumb to pick or pluck strings, and the nails of the other fingers—held together and slightly curled—to brush the strings on a down- or up-down stroke. This created a ringing, rhythmic sound that fitted well with either fiddling or singing. It was a bit primitive, but perfect for the raw sounds of the country string bands. Later, some players began "flat-picking"—using a triangular flat pick held by the thumb and fingers to alternately pick and strum. A third style, "finger-picking," uses picks formed like rings with projecting points that are slipped over the tips of the thumb and the first two fingers. This is the style used for the most complex and dazzling banjo playing.

The first major solo country artist to use the five-string banjo, an artist whose influence remains strong today, was Uncle Dave Macon. David Harrison Macon, a freight hauler turned musician, was born in Smart Station, Tennessee in 1870. A banjoist from his youth, he played primarily in the frailing style, but was also capable of a variety of other more complex picking styles. Macon, whose freight business was snuffed out by

One widely used system of classifying musical instruments, developed by Curt Sachs, begins by dividing all instruments into five main classes. String instruments fall into the class of chordophones (Greek chorde-string), but the banjo is unique among modern Western string instruments in borrowing its sound-amplifying principle from the family of membranophones, most of which are percussion instruments. Not surprisingly, the banjo's percussive quality is an important part of its musical contribution, even in the case of the melodic five-string banjo.

The usual country music banjo is a fretted instrument with five metal strings. Four of the strings run from a peghead, and the fifth from a peg set into the side of the neck, about a third of the way up its length. The body of the banjo is in fact very much like that of a modern drum, consisting basically of a plastic or calfskin head stretched over a round hardwood shell, and clamped to it by a tension ring running around the diameter of the head. The tension ring is clamped to the shell by sixteen or more hooks that are tightened individually to adjust the tension of the head, again like a modern drum. To this basic structure a third element is often added: a metal tone ring that surrounds the wooden rim and covers the rim's top edge, so that the head is actually clamped to the tone ring. This additional metal (cast brass or bronze in many more expensive instruments) adds volume and contributes its own character to the tone of the instrument. Another optional component of the banjo body is a "resonator": a chamber of wood or wood and metal attached to the back of the instrument. Sound holes around the resonator rim allow sound

the automobile, made his first public appearance in 1921, but he didn't become a full-time musician until he joined the Loew's vaudeville circuit in 1923. Performing with a fiddler, Sid Harkreader, he made his first recordings in July 1924. An ebullient, outgoing performer, his largely up-tempo repertoire was geared to grab an audience. One of his guaranteed showstoppers was "Uncle Dave Handles a Banjo Like a Monkey Handles a Peanut," in the course of which he played the banjo behind his back, over his head, and any other way it could possibly be held.

Macon was one of the first performers to work on the Nashville barn dance radio shows that preceded the Grand Ole Opry, and was among the first acts to appear on WSM's "Barn Dance," in late 1925, well before the name "Grand Ole Opry" was ever coined. He was among the Opry's major solo stars until Roy Acuff joined the show in the late thirties, and remained an Opry regular until his death in 1952. Along the way he inspired some others, two of whom continued in the Macon banjo-and-vocal tradition following his death: David "Stringbean" Akeman and Louis M. "Grandpa" Jones. Since Stringbean's tragic death it has been Grandpa Jones who carries on the Macon legacy, bringing it to mass audiences through his regular appearances on the top-rated TV show "Hee Haw." Ironically, Grandpa's style developed independently of Macon's.

While many banjoists of the 1920s were working in the frailing style or its variations, *coming from the back of the vibrating head to reinforce the sound coming from its front, and help project the sound. The scale length (length of the whole vibrating string) of the standard banjo is about 26.25 inches. The fifth string of the five-string banjo begins at the fifth fret, and the neck widens to accommodate the fifth string from that point to the body. The strings are attached to a tailpiece fixed to the end of the body, and the vibrations of the strings are transmitted to the head through a two-footed or three-footed wooden bridge sitting on it.*

Several different tunings are used on the five-string banjo, all permitting the fifth string to be used as a drone string. In the G-tuning, the most common, the fifth string is tuned to the G above middle C, the fourth string to the D below middle C, the third string to the G below middle C, the second string to the B below middle C, and the first string to the D above middle C. These notes form an open G chord, facilitating the combination of chord arpeggiation with melody lines that is characteristic of the five-string picking style. Other common open tunings are C, C-minor, and G-minor tunings. Several devices are used to permit open tunings in other keys, including capos (which clamp down all the strings across the width of the neck at any given fret); special pre-set tunings pegs (invented by Earl Scruggs and perfected by Bill Keith and Dan Bump) for fast retuning; and necks lengthened by three frets, which are tuned to open E-tuning, for example, and then capoed at the third fret for standard G-tuning. Various devices are used to capo the fifth string independently.

others were playing differently, among them a North Carolinian named Charlie Poole. Poole's approach to the banjo was a bit more complex than Macon's, as he played in a three-finger picking style that was particular to the region of North Carolina in which he grew up. Though he was not a great innovator, his playing gave the first hints of changes that would manifest themselves later in the work of Earl Scruggs. Another banjoist, the Chattanooga-based Homer Davenport, working with a group known as Jess Young and His Tennessee Band, played in a style even closer to the one Scruggs would develop, though there is no evidence that Scruggs ever heard him.

Still another unique banjo style of the 1920s was that of coal miner Dock Boggs, who first recorded in 1927. A white musician with blues influence in his playing, Boggs would pluck the melody of a song on his instrument as he sang the lyrics, an individualistic style rarely imitated.

In the wake of Jimmie Rodgers's success, by the early 1930s the guitar had become far more prominent than the banjo in country music and soon was the predominant instrument for vocal accompaniment. While the banjo generally had become less popular in string bands, four-string tenor banjos came to be used as rhythm instruments in the early Western swing bands of the Southwest. These began as small string bands in the early thirties and soon grew into larger groups. The East Texas Serenaders, a fiddle band that preceded the Western swing movement, had used tenor banjo. That example, and the tenor banjo's popularity among Dixieland bands—which had an enormous influence on the early Western swing bands—may well have inspired its use by the swing units. Among the early bands using tenor banjo were Milton Brown and His Musical Brownies (Ocie Stockard on banjo), and Bill Boyd's Cowboy Ramblers (Walter Kirkes on banjo). In Bob Wills and His Texas Playboys—the group that preceded the preeminent Western swing band, called simply the Texas Playboys—Bob's brother Johnnie Lee played tenor banjo. Then, from the mid-1930s until the early 1940s, Lee and Sleepy Johnson played it with the Texas Playboys. Joe Thames played tenor with Cliff Bruner's Texas Wanderers, and Marvin Mongomery was a featured member of the Light Crust Doughboys. However, as in jazz, the tenor banjo was gradually replaced by the rhythm guitar.

As drums became more acceptable for providing rhythm, and guitars proliferated in popular music, tenor banjo was used less, and by the forties it had largely disappeared, though Bob Wills used it occasionally throughout the fifties and sixties.

When Bill Monroe formed his original Blue Grass Boys in Atlanta in 1939, after splitting with his brother and partner, guitarist Charlie Monroe, that original group lacked a five-string banjo until David "Stringbean" Akeman joined in 1942. Stringbean's playing was strongly rooted in the frailing style of Uncle Dave Macon, and the banjo primarily added rhythm to the sound of the band. But late in 1945 the banjo's role in that group changed radically. Stringbean had left the Blue Grass Boys, and a replacement came in the form of Earl Eugene Scruggs, a native of North Carolina.

Scruggs grew up in Cleveland County, in western North Carolina, the same end of the state that produced Charlie Poole and other three-finger banjoists. Throughout his early youth he listened to a number of players in this style, including Snuffy Jenkins and Scruggs's cousin Smith Hammett. The style of his home region was based on a picking technique more complex than frailing. The thumb, index, and middle fingers picked the strings in a rolling syncopated style that created flowing cascades of notes. At the age of ten Scruggs found his own version of the style and developed it through his adolescence, playing with local groups such as the Morris Brothers, and working when he was fifteen with a local group, the Carolina Wildcats. In 1939 he was in South Carolina with the Morris Brothers. He worked in a factory during World War II, then returned to music, working with Lost John Miller. Late in 1945, he auditioned for Bill Monroe. The Blue Grass Boys already had Lester Flatt's singing and guitar, Chubby Wise's fiddle, and the bass of Howard Watts. The addition of Scruggs's banjo helped create the band that has set the standards for bluegrass music ever since.

Scruggs's role in the band was obvious from the beginning. He stood on stage rolling out a stream of banjo notes to incredulous audiences, at stage shows and on the Opry and other radio shows. Charlie Poole may have anticipated this technique to a degree, but he was greeted with none of the awe that Scruggs evoked. Banjoists throughout the South changed their perceptions of the instrument after hearing him, though not all were impressed: Uncle Dave Macon is reputed to have remarked, "He ain't one damn bit funny," while watching Scruggs play at the Opry. From late 1945 until 1948, when both Flatt and Scruggs left Monroe, the group's appearances and their Columbia recordings defined the bluegrass idiom. Soon Scruggs had imitators, who found their own variations on his style. One was Don Reno, Scruggs's replacement in the Blue Grass Boys, who had been toying with the three-finger style. Reno had auditioned for Monroe in 1943, and only military service prevented him from joining the band then. Another to follow in Scruggs's wake was the former clawhammer banjoist Ralph Stanley of the Stanley Brothers, one of the first bluegrass groups to follow Monroe. Reno's style differed considerably from that of Scruggs as he added licks picked up from steel and standard guitarists. He later formed a duo with guitarist Red Smiley (and more recently worked with guitarist Bill Harrell). Yet Scruggs still remained number one, even though Monroe picked up some talented players through the forties and fifties (one was Rudy Lyle, a hard-driving Scruggs-style player).

When Scruggs and Lester Flatt teamed up in 1948, after they left Monroe, Scruggs continued developing a style that set the standards for every five-string banjoist. One of the duo's earliest recordings was "Foggy Mountain Breakdown", a 1950 Mercury release that would become an enormous hit almost twenty years later as a theme song for the film *Bonnie and Clyde*. In 1951 they moved to Columbia, where Scruggs recorded "Earl's Breakdown." This instrumental session marked the debut of a new banjo tuner Scruggs had devised that permitted him to instantly alter the pitch of his B string and then return it to normal pitch. He used this new "Scruggs Tuner" again in 1951 on the recording of "Flint Hill Special," another popular instrumental number. The mysterious innovation caused Scruggs's growing group of followers much consternation as they rushed to emulate their idol.

By the late fifties, Scruggs had been discovered by the folk music audience, at that time a considerably more affluent and educated group than the average bluegrass audience, and Flatt and Scruggs became favorites on the college circuit. (Bill Monroe was ignored by many newcomers to bluegrass music, a wrong that was subsequently corrected by various Monroe partisans writing in folk publications.) Other highly talented banjoists appeared during those years. Sonny Osborne was an example. In 1951, at the age of thirteen, he began playing five-string banjo; within a year he was a member of the Blue Grass Boys. Following a brief absence, he again worked with Bill Monroe, then left to join his mandolinist brother Bobby. The pair joined with former Blue Grass Boys singer-guitarist Jimmy Martin to record for RCA, then recorded for MGM with Red Allen. Following Allen's departure they began recording as the Osborne Brothers for MGM, with Sonny's banjo prominently featured. Sonny's banjo innovations often included the use of non-standard banjos and one of the first electrified banjos in bluegrass; in 1970 he introduced a six-string banjo. Stylistically, Sonny borrowed licks from other stringed instruments. The Osbornes drew flak from bluegrass purists for both the amplification and the use of non-bluegrass instruments like drums, electric bass, and piano, but they stood firm in their intent to remain progressive.

Sonny Osborne wasn't the first to use an electric banjo, however. Buck Trent had done so earlier when he amplified a five-string and played it as part of Porter Wagoner's band, the Wagonmasters, in the sixties and early seventies.

The next major stylistic innovation on the five-string banjo came in the 1960s, with the emergence of William Bradford ("Bill") Keith. A graduate of Amherst College, Keith exemplified the urban bluegrass fans of that period. He developed a more complex approach to the banjo than Scruggs's. Known as "chromatic banjo," Keith's more melodic style became attractive to many up-and-coming players. He and his partner Dan Bump combined ideas with Scruggs to produce an improved pitch tuner that didn't require drilling holes in an instrument. A measure of Keith's credibility in bluegrass circles was his stay with Bill Monroe, who had expressed admiration for Keith as a musician. With unusual openness, Monroe has stated that Keith came in when his music "needed a boost." Keith subsequently went on to other projects, including the Jim Kweskin Jug Band, a more folk- and blues-oriented band, and later took up pedal steel guitar. But he remains primarily a banjoist, one of the most admired players of the past decade.

The way that the five-string banjo became ingrained in the American imagination bears examination. By the 1950s, the Scruggs five-string style had become so popular in bluegrass circles that it wasn't unusual for record companies such as the tradition-oriented Starday of Nashville to release entire LPs of five-string banjo, or to include a blurb on a bluegrass album stating that it "features the five-string banjo." Folksinger Pete Seeger's popular five-string banjo instruction book included information on Scruggs's playing (though Seeger himself worked closer to the frailing style) as early as 1954, and in 1957 the Folkways LP *American Banjo Scruggs Style*, brought the music to the folk audience, although it didn't feature Earl himself. When Flatt and Scruggs were selected to provide the soundtrack and theme song for the CBS TV show "The Beverly Hillbillies" and to make occasional appearances on the show, millions of people were introduced to banjos. In late 1962 Columbia released Flatt and Scruggs's version of "The Ballad of Jed Clampett," the show's theme song, and it became an enormous country hit. The use of "Foggy Mountain Breakdown" for the *Bonnie and Clyde* soundtrack also increased the pair's exposure as bluegrass artists, though by 1967, when the film was released, they were recording contemporary pop songs as well.

In 1969 Flatt and Scruggs separated in a dispute over their musical direction, and Earl Scruggs joined his sons in a contemporary country rock act known as the Earl Scruggs Revue. About the time that group debuted, in late 1970, Scruggs was featured on a Public Broadcasting TV special, "Earl Scruggs, His Family and Friends," later released as a soundtrack LP (Columbia). Many of Scruggs's bluegrass fans became incensed at what they saw as a sellout, and still more young people's attention was attracted. Flatt continued performing in a traditional vein until his death in 1979. More recently Scruggs, now an elder statesman of country banjo, has indicated interest in returning to conventional bluegrass, since the Revue disbanded several years ago.

The 1973 film "Deliverance" brought another vintage bluegrass banjo song onto the charts in the form of "Dueling Banjos," originally known as "Feudin' Banjos" and written by banjoist-guitarist Arthur "Guitar Boogie" Smith years before. The hit recording was done by Eric Weissberg, a New York studio musician. "Dueling Banjos" brought the banjo to the ears of many Americans, as the "Jed Clampett" song had a decade before.

For the most part new trends in banjo, or any other country instrumental style, don't come along often, so the new talents who have emerged in the 1980s are still defining themselves. Those who have attracted attention include Joseph "Butch" Robins, a young player whose style has remained bold yet solidly traditional. He's done solo recordings, and at one point held the banjo slot with Bill Monroe. Another is John Hickman, a virtuoso who works with two other bluegrass virtuosos, fiddler Byron Berline and flat-picking guitarist Dan Crary. Another youthful banjoist, Bela Fleck, shows a solid command of the instrument in a traditional vein, but can also create music with a fascinating variety of jazz, ethnic, and classical influences.

BANJO RECORDINGS

Various Artists

Tennessee Strings (Rounder 1033) is an anthology produced by Charles Wolfe, who is the author of an excellent book with the same title, dealing with early recorded examples of old-time pre-bluegrass Tennessee string-band music (see Part Four, Reading About Country Music). Among the banjoists included on this set are Uncle Dave Macon, and Homer Davenport, who was anticipating the Earl Scruggs bluegrass banjo style years before Scruggs was known to anyone.

Clawhammer Banjo (County 757) is an excellent anthology of contemporary clawhammer banjoists from the Virginia area, and although none of the players are "name" banjoists, the record proves that the older styles are not in danger of extinction.

Uncle Dave Macon

Laugh Your Blues Away (Rounder 1028) is an excellent album by the banjo-playing Opry star of the show's earliest days, concentrating on his more humorous numbers. Most of the material here has never been released in any other form; it includes onstage recordings made while he was an amateur performing at the Opry, private recordings, and test pressings of vintage recordings that were never issued. There are also some banjo duets with his longtime sideman Sam McGee, and a variety of material ranging from humor to hymns.

Grandpa Jones

The repertoire of Grandpa Jones goes back to his earliest recordings for King Records in 1944. Grandpa made a number of classic recordings over the years. Much of his excellent Monument material is currently out of print, but some of his earliest recordings are available, along with an abundance of recent work that shows his command of the older banjo styles to be formidable after several decades as a performer.

16 Greatest Hits of Grandpa Jones (Gusto SD–3008) makes available again some of Grandpa's best-known King recordings, starting with "It's Raining Here This Morning," one of his earliest records under his own name. This record shows his playing in a number of contexts and proves that his basic sound has remained essentially unchanged. More recently Grandpa has recorded for the tradition-oriented CMH label of Los Angeles, where he's had a chance to stretch out and play along with members of his family, including his wife Ramona, a fine fiddler. These records include some of the traditional material he grew up with; among them are *The Grandpa Jones Story* (CMH 9007), *Grandpa Jones Family Album* (CMH 90015), and *Grandpa Jones Family Gathering* (CMH 9026). All are double albums, replete with his work in a variety of different contexts, and all feature Grandpa's banjo playing prominently.

Snuffy Jenkins

Jenkins, a North Carolinian whose banjo style inspired Earl Scruggs and Don Reno, among others (although neither player imitated him), has recorded a couple of albums that show him in fine form. Teamed with fiddler Pappy Sherrill, he has recorded *33 Years of Pickin' and Pluckin'* (Rounder 0005) and *Snuffy and Pappy* (Rounder 0059). These entertaining records are an education in the Carolina banjo tradition that spawned Scruggs.

Earl Scruggs

To hear the Scruggs banjo playing that revolutionized bluegrass music, it is essential to hear his work with Bill Monroe and His Blue Grass Boys, with whom Scruggs worked from 1945 to 1948. That material is available on three albums also mentioned in the mandolin section: *Bill Monroe with Flatt and Scruggs* (Rounder SS06) and *Bill Monroe and His Blue Grass Boys: The Classic Bluegrass Recordings Volumes 1 and 2* (County Country Classics Series CCS–104, 105). The classic Columbia recordings of Flatt and Scruggs are also available on four fine albums, two from Rounder and two from County (their original Mercury recordings seem to be in limbo). Laced with plenty of Scruggs's banjo work, they are *Flatt and Scruggs: The Golden Era* (Rounder Special Series SS05), which includes his classic "Flint Hill Special," and *Don't Get Above Your Raisin'* (Rounder Special Series SS08). Two other compilations of Flatt and Scruggs Columbia sides from the early to mid-fifties are *The Golden Years* (County Country Classics Series CCS–101), which features the Scruggs tour-de-force "Earl's Breakdown," and *Blue Ridge Cabin Home* (County Country Classics Series P–14370). A few budget record bins may yield copies of the out-of-print *Live at Carnegie Hall* (Columbia Special Productions 8845). The soundtrack LP to the Public Broadcasting special *Earl Scruggs: His Family and Friends* (Columbia PC–30584), featuring Earl with Joan Baez, the Morris Brothers, and his sons, is also plentiful in budget sections. He's also prominently featured on the Nitty Gritty Dirt Band album *Will the Circle Be Unbroken?* (Capitol LKCL-9801) with Merle Travis, Maybelle Carter, Roy Acuff, Jimmy Martin, and Doc Watson. There are a number of Earl Scruggs Revue LPs that range from mildly interesting to dull, but one stands out: the 1973 *Live at Kansas State University* (Columbia PC–31758), another budget album easily available. It features an all-star lineup: Earl, his sons Gary and Randy, fiddler Vassar Clements, old Flatt-and-Scruggs dobroist Josh Graves, and drummer Jody Maphis (son of guitarist Joe Maphis). This is easily their finest album.

Rudy Lyle

Rudy Lyle's excellent banjo can be heard on four 1949 tracks on *Bill Monroe and His Blue Grass Boys: The Classic Bluegrass Recordings Volumes 1 and 2* (County CCS–104, 105).

Don Reno

Don Reno, the man who replaced Earl Scruggs in Monroe's band, never got a chance to do a recording session with Monroe. However, after he teamed up with Red Smiley, he began a prolific recording career with King. Though most of the King recordings are out of print, there are still albums of the vintage Reno and Smiley recordings available: *20 Bluegrass Originals* (Gusto GD–5028x), *Hymns, Sacred Gospel Songs* (Starday 693), *The World's Greatest 15 Hymns* (Starday 853), *16 Greatest Hits* (Starday/King 3001), and *Country Songs* (Starday/King 701).

The Stanley Brothers

There is quite a bit of the Stanley Brothers' material still available, more than could realistically be included in this list. However, one important new album is *The Stanley Brothers and the Clinch Mountain Boys: The Columbia Sessions Volume 1* (Rounder 5509), which makes available again some of the earliest recordings by the second great bluegrass band after Bill Monroe. The songs reflect Appalachian virtue, and the album offers a chance to hear Carter's excellent banjo work. There are other Stanley albums, including *20 Bluegrass Originals* (Gusto GD–5028X) and *Good Old Camp Meeting Songs* (Starday 805). Another fine gospel album featuring Ralph's banjo is *Uncloudy Day* (County 753). Ralph, since Carter Stanley's untimely death in 1966, has made numerous albums with a variety of musicians; one of the more recent recordings is *The Stanley Sound Today* (Rebel 1601). Check larger record stores for a complete listing.

Sonny Osborne

Sonny Osborne made a number of obscure recordings before joining Bill Monroe, but also did some recordings as a banjoist with Monroe that are available on Decca/MCA LPs like *Bill Monroe's Greatest Hits* (MCA 17), which has two songs with Osborne, "In the Pines" and "Footprints in the Snow." His early recordings with his brother Bobby are available on *The Osborne Brothers and Red Allen* (Rounder 5503) and *The Osborne*

Brothers (Rounder 5504), both taken from their classic MGM recordings. There are also more recent recordings done for CMH Records, among them *Bluegrass Concerto* (CMH 6231) and *I Can Hear Kentucky Calling Me* (CMH 6244). Another recording is *The Osborne Brothers and Jimmy Martin* (Collectors Classics CC–14), which details their association in the fifties before the brothers recorded for MGM.

Bill Keith

Bill Keith did a number of recordings during his stint with Bill Monroe, which are included on the following albums: *Bluegrass Instrumentals* (MCA 104) ("Sailor's Hornpipe," "Santa Claus"), and *Blue Grass Time* (MCA 116) ("Were You There?"). He's also prominent on the 1973 progressive bluegrass album *Muleskinner* (Ridge Runner 0016), his first solo album, *Something Bluegrass* (Rounder 0084), and on country-jazz guitarist Slim Richey's *Jazz Grass* (Ridge Runner 0009).

Butch Robins

Butch Robins, currently banjoist with Bill Monroe's Blue Grass Boys, can be heard on several albums, including two solo albums, *Forty Years Late* and *The Fifth Child* (Rounder 0086 and 0130), and his somewhat progressive *Fragments of My Imagination* (Rounder 0104). He can also be heard on Bill Monroe's *Master of Bluegrass* (MCA 5214).

John Hickman

Hickman can be heard on his *Don't Mean Maybe* LP (Rounder 0101) and on his album with Byron Berline and Dan Crary, *Berline, Crary, Hickman* (Flying Fish SH–3720).

Bela Fleck

Bela Fleck is a relative newcomer to recording solo, although he's done, among other recordings, a debut album titled for his group, *Tasty Licks* (Rounder 0106), a progressive bluegrass album with a variety of influences, and *Anchored to the Shore* (Rounder 0120), a slightly more tradition-oriented set. This solo album combines traditional instrumentals with some that go far into jazz.

BANJO INSTRUCTION

All books listed here are in print at this time. They can be bought in book stores, music and record stores, or directly from the publisher or distributor, listed in the last chapter of this part of the book.

How to Play Banjo by Tim Jumper (Music Sales) is a basic instruction method for the beginner. It uses tablature to show ways to pick out a melody, up-picking, chords, rhythms, and accompaniment styles, and includes a special section on playing bluegrass.

The Banjo Songbook by banjoist Tony Trischka (Music Sales) traces the development of three-finger picking from classical banjo playing (yes, there was such a thing) up through transitional styles into the classic Scruggs style, and includes special sections on the Scruggs and Don Reno styles along with other varied instruction.

Bluegrass Banjo by Peter Wernick (Music Sales), written by the fine banjoist with the group Hot Rize, gives excellent tips on getting into the basic bluegrass styles, for players from elementary to advanced. Various sections deal with playing in groups, care of the instrument, and more. A record is included.

Clawhammer Banjo by Miles Krassen (Music Sales) takes the player into the sort of music that scores of country banjoists in the 1920s (and before) specialized in. This book shows the styles of some of the greatest, and if you're planning to take up Uncle Dave Macon's or Grandpa Jones's styles, this should be required reading.

How to Play the Five-String Banjo by Pete Seeger (Music Sales) deals little with country music as such but does give basic tips that can at least get you started.

Melodic Banjo by Tony Trischka (Music Sales) looks at the melodic styles pioneered by Bill Keith, Alan Munde, and others of the post-Scruggs era. It deals in depth with all of these players (and others) and explains the techniques for both right and left hands, blues runs, improvisations, and other aspects of the style. Comes complete with record.

Old-Time Mountain Banjo by Art Rosenbaum (Music Sales) deals with the pre-Scruggs era of old-timey banjo, based on the styles of traditional banjoists.

Bill Keith Banjo by Tony Trischka and Bill Keith (Music Sales) transcribes twenty-two songs and breaks by Keith and carefully analyzes not only his complex style but the physical setup of his banjo.

Earl Scruggs and the Five-String Banjo (Peer Southern Publications) has been the virtual bible of bluegrass banjoists for decades; it shows the basics of how Scruggs-style banjo is played in 156 pages, with diagrams and photos. The book was written by Scruggs, so the information is about as credible as it could possibly be. A record is available to accompany the book at extra cost.

Melodic Clawhammer Banjo by Ken Perlman (Music Sales) explains the more modern approach to clawhammer, and describes the way to play Appalachian fiddle tunes, string band songs, hornpipes, and Irish numbers. An instruction recording is included.

Banjo Fiddle Tunes (Mel Bay) features five-string banjo solos in the melodic styles pioneered by Bill Keith and others.

Banjo Pickin' Solos (Mel Bay) features a collection of five-string banjo solos written in bluegrass, double-thumbing, and frailing styles.

Bluegrass Banjo (Mel Bay) by the legendary Sonny Osborne is another excellent instruction book on the style by one of the instrument's innovators.

E-Z Banjo Solos by Neil Griffin (Mel Bay) is a book of simple banjo solos arranged for the beginner, in tablature.

Deluxe Bluegrass Banjo Method by Neil Griffin (Mel Bay) is a detailed instruction book that looks at all aspects and styles of bluegrass banjo playing; a cassette tape is available at extra cost.

Advanced 5-String Banjo Technique by Neil Griffin (Mel Bay), the companion to *The Deluxe Bluegrass Banjo Method*, deals with more advanced techniques.

Frailing the Five-String Banjo by Eric Muller and Barbara Koehler (Mel Bay) analyzes the frailing style. A recording is available at extra cost.

Three-Finger Pickin' Banjo Songbook by Mike Bailey (Mel Bay) contains easy arrangements of banjo favorites. Cassette available at extra cost.

Anthology of Five-String Banjo Styles (Mel Bay) features solos in a variety of current styles.

Banjo Artistry by Mark Barnett (Mel Bay) features original solos for the five-string banjo.

Clawhammer Banjo Solos by Alec Slater (Mel Bay) deals with modal and Irish styles, both closely related to early American country styles.

The Complete Banjo Book by Neil Griffin (Mel Bay) is another exhaustive study of all aspects of five-string banjo.

Mel Bay's Tenor Banjo Melody Chord Playing System (Mel Bay) deals with the sort of styles that work well with banjo showpieces; it might be a good source for the banjoist who wants to work in a thirties-style Western swing band.

Homespun Tapes also has an excellent six-tape course by Bill Keith, detailing every aspect of the melodic banjo style he pioneered. It starts with beginning bluegrass styles, goes through the basics of the Keith style, teaches backup banjo, fiddle tunes, and how to use different tunings in the Keith style.

BASS

Bass fiddles have been around country music for many years, but their position was not a prestigious one. That changed, however, as the music developed, as various substyles emerged, and as the instrument gained audibility.

Cellos were used by the early string bands for some time to give a lower end to a band's sound; often they were bowed. Many string bands didn't use any such instrument, however, preferring guitar/mandolin/fiddle/banjo combinations instead. Dr. Humphrey Bate, the earliest string-band leader to perform on the early Nashville barn dances that preceded the Grand Ole Opry, included a cello in his earliest group, the Castilian Springs String Band, in the early 1900s. By the time he had begun playing in Nashville in the mid-1920s, the band had a standup string bass played by a regular bassman, Oscar Albright.

Many smaller units continued without the bass, but by the early 1930s the larger bands were turning toward them. In the Southwest, Otto Gray's Oklahoma Cowboys continued using a cello, but as the early Western swing bands came together, most utilized bassists—the Light Crust Doughboys (after they were together a couple of years) and Milton Brown and His Brownies are examples. It was probably in such southwestern bands that bass players first were taken seriously, as shown by the heavy bass rhythms on some early Western swing recordings. For example, the Light Crust Doughboys' "Pussy, Pussy, Pussy" featured a slapped bass that anticipated the rockabilly sound by nearly twenty years. Yet this wasn't always the case. Eldon Shamblin, who played guitar with Bob Wills's Texas Playboys in the thirties and forties, and who is considered one of the great rhythm guitar players, once said in an interview that he came to his style of adding bass runs on the guitar in between his chords as a way of compensating for the mediocre bass players Wills hired: often these were players who would slap the bass more than actually play it. In all fairness, it should be said that Wills had several fine bassists, including his cousin Em Lansford, Teddy Adams, and his brothers Luke and Billy Jack Wills.

In the Southeast, country groups adopted bass players, but they were often more important as baggy-suited comedians than as serious musicians. This is not to say that some didn't (or couldn't) play well, but most were relegated to playing the fall guy or

157

The Fender Precision Electric Bass

being the butt of the band's cornball jokes. Among the better-known musicians who did this were Lonnie Wilson, who created the character of "Pap" that he used with Roy Acuff, and Joe Zinkan, who was "Cowboy Joe" with Pee Wee King's early Golden West Cowboys. Even Bill Monroe's Blue Grass Boys, noted for their deadly serious approach to the music Monroe founded, had a bassman-comedian in Cousin Wilbur for a time. This continued through the forties; Hank Williams utilized both Hillous Buttrum and Cedric Rainwater for this purpose in the Drifting Cowboys. Another popular bassist-comedian was Joel Price, who worked with Monroe and later with Little Jimmy Dickens, and as a staff musician on the Opry.

However, by the time Price came along things were beginning to change. The standards for making records and for performance had begun to rise, to the point that getting someone to stand onstage in a silly outfit thumping a bass just didn't cut it anymore. Muffed notes and sloppy playing were beginning to show through. Also, bassists themselves were becoming more precise players. A few of the comedians made the transition quite well, among them Joel Price (who met the exacting standards of Bill Monroe and worked on the Opry for some time), and Joe Zinkan, both of whom worked on many recordings over the years. A popular bassist in Nashville, beginning in the late forties, was Ernie Newton, formerly of the Les Paul Trio (along with Jimmy Atkins, Chet's brother). He worked extensively with Red Foley and did numerous recording sessions in the fifties. Another bassist was Bob Moore, whose formidable musical talents made him a virtual fixture on many of the country recording sessions held in Nashville in the fifties and sixties. At last count he had played bass in some 18,000 sessions.

In 1951, the Fender instrument company introduced a new type of bass, the Precison solid-body electric bass. To country bands, particularly those who worked the road a lot, it was a godsend. For years the stereotype of the pre-bus/van era for country bands was a Cadillac with a bass fiddle strapped to the top with the rest of the luggage. The Precision, or P-Bass, changed all that. It was fretted, which meant it could more easily be played accurately, and its volume and tone could be adjusted over a much wider range than those of an acoustic bass. Its sound could carry in a large hall, and it could be transported with comparative ease. One of the first groups to use it was Little Jimmy Dickens's band, the Country Boys.

There wasn't a huge defection to electric basses at first. Many bands continued to use the standup bass and it remained widely popular in commercial country music for a time. It also figured prominently in rockabilly, as Bill Black, a former country bassist, began slapping it behind Elvis Presley in the Sun studios. But by the late 1950s even Black had begun using a Fender bass, and by the early 1960s more and more country bands were making the switch to electric bass, even though traditionalists, particularly in bluegrass, continued to resist the trend. Through the fifties and sixties the transition from standup to electric bass occurred hand-in-hand with the increasing use of drums in country music. (Trying to mike an acoustic bass to match the volume of a full drum set is just begging for feedback trouble.) Of course the influence of rock 'n' roll had a lot to do with both of these developments.

Acoustic or "standup" bass (Al Atherton)

The bass (known as the double bass to classical musicians) is the largest member of the violin family, and the lowest in pitch: its four strings (each with a vibrating length of about 42 inches) are tuned, at intervals of a fourth, an octave lower than the four lowest strings on the guitar: the lowest bass string is two octaves below the E below middle C, not far from the lower limit of human hearing. The form of the traditional acoustic bass resembles that of a violin or cello: its body has an arched top and f-holes, and the neck is unfretted. The strings (usually gut or nylon, the lower two weighted with metal cores) run from a scroll-shaped peghead to a tailpiece attached to the end of the body. The strings' vibrations are transmitted to the body of the instrument by a bridge, which bears on the top with two feet. Beneath one of the feet, inside the instrument, is a sound-post, which fits tightly between the back and the top of the bass so that string vibrations are transmitted to the top almost entirely by the other foot of the bridge. In country music, the acoustic bass is most often plucked with a downstroke, often with first and second fingers together; sometimes the hand "slaps" the string, which contributes a percussive quality to the note. Playing with a bow seldom fits country styles.

The electric bass looks like an oversized electric guitar, usually of the solid-body type. It has four steel or steel-core strings whose vibrations induce a corresponding alternating current in wire coils surrounding magnets mounted on the top of the instrument, beneath the strings. Because the volume of the notes on an electronic instrument can be electronically amplified to almost any level, the amplitude of the strings' vibrations is of much less importance than it is when the strings of an acoustic bass have to set the great surface area of the standup bass's top in motion. For this reason, the strings of the electric bass are shorter (standard scale length is about 34 inches), but they are tuned to the same notes as those of the acoustic bass. Electric basses are usually fretted, although many models can be ordered without frets. Theoretically, the electric bass should be capable of sounding almost exactly like the stand-up bass; given precisely the right electronic equalization, perhaps it can. In practice, although the fundamentals (the notes to which the string is tuned) are the same for the acoustic and electric instruments, the overtone ratios (which give all instruments their various characteristic tones) generated in the electric bass's circuitry and loudspeaker are not the same as those of the acoustic bass. Each instrument has its musical advantages: the standup bass sometimes seems to create a much more solidly rooted foundation for the music than the electric. On the other hand, the notes of the electric bass often have greater definition. The electric bass is often played with a flat pick, as well as being plucked like the upright. A third kind of bass, much less widely used, is the bass guitar (similar to the Mexican guitarrone). Not much bigger than an acoustic guitar, it provides bass fundamentals at greatly reduced volume in a portable package.

There are those who still prefer the sound of the traditional standup bass, often for record sessions. Willie Nelson, for example, who always uses Bee Spears as his regular electric bassist, cut his *Over the Rainbow* (Columbia FC–36883) album in 1980 using all acoustic instruments, including dual standup basses (Bob Moore played one of them). The acoustic bass sound will undoubtedly always be popular, particularly in bluegrass—although it doesn't cut like an electric does, its solidity cannot be duplicated.

It's not easy to describe bass styles in country music because most variations are very subtle. Most country bass playing is simple but precise both rhythmically and harmonically, but within that restricted framework individual players develop interesting variations. As the music itself has broadened, some rock techniques and sounds (fuzztone, for example) have become more acceptable, depending on the music being played. The use of the flat pick instead of the fingers can make a significant difference, on the plus or minus side, in the flow and pulse of the bass line. The essential idea is to complement the music. As the main link between rhythm and harmony, and with its close kinship to the guitar, the bass has come to have a unique and important role in country music.

COUNTRY BASS RECORDINGS

There are no "country bass" records as such, but here are some that will give you an idea of how the bass works in a variety of country music contexts. All of these records are in print; notes and discographies don't always tell who's playing on them.

For standard country bass, any of the Hank Williams recordings, such as *24 Greatest Hits* (MGM SE–4755–2), will show the purist country bass styles. Just about any other record by any singer of this period will do the same.

For good examples of the bass styles used in the honky-tonk idiom, listen to the bass work on Lefty Frizzell's *Treasures Untold* (Rounder SS–11), particularly Bill Callahan's playing on "Shine, Shave, Shower" and Artie Glenn's loping bass on "Run 'Em Off." But for the "walking" or "shuffle" bass that was an integral part of honky-tonk, listen to *Ray Price's Greatest Hits* (Columbia PC–8866), in particular to songs like "Crazy Arms" and "City Lights," and to the work of Bee Spears of Willie Nelson's group on the Willie Nelson/Ray Price album *San Antonio Rose* (Columbia JC–36476).

Western swing bass playing can be heard on any of the Bob Wills albums. A particularly hot bassist was Sam Lansford, who plays tough, driving accompaniment on "Osage Stomp," the first recording Wills and the Texas Playboys made in 1935 for Columbia. For later examples, check out *Twenty-four Great Hits by Bob Wills* (MGM 2-5305). The "Osage Stomp" cut is on *The Bob Wills Anthology* (Columbia PG–32416).

Rockabilly bass playing had its origins in the late thirties, though few people realize it today. The stopped bass on the risque Light Crust Doughboys song "Pussy, Pussy, Pussy," particularly in the final part of the song, anticipated the playing of rockabilly bassmen like Bill Black by a good twenty years (available on *Hot As I Am*, Rambler 105). But the most definitive rockabilly bass work is available on the Elvis Presley LP *The Sun*

Sessions (RCA AYM–1-3893, previously AFM–1-1675), which features the work of Bill Black prominently throughout, particularly on "Blue Moon of Kentucky," "Mystery Train," and "Good Rockin' Tonight," where he uses a walking beat not unlike that used by the later shuffle bassists.

BASS INSTRUCTION

There aren't a lot of country bass instruction books around, but some have been published in the past few years that can help the aspiring country bassist get a line on the stock patterns that are a part of playing bass in a country or bluegrass band.

Bluegrass Bass by Ned Alterman and Richard Mintz (Music Sales) is a book basic enough to be used by any country bassist even if he isn't concentrating on the bluegrass field. There are a number of tunes included, with notation in both standard form and tablature. Among the subjects dealt with are scales, chords and progressions, runs and lines, slap bass (important for rockabilly enthusiasts), and backup styles for country and blues.

Mel Bay's Electric Bass Method, Volumes I and II (Mel Bay), is a basic but excellent general introduction to the electric bass, giving information on hand positions and other rudiments for learning the instrument. There are sections on theory, and technique for playing everything from country to jazz and rock. A cassette version of this method is also available.

Mel Bay's Learn to Play Bluegrass Bass (Mel Bay) is another very basic beginner's text on the theory of playing bluegrass accompaniment.

Country Electric Bass by Jay Friedman (Ernie Ball) offers special instruction in playing country bass guitar, with exercises for developing technique.

DOBRO

The National Duolian resophonic guitar, generically a dobro (Country Music Foundation)

The history of the dobro—also called the resophonic or resonator guitar—is closely intertwined with that of the steel guitar, which is discussed in detail in a later chapter. To avoid repetition, the present chapter concentrates on the history of the dobro alone. The name "Dobro" is a product trademark, but it has become a generic term among musicians for the resonator-equipped Hawaiian guitars invented by the Dopyera Brothers in the 1920s and now produced by several companies. To avoid any confusion, the capitalized word "Dobro" will designate the original Dopyera instruments and those produced by their successor company, the Original Musical Instrument Company; lower-case "dobro" will indicate any model, regardless of its manufacturer.

The Dobro was the creation of a Los Angeles instrument repairman named John Dopyera. The year he built his prototype, 1925, was a time when door-to-door salesmen were traveling the country selling inexpensive Hawaiian guitars along with lessons, and musicians like Sol Hoopii were making popular recordings that showed their virtuosity on the steel guitar. Correspondence courses were available, and even major manufacturers like Gibson and Martin had Hawaiian guitars on the market. Dopyera's idea stemmed from a local guitarist who asked if there were any way he could get more volume out of his standard Hawaiian guitar, which was basically a standard guitar with a raised nut to facilitate fretting the steel strings with a bar. (Electrical amplification for stringed instruments was not yet perfected.)

Dopyera devised a unique system of aluminum resonating cones that would amplify a guitar's sound. Using three cones connected by a T-shaped bridge, he created the prototype, later known as the National Tri-Plate model. John's brother, Rudy Dopyera, devised another refinement: using metal to build the bodies. Subsequently thirty-six metal-bodied instruments were built by hand. After obtaining patents and deciding on an entire line of models, including one with a larger, single-cone type of resonator, they formed the National Instrument Company with a group of investors and began production. The term Dobro originated in 1929, when the Dopyeras (now including brother Ed) quit the National company and began manufacturing under the name Dobro, for DOpyera BROthers. Control of the Dobro patents passed among several companies until they expired. National became a competitor for a time, until the company and the Dopyeras reunited in 1932. During the thirties Dobros became enormously popular, in part due to continuing interest in Hawaiian music, but primarily due to the interest of country players. National was bought by Valco in the 1950s. Today the Dopyera family operates the Original Musical Instrument Company.

A large number of country musicians were playing non-resophonic Hawaiian acoustic guitars in the late twenties, most nobably Jimmie Tarlton, of the team of Darby and Tarlton, as well as Howard Dixon of the Dixon Brothers. The Hawaiian guitar was also used on some of Jimmie Rodgers's popular recordings, which gave that sound even greater exposure (and may have done as much as anything to increase the popularity of the Hawaiian guitar in country music, judging from the artists who later started using it as accompaniment). Among Rodgers's accompanists were Ellsworth Cozzens, Cliff Carlisle, and Joe Kaipo. Carlisle, who had originally played a standard Hawaiian guitar, later

---

The resophonic, ampliphonic, or "dobro" variant of the Hawaiian steel guitar has a distinctive acoustic sound. The instrument is distinguished by a large circular resonator, generally a perforated cone of one or more layers of thin metal, that takes up most of the lower bout. The bridge rests on the cover of this resonator. The dobro is usually strung with six strings, but there are also eight-, ten-, and twelve-string models. The resonator increases the volume of the instrument without electronic amplification; two or more small sound holes in the upper bout add tonal richness.

A six-string resophonic guitar is typically tuned with the lowest string sounding the G an octave below the G below middle C. The intermediate strings are tuned to the B, D, G, and B above that, and the highest string to the D above middle C. The instrument usually is played like a Hawaiian guitar: held horizontally across the lap, with a slider bar of metal or ceramic in the left hand, and picks on the thumb and one or more fingers of the right hand. (See "Steel Guitar.")

teamed up with his brother Bill and another dobro-picking associate named Fred Kirby, playing adaptations of black blues and Jimmie Rodgers numbers.

It was Roy Acuff, however, who truly helped ingrain the dobro sound in country music. His original band, the Tennessee Crackerjacks, playing around Knoxville during the thirties, was the first large group to feature a dobroist, Clell Summey. A revised lineup, known as the Crazy Tennesseeans, still including Summey on dobro, began recording for ARC (forerunner of today's CBS Records), and Summey's playing was clear on such early hit numbers as "Great Speckled Bird." The popularity of that number gradually eroded the Grand Ole Opry's reluctance to add new talent to its lineup, and by late 1938 Acuff and his band—now known as the Smoky Mountain Boys—were regulars on the Opry. Clell Summey soon left (he later became known as comedian "Cousin Jody" on the Opry) and was replaced by Pete Kirby on dobro. Kirby, who continues to work with Acuff today, is also known in his more comedic role in the band as "Brother Oswald." His dobro work has been a part of the Acuff sound for most of the past forty years.

However, the dobro has had its ups and downs with Acuff. According to Acuff's biographer, Elizabeth Schlappi, at one point Acuff and Kirby tried an amplified dobro with disastrous results. From 1955 to 1962, Acuff dropped the dobro sound from his act, and Kirby played guitar. Perhaps once or twice on a show, he would play dobro. However, in recent years the dobro has returned to the forefront of Acuff's band—it is a fine complement to his raw, unvarnished singing.

Other groups began using dobros by the forties, among them the band of Esco Hankins, an Acuff-style singer. Wilma Lee and Stoney Cooper, favorites over WWVA in Wheeling, West Virginia, also featured the dobro, as did Mac Wiseman's bluegrass band. A musician who worked with all of these bands, Burkett "Josh" Graves, emerged in the fifties as a premier dobroist. He was an important force in maintaining the instrument's popularity, and was also responsible for establishing the dobro within the bluegrass idiom. Graves joined Flatt and Scruggs in early 1955, working as the band's comedian as well as dobroist. While Kirby always remained close to the Hawaiian techniques that he'd learned when he started playing, Graves was a far more energetic player. He approached the dobro with a style of his own, not unlike the "rolling" finger-picked style with which Scruggs was revolutionizing banjo music at the same time. Instrumental numbers like "Shuckin' the Corn" were built around Graves and became virtual standards in the Flatt and Scruggs repertoire. Another steel guitarist and dobroist popular during the 1950s was Shot Jackson, a conservative player with a technique not unlike Kirby's. (Unlike either Kirby or Graves, however, Jackson also played plenty of electric steel.) But without question it was Graves who set the standards for other players in the fifties.

During that time, the dobro sound was largely confined to hard-core, traditional groups like Acuff's and the Flatt and Scruggs organization. It was rarely heard on the more conventional Nashville country and western recordings of that time. Through most of the sixties, Graves continued to dominate the dobro idiom. However, by that decade's end, new styles and players were emerging, most notably Mike Auldridge, a veteran of top bluegrass bands in the Washington, D.C., area (a veritable hotbed of bluegrass activity from the fifties to the present). Auldridge, a descendant of onetime Jimmie Rodgers steel accompanist Ellsworth Cozzens, became noted not only for his brilliant playing techniques but also for his ability to devise original and sympathetic accompaniments for singers and other instrumentalists. His musical roots were varied, and he was a fan of big-band music as well as bluegrass. After working with the acclaimed bluegrass band the Country Gentlemen, he now works with the equally brilliant contemporary group the Seldom Scene, and has performed and recorded with a number of other artists from steel-guitar virtuoso Jeff Newman to Linda Ronstadt and Emmylou Harris, creating music that never sacrifices the mood of a number for a few seconds of flashy licks.

Interest in the dobro as used by country performers also developed in rock music circles by the late 1960s. Rock musicians' fascination with the electric and acoustic bottleneck styles used by black blues guitarists was joined by interest in country dobro, notably in San Francisco–based rock singer Boz Scaggs's first LP in 1969, which featured a straightforward version of Jimmie Rodgers's classic "Waitin' for a Train" with dobro accompaniment. Still more interest came in the early seventies as the popularity of folk-rock singer-songwriters continued. Not only did these performers use pedal steel on their records, they also used dobros on occasion. A young folk/bluegrass sideman named David Bromberg began playing it on some recordings, such as vocalist Paul Siebel's 1970 LP *Woodsmoke and Oranges* (Elektra EKS-74064). The fascination with country music expressed by Siebel, as well as Linda Ronstadt, the Grateful Dead, the Byrds, Townes Van Zandt and Gram Parsons also brought them more into contact with country instruments.

Bluegrass festivals attracted an increasing number of followers, particularly young people, by the mid-seventies, and more amateur musicians became interested in banjo, mandolin, and dobro. By this time Original Musical Instrument (OMI), still controlled by Ed Dopyera and his family, was back in business making Dobros again. But now other manufacturers of resophonic guitars had appeared, among them Shot Jackson, who founded the Sho-Bud pedal steel guitar concern with Buddy Emmons in the late fifties. Jackson, who sold Sho-Bud to Gretsch some years ago, manufactured a resophonic guitar known as a "Sho-Bro." The OMI Dobros were built and styled as the Dopyeras had originally built them, and today OMI remains the predominant manufacturer.

Dobros gradually became more common on commercial country recordings, such as Tom T. Hall's 1971 hit "The Year that Clayton Delaney Died," arranged in the style of the old Jimmie Rodgers recordings. Emmylou Harris and Linda Ronstadt have also used dobros on occasion, often with Mike Auldridge featured. The popularity of both artists has given Auldridge exposure outside bluegrass circles that he might never have gotten otherwise. Considered a master of the instrument, in recent years Auldridge has played an eight-string dobro on some occasions. Lloyd Green, the legendary pedal steel guitarist, also played some excellent dobro on the hit recordings of Don Williams.

Another important dobro stylist who will undoubtedly gain attention is Jerry Douglas. Raised in eastern Ohio, Douglas was impressed with the playing of Josh Graves as well as that of Oswald. By the time he was thirteen he was playing part-time with bluegrass-style bands, but later in his teens became a follower of the Auldridge style and wound up as an occasional member of the respected Country Gentlemen. Like Auldridge, Douglas was somewhat broader than many instrumentalists in his musical tastes, unafraid to include pop influences in his playing. He worked with J. D. Crowe's contemporary bluegrass band, as well as with the progressive bluegrass band Boone Creek, which disbanded in 1978. In 1979, having gained a considerable reputation from his work on recordings with Emmylou Harris and with Buck White and the Down Home Folks, he recorded a solo album for Rounder (0093), *Fluxology* (Douglas's nickname is "Flux"), that featured traditional numbers as well as unusual choices like the Burt Bacharach standard "I Say a Little Prayer for You" and original numbers. Douglas also joined Buck White and the Down Home Folks, a group that plays a number of styles beyond bluegrass, including Western swing (their version of "San Antonio Rose" features a Douglas solo with an extremely credible Western swing flair to it). With such an eclectic approach it seems likely that Douglas will be a major dobro innovator of the future.

DOBRO RECORDINGS

Various Artists

Steel Guitar Classics (Old Timey 113—described in the steel guitar discography) is an anthology primarily of acoustic steel performances by some of the earliest acoustic Hawaiian guitarists. It is difficult to tell who is and isn't using dobro, though it's virtually certain that the two Roy Acuff tracks feature one.

Pete "Brother Oswald" Kirby

Without a doubt, Oswald's most enduring work was done with Roy Acuff on his Columbia recordings of the forties. Regrettably, nearly all of that material is now out of print. However, Oswald also played on many of the rerecordings Acuff made through the fifties and sixties, and these give an excellent idea of his role in the Smoky Mountain Boys. *Roy Acuff's Greatest Hits, Volumes 1 and 2* (Elektra 9E-302, -303) include many recordings that feature Oswald's crying, shivering, Hawaiian-based playing behind Acuff. He's also playing with Acuff on the landmark LP *Will the Circle Be Unbroken* (Capitol LKCL-9801) with the Nitty Gritty Dirt Band, Doc Watson, and others. "Os" has also recorded several albums with other musicians that feature his playing as the instrumental lead. Two of the best are *Brother Oswald* (Rounder 0013) and *That's Country* (Rounder 0041), done with longtime Smoky Mountain Boys lead guitarist Charlie Collins.

Josh Graves

Without question, Graves's most enduring work is on those legendary Flatt and Scruggs Columbia recordings of the fifties and sixties. Though many of the Columbia albums are out of print, one album of reissued Columbia material is available that features Josh at his best with them. *Blue Ridge Cabin Home* (County Country Classics Series 14370). It includes his playing on just about every track and includes his showpiece, "Shuckin' the Corn." An excellent recording from the early sixties reissued in 1979 is *Josh Graves and Friends* (Cowboy Carl 102). This set features fifteen numbers, including one with Brother Oswald, and has some of Josh's finest recorded work. He can also be heard on the Earl Scruggs Revue's *Live at Kansas State University* (Columbia PC–31758) and on *King of the Dobro* (CMH 6252), which features him playing bluegrass and country standards with more contemporary backing.

Tut Taylor

Taylor is another excellent dobroist who sticks fairly close to traditional styles. Among his albums are *The Old Post Office* (Flying Fish 008) and *Friar Tut* (Rounder 0011).

Mike Auldridge

There are plenty of Mike Auldridge albums available on a variety of labels, any of which will give you a good idea of what he's doing. Two excellent ones are *Mike Auldridge and Jeff Newman* (Flying Fish 080), which features him working with the longtime expert of pedal steel instruction on a number of songs, and *Mike Auldridge and Old Dog* (Flying Fish 054), a more basic bluegrass-oriented record. He's also done recordings with the Seldom Scene such as *Act Four* (Sugar Hill SH–3709), with Linda Ronstadt—*Heart Like a Wheel* (Capitol 11-358), and with Emmylou Harris—*Elite Hotel* (Warner Brothers MS–2230) and *Luxury Liner* (Warner Brothers BSK–3115). The last three records show Auldridge in a studio backup capacity more than the others.

Jerry Douglas

Jerry has one solo album on the market now, *Fluxology* (Rounder 0093), which includes some bluegrass favorites and some decidedly non-bluegrass material like the Burt Bacharach pop tune "I Say a Little Prayer," and other unusual numbers. His playing is prominent on Emmylou Harris's *Roses in the Snow* (Warner Brothers BSK–3422) and Ricky Skaggs's *Sweet Temptation* (Sugar Hill SH–3076) and *Waitin' for the Sun to Shine* (Epic FE–37913). He's also on the Buck White album *More Pretty Girls Than One* (Sugar Hill SH–3710).

DOBRO INSTRUCTION

Homespun Tapes, known for its excellent instruction courses for fiddle, guitar, mandolin, and bass, has a dobro package that will work well for the beginner or intermediate player and will give even advanced players some new tips. Stacy Phillips's *Bluegrass Dobro* is a six-tape course that deals with the basics (tunings, using the bar, vibratos, etc.), slanting the bar, the various musical elements of bluegrass, rolls, backing instruments or singers, scales, and getting pedal steel guitar effects out of a dobro. There are printed tablature supplements to the tapes.

Stacy Phillips has also written an excellent instruction book, *The Dobro Book* (Music Sales), a comprehensive guide to dobro styles. It includes tips for cultivating smooth left and right hand techniques, bar slanting, playing chords, tunings, history, how to adapt a standard Spanish guitar for use as a dobro and instructions for playing bluegrass, blues, country, and Western swing (Bob Dunn's playing is examined). It includes a recording.

How To Play the Dobro G-Tuning by Doug Jernigan (Emmons Guitar Co.), a course taught by an excellent pedal steel and dobro player, offers an LP recording of ten songs in the G-tuning, and a corresponding set of diagrams for each song.

Modern dobro master Mike Auldridge has created a set of fine dobro instruction tapes that, when you feel you're ready to keep up with his superb playing, allow you to turn down his channel and fill in for him, with accompaniment (Mike Auldridge).

Dobroist Dan Huckabee also offers a tape instruction course (Dan Huckabee).

DRUMS

Gretsch Jazz drums played by Phil Lee (France Menk)

Drums. That five-letter word once had the impact of a four-letter word in country music circles. At the time the first country recordings were made in 1922, drums just weren't used in that kind of music. Even when the much looser Western swing of Milton Brown and His Musical Brownies was burbling up from Fort Worth, Texas, the instrumentation included drums only when the Brownies' contracts specifically called for them. Gene Krupa and others might have been hot in New York and Chicago, or even in larger southern cities with sophisticated populations, but it was another story in the rural areas where fiddlers, banjoists, and guitarists held sway.

The first known country performer to challenge that attitude was Jimmie Rodgers, who recorded "Desert Blues" and "Any Old Time" on February 21, 1929, in New York. He had a six-piece pop orchestra backing him, including an unknown "trapman." According to Nolan Porterfield's discography in his book *Jimmie Rodgers* (University of Illinois Press), Rodgers never again recorded with drums.

Other early country artists may have tried drums, but the major breakthrough after that seems to have come when Bob Wills, then just starting his Texas Playboys organization, hired jazz drummer Smokey Dacus to work with the group. This was unusual even in Western swing, where drums weren't used by most of the smaller Western bands influenced by the Milton Brown style. Wills, however, was developing a much larger band that included several horns. This needed a stronger rhythmic pulse than a string bass alone could provide. Dacus remained with the Playboys until 1940, when he was replaced by the excellent Gene Tomlins. Wills continued to use drums through the

World War II years and beyond, employing some excellent Dixieland-based drummers including Monte Mountjoy and Johnny Cuviello, as well as his younger brother, Billy Jack Wills. When Wills dropped his large horn sections, he brought fiddles and amplified guitars into the front line of the band. In this instrumentation, drums remained essential for maintaining a strong, defined beat for dancing.

Only a few bands used drums in the Texas and Oklahoma region in the late thirties and early forties. One group that did was Bob Skyles and His Skyrockets, an Oklahoma novelty group whose music was on the extreme edge of Western swing. The band was equipped with a full drum set. Adolph Hofner's San Antonians included a drummer by 1941.

In 1943, Bob Wills relocated to the West Coast, but even before that other Wills-style bands proliferated there. One was the Rhythm Wranglers, led by Western movie star Ray Whitley. Their drummer was Muddy Berry, a former big-band drummer who later worked with Spade Cooley, then with Tex Williams's Western Caravan, and again with Cooley in the late forties. After World War II the Texas and Oklahoma bands began regularly including drummers, and in these smaller bands the lineup of twin fiddles, steel guitar, piano, guitar, bass, and drums became standard.

But drums were still generally forbidden in Nashville in the late forties. They remained taboo on the Opry, and on most country records produced in Nashville and elsewhere. Wills, at his first "Grand Ole Opry" appearance late in 1944, was told to hide his drummer behind a curtain. At the last moment he ordered the drums moved out on stage. The Opry staff was not pleased.

An excellent drummer (and WSM staff musician) named Farris Coursey, who worked on sessions in the late forties and early fifties, seems to have been virtually the *only* studio drummer for country recordings in the late forties. But Coursey was rarely permitted to stand out on a country record. The powers-that-were in the early Nashville music scene wanted percussion felt but not actually heard, and often preferred to have a guitarist slap his strings, to get a more subtle rhythmic push. One of the few Nashville-based artists daring to use drums was Pee Wee King, whose Western swing–inspired band, the Golden West Cowboys, included percussionist "Sticks" McDonald. Otherwise, rhythm guitarists like Jack Shook (and later Ray Edenton) were used to play a percussive rhythm on muted strings (dead-string style). As for Coursey, he played on quite a few hits. He performed the memorable "rag-popping" on Red Foley's "Chattanoogie Shoeshine Boy" by slapping his thighs.

The general aversion to drums in Nashville continued even into the fifties, though backup bands elsewhere began to use them. In 1954 Carl Smith, then one of the top singers in the country, decided to add drums to his band. He hired Murrey "Buddy" Harman, a local big-band drummer, and took considerable flak from fellow artists. Harman went on to become one of the most recorded musicians in town, working on scores of country hits over the years. But drums remained forbidden at the Opry; Harman recalls that Opry management finally permitted just a snare drum, played with brushes (no sticks), and they decreed that it be kept behind a screen so the audience couldn't see it. After rock 'n' roll hit, a new Opry strawboss named Dee Kirkpatrick, wanting to dissociate the Opry from anything that even resembled rock (they'd told Elvis to go back to truckdriving in 1954), banned drums as a symbol of what he considered to be "devil's music." However, the Opry gradually moderated its position, and in the early 1960s it became common to see a snare onstage with a drummer using brushes on it. For fifteen years that remained the norm.

After Elvis hit big in 1956, Nashville's music industry felt the impact. Drums took on a new significance when country record sales experienced a decline and many bands followed Carl Smith's lead in adding a drummer to the lineup in order to sound more "with it." In some cases they also sacrificed their fiddlers and/or steel players. There was also a sudden relaxation of the unwritten ban on drums in the studios.

One performer who took notable advantage of that was Ray Price, who began working with a $^4/_4$ tempo he and Buddy Harman developed in the mid-fifties. Known as the "Texas shuffle," it was a characteristic of most of Price's recordings from 1956 into the sixties. It became an essential element of the honky-tonk style, and was employed by scores of other country singers, including Faron Young, Charlie Walker ("Pick Me Up On Your Way Down" is an excellent example), and Mel Tillis.

All of this meant an increase in Buddy Harman's session work as drums became prominent on more Nashville recordings. By 1960, only a handful of artists (largely bluegrass performers) were touring without drums. But even bluegrass had the inevitable exception: the Osborne Brothers, who'd been using Buddy Harman on records since 1958. Although it was their record company's idea, the Osbornes had no problem accepting drums for studio sessions, and eventually added a drummer and electric bass to their touring band as well. (For years they took heat about this from bluegrass purists who conveniently forgot the World War II years when Bill Monroe's Blue Grass Boys had altered the traditional bluegrass instrumentation by including accordionist Sally Ann Forrester.)

A number of country drummers went on to become stars themselves. Roger Miller, for example, had played drums in Faron Young's band; during the early sixties Jack Greene had drummed for Ernest Tubb's Texas Troubadours until he had his own hit with "There Goes My Everything" in 1965.

In most cases drummers remained in the background. They rarely did anything more than keep the beat for other artists, and drum solos were infrequent. However, the revitalization of rock in the middle and late sixties brought a more creative approach, and one of the offshoots of that was an interest among rock musicians in recording in Nashville. As a result, some country session drummers, such as Jerry Carrigan and Kenny Buttrey, were brought into working proximity with rock and had an opportunity to vary their playing. Certain country records and backup bands began reflecting influences from the rock world, including heavier, more defined drumming. The first stirrings of this "outlaw" movement in country music found two drummers working as close associates with the respective singers who employed them: Richie Albright with Waylon Jennings's Waylors and Paul English with Willie Nelson's band. These two drummers became highly visible to fans and were important contributors to the heavier rock-influenced sound of the Outlaw period. Albright, for example, coproduced some of Waylon's records.

There was no question that the controversy over drums in country music had pretty much ended by the 1960s. Only bluegrass bands and other groups playing traditional older country styles continued to exclude them as a matter of course. And not long after the Grand Ole Opry moved from the Ryman auditorium to the new Opry House at Opryland (in 1973) space was made available on the Opry stage for full drum sets.

COUNTRY DRUM RECORDINGS

Not surprisingly, there are no country drum records as such. There are certain albums, though, in which the drums figure prominently enough to justify mentioning them as examples of specific styles.

The classic "shuffle" beat, developed for Ray Price by drummer Buddy Harman in the mid-fifties, can be heard on two records, *Ray Price's Greatest Hits* (Columbia CS–8866) and *Night Life* (Columbia Limited Edition Series LE–10061), both of which have numerous shuffle-tempo tunes of the kind that are now a staple of country music. Johnny Bush, Moe Bandy, Gene Watson, and other Texas singers have kept the shuffle very much alive, even though Price has largely abandoned it.

Western swing drumming styles can best be heard on several Bob Wills albums, most notably *The Bob Wills Anthology* (Columbia PG–32416), which contains some of his original Columbia recordings with not only his original drummer, Smokey Dacus, but with a variety of other fine drummers. The two-record *24 Great Hits By Bob Wills and His Texas Playboys* (MGM 2-5305) demonstrates the role drummers like Billy Jack Wills and Johnny Cuviello played in his postwar bands from 1947 to the early fifities. *For the Last Time* (United Artists UA LA–216-J2), recorded in 1973, has Smokey Dacus playing again on a number of Wills classics of the past, the newer, higher fidelity recording techniques making it possible to better hear the subtleties of the style. To hear Western swing drumming moving closer to rockabilly, listen to *Billy Jack Wills and His Western Swing Band* (Western 2002) and *Crazy, Man, Crazy* (Western 2004).

For rockabilly drumming the Sun recordings, reissued on the Charly label in Britain, or the Sun label in America, show the variety of styles available. On the Sun label, Carl Perkins's *Original Golden Hits* (Sun 111) and *Blue Suede Shoes* (Sun 112) feature the drumming of W. S. "Fluke" Holland, the great rockabilly/country drummer who has worked with Johnny Cash for the past couple of decades. Holland's snappy drumming was an essential part of the early Perkins sound. Another rockabilly drummer from the Sun stable was Jimmy Van Eaton, who did countless sessions. He can best be heard on Jerry Lee Lewis's *Original Golden Hits, Volume 1* (Sun 102) in such classics as "Whole Lotta Shakin," "Great Balls of Fire," and "Breathless." D. J. Fontana is also an essential rockabilly drummer who, like Holland and Van Eaton, had a solid country background before coming into rock. He did not drum on the Sun recordings, but played on all of

Elvis's early RCA records, including *Elvis Presley* (RCA LSP-1254) and *Elvis* (RCA LSP-1382).

DRUM INSTRUCTION

When drums first became widely used in country music it was swing drumming styles that were the dominant influence; more recently, rock styles have become very important, and a good country drummer today should be comfortable with both. There is very little instructional material aimed specifically at country drummers, though many methods include some material on the subject.

There is one book we know of on the subject of country-oriented drumming. It's titled *Country Drumming—A Complete Method* (Thomas Frederick) and is designed for players from beginners to advanced drummers.

The Recording Drummer (Music Sales) is by Clyde Brooks, Dolly Parton's drummer. This excellent book covers a wide variety of playing styles, including country and country-rock. It also deals with the special requirements of the studio recording stituation (some of which also apply to live performances) such as miking techniques, how to muffle the drums, and preparing the drums for recording.

FIDDLE

If one instrument symbolized country music, square dancing, and rural music in the days before the guitar came to the fore, it was the fiddle. And although the guitar has remained dominant, the fiddle, despite occasional lapses in popularity, has remained one of country music's essential instruments, along with banjo and the steel guitar. The renewed popularity of bluegrass and Western swing, as well as the resurgence of honky-tonk and other more traditional styles, means that the fiddle is once again riding high.

Among country music instruments, the fiddle has one of the longest pedigrees. It's impossible to trace the complete history of the fiddle in America but some general explanation of its place in country music can be made. Fiddles were almost certainly in America by the 1600s. Many early settlers undoubtedly brought them, and with them many of the hornpipes and other fiddle tunes that had been particularly popular in the British Isles, tunes that have survived in varying forms for centuries, such as "Soldier's Joy."

Fiddles had some important advantages. They could be taken anywhere (something you couldn't say for harpsichords), were much less expensive than keyboard instruments,

The violin of today is essentially indistinguishable in design from its forebears of the sixteenth century: four strings running along a fretless neck and across a bridge that rests on a small body with two f-holes. Inside the body, a sound post fitted tightly under one foot of the bridge transmits vibrations to the back of the instrument, while the other foot performs the primary sound-producing task of transmitting vibrations to the top. Tuning is achieved with pegs at the top of the neck, which are turned to tighten or loosen their individual strings. The fourth string is tuned to G below middle C, the third, second, and first strings to D, A, and E above middle C, respectively.

In country music terms, a violin is a fiddle, often with steel rather than gut or nylon strings, and with a flatter bridge than a classical instrument. Playing style is the major distinguishing feature. In traditional country playing, the basic technique is a constant rhythmic bowing; plucked pizzicatos and other classical fancywork are not often heard. Even so, there is no lack of virtuosity in country fiddling, and a great variety of styles has developed over the past five decades as the music itself has developed in many directions.

and being fretless were even easily homemade. Fiddles were perfect for either formal or informal dancing. A good fiddler was an invaluable spiritual asset in colonial communities, which often needed music to boost morale. Inevitably there were hyper-religious folk who frowned on such things, and the slogan "the Devil is in the fiddle" was thrown about by many preachers who felt that playing any sort of music for enjoyment (outside of hymns, of course) was the perfect way of undermining people's moral fiber. It was a stigma that overzealous ministers later tried to attach to the waltz, to ragtime, to jazz, and to rock music, with no greater success.

Fiddlers were particularly important on the frontiers of settlement, where all the dangers were multiplied several times, and where portability was essential. Informal square dancing provided a sense of community at a time when that was desperately needed. The music remained based largely in the English, Irish, and Scottish fiddling traditions of the Old World. The dances—the forerunners of today's square dances—became less formal than they were in the more polished, wealthy plantation society of Virginia and in the cities of Philadelphia and Boston. Different regions of the country gradually developed their own approaches to fiddling, as the number of fiddlers multiplied and songs and playing styles were passed from fiddler to fiddler, from generation to generation.

Through the nineteenth century, fiddling continued to develop as an important part of American culture. It was popular in the armies of both sides during the Civil War, particularly when units were in their winter encampments. By then fiddling contests were an essential part of community life, in their own way almost as important as sports events. Some were huge, elaborate affairs with a carnival-like atmosphere. A prize-winning fiddler was considered an asset by many towns, and square dances, now far less formal than their earlier forms (but still with a highly defined set of rules), were routinely held, with the fiddlers playing their own variations of many of the early tunes, as well as newer, original compositions. Fiddling even made its way onto political podiums (a tradition upheld today by West Virginia Senator Robert Byrd, an above-average fiddler).

In the Southwest, square dances were more often than not held in the form of "house parties," in which rooms were stripped of their furniture to permit dancing. A Texas family named Wills produced some of the finest fiddlers in the state. Black musicians also fiddled, many of them playing the same traditional tunes as whites. Even in the earliest days of New Orleans jazz, the fiddle was important. All of these influences would later have a profound effect on the direction of country music.

The first commercially recorded country music disc was a fiddle tune, recorded by Victor in 1922 (but not released until 1923) by A. C. "Eck" Robertson, a Texas-based fiddler and longtime contest winner. The song itself was the old traditional "Sallie Goodin." However, the first country record actually released came from a Georgia-based fiddler named Fiddlin' John Carson. Though recorded over a year after the Robertson disc, it was still the first release because the Robertson disc came out only after the Carson recording proved to be a successful seller. Many of the early country recordings were done by fiddlers in the Southeast, often backed by guitars. Henry Ford, by sponsoring fiddle contests, acted to preserve old-time fiddling on the premise that it was a way of maintaining traditional American music and values. The earliest country radio shows also featured fiddling. Among those who played an essential part in such shows were Tommy Dandurand and the Barn Dance Fiddlers on Chicago's "WLS National Barn Dance," and Uncle Jimmy Thompson, one of the earliest performers on Nashville's "WSM Barn Dance."

Another enormously popular fiddler of the 1930s was Arthur Smith, who often recorded with Sam and Kirk McGee (as Arthur Smith and the Dixieliners) and with the Delmore Brothers (as the Arthur Smith Trio). Smith was a fine traditional fiddler, but had a smoother style that made him one of the more sophisticated players around at the time. His versatility took him from the Grand Ole Opry in the 1930s to Jimmy Wakely's Western group in the 1940s. (He also wrote the song "Beautiful Brown Eyes.") Another fiddler with advanced ideas was Clayton McMichen, who recorded with Jimmie Rodgers and later led a group known as the Georgia Wildcats. McMichen was influenced somewhat by Dixieland jazz, and often mixed pop- and jazz-flavored numbers into his repertoire (though his sound had little if anything to do with Western swing music). Interestingly, McMichen was a part of one of the early "hillbilly"-style bands, Gid Tanner and His Skillet Lickers, and could play hoedowns with the best. Toward the end of his career, he ran a Dixieland band, then enjoyed a brief revival when he was rediscovered. He had returned to old-time fiddling before his death in 1970.

The fiddle's place in country music changed as vocalists eclipsed the string bands in audience appeal. Much of that change was due to the stardom of Jimmie Rodgers, which paved the way for Gene Autry and others. The fiddle was now largely used as an accompanying instrument, and although it remained dominant as a lead instrument in the older styles of music, it came to function most often as a backup instrument, at least in the mainstream of country music.

While traditional fiddle styles were dominant in the Southeast, the Southwest had its own traditions. Southwestern fiddlers often played the same tunes as their eastern cohorts, but gave them unique regional flavors. There were other cultures that influenced their fiddling: black blues music (sometimes sung, sometimes played on guitars or even occasionally on the fiddle), Mexican music, and ragtime crept into southwestern fiddle music. Certain tunes like "Billy in the Low Ground" and "Big Taters in the Sandy Land" were peculiar to that area. The Texas fiddle style had its own exponents in virtuoso fiddlers like Eck Robertson, John Wills, his son Bob Wills, and Daniel Huggins Williams, all active in the 1920s and 1930s. Bob Wills, in particular, was an up-and-coming West Texas fiddler. As a boy he'd learned from his father and his grandfather (Tom Wills), and he was influenced by the singing of black field hands to conceive his own way of doing things on the fiddle. Left-handed fiddler Daniel Huggins Williams was influenced by ragtime music. Another Texas fiddler, Prince Albert Hunt, had some melodic twists in his playing that anticipated the style that would become known as Western swing.

But it was Bob Wills who would define Texas-style fiddling. In his hometown of Turkey, Texas, Wills was enormously popular with young people, who flocked to hear him. Being a top fiddler in Texas was like playing football, an easy way to status and respect. Along with singer Milton Brown, Bob Wills formed the original Light Crust Doughboys in 1931. When Milton Brown left in 1932, Wills recruited vocalist Tommy Duncan. Bob played a variety of styles with the Doughboys before splitting with the band's financial benefactor and "leader," W. Lee O'Daniel. He began his own band, the Playboys, in Waco, Texas. Tommy Duncan also quit the Doughboys to go with Wills. After some struggles as the Playboys, they moved to Oklahoma, added more musicians, and changed their name to the *Texas* Playboys. Wills also brought in jazz/swing fiddlers who would have a wide impact on the sound of country fiddle.

There was ample precedent for fiddlers playing jazz. Some of the earliest New Orleans jazz musicians were fiddlers. And in the thirties the team of guitarist Eddie Lang and violinist Joe Venuti was quite popular. It was inevitable that white players would try to play what was often called "hokum" music (a nickname for jazz improvisation). Among the earliest Western swing fiddlers in this vein were Musical Brownies Jesse Ashlock, Cliff Bruner, and Cecil Brower (the latter a formally trained violinist). After the Brownies disbanded following Milton Brown's death in 1936, Ashlock went with Bob Wills, who enjoyed his playing and wanted it in his band. Wills, despite his long association with the style, never learned to play it, but it is often inaccurately referred to as "Bob Wills" fiddling anyway.

Two other superb swing fiddlers were J. R. Chatwell and Louis Tierney. Johnny Gimble has credited both Cliff Bruner and Chatwell with influencing his playing. Chatwell's style was characterized by its thick tone and biting high notes, and a rhythmic strength equaled only by his idol, black jazz fiddler Stuff Smith. Tierney, who doubled on saxophone, had a style similar to Chatwell's, though his touch was lighter. There was an entire cadre of swing fiddlers by the late thirties, people like Joe Holly, Cotton Thompson, and Buddy Ray, all of whom played exciting, driving improvisations. Ashlock earned the respect of Joe Venuti himself.

This fiddle style would, in a somewhat simplified form, become a part of mainstream country music by the 1940s, particularly in the genre known as honky-tonk music. The fiddlers improvised lines behind vocalists and soloed on instrumental breaks. The twin fiddles that remain a keystone of the honky-tonk sound have their roots in bands like the Musical Brownies, which often used twin fiddles. (Gid Tanner's group and other old-timey bands also used twin fiddles in the 1930s in the Southeast, but it's unclear whether this influenced the Western bands.)

Other great fiddlers in the swing idiom emerged through the forties. Tommy Jackson worked in Cincinnati and Nashville and fiddled on some of Hank Williams's early recordings. Keith Coleman, who worked with the Texas Playboys and later with Hank Thompson's Brazos Valley Boys, could often evoke the driving sound and improvisational flair of Chatwell. Others, Max Fidler and Billy Hill among them, freelanced among the West Coast swing bands, including that of Spade Cooley (himself an Oklahoma-bred, classically trained fiddler who used up to *four* fiddles in his late 1940s swing bands). Karl Farr of the Sons of the Pioneers could swing superbly. Along with his guitarist brother, Hugh, he could create music that evoked Lang and Venuti transplanted to Western skies. Johnny Gimble, who joined Wills in 1949, later became a top Nashville studio fiddler. In 1974 he was named instrumentalist of the year by the Country Music Association, and remains America's best-known swing fiddler. In the past decade, Western swing fiddling has gained new audiences, many of whom weren't even alive when Wills was in his heyday.

In the late thirties, while all the Western swing activity was going on in Texas and the Southwest, Bill Monroe was creating bluegrass music, of which fiddle music is a prime component (Monroe was greatly influenced in this by his uncle Pen Vandiver). The original fiddler in his first Blue Grass Boys band was Fiddlin' Art Wooten, whose style was based in the traditional southeastern styles. By the mid-forties Chubby Wise, a more innovative fiddler, joined the group. Wise, who worked with the Blue Grass Boys at the same time Lester Flatt and Earl Scruggs did, was a smoother, bluesier player, though his roots were also in the old-time styles. His use of double-stops could add a certain eeriness to a song, and his infusion of blue notes gave Monroe's music an even greater depth. Many other fiddlers have gone through Monroe's groups in the last three decades, including Vassar Clements and Richard Greene in recent years, both of whom have had considerable impact. Kenny Baker has fiddled with Monroe for many years, gaining a reputation as one of the most distinguished bluegrass fiddlers of all time, a long way from his early days playing swing and honky-tonk.

The bayou country of southern Louisiana spawned another influential fiddle style. The region was inhabited by people whose French-Canadian ancestors were deported from Canada by the British in 1755. They were originally called "Acadiens," a name that was gradually transformed into "Cajuns." The Cajuns retained their French-Canadian culture and added to it input from their new home to create a unique culture, one different from that of either Canada or the American South. The new culture included the unique Cajun music, which featured fiddles and accordions. Cajun music spread to other parts of the region, including east Texas. As early as the 1920s and 1930s record companies were recording such Cajun groups as the Hackberry Ramblers (which briefly included mandolinist Tiny Moore), who combined Cajun sounds with Western swing, a perfect mix for dancing. But the record that brought Cajun music to national attention was fiddler Harry Choates's 1946 version of "Jole Blon" (Cajun for the French *jolie blonde*: pretty blonde). Choates's recording became a huge success and gave many country listeners their first substantial taste of Cajun music. Choates had a flowing, infectious style that was both listenable and danceable, and his loose, spontaneous vocalizing was perfect for the honky-tonks and dancehalls he played. Choates unfortunately had a serious drinking problem that helped kill him in 1951 at the age of twenty-nine. Choates's influence has continued through the music of fiddlers like Doug Kershaw and Rufus Thibodeaux, the latter a veteran of a number of Nashville groups and in recent years a member of Cajun country singer Jimmy C. Newman's group.

Link Davis was another Cajun fiddler with a varied background. A former member of Fort Worth's Crystal Springs Ramblers, a Western swing band, Davis doubled on sax and contributed bluesy vocals to Cliff Bruner's band in the forties. He was also a fine fiddler, and composed the Cajun classic "Big Mamou."

In the fifties, a new Cajun duo emerged: Rusty and Doug Kershaw. Born in Tiel Ridge, Louisiana, the Kershaw Brothers began working with a group that played not only Cajun, but also country boogies and straight country and western. They made their first recordings in Louisiana in 1953. Their music had non-Cajun elements and was popular enough to get them a contract with Nashville's Hickory Records. In 1961 they had two Cajun-oriented country hits with "Louisiana Man" and "Diggy Diggy Lo," both of which enjoy popularity far beyond the bayous; in fact, the first of these has acquired the status of a country classic. The Kershaw brothers separated musically in 1964. After signing with Warner Brothers records, Doug became a popular performer on both the country and rock circuits. He dressed in velvet, and his flashy Cajun fiddling, backed by loud rocking music, was both visually and musically impressive.

As trends have changed in Nashville, fiddles have undergone various "in" and "out" phases, in response to increasingly structured commercialism. In the recordings of the forties the instrument was in enormous demand, as evidenced most notably by the work of Hank Williams, who was backed on his early records by Tommy Duncan, and later by his regular Drifting Cowboys fiddler, Jerry Rivers. However, when Elvis Presley arrived at the pinnacle of success around 1956, bringing with him radical changes in the popular music scene, many younger country singers decided to join him. Fiddlers and steel guitarists, symbols of the "hillbilly" sound, were unceremoniously dumped from bands (as drums began to be accepted) in a play for more youthful audiences. But as Nashville regrouped, hard-core, twin-fiddle honky-tonk music returned with Ray Price, who recorded such hits as "Crazy Arms," "My Shoes Keep Walking Back to You," and "City Lights," featuring heavily bowed fiddle lines played in improvisational styles. A few swing fiddlers, such as Wade Ray, began working on the road with Price and other honky-tonk bands. Others, like Dale Porter, could play swing or honky-tonk and thus found plenty of work in Nashville's studios.

The coming of the pop-oriented Nashville Sound hurt fiddlers who didn't read music. Those who did were considered "violinists" (one was Cecil Brower, a former member of the Musical Brownies), but few of them played much country; most were members of symphony orchestras or else played behind smoother country singers like Eddy Arnold.

There were some country artists who never abandoned fiddles. One was George Jones, who once stated, "You'll always hear a fiddle on a George Jones record." That's generally true, but on some occasions the fiddles actually have been carefully arranged violins. Bluegrassers and other traditional artists like Roy Acuff continued to use fiddles, as did Little Jimmy Dickens and Carl Smith. However, in the mid-1960s one hard-core group that did not use fiddles, preferring instead to emphasize electric bass and guitars, was the musicians of Bakersfield, California, such as Merle Haggard and Buck Owens. Their classic recordings do not utilize fiddling at all, though after Haggard became interested in performing Western swing he taught himself the fiddle in a matter of months.

By the late sixties even certain rock bands were interested in using fiddles, as well as in playing more country-oriented sounds. Johnny Gimble and Shorty Lavender (another studio fiddle great) recorded with the band Mother Earth (featuring vocal star Tracy Nelson, whose post-Nashville work is now available on albums from Rounder and Adelphi). Doug Kershaw's popularity also gave the fiddle greater exposure among young people—to many who'd never heard of Harry Choates, Kershaw provided an introduction to Cajun music. Former Blue Grass Boy Richard Greene became a part of the popular California-based rock band Seatrain for a time, bowling audiences over with a highly amplified, supercharged fiddle version of "Orange Blossom Special."

The Western swing revival, largely a result of singer Merle Haggard's love of the music, brought the Bob Wills sound back into vogue. Suddenly Wills, who'd had a crippling stroke in 1969, became a major influence again. Younger fiddlers, listening intently to the old recordings and to live performances of ex-Playboys like Gimble, Joe Holley, Keith Coleman, and Jesse Ashlock, learned the style themselves. Among the excellent neo-swing fiddlers were Andy Stein of Commander Cody and His Lost Planet Airmen, Link Davis, Jr. (son of the legendary Cajun-swing fiddler), Richard Casanova of the swing revival band Asleep at the Wheel, and Sid Page, a former classical and jazz fiddler who worked with the swing-jazz–oriented group Dan Hicks and His Hot Licks. All of this meant renewed appreciation and popularity for the older fiddlers.

Another important fiddler of the revival period of the seventies was Vassar Clements, a former Blue Grass Boy, and sideman with Jim and Jesse, and with Faron Young. Clements had become a popular Nashville session player in the late sixties, and had gone with the Earl Scruggs Revue in the early seventies, where his command of bluegrass and swing and his ability to play respectably in even a hard-rock context, made him popular among young people. He became an artist for all styles, and one recording, *Hillbilly Jazz* on Flying Fish, became a popular introduction to modern Western swing. Vassar

Clements continues to record and perform in a variety of musical forms, from bluegrass, to rock, to jazz (including forties-style bebop), all with equal finesse.

The revived popularity of honky-tonk music in the early seventies, particularly the music of Moe Bandy, a singer solidly in the Ray Price/George Jones tradition, revived the fiddle on country records. Nashville studio fiddlers like Johnny Gimble and Buddy Spicher (another fiddler able to play bluegrass, Cajun, or swing) were virtual fixtures on Bandy recordings. Meantime another fiddle style was forming out of a unique fusion of jazz, bluegrass, ethnic, and classical music—a fusion to which mandolinist David Grisman lent the name "Dawg music." This style covered a lot of ground. Two players associated with Grisman stand out here: Darol Anger, a delightfully eclectic fiddler capable of handling any style (including Grisman's), and Grisman's former fiddler-guitarist Mark O'Connor, a champion fiddler able to play traditional Texas fiddle styles, avant-garde jazz, rock, bluegrass, or swing. These two fiddlers are not strictly country, but their ways of combining a variety of influences will undoubtedly be influential for years to come.

Although fiddles have not been prominent on many of the Texas "Outlaw" recordings of the seventies, Willie Nelson often uses Johnny Gimble onstage and on recordings (he also appeared with Willie in the movie *Honeysuckle Rose*). The Nelson album *Over the Rainbow* features Gimble swinging away behind Willie on a number of old pop songs, backed by a jazzy acoustic band.

It's safe to say that more labels are offering a greater variety of fiddling than ever before.

FIDDLE STYLES

There are so many variations in fiddling styles that this can't even hope to be a comprehensive guide to every one. Most players learn the differences with experience and from interaction with other fiddlers. Here it is possible to look over the general categories of fiddling a bit more closely than in the preceding historical section.

OLD-TIME

Old-time fiddling styles are by and large the linear descendants of the fiddling popular in the British Isles, the music that the earliest settlers from those areas brought with them to America. Among this music were hornpipes, reels, and other tunes that had been around for many generations. Their styles are best known through tunes like "Fisher's Hornpipe," "Arkansas Traveller," "Sallie Goodin," "The Eighth of January," and other traditional tunes that took on a distinctively American character the more they circulated through various regions of the country. These songs have remained popular with fiddlers over the years. Not every fiddle classic is centuries old, however: that old warhorse, "Orange Blossom Special," was written by Ervin Rouse in the 1930s. (It continues to be popular with listeners, but many fiddlers consider it to be the "Melancholy Baby" of old-time fiddling. Because of the facile bowing techniques involved in playing it, many old-time fiddler's organizations have banned it in contests.) Every region of the country has its own fiddle styles. Today, for the most part, old-time contest fiddling is done solo, with only a guitar or banjo for backing.

SQUARE DANCE

Square dance fiddling is, for the most part, a variation on old-time fiddling, built around specific numbers played for dancers. Though early square dancing in America was quite informal, it gradually assumed unique traditions to the point that today there are square-dance organizations throughout America.

BLUEGRASS

Bluegrass fiddling also descends from the old-time fiddle styles. However, the roughness characteristic of old-time fiddle music is gone in bluegrass (Arthur Smith's work in the 1930s anticipated the smoother sound of bluegrass fiddlers). It is also more sophisticated, harmonically and rhythmically, than old-time fiddling, with strains of blues running through it. In mainstream bluegrass, the fiddle, like every other instrument, has a very definite and highly defined role in a band, often serving to kick off a number, and fading in and out behind either the instrument that's soloing or behind the vocalist(s).

CAJUN

Cajun fiddling's origins have already been explained. It has its own unique rhythmic patterns, often manifesting themselves in waltzes or other more up-tempo beats. It often includes droning strings, double-stops and a heavy, rhythmic bowing technique. Doug Kershaw, something of an extremist in this area, has been known to tear up several bows per performance.

WESTERN SWING

There are actually two distinctive aspects of Western swing fiddling, as noted developmentally above. The first is the traditional blues-tinged Texas-based style that Bob and Johnnie Lee Wills excelled at in songs like "Big 'Taters in the Sandy Land" and "Liberty." There were also considerable blues influences in other Wills originals, such as "Bob Wills Special," and "Osage Stomp," an adaptation of an old black number known as "Rukus Juice and Chitlin'." The second style is the jazzier "takeoff" style played by Cliff Bruner, Jesse Ashlock, Buddy Ray, Cecil Brower, Louis Tierney, J. R. Chatwell, and others. This style was developed by a number of musicians. The most obvious influence was jazz violinists like Joe Venuti, Stuff Smith (a considerable influence on Chatwell, Ray, and Gimble), and Stephane Grappelli, but horn players—mostly those playing Dixieland and swing—were also influences on Western swing fiddlers. One story about Johnny Gimble, quoted by Charles Townsend in his excellent biography of Bob Wills,

San Antonio Rose, states that Gimble once jammed with Dixieland clarinetist Pete Fountain and found he didn't have to alter his style a bit.

HONKY-TONK

One of the most fundamental instruments in the honky-tonk genre is the fiddle, either a single fiddle or twin fiddles, the latter tradition coming directly from Western swing (though it had been used in old-time country as well). However, in this style the playing is often not as hot or improvised as in standard Western swing. The twin fiddles (or solo fiddle) often play the instrumental introduction to a number, and one or both will play some fills behind the vocalist, often long phrases replete with finger vibrato or semi-improvised phrases. Everyone from Ray Price to Moe Bandy has used twin fiddles, while Hank Williams, for example, used a single fiddle on most of his hits. Johnny Gimble and Buddy Spicher have provided much of the twin-fiddling on Moe Bandy's recordings.

MODERN

A number of fiddlers who have worked in bluegrass have, in more recent years, taken their playing into more contemporary areas such as country rock and similar styles. They've drawn on a number of musical influences from non-country areas such as jazz, blues, swing, ethnic music, and even rock. At times they use amplified fiddles; at other times they play acoustic instruments next to a microphone. In the forefront of this group was Richard Greene, a former member of Bill Monroe's Blue Grass Boys (and later the folk-oriented Jim Kweskin Jug Band), who worked with the group Seatrain, as a sideman on numerous albums by other artists, with David Grisman in the Great American Music Band, and finally on his own as a solo artist. Greene incorporated swing, bluegrass, avant-garde jazz, and other modern styles into his music. Byron Berline is another player who has remained closer to traditional styles, but nonetheless has recorded with the Rolling Stones and worked with the mid-seventies' Flying Burrito Brothers. Berline is a superb bluegrass fiddler with many awards to his credit. After forming his own progressive bluegrass band, Country Gazette, he went on to another modern bluegrass band known as Sundance. He recorded a superb (1980) LP, *Outrageous*, that featured his work with a driving electric band, playing original tunes with a heavily country-rock flavor. Vassar Clements continues to pursue a variety of music, from bluegrass to jazz to old-time fiddling, playing with a solid command of the bow and adding phenomenal double-stops.

As mentioned, Dave Grisman's "Dawg music" has its own fiddle exponents in Darol Anger and guitarist-fiddler Mark O'Connor, who also blend a variety of styles. Both have recorded solo albums that demonstrate their own unique approach to music, as well as their respect for the variety of styles that influenced them.

FIDDLE RECORDINGS

TRADITIONAL/OLD-TIMEY

Fiddlin' John Carson

Fiddlin' John Carson, a Georgia-based fiddler and singer whose grandfather was a fiddler in Ireland, was one of the top fiddlers and showmen in the Atlanta area. In 1922 he was one of the first country performers to play music over a radio station. He appeared in a newsreel of old-time fiddling in 1923 that was noticed by Polk Brockman, an Atlanta record distributor, and Brockman recorded him in June 1923. The songs "Little Old Log Cabin in the Lane" and "The Old Hen Cackled" were first sold only in the local area and did well enough to be more widely distributed. *The Old Hen Cackled and the Rooster's Going to Crow* (Rounder 1003) features many of Carson's classic recordings, showing some of the earliest and best examples of old-time fiddling. An essential fiddle record of raw, compelling music.

Gid Tanner and His Skillet Lickers

Gid Tanner was another 1920s fiddler whose roots were in Georgia; for a time he was one of Carson's rivals on the Georgia fiddlers' contest circuit. Tanner's music included many traditional songs from the nineteenth century. He recorded extensively from 1924 to 1934 with a loose group of musicians collectively known as the Skillet Lickers, which included blind guitarist Riley Puckett, and another fiddle legend, Clayton McMichen, whose playing was much smoother than Tanner's, as was the playing of Lowe Stokes. *Hear These New Southern Fiddle and Guitar Records* (Rounder 1005) shows the ebullient chemistry of the group, and much fine fiddling in the contrasting styles of Tanner, McMichen, and Stokes.

Arthur Smith

Arthur Smith (not to be confused with Arthur "Guitar Boogie" Smith) had enormous popularity in the South during the 1930s, in part because of his association with the Grand Ole Opry. Smith's fiddling made extensive use of double-stops, and the bluesy overtones in his playing made him sound far ahead of his time. *Fiddlin' Arthur Smith and the Dixieliners, Volumes 1 and 2* (County 546 and 547) includes recordings he made in the late 1930s and early 1940s with the Delmore Brothers; on some cuts he uses a second fiddler, Tommy Magness. The sound is clear and the blues elements on songs like "Fiddler's Blues" are plain to hear. Smith's playing undoubtedly contributed to what later became the bluegrass fiddle style.

BLUEGRASS

There are countless recordings of bluegrass fiddling both old and new. The albums included here are a tiny fraction of what's out, but are representative of the bluegrass style.

Bill Monroe and His Blue Grass Boys

A number of great bluegrass fiddle performances, and some of the most important, are on the postwar recordings of Bill Monroe and His Blue Grass Boys from 1945 to 1949. These feature the work of Chubby Wise, one of the fiddlers who established many of the ideas that are still fundamental parts of the bluegrass fiddle style, drawing upon earlier old-timey fiddlers. Among these albums are *Bill Monroe with Lester Flatt and Earl Scruggs:* (Rounder SS–06 and *The Original Blues Band*) and *Bill Monroe and His Blue Grass Boys: The Classic Bluegrass Recordings, Volumes 1 and 2* (County Country Classics Series 104 and 105), all of which feature Wise prominently.

Lester Flatt and Earl Scruggs

No less important are the recordings of ex-Blue Grass Boys Lester Flatt and Earl Scruggs, who left Monroe to form what became one of the most popular bluegrass units of all time. Flatt and Scruggs had a number of fine fiddlers, including Chubby Wise, Benny Martin, Paul Warren, and longtime Roy Acuff associate Howdy Forrester. Many of the Flatt and Scruggs Columbia recordings have been reissued, featuring all of these fiddlers. Among the reissued LPs are *Flatt and Scruggs: The Golden Era* (Rounder SS–05), *Don't Get Above Your Raisin'* (Rounder SS–08), *The Golden Years* (County CCS–101), and *Blue Ridge Cabin Home* (County County Classics Series 14370).

Vassar Clements

Crossing the Catskills (Rounder 0016) features one of the finest modern bluegrass fiddlers (who also works in more contemporary styles and contexts). The material includes old songs like "Paddy on the Turnpike" and "Florida Blues," as well as some tunes like "Faded Love," done up in a different but still traditional style.

Byron Berline

Berline, another fiddler who can play either bluegrass, swing, or more modern styles, plays it straight and close to the ground on *Dad's Favorites* (Rounder 0100), a tribute to his father, also a fiddler. He's backed by a number of top bluegrass players, including Doug Dillard, Dan Crary, and John Hartford. It's interesting to contrast this playing with the more modern material Berline has done.

Kenny Baker

Coming from a straight country and Western swing background, ex-coal miner Kenny Baker evolved into one of the greatest bluegrass fiddlers of all times when he joined Bill Monroe's Blue Grass Boys. Solidly ensconced in the traditional, standard bluegrass style of fiddling, *Kenny Baker Plays Bill Monroe* (County 761) features an all-star group (including Monroe himself on mandolin). Several of the tracks were numbers he excelled at and recorded with Monroe, while others were written by Monroe and never previously recorded. *Farmyard Swing* (County 770) is in a similar vein, with a number of traditional fiddle numbers such as "Arkansas Traveller," "Lost Indian," "Smokey Mountain Rag," and some Baker originals with bluegrass luminaries like Sonny and Bobby Osborne providing the backup.

Buddy Spicher and Benny Martin

Benny Martin, who recorded on his own as well as with Flatt and Scruggs and other top bluegrass bands, teams up on *The Great American Fiddle Collection* (CMH 9025) with veteran studio fiddler Buddy Spicher, who can play bluegrass, old-time fiddle, jazz and Western swing with equal aplomb. They are heard here on two records with twenty-five old-timey and bluegrass numbers such as "Sweet Bunch of Daisies," "Lee Highway Blues," "Silver Bell/Red Wing," "Tennessee Waltz," "Down Yonder," and others, played with pretty much straight bluegrass instrumentation. Martin's more traditional bluegrass playing contrasts nicely with Spicher's style, and it's fascinating to hear two masters of the field with such different approaches.

WESTERN SWING

The East Texas Serenaders

This group, which can be heard on *The East Texas Serenaders: 1927–1936* (County 410), was one that pioneered the idea of a more pop-and-ragtime oriented approach to Texas fiddle music. While there wasn't the sophistication of the Bob Wills or Milton Brown styles that later became essential to pure Western swing, the slight blues and pop overtones in the fiddling of Daniel Huggins Williams anticipated the development of the swing idiom in the Southwest by several years.

Milton Brown and His Musical Brownies

Country and Western Dance-O-Rama (Western 1001) is a ten-inch LP, a reproduction of an album originally released in the mid-1950s by Decca. Milton Brown was a singer who worked in the Light Crust Doughboys with Bob Wills. He quit in 1932 and formed his own band, the Musical Brownies (which recorded for Victor and then for Decca), before Bob Wills formed the Playboys. The Brownies included two superb fiddlers: Cecil

Brower and Cliff Bruner, both of whom can be heard here on numbers like the traditional "Washington and Lee Swing" and "Beautiful Texas." This is the most basic sort of twin fiddle arrangement, much like the ones still used in Western swing and honky-tonk bands.

Bob Wills

Bob Wills—Keepsake Album (Longhorn 001; available from Club of Spade Records), recorded in the early 1960s, represents the only time that Wills ever recorded an entire album of fiddle numbers without his Texas Playboys band behind him. It was done informally, sitting around with some friends and a bass, guitar, and banjo for some rhythm, as Bob played songs like "Big 'Taters in the Sandy Land," "Put Your Little Foot," and other traditional Texas fiddle tunes that he grew up with. Although he had cut some recordings in the 1930s like this (his first record in 1929 wasn't much different), he was always known for his work with the Playboys. Here his own ability as a fiddler is up front, and the music is enriched by colorful stories between numbers. He even recreates the first fiddle tune he ever played with a story that should inspire even the most apprehensive beginner. This isn't Western swing as such, but it is an excellent look at its roots.

The Bob Wills Anthology (Columbia PG–32416), a two-record set, features some of the greatest Wills recordings from 1945 and 1946. Not only is Wills himself prominent, but some of the great, jazz-influenced fiddlers who worked with him, like Jesse Ashlock, Joe Holley, Sleepy Johnson, Louis Tierney are heard. As it was always Bob's nature to call out the name of his soloists, it's easy to hear, and gradually to distinguish, the varied approaches of each of them. Ashlock and Holley, for example, were always driving, intense swingers while Tierney reflected a somewhat cooler approach. *24 Great Hits by Bob Wills and His Texas Playboys* (MGM 2-5305) contains tracks made from 1947 to 1954, and reflects the smaller but more amplified Texas Playboys of the postwar era. Some of Johnny Gimble's finest fiddling is on this set, particularly on "Boot Heel Drag." Joe Holley is heard on several tracks and Keith Coleman on several others. Again, Bob's calling out the names of his soloists makes it quite simple to distinguish the fiddlers from each other.

Bob Wills (Time-Life Country Classics 07), part of Time-Life's Country Classics series, is a forty-song, three-LP anthology of classic Wills material drawn from throughout the musical high points of his career, from 1935 to 1961 (after that, the quality of his recordings began to drop precipitously). More than twenty-five percent of the cuts are previously unissued, and among the strong fiddle numbers are "Smith's Reel," performed alone with Sleepy Johnson's guitar; "Liza, Pull Down the Shades," featuring excellent hot fiddle from Jesse Ashlock; and a previously unissued version of Wills's "New San Antonio Rose," featuring both fiddles *and* horns (unlike the better-known version that featured only horns). Joe Holley and Wills interact brilliantly on "Miss Molly," and Louis Tierney swings out on "Take Me Back to Tulsa." One of the strongest fiddle numbers, however, is the 1961 "Jobob Rag," featuring some smooth but swinging interaction between Wills and fiddler Joe Holley.

Johnny Gimble

The Texas Fiddle Collection (CMH 9027), a 1980 recording, features probably the finest and easily the best-known swing fiddler around today, from his stint with Bob Wills, his studio work, and work with Willie Nelson and Merle Haggard. On this recording, Gimble looks at not only Western swing but some of the traditional fiddling from earlier days. On certain tracks, he plays with a small acoustic band, as Wills did in his pre-Playboys days, doing songs he remembers from his own Texas boyhood. On other tracks he uses people like Eldon Shamblin, his old mentor, and ex-Musical Brownie Cliff Bruner to delve into the more developed band sounds, going from waltzes like "Goodnight Waltz" and "Texas Jole Blon" to swinging pop numbers like "Tuxedo Junction" and "On the Alamo." For a basic trip through the entire area of Texas fiddling, with Gimble, Bruner, and other greats, this is an excellent start.

Curley Lewis

Curley Lewis is not known on the same level as Johnny Gimble or Buddy Spicher, yet his fiddling is well worth mention, as he was long a stalwart of Johnnie Lee Wills's band in Tulsa. He spent nearly a decade with Hank Thompson's Brazos Valley Boys as well. Lewis's fiddling on *Shenandoah* (Hi-Spot; available from Keith Kolby) moves between the breakdown style of Wills (he won a Bob Wills–sponsored contest when he was eleven), and driving swing, executed flawlessly and with a fair amount of humor. He varies his repertoire from traditional to swing and pop and creates an album that is a gem.

CAJUN

Harry Choates

Harry Choates was the Hank Williams of Cajun music. A brilliant fiddler, songwriter, and vocalist, he boozed himself into an early demise. Choates—who wrote the immensely popular "Jole Blon" (not included here due to contractual problems)—opted for a non-traditional Cajun sound with heavy Western swing overtones. His ebullient personality comes through on every one of the sixteen tracks of *The Fiddle King of Cajun Swing* (Arhoolie D–7000) and shows a clear precedent for the later Cajun wildness of Doug Kershaw. And if you want the original "Jole Blon," it's still available (from Down Home Music) as a single on the "D" label.

Rusty and Doug Kershaw

Coming from the Louisiana bayous, Rusty and Doug Kershaw were an electrifying team at their best, combining standard country music with Cajun sounds and exposing their music to many people for whom Cajun had been merely "Jambalaya" and "Jole Blon."

Rusty and Doug Kershaw—The Cajun Country Rockers (Bear Family BFX–15036; available from Down Home Music), a German reissue of their 1956–1961 Hickory recordings, includes the original version of "Louisiana Man," "Cajun Joe (The Bully of the Bayou)", and "Diggy Diggy Lo," all Cajun standards of today.

HONKY-TONK

Since honky-tonk fiddling is basically an offshoot of Western swing fiddling and is primarily used for backing a singer, the most effective way of hearing it is to listen to some vocal recordings where it plays a prominent role, such as those of Hank Williams.

There really isn't such a thing as a Hank Williams LP that features only Hank's regular fiddler Jerry Rivers, for he used a number of fiddlers on his earlier sessions, including the great studio musicians Tommy Jackson and Dale Potter, before Rivers began recording with Hank (along with the rest of the Drifting Cowboys) in early 1950. There is much to be learned from the sympathetic fiddling behind Hank's vocals. Any of the ubiquitous Hank Williams repackages on MGM will give you plenty of insight into the basics of honky-tonk fiddling. You can hear Rivers on sides like "Long Gone Lonesome Blues," "Why Don't You Love Me," "Cold, Cold Heart," "Hey, Good Lookin'," and "Jambalaya," while Jackson is the fiddler on "Move It on Over" and "I Saw the Light." "Lost Highway" features Dale Potter. Rivers has since recorded various LPs with members of the Drifting Cowboys, but you can get a real idea of his style on the Hank Williams original recordings, playing in his most appropriate context.

Back in the fifties Ray Price also used a typically heavily bowed honky-tonk fiddle on such hits as "Crazy Arms," "I've Got a New Heartache," "City Lights," and "My Shoes Keep Walking Back to You." I'm not sure of the fiddler, but these are classic honky-tonk recordings, well worth listening to on *Ray Price's Greatest Hits* (Columbia CS–8866). *Note:* Don't think you'll find this style of fiddle on his later recordings; he gradually went for a pop sound that featured violins but no fiddles. One notable exception to this is his 1980 LP with Willie Nelson, *San Antonio Rose* (Columbia JC–36476), which features Johnny Gimble playing the same style of fiddle heard on those earlier recordings. There Price returns for a time to the sound that established him.

On a more current note, Moe Bandy has used the honky-tonk fiddle style on all of his albums, usually utilizing Johnny Gimble and/or Buddy Spicher to do the honors. Albums such as *Hank Williams, You Wrote My Life* (Columbia C–34091), *The Champ* (Columbia JC–36487), *I'm Sorry For You, My Friend* (Columbia 13-33379), and just about any of his others will reveal plenty of fine fiddling.

MODERN COUNTRY FIDDLE

These albums correspond to the fiddle styles mentioned earlier; the music itself is far more varied than in the other styles.

Darol Anger

Darol Anger, longtime associate of progressive mandolinist David Grisman, combines bluegrass, country, swing, jazz, and various ethnic musics on *Fiddleistics* (Kaleidoscope F–8), his first solo album, to create music with great textures and tensions. He plays straightforward acoustic fiddle for the most part (though he uses an electric fiddle on the old Charlie Parker bebop standard "Moose the Mooche"), and uses material by Grisman and Tony Rice, as well as songs of his own.

Vassar Clements

Though the songs on *Hillbilly Jazz* (Flying Fish 101), a two-record set, are mostly old swing classics, country standards, and jazz numbers, the approach is streamlined and modern, with Vassar pushing down hard on his fiddle to create thicker tones than most electronic devices could provide. He plays in a swinging style, but with surprisingly little of the lightness that characterized many of the best fiddlers. It sounds distinctly like the Clements style used in other ensemble situations.

Richard Greene

This progressive fiddler, working with some of the David Grisman crew and some traditionally oriented players and using overdubs to created massed fiddles, plays a variety of material on *Ramblin'* (Rounder 0110), from Bach to old pop songs like "New Orleans" (on which the overdubbing works particularly well), to traditional bluegrass numbers such as "In the Pines" and "Uncle Pen."

Byron Berline

Berline, who's played straight bluegrass—but who's also played with the Eagles, Linda Ronstadt, the Rolling Stones, Bob Dylan, and the Byrds—is playing hard-core electronic country-rock fiddle on *Outrageous* (Flying Fish FF–227). He works here with a tough, rocking band including former Elvis lead guitarist James Burton and ex-Emmylou Harris guitarist Albert Lee. There are a variety of styles weaving in and out of Berline's searing fiddling: jazz, blues, and plenty of country-rock.

FIDDLE INSTRUCTION

Learn to Play Country Fiddle by Frank Zucco (Mel Bay) is a very basic, beginner's-level book on learning the fundamentals of country, folk, and bluegrass violin.

Deluxe Country Fiddling Method by Craig Duncan (Mel Bay), written by a working fiddler, explains techniques and styles of current fiddling.

Anthology of Fiddle Styles by David Reiner (Mel Bay) deals with a number of country and rural fiddle styles, including Scandinavian fiddling, folk fiddling, Texas, Cajun, and other styles. A cassette is also available.

Country Fiddling for Four Violins by Burton Isaac (Mel Bay) has arrangements of country tunes for four fiddles. Spade Cooley often used such arrangements.

Great Country Fiddle Solos by Frank Zucco (Mel Bay) is the follow-up book to his *Learn to Play Country Fiddle*, continuing the instruction through intermediate levels. There are a number of fiddle solos that can be played independently of the instruction.

A *Hundred Favorite Fiddle Solos* by Bill Guest (Mel Bay) includes some solos composed by him, arranged for either twin or solo fiddles.

The Bluegrass Fiddler (Mel Bay) is a collection of a number of bluegrass-oriented fiddle favorites.

Old Time Fiddle Solos (Mel Bay) deals with the old-time, pre-bluegrass fiddle styles that came down from the earliest American fiddlers with British Isles roots.

Folk Fiddle Styles by Burton Isaac (Mel Bay) includes bluegrass and country fiddle solos on well-known jigs, reels, and tunes, with guitar accompaniment.

Beginning Old-Time Fiddle by Alan Kaufman (Music Sales) is a comprehensive book for the beginner that uses both standard notation and a new tablature form for fiddle. It gives extensive instruction on the old-time styles, as well as basics such as how to hold and move the bow, and an entertaining history of the old-time fiddlers of the past. It also includes tunes in the style of a number of the great fiddlers of the 1920s and 1930s. It includes a fiddle discography and an instruction record.

Violin Pieces Country Style by Betty McDermott (Music Sales) is a very basic book for violin students with an interest in country music. It includes piano accompaniments.

Appalachian Fiddle by Miles Krassen (Music Sales) includes fifty-eight transcriptions of breakdowns, jigs, hornpipes, and other tunes from the distant past of old-timey fiddle. It also includes instruction on old-time fiddling, such as double-stops.

Play Old Time Country Fiddle by Jerry Silverman (Chilton Book Co.) contains seventy-five fiddle tunes with words and chords, and twenty-five square dances with complete calls and instructions.

Bluegrass Fiddle by ex-Bill Monroe Blue Grass Boy Gene Lowinger (Music Sales) is an excellent, comprehensive guide by one who has played with the master. Includes twenty-nine bluegrass and fourteen traditional tunes.

The Fiddle Book by Marion Thede (Music Sales) includes 150 traditional fiddle tunes, all transcribed from the playing of country fiddlers.

Jazz Violin by Matt Glaser (Music Sales) is not really country, but for the player interested in getting into Western swing playing, it is essential. Glaser was assisted by the current master of jazz violin, Stephane Grappelli; he gives extensive information on Grappelli's playing, often using transcriptions from his recordings and from the recordings of others. Everything here is in standard notation, no tablature.

Vassar Clements/Fiddle by Matt Glaser (Music Sales) looks at the style of one of the most electrifying and eclectic fiddlers around today, another ex-studio musician and Blue Grass Boy who's become respected by rock musicians and retained his credibility with traditionalists as well. There are extensive notes on the seventeen transcribed songs, as well as analytical sections on the more complex parts of each number, for added understanding.

Bluegrass Fiddle Styles by Stacy Phillips and Kenny Kosek (Music Sales) is an excellent collection of seventy songs, in the manner they were performed and recorded by twenty-five fiddlers, including Chubby Wise. The title is somewhat misleading since the book includes Johnny Gimble's swing favorite "Fiddlin' Around." There's also instruction on playing fiddle with a bluegrass group, fiddle maintenance, and other information.

Bluegrass Fiddle for Beginners by Warren Kennison (Alfred Music) introduces bluegrass fiddling to the player with no previous experience on the fiddle. It begins with basic information on tuning, bowing, and reading tablature. The book includes twenty bluegrass standards, and gradually introduces more advanced techniques as it goes along.

Swing Fiddle (Homespun Tapes) is a six-cassette course by well-known fiddler Matt Glaser. The tapes cover just about all of what qualifies as Western swing, including the Texas-based traditional fiddle styles of Bob Wills, Benny Thomasson, and Johnny Gimble; old-time styles and songs like "Leather Britches"; variations on the old tunes; and the jazzier styles of Wills alumni Joe Holley, Keith Coleman, and others. The series ends with beginning jazz fiddle, in the styles of Joe Venuti and Stephane Grappelli. Complete transcriptions come with the tapes, and you can order any one, or all six at a discount.

Bluegrass and Country Fiddle by Kenny Kosek (Homespun Tapes) is a six-cassette instruction method with written transcriptions and extensive, detailed lessons. It's structured to lead you at your own pace through traditional songs, improvising harmonies, double-stops, harmonizing chord changes, and licks characteristic of greats like Vassar Clements and Benny Martin. You can order one cassette or save by ordering all at the same time.

GUITAR

Ray Whitey's Gibson J200 acoustic guitar (Country Music Foundation)

It's safe to say that no single instrument is as synonymous with country music as the guitar. It has become a basic part of the country music stereotype, whether in the hands of a denim-clad farmer or a rhinestone or Telecaster cowboy. It dominates the Opryland corporate logo, and an eight-foot-deep guitar-shaped swimming pool sits at the top of Music Row in Nashville, a copy of Webb Pierce's 1950s original.

But the guitar wasn't all that popular in the early days of country music. Arriving in America with early European settlers, it had enjoyed a limited popularity (especially as a ladies' instrument) during colonial times, and that popularity grew slowly. Until the early 1800s the guitars played in America were almost exclusively of European manufacture. Then guitar makers gradually began to emigrate to America, among them Christian Friedrich Martin, who brought his guitar-making talents to New York City, then moved to Nazareth, Pennsylvania, not far from the Delaware River, and began manufacturing instruments that helped set the standards for American acoustical guitars.

In the years following the Civil War, America's Industrial Revolution began in earnest. For the first time it was possible to mass-produce guitars, making them more widely available. Another development was the appearance of the first steel-string guitars, which had more volume than gut-string models, and a solid, ringing tone. But most rural southern string bands preferred fiddle, banjos, and mandolins. The sound of gut-string guitars simply didn't project when played in a group that included steel-string banjos and mandolins, and although the steel-string guitars were an improvement, the early mass-produced models were often poorly constructed, with small bodies that still didn't have enough volume to hold their own in the string bands.

The first southern musicians to use guitar were black, playing their forms of country dance music. The blues form was also developing. Although many black musicians played fiddles, mandolins, and banjos, none of these instruments were appropriate for accompanying blues singers or playing instrumental blues. To produce "blue" notes it was necessary to bend notes—shift the pitch slightly after the note was sounded. That could be done much more easily and clearly (by stretching the string across the neck) on a guitar than on the other instruments. Whites took notice of black musicians' guitar playing, and the number of white players increased. Sam McGee, who would become one of the early stars of the Grand Ole Opry, had fooled with a guitar, but found his true inspiration when he heard two black railroad workers playing guitars at his father's store during their lunch break. By the early 1900s guitars were showing up more often in country string bands.

Another boon to the guitar's fortunes in America was the advent of mail-order catalogues, which made many of the less expensive guitars (and occasionally some top-quality models as well) widely available. Many country players got their first guitar through a Sears, Roebuck or Montgomery Ward catalog. In the early 1900s there were more top-quality guitars around than ever before. Martins, Washburns, and Maurers were available, and the Gibson company—which began in the mandolin and guitar shop of Kalamazoo, Michigan eccentric Orville Gibson—was just beginning production. Most early country guitarists, however, used inexpensive models they mail-ordered from Sears or Montgomery Ward.

By the late 1920s, guitars had become standard for most string bands and Martins and Gibsons began replacing cheaper instruments. Guitarists like Roy Harvey, who worked with Charlie Poole and his North Carolina Ramblers, and Gid Tanner's guitarist Riley Puckett began working in new ideas for the guitar, injecting rhythmic bass runs in their playing that enhanced the sound of the bands they worked with.

But if one individual brought the guitar to prominence among country performers, it was Jimmie Rodgers, the first true country music singer. His guitar playing, always prominent on his recordings, made the instrument noticeable. Countless young people throughout the South began playing the guitar and singing in the Rodgers style. (Rodgers was the first country singer to endorse a guitar and have one named after him, when Weymann introduced its Jimmie Rodgers Special model in 1930. In fact, Rodgers generally preferred Martins, but often used custom-built models such as the Weymann.) By the 1930s, the guitar was firmly entrenched in country music, and another singer who would extend its popularity even farther than Rodgers had done was just getting his start.

Orvon Gene Autry, an Oklahoma telegrapher who enjoyed the Rodgers style, began recording in 1929 and metamorphosed into "America's Singing Cowboy." He became one of the stars of Chicago's "WLS Barn Dance" and had a huge hit in 1931 with his

There are several variations of the fingered (as opposed to the slide) acoustic guitar used in country music. The variations are primarily in the number, material, or tuning of the strings; they include: the classic guitar with six nylon strings; the twelve-string guitar (the four bottom strings each paired with a string tuned an octave above it, the two top strings paired with a string tuned in unison with them); and the high-string guitar (like the twelve-string minus the six normally tuned strings). The standard country music guitar, however, is a fretted instrument with six metal strings tuned to intervals of a fourth, except for the second string, which is tuned a major third above the third string. The lowest string on the guitar is tuned an octave below the E below middle C. The remaining strings are tuned to the A, D, G, B, and second E above that.

The body of the instrument is a resonant chamber with a flat top with a sound hole. The strings run from tuning machines (geared pegs) at the head of the instrument, down the fretted neck and past the sound hole, to a bridge, usually rectangular, glued to the top. Wood or plastic pins hold the six strings in holes drilled in the bridge (the strings have balls wired to their ends to permit this), but just before entering these holes the strings pass over a narrow saddle, made of bone, or sometimes hardwood or ceramic, which is set into a slot in the bridge. This saddle acts like a lever to transmit the vibrations of the strings (which occur in several planes) to the top, which amplifies them. (Unlike the violin, bass, and other stringed instruments played by bowing, the guitar, mandolin, and other plucked stringed instruments do not have a sound post inside the body under one end of the bridge.)

The sound of an acoustic guitar can be amplified by a contact mike on the top or built into the bridge, a miniature mike inserted through the sound hole, an accessory magnetic pickup in the sound hole, or variations of such devices. Today,

composition "That Silver Haired Daddy of Mine." Autry loved Martin guitars, for the balance their fullness and depth provided for his voice. Martin had been making a large-bodied D (for "dreadnought") model since 1917 that met his requirements. In 1932 another WLS singer named "Arkie the Woodchopper" ordered a D-2 model dreadnought with his name inlaid in pearl on the fretboard. The D-2 (which had the famous Martin herringbone pattern wooden trim) subsequently became known as the D-28. A year after Arkie got his customized instrument, Autry ordered a Martin dreadnought, but had his outfitted in Martin's elaborate style 45, which featured plentiful abalone trim. His model became the first D-45, and these two guitars, the D-28 and D-45, set the standards for many country guitars throughout the thirties and forties.

Not surprisingly, the Gibson company wanted a jumbo acoustic of its own to compete with the Martins being used by many country musicians. When singing cowboy film star Ray Whitley met Guy Hart, then president of Gibson, Whitley suggested possible improvements to Gibson's guitars. Hart invited him to the Gibson factory in Kalamazoo, *improved contact mikes are often used with acoustic steel string guitars, but most true electric guitars have electromagnetic pickup devices located below the steel strings. As a string vibrates it disturbs the magnetic field of its individual pickup and the resulting signal is electronically amplified to produce sound via a loudspeaker. Various controls permit adjusting volume, tone, and equalization, and may also permit adding reverberation, harmonically blurred "fuzztones," or other effects. Because they do not depend on an acoustic sound chamber to produce tones by means of air vibration, electric guitars are often built with very thin hollow bodies, or with solid bodies of wood or metal hollowed out just enough to accommodate the electronic components.*

Both acoustic and electric guitars are commonly played with fingertips, fingernails, flat picks, or finger- and thumb-picks, which fit over the fingers and thumb of the picking hand, and act somewhat like extensions of the fingernails. On steel string guitars, flat-picking is generally preferred both for playing full chords (three or more notes simultaneously, perhaps interspersed with bass notes or bass runs) and for playing single note melodic passages. Finger-picking style on steel-string guitar may consist of simple chord arpeggiations, as in folk guitar, but can also display a special kind of highly rhythmic, often syncopated and raggy interplay between steady bass string notes and chord arpeggiations, combined with passing tones and melody notes, often moving through a number of chord voicings up and down the neck. Some skilled players develop a technique of holding the flat pick between thumb and first finger and simultaneously finger-picking with the remaining fingers, which allows them to switch instantly from flat-picking to finger-picking styles. Other players achieve a similar effect by using just a thumb-pick, which they grasp with the thumb and first finger for flat-picking passages.

---

where the company's engineers listened to Whitley's ideas. In 1938 they presented him with the SJ (for Super Jumbo) 200, a large-bodied guitar with a rounder lower bout than the dreadnoughts, that was perfect for accompaniment; many vocalists appreciated its quality. Over the years Whitley, Gene Autry, Jimmy Wakely, Eddy Arnold, Porter Wagoner, Hawkshaw Hawkins, Lefty Frizzell, Emmylou Harris, Elvis, and countless other stars have used SJ-200s.

All this guitar design and sales activity stemmed to a considerable extent from the popularity of Autry, Whitley, and other singing cowboys. The singing cowboy phenomenon itself had struck America during the Depression years, when the country seemed to be in need of some sort of hero. When Sears came out with the inexpensive "Gene Autry" model in the 1930s, some of the millions sold put their owners on the road to a career in country music.

By the mid-thirties a new type of guitar was coming onto the scene: the electrically amplified guitar, which caused considerable controversy among country musicians. Even though electric Hawaiian guitars had been available since the early 1930s, when Rickenbacker developed its "frying pan" model, amplification was generally discouraged among country players. Many felt it inappropriate to rural music, including Grand Ole Opry founder George D. Hay, whose "keep it down to earth" dictum carried the clout of the Magna Carta among the show's performers.

Even electrically amplified steels weren't used by country artists until 1934, when a steel guitarist named Bob Dunn brought along a converted Martin with a Volu-Tone pickup when he joined Milton Brown and His Musical Brownies, one of the original Western swing bands, in Fort Worth. Still, nobody was bothering with electrics. Lloyd Loar, who played an important part in creating classic Gibson models such as the L-5 guitar (played by Mother Maybelle Carter), the F-5 mandolin (played later by bluegrass pioneer Bill Monroe), and the Mastertone banjo (played by Earl Scruggs and others), left Gibson to start his own company, Vivi-Tone, and patent an electric model in 1935— one that attracted little enthusiasm. In 1936, Gibson introduced its ES-150 (electric Spanish) guitar and amplifier and its EH-150 (electric Hawaiian) steel guitar. Neither got the greatest reception among country players, except in Texas and Oklahoma where Western swing players, who often tried their hands at pop and jazz, were far more open-minded about such things. One of the first to play an ES-150 was Muryel "Zeke" Campbell of the Light Crust Doughboys, who had an original style of playing lead on a single string.

Electrics went over far better with jazz players, and the ES-150 would forever become associated with jazz guitar innovator Charlie Christian, its bar pickup immortalized as the "Charlie Christian pickup." In part because many Western swing players were Christian fans, amplified guitars of all types became very important in that music. However, in the remainder of the country music field they were still regarded with some suspicion. Sam McGee brought one once to the Opry in the early forties, and was told by George D. Hay to leave it home from then on. An early solid-body model had appeared around 1935, made by Rickenbacker. Known as the Electro, it was built with a Spanish guitar neck on a small body, not unlike the Rickenbacker steels of the period. Some country players used it, but it was ahead of its time. Even Bob Wills, who was known for his progressive views, wouldn't let his guitarist Eldon Shamblin use an Electro because it didn't look enough like a guitar.

Things began changing by the early 1940s. Acoustic guitars were still enormously popular, but electrics began to do much better as younger, more liberal-minded musicians came along. One of these was Merle Travis, who used a Gibson L-10 with a DeArmond detachable pickup (many players preferred this kind of set-up to buying an electric with built-in pickup). When Ernest Tubb had a hit in 1941 with "Walkin' the Floor Over You," a number that featured prominent electric lead guitar, he became one of country music's top singers and soon joined the Grand Ole Opry. Apparently the fans were more open-minded than most purists realized, for between Tubb, Pee Wee King, and Paul Howard, the Opry's ban on electric instruments finally fizzled.

Electric guitars were firmly established by the end of World War II. Martins and Gibsons continued to dominate the acoustic market, with Martin dreadnoughts in particular gaining exposure through the work of Lester Flatt and other bluegrass guitarists. Before the war there had been no virtuoso country guitarists of any important stature. Guitar was primarily for accompaniment and was not perceived as a solo instrument for country music purposes. The first stand-out guitarists emerged in the mid-to-late forties. Singer Floyd Tillman, who composed such country classics as "Slippin' Around" and "Gotta Have My Baby Back," began playing his own instrumental breaks on an electric guitar, and in the immediate postwar years guitarists like Arthur Smith, who came to prominence with his 1947 hit recording of "Guitar Boogie," appeared. Merle Travis, who played in the thumb-and-finger style he'd learned from his neighbors in Ebenezer, Kentucky and had played over WLW before the war (inspiring a youthful Chester Atkins, who heard Travis's broadcasts when he was a teenager), went to California and quickly became noted not only for his superb country and western compositions ("Divorce Me C.O.D." and "No Vacancy") and hit recordings, but also as an exciting and innovative guitarist.

Travis's style, originally designed for solo guitar and rooted in black ragtime guitar, was most infectious. Travis was also the first known country singer to accompany himself on a solid-body Spanish guitar, one built for him in 1946 by inventor Paul Bigsby. Another solid-body maker closely studying the country music market was Clarence Leo Fender of Orange County, California. Fender had built a solid-body Spanish guitar in 1944 and gotten a patent on it (it looked somewhat like the small Rickenbacker Electro, though it was different under the skin), but had abandoned the project and was manufacturing amplifiers and steel guitars. Many Western swing players liked his steels, and Fender had numerous contacts in the California country and western scene. In 1949 Fender marketed his first serious solid-body model, the Broadcaster, which had strings installed through the back of the instrument. The Broadcaster had much of the twang of the steel guitar, a radically different sound from other standard electrics of the period.

The Fender Broadcaster (soon renamed "Telecaster" because the Gretsch Instrument Company already had "Broadcaster" drums) first found favor with country players like Jimmy Bryant, who earned the admiration of jazzmen for his clean and rapid playing. By the early fifties Fender was firmly established as a musical instrument manufacturer, and the "Tele" became for many *the* solid-body country guitar. The Gibson company, who had turned Les Paul down before World War II when he suggested marketing a solid-body electric, reconsidered, and in 1952 they unveiled the first Les Paul solid-body, an instrument with an unprecedented ability to sustain sounds.

Other prominent country guitarists emerged in the late forties and early fifties, all fine solo artists whose influence went far beyond country. One was Chet Atkins, the young Merle Travis fan from Tennessee's Clinch Mountains. Chet's playing style owed much to Travis, though he approached the instrument differently. He was also interested in other forms of music (his brother Jim had worked with Les Paul's trio before and during World War II), including pop, jazz, and classical, which gave his playing far more sophistication than many country players of the time. This sometimes hurt him: he was let go by several employers during the time he worked as a sideman on radio because they thought his style "way out" for country audiences. In 1947 producer Steve Sholes signed him to RCA Victor as the label's answer to Merle Travis, who was then riding a wave of solid hits over at Capitol. Chet sang—poorly—on some of his early recordings, but soon moved to doing instrumentals almost exclusively. His style showed debts to Travis, and to Les Paul and Django Reinhardt, the legendary French gypsy jazz guitarist whose incandescent playing inspired many country players (including singer-guitarists like Don Gibson and Willie Nelson). Chet became highly popular as an RCA artist, emerging as country music's best-known guitarist, and among the finest it has produced. In his work with classical and jazz players Atkins proved that country musicians aren't necessarily limited to one type of music.

Another formidable guitar stylist of the 1950s was Joe Maphis. Born in Virginia, Maphis caught onto the idea of playing fiddle tunes on the guitar, developing a smooth, rapid-fire technique that earned him the title "King of the Strings." Although he started out as a comedian, his abilities on a number of stringed instruments, including his awesome guitar playing, soon brought him acclaim. He and his wife and music partner, Baltimore-born singer-guitarist Rose Lee, moved to the West Coast and worked in live television with their friend Merle Travis on shows including the popular "Town Hall Party." Maphis has become a legend. His famous doubleneck guitar (designed by young Semie Mosley in 1954) is enshrined in the Country Music Hall of Fame. The Maphises were signed to Capitol records and also did session work. A popular L.A. studio musician, Maphis did soundtracks for *Thunder Road* and other films, and played on some of Ricky Nelson's early sessions (he could play either country or rockabilly with the best of them). He and Rose Lee also introduced a twelve-year-old Barbara Mandrell to the performing world on their show, playing pedal steel and sax.

Hank Garland and Grady Martin were two other important guitarists of the fifties. Both could play funky country or blues licks or flat-out jazz, depending on the assignment. They became virtual fixtures in the Nashville studios, much like Chet Atkins, though neither did the production work that eventually became such an important part of Atkins's contribution. The pair often worked as a team and played on a huge chunk of the popular country recordings of the fifties. Nowdays Martin primarily plays live shows as part of Willie Nelson's backup band. Garland's career was shattered by a 1961 automobile accident that nearly killed him; he now plays mainly around his home base of Spartanburg, S.C.

Through the fifties guitar technology expanded and new models became popular, including the Stratocaster, a model introduced in 1954 by Fender, which took the advice of California country players and made a very playable guitar whose contours wouldn't dig into players' ribs when held close to the body. The Stratocaster went on to great things in rock music, but like the Telecaster it came into being largely through the efforts of Leo Fender working with country musicians. In 1955, Gibson introduced the hollow-body Byrdland, a guitar incorporating design suggestions made by both Hank Garland and his friend Billy Byrd, Ernest Tubb's longtime lead guitarist. The Byrdland distinguished itself as a jazz and rock instrument. The first Chet Atkins models, built by Gretsch, appeared in 1955, beginning a twenty-four-year series of those instruments.

Guitars became even more prominent in Nashville and elsewhere after the country music business was sent reeling by the rock 'n' roll boom of the fifties. Fiddles and steels were temporarily shunted aside in favor of a guitar-dominated sound that could grab audiences without sounding "hillbilly." This idea became the much praised (or condemned, depending on whom you talk to) "Nashville Sound," with its heavy pop and rock influence.

Another group of guitar stylists emerged from bluegrass. Lester Flatt, previously of Bill Monroe's Blue Grass Boys, teamed up with Earl Scruggs and helped to define bluegrass guitar with his rhythm playing and bass runs (the best-known of which has been forever immortalized as the "Lester Flatt G-run"). Flatt was of course influenced by earlier players, among them Roy Harvey (whose playing with Charlie Poole and the North Carolina Ramblers anticipated bluegrass guitar styles by twenty years), but Flatt polished those influences and added his own ideas to create the style that many bluegrass guitarists still try to emulate.

There were still other fine bluegrass guitarists, such as the Stanley Brothers' George Shuffler, whose brilliant "crosspicking" style, played with a flat pick, is complex and difficult to master. Bill Napier applied mandolin picking techniques to the guitar.

New guitar styles became prominent as the 1960s began, among them the "chicken pickin' " styles that developed in California, particularly around Bakersfield, where people like Joe Maphis, Tommy Collins, Buck Owens, and Merle Haggard were working. By the mid-sixties this style, usually played on a Fender Telecaster with as much treble as possible, was often featured on solo breaks and instrumentals.

A new generation of country players with a broader musical background emerged, including ex-rock 'n' rollers. One of these was Jerry Reed, a former rocker who became one of Nashville's top guitarists in the sixties. He expanded upon the Chet Atkins and Merle Travis styles, picking with more fingers (he recently switched to flat-picking, however). Another was Glen Campbell, who worked with a number of rock bands but made his reputation playing country and pop in the studios. Both Reed and Campbell emerged from the studios into careers as solo performers, a change from performers who had gained most of their experience and reputation working on the road. Reed and Campbell, along with Roy Clark, were among the first instrumentalists of the sixties to become celebrated for their singing as well as their guitar work, something that hadn't happened since Floyd Tillman, Hank Snow, and Merle Travis emerged in the forties, and singer Billy Grammer in the fifties.

Rock music began influencing country guitar playing in another way in the late sixties, as more devices that altered tone became available. As had been the case with the first electric guitars, there were plenty of country pickers who had no use for fuzztones and phase shifters, but younger players generally didn't agree with that point of view, and electronic modification became part of country guitar playing too.

PLAYING STYLES

It would take a far larger section than we have room for to discuss in detail all the country guitar styles that exist, for there are countless variations and idiosyncratic forms used by amateur and professional players. However, here are some of the most prominent styles.

ACOUSTIC

The so-called Merle Travis style which uses the thumb to keep a rhythmic, syncopated bass accompaniment while the other fingers play both melody and harmonies on the treble strings, started before Travis heard it as a youth in Kentucky, played by his neighbors. Travis's playing on the 50,000-watt WLW radio in Cincinnati in the late 1930s and early 1940s brought it to the ears of a number of people including young Chet Atkins, who learned it in his own way. In the late forties, Atkins had a number of hits playing his own version of the Travis style. This style likewise influenced Scotty Moore, who used it on most of Elvis Presley's earliest recordings for the Sun label, making it a rockabilly guitar style as well. The wide popularity of the style started with Travis, however, and its influence has been pervasive. Although it started on acoustic guitar, it is equally popular on electric.

Doc Watson has also given his name to a guitar playing style. Blind since birth, Watson was virtually unknown until the early sixties, when he was discovered as an American folk music revival was beginning. Although he had often played country (and occasionally even "Blue Suede Shoes") on electric guitar, it was his acoustic picking that put him over with the folk and later the bluegrass audience. Doc Watson's ability to play rapid-fire solos, often taken from fiddle tunes, elevated him to virtuoso status. There are any number of variations on this style.

There also are numerous bluegrass guitar styles. The classic style is that of Lester Flatt, which combines chords and bass runs. There are guitarists doing things similar to Flatt, including old-timey guitarist Roy Harvey, but Flatt developed the style with Bill Monroe's Blue Grass Boys and during his partnership with Earl Scruggs.

While with the Stanley Brothers, George Shuffler developed a distinctive "cross-picking" style that owed a lot to mandolinists. It is a difficult style, not easily mastered. Another mandolin-derived guitar style came from Bill Napier, who preceded Shuffler with the Stanley Brothers. A former mandolinist, he adapted the tremolo notes of the mandolin to the guitar.

Clarence White was yet another legend. One of the finest bluegrass flatpickers of all time, White's clear, clean picking style became widely respected through his work with the Kentucky Colonels bluegrass group in the early to mid-sixties. His playing, often done on an old Martin D-28 herringbone, was always appropriate to the moment. In the late sixties he went electric with the Fender Telecaster and earned an impressive reputation for his abilities, particularly his work behind the former folk-rock band, the Byrds, who were trying their hand at country-rock. White and Byrds drummer Gene Parsons also developed the Parsons-White String Bender, a device that could be built into a Fender Telecaster or other solid-body guitar that could handle its mechanism. It would bend the second (B) string when the player pushed down on the guitar. The pull against the strap activated a plunger built onto the strap button, which created a sound reminiscent of a pedal steel slide. White continued working in the country-rock and bluegrass fields, recording in both contexts and earning increasing respect.

The Maybelle Carter guitar style may not have been bluegrass (it preceded that style by over a decade), but its influence on bluegrass and folk music makes it highly important. Known as the "drop-thumb style," it resembles the Merle Travis style, but the roles of the rhythm and bass strings are reversed. The melody is played on the bass strings with the thumb while a rhythmic chord accompaniment is played by brushing the treble strings. This can best be heard in her recordings of "Wildwood Flower" or any of the other classic Carter Family recordings; many of the songs were adapted to fit her guitar work. The style as she played it used two finger picks for the treble strings and a thumb pick to make the bass string melody prominent. This style has never gained the celebrity status of the Travis style. It has been equally important, but its influence was probably greater in folk music than in country.

ELECTRIC

The Merle Travis style is used with electric as well as acoustic guitars. Some of the other prominent electric guitar styles are discussed here.

The "Telecaster" sound, named after the Fender guitar on which it is normally played, uses the natural twang of the instrument and its treble emphasis to get a distinctive sound that cuts through a band. Solos are often played on either the highest or the lowest strings. On the lower strings, they sound twangy. The late Don Rich often used this style on Buck Owens classics such as "Tiger by the Tail" and "Act Naturally." Usually reverberation is added on the amplifier. Basic to the style is a kind of musical stutter often accompanied by bending the strings. Many of Merle Haggard's classics, such as "Swingin' Doors" and "The Fugitive" feature Roy Nichols or Phil Baugh playing in this style. It can also be heard on many trucker classics of the sixties. The low-string sound opens the Dave Dudley classic "Six Days on the Road." Waylon Jennings uses a similar sound. It's uncertain just where this sound originated, but it seems that the Owens and Haggard records of the early to mid-sixties crystallized it. It's also known as "chickin' pickin'." A variation on this is the bass-string "boom-chukka" that is the foundation of the Johnny Cash sound. It was devised by Cash's original lead guitarist, the late Luther Perkins, who stumbled on the simple style while trying to work out accompaniment on Cash's early Sun recordings of the mid-fifties. Perkins usually played on a Telecaster to produce this sound.

The rapid-fire Joe Maphis guitar style is a product of his interest in playing fiddle tunes on the guitar. It is one of the most difficult techniques and must be learned slowly, hitting each note cleanly and clearly, gradually building up speed until the notes flow smoothly and evenly. It is a flashy style, one that can grab an audience quickly.

Western swing electric styles are a bit more complex, and many draw on jazz guitar techniques. That makes it mandatory to have at least a working knowledge of the music of swing guitarists, especially Django Reinhardt and Charlie Christian, for they were the masters many prominent swing guitarists listened to. For Western swing rhythm playing, the style of Eldon Shamblin, featuring driving rhythm with bass runs, is one of the most harmonically sophisticated guitar styles found anywhere. Shamblin combines clear, mellow jazz chords with rich bass runs, a style he developed while playing for Bob Wills in the late thirties, and which evolved into the cohesive style that he has since used with Merle Haggard and on other contemporary recordings he's made since being "rediscovered" by Haggard in the early seventies. Unfortunately, Shamblin hasn't put his secrets down in book form yet, but we can hope that he will do so.

GUITAR RECORDINGS

Arthur Smith

Following World War II, one of the first serious country guitar instrumentalists to emerge was Arthur Smith, a featured member of a group called the Rambler Trio. Around 1946 he recorded a number titled "Guitar Boogie," which bore considerable resemblance to the guitar break taken on the Delmore Brothers' "Hillbilly Boogie." A straightforward boogie-woogie solo, Smith recorded it with a Martin acoustic for the Super Disc label. MGM picked up Smith's recording and issued it in 1947. It not only became the first country guitar instrumental to sell a million copies, it helped to establish the boogie-woogie guitar idiom in country music (although "Zeb's Mountain Boogie," released on Bullet in 1945, was probably the first country boogie instrumental). Country boogie became a stepping stone to what would become rock 'n' roll in the mid-1950s. *Guitar Boogie* (MGM 662-003) features some of Smith's early MGM recordings. The "Guitar Boogie" here seems identical to the Super Disc version, but in any case there's much to learn from on this disc and Smith's versatility manifests itself on other instruments as well ("Banjo Boogie," "Mandolin Boogie").

Merle Travis

The Best of Merle Travis (Capitol SM–2662) is a reissue of an earlier LP that features Travis on a number of his 1940s honky-tonk hits and a few of his acoustic coal-mining ballads, including "Sixteen Tons" and "Nine Pound Hammer." His guitar can be heard, though not in the sort of context that permits hearing any substantial amount of solo work. Fortunately, there are other Travis LPs that concentrate more on guitar-oriented material. Among them an LP issued by the late Jimmy Wakely's Shasta label, *The Guitar Player* (Shasta SH–523). The time is mostly the early to mid-1950s, and except for one 1976 track the setting is Jimmy Wakely's CBS radio show, where Travis was often a guest. Here he is playing at the top of his form, particularly on "Texas Tornado," "Gambler's Guitar," "I'll See You in My Dreams" and the effervescent "Guitar Rag."

Guitar Standards (CMH–9024) features all instrumentals on a two-record set that concentrates solely on interpretations of pop tunes played in Travis's distinctive style now. *Travis Pickin'* (CMH 6255) is an extension of *Guitar Standards*, but here he performs in a solo acoustic context, still playing mostly pop tunes. With no other accompaniment, it is possible to hear the Travis style in its most self-contained manner: lead, rhythm, and bass all coming out of one guitar and one pair of hands. *The Atkins-Travis Traveling Show* (RCA APL–1-0479) is a fine reunion between Travis and the man who in many ways is his best-known protege. Putting aside all the cornball novelties that were specially written for them to sing on the LP, it's fascinating to hear Travis playing along with Atkins's more lavish style and note the difference. *Walkin' the Strings* (French EMI 1550801) is a 1984 reissue of a 1950s album of acoustic instrumentals recorded for Capitol Records radio transcriptions in the late forties. One of the rarest Travis LPs, it captures the essence of the Travis style. (Available from Down Home Music.)

Chet Atkins

A *Legendary Performer Vol.* 1 (RCA CPL–1-2503) features the work of the man who is easily the best-known country guitarist of all time, and who is a true musical innovator. A visionary who used Merle Travis's guitar style and his interest in jazz and pop music as a springboard, Chet Atkins played an enormous role in upgrading the talents of country guitarists. The bulk of his work as a solo artist has been for RCA. *The Legendary Performer* set includes a number of early and obscure sides from his earliest RCA sessions (including some with Homer & Jethro as sidemen) and a few interesting tracks from later sessions, along with a beautiful and informative booklet loaded with Atkins memorabilia and photos.

Now . . . and Then (RCA VSPX–6079) was issued originally in 1972 to commemorate Atkins's twenty-fifth anniversary with RCA (a label he left in 1982). This album brings together his best-known material on two LPs, from "Canned Heat," a 1947 number heavy on Travis licks, to the excellent 1972 "Knee Action," which succeeds even with the string arrangements. It provides a valuable summary of his entire career.

Chester & Lester/Guitar Monsters (RCA AYL–1-3682) brings together two guitar greats. Chet's late older brother Jim played guitar in the Les Paul Trio in the 1940s, and Les himself was a formidable influence on Chet's playing. (On the other side of the coin, Les began his career as a hillbilly singer-guitarist named "Rhubarb Red.") On these two outstanding records, the emphasis is on swinging, tight country/jazz improvisations served up with generous portions of humor.

Chet Atkins and Doc Watson; Reflections (RCA 2AHL–13701), an engaging collaboration between two virtuoso guitarists, in many ways captures the best in both men. Atkins's nylon string fingerpicking manages to complement Watson's steel string flatpicking seamlessly. Possibly excepting one cornball ditty ("Me and Chet Made a Record") the music here makes the listener yearn to hear Chet continue to play this close to his roots.

Phil Baugh

Country Guitar (Longhorn T–502; available from Keith Kolby) is a brilliant recording that was originally issued in the 1960s. On the title track Baugh, an obscure but even then brilliant player, manages to mimic some of the best guitarists in the business on a Fender Telecaster. The album languished in obscurity until writer Charlie Burton found a copy in a tiny record store in the early 1970s and tracked Baugh down. Using a volume pedal as his only effect device, Baugh created some truly incredible music, pulling steel guitar sounds out of this austere setup (Vern Stovall, in whose band Baugh worked, sings on several tracks). Baugh is in Nashville these days working regularly in the studios, and Longhorn reissued this album several years ago with other tracks added. You may have heard Baugh and not known it, even twenty years ago. It was he who played many of those screaming Telecaster leads on such early Merle Haggard hits as "Swinging Doors." *Country Guitar* is his finest hour.

Joe Maphis

At this writing, all of Joe Maphis's brilliant solo recordings for Columbia are unavailable, though it appears that Germany's Bear Family Records is soon to release some of the best material, along with duet tracks by Maphis's protege Larry Collins (of the Collins Kids rockabilly duo) and solo recordings by Collins. However, Maphis did a prodigious amount of recording for the Los Angeles–based CMH Records in the late 1970s and early 1980s. Unfortunately, many of those albums, including *Grass 'n' Jazz* and *Boogie Woogie Flat-Top Guitar Pickin' Man*, are out of print. One still available is *The Joe Maphis Flat-Picking Guitar Spectacular!!* (CMH 9030), which consists largely of acoustic duos with Arthur "Guitar Boogie" Smith, Merle Travis, and banjoist Zen Crook.

Don Rich

The guitar of the late Don Rich was an integral component in the sound of Buck Owens's music in the 1960s and 1970s. His twanging Telecaster leads on hits like "Tiger by the Tail" and "Act Naturally" were simple but effective within the spare context of Owens's music. Rich died in a 1974 motorcycle accident and Owens, whose string of hits was leveling off, never really had the same act after that. Listen to *The Best of Buck Owens* (Capitol ST–2105) and *Buck Owens* (Time-Life STW–114).

Clarence White

Clarence White became a bluegrass guitar legend with the Kentucky Colonels, playing single-string leads of a sort few before him had ever thought of. Jazz influences were clear in his music, and that he managed to innovate within the staid traditions of bluegrass was a tribute to his ingenuity. Some of his earliest work is available on the Kentucky

Colonels' *Livin' in the Past* (Sierra 4202), which includes some early acoustic leads and works through to the sixties, all through recordings of live performances. Another excellent LP is *Nashville West* (Sierra 8701), which details—again through live performance tapes—White's early experiments with electric guitar.

White later began to use a Fender Telecaster with the string-bending device he helped to design to give him pedal steel-like effects. It was that instrument, combined with his brilliant ideas, that made him so important to the Byrds' country-rock experiments. He can be heard prominently on their *Sweetheart of the Rodeo* (Columbia CS–9670) and *Dr. Byrds and Mr. Hyde* (Columbia PC–9755). After leaving the Byrds, White began combining rock influences with a return to acoustic progressive bluegrass. He started recording his first solo LP for Warner Brothers in 1973, but was killed by a drunk driver before he could complete it. Four cuts from those sessions are available on *Silver Meteor* (Sierra 8706), a California country-rock anthology. (Available from Down Home Music.)

Grady Martin

Sad to say, virtually all of Grady Martin's solo recordings are no longer in print, including his brilliant *Dance-O-Rama* ten-inch LP recorded in the mid-fifties. However, he can be heard playing acoustic nylon-string guitar on such Marty Robbins recordings as "El Paso" or any of the Robbins *Greatest Hits* sets. Martin played piercing electric guitar leads on some of Johnny Horton's rockabilly-oriented tracks, including "I'm Coming Home," "Honky-tonk Man," and "Honky-tonk Hardwood Floor," all available on *Rockin' Rollin' Johnny Horton* (Bear Family BFX–15069), a German import, or on Horton's *Honky-tonk Man* (Columbia CS–8779), still in print after more than twenty years. Martin can also be heard playing lead guitar on many of Willie Nelson's current LPs.

Ray Edenton

Ray Edenton came to Nashville in 1953 hoping to be a lead guitarist, but the excellence of several other lead men convinced him to concentrate on rhythm guitar, which he's played on thousands of sessions over the past thirty years. He did one solo LP for Columbia (out of print), but can best be heard in a backing capacity on *Patsy Cline's Greatest Hits* (MCA 12). A rare Edenton lead can be heard on Marty Robbins's 1956 recording of "Singing the Blues," available on *Marty Robbins' Greatest Hits* (Columbia PC–8639). The famous Edenton high-string rhythm guitar can be heard on the Everly Brothers' *Rip It Up* (British Ace), a British import chronicling some of the duo's recordings originally made for the Cadence label in the 1950s. On these cuts Edenton and Don Everly created the driving rhythm guitar that helped establish Edenton as a top-level Nashville session player. *24 Golden Hits of the Everly Brothers* (Arista AL9-8207) also includes some of these recordings.

Eldon Shamblin

Eldon Shamblin played on dozens of recordings by Bob Wills and His Texas Playboys. Listen closely: if you hear smooth chords and seemingly effortless bass runs on the strings, you're probably listening to Eldon, who worked on and off with Wills from 1938 to the 1950s and on various Western swing reunion LPs in the 1970s and 1980s. The best chronicles of his days with Wills are on *The Bob Wills Anthology* (Columbia PG–32416), *Bob Wills* (Columbia Historical Series FC–37468), *Bob Wills* (Time-Life Country Classics Series 07), *24 Great Hits by Bob Wills and His Texas Playboys* (MGM 2-5305), and *The Rare Presto Transcriptions Volumes 1,2,3* (Cattle CAT–20, a German import).

Shamblin's later work can be heard on Merle Haggards's *A Tribute to the Best Damn Fiddle Player . . .* (Capitol SN–16279), Bob Wills's 1973 *For the Last Time* (United Artists LMBL–216), and *S'Wonderful* (Flying Fish 035), a collaboration between Shamblin, the late jazz violinist Joe Venuti, steel guitarist Curly Chalker, and mandolinist Jethro Burns. He can also be heard on Tiny Moore and Jethro Burns's *Back to Back* (Kaleidoscope F–9) and Moore's *Tiny Moore Music* (Kaleidoscope F–12). Shamblin also recorded a solo LP for Delta Records.

Lester Flatt

Flatt can be heard on any of the Bill Monroe or Flatt and Scruggs recordings listed in the banjo or mandolin sections, or on the LPs he recorded with his band, the Nashville Grass, for CMH in the 1970s. These include *Fantastic Pickin'* (CMH 6232), *Heaven's Bluegrass Band* (CMH 6207), *Lester Flatt's Greatest Performances* (CMH 6238), *Pickin' Time* (CMH 6226), *A Living Legend* (CMH 9002; two LPs), and *Lester Flatt's Bluegrass Festival* (CMH 9009; two LPs).

Scotty Moore

For the aspiring rockabilly musician, Scotty Moore is required listening. His style, rooted deeply in that of Merle Travis but replete with blues overtones, virtually defined the idiom. The best place to hear Scotty is on the records that made his reputation: Elvis Presley's earliest recordings for Sun and RCA. *The Sun Sessions* (RCA AYM–1-3893) details his earliest work with Presley, and one can hear licks that have never really become dated. Any of Presley's early RCA albums, such as *Elvis Presley* (RCA AFL–1-1254e) or *Elvis* (RCA, two vols.: CPL–1-0341/-1349) afford plenty of other classic licks from Scotty. More recently, *Elvis: A Golden Celebration* (RCA CPM6-5172), a six-LP boxed set of early, unreleased Elvis material from TV and live performances, shows some of Scotty's wildest, most savage playing.

Hank Garland

Like Grady Martin, Hank Garland is now largely represented by recording session work. His solo efforts are mostly out of print, but the majority were in a jazz context. The country recordings he did for Decca in the late 1940s and early 1950s are long unavailable. He can be heard playing the lead on Patsy Cline's "I Fall to Pieces," and playing on a variety of Don Gibson's RCA recordings (*Rockin' Rollin' Don Gibson, Volumes 1 and 2* [Bear Family Records BFX–15089, –15097]). But unless one is willing to do extraordinary amounts of research, turning up Garland solos is not easy at this time.

Doc Watson

It's hard to believe that Doc Watson, now considered one of the great traditional bluegrass guitar virtuosos, actually spent time working in an amplified country and western band in North Carolina. But before he was discovered by folk music researchers, that's what he did. Today he often records with a rhythm section and numerous guest pickers, but *On Stage* (Vanguard VSD–9/10), a double set, was cut back in the late 1960s when he toured with just his son Merle backing him up. It may not be his finest Vanguard album, but any drawbacks are more than compensated for by hearing him work to a live audience, recalling the music that inspired him—the music of Travis, the Delmores, and Jimmie Rodgers—and demonstrating his own awesome abilities as a finger-picker and as a rapid-fire flatpicker. It is a true classic.

Maybelle Carter

"Wildwood Flower" on *The Original Carter Family—Legendary Performers, Vol. 1* (RCA Victor CPM–1-2763) is a track that was recorded in 1928 when the Carters were just getting started on records (though it wasn't their first session). Maybelle's lick on this song's opening has become one of the best-known guitar riffs in either country or folk music (her influence extended into both areas). While there is some controversy as to whether her drop-thumb style was actually influential in country music as a whole (not many country players have named her as an influence, though Hank Garland and others were very clear in describing her impact on them in the early days), her influence in bluegrass circles can still be heard. Her method of playing melody on the bass strings with a thumb pick while brushing chords with her index finger is far easier to listen to than it is to learn, for it required the sort of coordination it takes to play the Merle Travis style. Of course, the Carter recording of "Wildwood Flower" has long been a country classic.

Jerry Reed

Although Jerry Reed, the composer of the rockabilly classic "Guitar Man," available on *The Best of Jerry Reed* (RCA), today is known by millions for his appearances as an actor in films and television, country fans and guitar enthusiasts know that his abilities as a guitarist are awesome. Reed's style brings into play more picking fingers than the standard Travis style. Samples of his picking can be heard on most of his RCA albums.

GUITAR INSTRUCTION

FOR BEGINNERS

Private Guitar Lessons, Books 1 and 2, by Bob Baxter (Music Sales) doesn't deal strictly with country, but it could be an excellent alternative to a teacher. Written by a veteran California guitar instructor, it draws on his years of experience in teaching and writing manuals to give the beginning guitarist step-by-step basic instruction. Book 2 gets into basic fingerpicking (important to anyone aspiring to play like Chet Atkins or Merle Travis) as well as the Carter Family style. A recording accompanies the books.

First Guide to Guitar by John Pearse (Music Sales) is not as elaborate as Baxter's manual, but is a very simple, sixteen-lesson guide to basic chords, hand positions, and other fundamentals. Later on, it gets into fingerpicking, including the style of country guitarist Sam McGee.

Teach Yourself Guitar by Harry Taussig (Music Sales) is a basic instruction manual geared to the beginner, dealing in basic chords, accompaniment, and other simple techniques. Although the major thrust of the book is toward folk, rather than country, styles, it can be a valuable volume for the beginner without a teacher.

FOR INTERMEDIATE TO ADVANCED PLAYERS

Baxter's Complete Guitar Accompaniment Manual by Bob Baxter (Music Sales) applies to polishing your sound when accompanying your own singing or the playing of others. It also gives pointers on reading music and developing your playing.

Baxter's Guitar Workshop by Bob Baxter (Music Sales) is from Baxter's CBS "Guitar Workshop" TV series. Among his guests were prominent country players like the late bluegrass flatpicker Clarence White, Doc Watson, John Hartford, and others. In standard notation and tablature, Baxter explains some of their techniques and music.

Flat-Pick Country Guitar by Happy Traum (Music Sales) is by a veteran country-folk guitarist and originator of the Homespun Tapes instruction method. Happy Traum's excellent book lays out the standard flatpicking techniques as applied to the music of Doc Watson, the Carter Family, and even Nashville-style country and country-rock. Runs, breaks, and solo passages are demonstrated in both standard notation and tablature, and better yet, the music included here works on acoustic or electric guitar.

Doc Watson by Doc Watson (Music Sales). Without a doubt, Watson is the finest bluegrass lead guitarist around, a fluent flatpicker who can as easily slip on finger picks and play brilliant Merle Travis-style guitar. This book lays out in notation and tablature thirty of his songs as he recorded them. For the player wishing to concentrate on rapid-fire guitar soloing and general virtuosity, this is a fine way to get started.

Nashville Guitar by Arlen Roth (Music Sales) is one of the few books written on the subject of electric country picking. It comes with a sound recording to demonstrate the techniques included in the book. Appropriate attention is given to the acoustic player as well. The book illustrates the styles of Doc Watson, the late Clarence White, the late fingerpicker Sam McGee, the Delmore Brothers, Merle Travis, and Mother Maybelle Carter. There are also chapters on playing lead electric guitar, bluegrass, and even rockabilly, as well as special instruction on string-bending and getting steel guitar effects from a standard guitar. A must for the country musician planning to play electric.

Old-Time Country Guitar by Fry Bledenberg and Stephen Cicchetti (Music Sales) is an instruction manual dealing with pre–World War II guitar styles of rural string-band music, dating from a time before there were electric guitars, or even bluegrass. The book illustrates the playing of Sam McGee, Dick Justice, and other more obscure players, and includes waltzes, rags, blues, and the traditional buck-dance and gospel songs from that period. The book comes with a sound recording demonstrating some of the techniques covered in the text.

Anthology of Fingerstyle Guitar by Tommy Flint (Mel Bay) looks at a variety of fingerstyle guitar playing methods, not just country, and includes basic instruction and pointers for everything from blues to ragtime. A stereo cassette can be purchased at additional cost.

Fun with the Guitar (Mel Bay), a simple method book to help beginning guitarists play instantly, uses photos and other visual aids. No real country licks, but worthwhile for the person just getting into the instrument.

The Merle Travis Guitar Style by Merle Travis and Tommy Flint (Mel Bay) gives a complete course for the intermediate to advanced player, with photographs and music in both notation and tablature. It does miss some of the subtleties of the Travis style (such as the fact that he occasionally picks with more than just his thumb and index finger), but it is nonetheless a pretty definitive look at one of the most influential guitar styles of all time, one essential for the well-rounded country player to know.

Learn to Play Bluegrass Guitar by Tommy Flint (Mel Bay) is an excellent look at basic bluegrass guitar licks, runs, and so forth.

Authentic Bluegrass Guitar by Tommy Flint (Mel Bay) is a collection of solos and technical tips on playing bluegrass guitar collected from Muhlenberg county, Kentucky, the birthplace of none other than Merle Travis, a decidedly non-bluegrass picker. But then Rosine, the home of bluegrass founder Bill Monroe, is in the neighboring county.

E-Z Way Bluegrass Guitar by Tommy Flint (Mel Bay) gives some simple bluegrass flat-picked guitar solos in a method designed for beginning bluegrass players.

Country Guitar Pickin' by Tommy Flint (Mel Bay), apparently designed for both the electric and acoustic player, deals with the voicings, techniques, and effects used by country lead guitarists, with a tendency toward modern country sounds.

Chet Atkins' Style for Guitar Volume I (Mel Bay) is a basic introduction to the Atkins style. The influence of classical guitar technique on Chet's playing is clear in this volume.

Deluxe Album of Folk, Country and Bluegrass Guitar Tunings (Mel Bay) is an unusual collection of solos that demonstrate the wide variety of tunings other than the standard E-A-D-G-B-E available to the guitarist.

Guitar Country Licks by Jay Friedman (Ernie Ball) deals with solo picking for the country guitarist. It is laid out with tablature and regular notation, and is geared for everyone from beginners to advanced players.

Flatpickin' Bluegrass Guitar I by Ron Freshman (Ernie Ball) covers rhythm accompaniment in bluegrass guitar, beginning with basic strums and going to alternate bass note chording, from the basics to complex improvisations.

The following sets are from the *Homespun Tapes* series founded by Happy Traum. Each is a course consisting of from three to six cassettes, and printed tablature. The instructors of the various courses include some top professionals.

Happy Traum's *Guitar for Beginners* starts you out with the basics. The first lesson alone introduces you to a dozen numbers, while later lessons bring the total to seventy complete songs. The system teaches you to play by ear as well as chord theory.

Fingerpicking Styles, also taught by Traum, deals with blues as well as country fingerpicking styles. There is also instruction in the Merle Travis style. The blues styles might well help you see where Travis's style came from and give you a few ideas on forming your own style.

Traum teaches a basic *Flatpicking* course in six cassettes that include instruction in basic strums, bass runs, the Maybelle Carter style of picking out melodies with chord accompaniment, hammer-ons and pull-offs, tremolos, fiddle tunes, break-downs, and more advanced material, including intros to songs and improvised endings. The songs here are by and large old country and bluegrass tunes.

Russ Barenberg, a superb bluegrass flatpicker, teaches a six-hour course in *Advanced Flatpicking*. Barenberg, an expert in the bluegrass flatpicking style of the late Clarence White, goes through a number of complex styles, including fiddle tunes flatpicked on solo guitar (something Doc Watson, Dan Crary, and pioneer flatpicker Joe Maphis have built their reputations on), as well as crosspicking (the style George Shuffler made famous with the Stanley Brothers), and other techniques.

Dan Crary, one of the foremost acoustic flatpickers today, teaches a specialty course in *Flatpicking Fiddle Tunes* that compiles a number of old fiddle tunes and variations on them and shows how to play them with increasing speed. He teaches crosspicking, and a number of other pointers for the advanced flatpicker interested in this sort of technique.

Merle Watson, Doc Watson's son and longtime partner, teaches *Country Guitar Styles*, an excellent course that includes thirty songs and instrumentals on a special three-tape series. On the final tape Doc joins in to provide insights into the twin acoustic guitar style they've used onstage for so many years, taking apart some of the songs they've made famous, such as "Blue Railroad Train" and "Windy and Warm." The first two tapes cover basic fingerpicking; the second tape also covers slide guitar.

HARMONICA

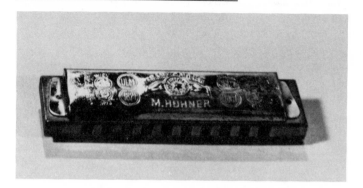

The earliest known ancestor of the mouth harmonica, a multiple-pipe reed instrument known as the sheng, was developed around 3000 B.C. in China, during the reign of Emperor Nyn-Kwas. A sheng was transported to Europe in the 1700s and is said to have brought with it the principle of producing tones by means of free reeds—that is, reeds that are not controlled by direct pressure of the lips or tongue, but are free to vibrate in a column of air blown past them. The principle was first adopted in the Western world for pitch pipes, and is used to this day. The pipes of the sheng, the Japanese sho, and many related instruments share a common air chamber that has a single mouthpiece. Each pipe contains a reed fastened at one end but free at the other; the length of the pipe and the reed determines the pitch of the tone. The pipes are made to sound by covering or uncovering fingerholes while blowing into the mouthpiece.

The modern harmonica has a series of separate air chambers each divided into two parts, one with a reed that vibrates to produce a single note when the player exhales, the other with a reed that vibrates to produce a harmonically related note when he inhales. The instrument is moved in front of the lips to bring the chambers into blowing position, and neighboring chambers that are not to sound for a given note are stopped by the tongue or by shaping the lips. Mechanically simple harmonicas—those favored by many country and blues players—play in a single key. They are not expensive, so it is easy to have one or more instruments for each key that may be used. More complex—and more difficult—"chromatic" harmonicas have controls that permit shifting keys and scales on a single instrument.

The basic design of the modern harmonica was created in 1821, when a sixteen-year-old German clockmaker named Christian Friedrich Ludwig Buschmann put fifteen pitchpipes together to create what was known as the "mund-aeoline" (German for "mouth-harp"). Another German clockmaker built them for a while and then, in 1857, twenty-four-year-old Matthias Hohner began mass-producing them in Trossingen, Germany, on the same spot where the Hohner factory stands today. Around the early 1860s, before the American Civil War, Hohner sent a few samples to cousins who had emigrated to America. They asked for more, and in the course of the Civil War harmonicas became popular with both Union and Confederate troops. After the war, the instrument remained popular. In the late nineteenth century rural white and black farmers formed small bands for their own enjoyment; harmonicas were often added to these groups. For black Americans the harmonica was a bow to modern technology; for many years before its arrival they had played homemade "quills," three pieces of hollow cane of different lengths, bound together and held to the mouth. The advantages of the new instrument were obvious: the harmonica was louder, had a greater range of notes, and came pre-assembled.

Harmonicas were popular in white string bands by the late 1880s, and were used along with the stringed instruments. By the turn of the century they had become a part of the developing blues form. Hohner's Marine Band model—its best seller, at a price of fifty cents—was introduced in 1896. The design of the current Marine Band Hohner is virtually identical.

In the 1920s harmonicas were popular in black jug bands, as well as with country and blues players. In the 1930s, classical music was added to the harmonica repertoire by players like Larry Adler, who played pop, jazz, and classical material, and John Sebastian (father of the well-known folk-rock songwriter of the 1960s). These two were among the first harmonica players admitted to the American Federation of Musicians in 1948. Adler recorded one of the earliest jazz harmonica performances, with guitar virtuoso Django Reinhardt, in France in 1937.

The first major country harmonica player was DeFord Bailey. Bailey was black, but despite Southern racial attitudes he began appearing on the WSM "Barn Dance." He opened the show on the night in 1927 when George D. Hay dubbed it "Grand Ole Opry" and introduced Bailey, who played his "Pan American Blues," a frenzied, rushing train number. As Peter Guralnick's excellent chapter on Bailey in his book *Lost Highway* notes, in the year 1928 Bailey played on forty-eight of the fifty-two Opry broadcasts, twice as many as any other performer. He toured with Roy Acuff and Bill Monroe in the late thirties. However, the Opry grew more conservative as its stature increased and Bailey's star began to fade. Finally, for rather murky reasons, he was abruptly dismissed from the show in 1941. Bailey continued to live in Nashville, playing on Opry reunion shows but rejecting all recording offers, until he died in 1982. He was one of the first musicians to record in Nashville, in 1928.

Lonnie Glosson never became the legend Bailey did, but his influence was immense. Glosson first emerged in the thirties in the Arkansas-Missouri area as a vocalist, harmonica player, and guitarist, and he gained a following over KMOX radio in St. Louis. Glosson specialized in making a harmonica "talk," as black players had been doing for some time. One of his later recordings, "I Want My Mama" (cut in the 1950s), demonstrates just how effective his imitations could be. Over the years he recorded for a number of labels, including Decca and Mercury.

One of Lonnie Glosson's young fans, Wayne Raney, became his protege and eventually greatly increased the harmonica's popularity in country music. Raney was born in Arkansas in 1921. Because of a crippled foot he was unable to handle heavy farm work and he spent a lot of time listening to Glosson over KMOX. Around 1938 Glosson and Raney met in Little Rock and teamed up, playing harmonica duets; Raney later worked alone, in Texas. By that time other country acts were using harmonicas, among them the Rice Brothers Gang, who featured a large chromatic model on solos and behind vocals. Also working the South was Jimmy Riddle, who played for a time with the Swift Jewel Cowboys in Memphis and, after World War II, worked for some years backing up Roy Acuff as one of the Smoky Mountain Boys. It was Raney, however, who truly popularized country harmonica. Unlike most of the other players, Raney could also sing. In 1941 he went to work for WCKY radio in Cincinnati, one of the Midwest's most powerful and influential country stations. His radio show sent harmonica sales skyrocketing in the years following World War II. Raney peddled harmonicas mail-order on his show, referring to them as "talking harps." There were rumors that Raney was selling an average of a million harmonicas a year between 1945 and 1950.

Even more important to country harmonica history was Wayne Raney's work with the Delmore Brothers, the old-timey group who worked at Cincinnati's WLW radio (they'd previously worked on the Grand Ole Opry). Following the war, the Delmore's had moved towards a blues- and boogie-woogie–oriented style that set them apart from many other duos. They began working with Raney and featured his playing on such Delmore classics as "Freight Train Boogie" (recorded for the Cincinnati-based King label), thereby enhancing his reputation even further. In 1947, Raney began cutting his own records for King, with the Delmores often backing him. The Delmores' 1949 hit, "Blues Stay Away from Me," prominently featured Raney's playing. At the same recording session he cut a song titled "Why Don't You Haul Off and Love Me?", which became a huge hit for him. His old friend Lonnie Glosson did the backup harmonica work on the record. Raney's popularity faded in the fifties, particularly after his work with the Delmore Brothers ended with Rabon Delmore's death in 1952, but he remains active musically.

Raney wasn't the only harmonica player in the early fifties. Harmonica Frank Floyd was the first white musician to record for Sam Phillips's then blues-oriented Sun Records, in Memphis in 1952. Floyd, a medicine-show veteran, could play two harmonicas at once (one through his nose!), and also pioneered the "eeffing"—"ee-(gasp)-ah"—that the late Jimmy Riddle and his partner Jackie Phelps often engaged in on the "Hee Haw" TV show. Floyd also played harmonica on one side of his mouth and sang his own wild songs out the other. There was also Onie Wheeler, whose Raney-influenced music landed him a recording contract with Columbia in the early fifties, and who produced some excellent semi-rockabilly material, such as his hit "Onie's Bop." Wheeler later recorded for Sun and played some fine harmonica on the unusual acoustic rockabilly recordings of the late Jimmy Murphy. Wheeler went on to work with Roy Acuff's Smoky Mountain Boys when Riddle moved over to piano; he remains there today. An example of harmonica on recordings of the early 1950s is Red Foley's popular Decca cut, "Old Kentucky Fox Chase," which features a harmonica player (possibly Lonnie Glosson) mimicking the hounds. Terry Fell's original recording of the now-classic "Truck Drivin' Man" also featured harmonica.

The importance of harmonica in country music and on country records faded somewhat after Elvis Presley and rock 'n' roll rolled over America; at the same time it became more important in folk music and the blues. Actually, harmonicas had never lost ground among blues singers (though the larger, horn-dominated urban blues bands seldom featured them). As amplified guitars became a part of the blues sound in the postwar years, a new technique for playing harmonica came into vogue. The harp itself was cupped in the hands along with an inexpensive microphone plugged into a guitar amplifier. With a bit of vibrato or reverb added, and the expanded dynamic range that amplification provided, the instrument took on new dimensions. The chief exponents of this new style were Chicago's Little Walter Jacobs, James Cotton in Memphis, and Sonny Boy Williamson II (a.k.a. Rice Miller) in Arkansas. Little Walter came to prominence with Muddy Waters's Chicago blues band, and through his 1950s instrumental number "Juke." Cotton began working in Memphis in the early fifties and played on many of the early Sun blues recordings. Williamson's recordings for the Trumpet and Chess labels, his "King Biscuit Time" radio show over KFFA in West Helena, Arkansas, and his occasional European tours, brought him legendary status.

Young white musicians heard both blues and folk harmonica players, but it was the blues players who had the greater impact on them, particularly those living in the South. One of these young Southern musicians was a Texas singer named Delbert McClinton. In 1962 McClinton recorded some harmonica riffs behind another Texas singer named Bruce Channel on a song titled "Hey, Baby." The song became one of the biggest hits of the year in America and did quite well in England. When McClinton and Channel toured there later in the year they were put on a bill with a rising group known as the Beatles. Delbert reportedly met John Lennon and taught him the rudiments of playing the instrument. The first official Beatles' record, "Love Me, Do" (1962), was kicked off by Lennon's warbling harmonica. Throughout the 1960s the blues harmonica style gained popularity through the music of the Rolling Stones, John Mayall, Paul Butterfield, and other British and American white blues musicians. Hohner even introduced a "Blues Harp" model.

A major link in the chain that connected these widespread blues sounds of the sixties back to country music was a young Southerner named Charlie McCoy. A multi-instrumentalist born in Oak Hill, West Virginia, McCoy had been under contract to Nashville's Monument Records since the early sixties. Influenced by the black blues players, McCoy could play literally anything on the harmonica, from Little Walter's "Juke" to the Wayne Raney sound. He became indispensable in the Nashville studios where he worked scores of sessions. He also played harmonica on Bob Dylan's 1966 recording of "Obviously Five Believers" and later did outstanding work in the early seventies with Area Code 615, an early "progressive" country group made up of outstanding Nashville-based instrumentalists. In the early seventies, Charlie McCoy's own instrumental versions of "Today I Started Loving You Again," "I'm So Lonesome I Could Cry," and "I Don't Really Want to Know" became impressive hits. He won Country Music Association awards and Grammys during that period, and deserves most of the credit for bringing the harmonica back to popularity in country music.

The harmonica's renewed prominence in country music became still more evident when it began to be heard behind Willie Nelson and Waylon Jennings in the mid-seventies, both on records and in their on-stage backup bands. Willie and Waylon, along with the other "outlaws," began to change the face of the country music industry, not so much through revolution as through re-exposing the roots that many had forgotten. The harmonica became one symbol of their sound. Jennings has had several harmonica players in recent years, including Don Brooks, Roger Crabtree, and Gordon Payne. The superb blues-tinged harp of Mickey Raphael has been an integral part of Nelson's sound for several years; P. T. Gazell served a similar function with Johnny Paycheck's group. And Delbert McClinton, who has emerged as a country blues artist in his own right, never abandoned the harp. The styles of all these players combine country with blues—often played in the style of the electric bluesmen like Little Walter—to hauntingly complement the wide range of human emotions covered in the finest modern country songs.

HARMONICA RECORDINGS

DeFord Bailey

Unfortunately, no label has had the foresight to do a good reissue series on DeFord Bailey, even though his legend has spread far beyond Nashville and the Opry. What is available is scattered over several albums. Probably the best samples of his playing are found on two tracks of an album titled *Nashville: The Early String Bands Vol. II* (County 542), an anthology that features a number of the early string bands that appeared on the Opry and WSM in the mid-1920s. It includes "Pan American Blues" and "Muscle Shoals Blues" by Bailey, and the surrounding tracks demonstrate the context in which his work was then heard.

Wayne Raney

Although Raney can be heard on many of the Delmore Brothers reissues, *Songs from the Hills* (King LP–588), the only album he ever recorded for King, was recently reissued with the original cover and liner notes. The album contains Raney's best material, including his 1950 hit "Why Don't You Haul Off and Love Me?", the haunting "Lonesome Wind Blues," "Lost John Boogie," and some songs that feature Lonnie Glosson backing Raney's vocals. "Jack and Jill Boogie," performed with the Delmores, features some of the rawest, most menacing country harmonica ever recorded. More recently, *When They Let the Hammer Down* (Bear Family BFX 15167), featuring hot boogie numbers by both Raney and the Delmores, has appeared.

Harmonica Frank Floyd

Harmonica Frank Floyd actually goes back considerably farther as a performer than Wayne Raney, but he wasn't discovered for recording purposes until the early fifties, when Sam Phillips spotted him. He has at times been mistaken for a black blues artist because of the rawness of his style. His Sun recordings include his famous talking blues "The Great Medical Menagerist," the risque "Swamp Root," and "Step It Up And Go," along with some of the rockabilly-style recordings he made with Larry Kennon in the fifties.

Charlie McCoy

Most of Charlie McCoy's Monument albums, except some of the early ones, are still available, and you can pretty much take your choice. *Greatest Hits* (Monument MG–7622) has "Today I Started Loving You Again" and the other well-known hits, but there's good McCoy on all the albums.

Mickey Raphael

Raphael's great work with Willie Nelson in some ways epitomizes the current use of amplified harmonica in country music, adding touches of blues to straight country sounds. Willie Nelson albums such as *Willie Sings Kristofferson* (Columbia JC–36168), the two-record *Honeysuckle Rose* movie soundtrack (Columbia S–2-36752), or the Nelson–Leon Russell duet LP *One for the Road* (Columbia KC–2-36064) give some fine examples of Mickey's playing. But it can probably best be heard on *Willie and Family Live* (Columbia KC–2-35642) where he stretches out with the band in live performances. It's to be hoped that Raphael will soon record an album of his own.

P. T. Gazell

Gazell has been as prominent in Johnny Paycheck's band as Mickey Raphael has in Nelson's. On *Pace Yourself* (Sugar Hill 3073) he tackles some unusual selections (the "Flintstones" theme; "Greensleeves") as well as some fairly straight acoustic country and bluegrass numbers, played with a traditional bluegrass band that includes Ricky Skaggs and dobroist Jerry Douglas. They play "Roanoke," "Hold the Woodpile Down," "Billy in the Low Ground," and a "British Isles Medley" of traditional songs. This repertoire—a considerably more traditional kind of country than his work with Paycheck—shows an interesting approach to traditional country harmonica work.

HARMONICA INSTRUCTION

We haven't located any books that deal strictly with country harmonica. Some of the following general books should give some insights, however. Listening to the records previously listed will help even more.

Basic Harmonica Instructions (Hohner) is a simplified method for blues, rock, and folk playing with non-notation method of instruction, using arrows to indicate whether to blow or draw (exhale or inhale) for the right notes, and numbers to tell you which hole to play. It includes twenty pages of instructions and ten arranged songs.

Let's Play the Harmonica (Hohner) has twenty-eight pages of instructions for the Marine Band–type harmonica (the kind generally used by country players). The songs are arranged with blow or draw arrows and include "Dixie," "Home, Sweet Home," "Old Black Joe," and others.

The ABC of Harmonica Playing (Hohner) features more basic instructions, written in question-answer form. Included in its sixteen pages are several exercises and instruction charts.

Blues Harp by Tony "Harp Dog" Glover (Music Sales) might seem rather irrelevant to country music, but it is definitely not so. Many of the players covered here were enormous influences on Charlie McCoy, Delbert McClinton, and Mickey Raphael.

Blues Harp Songbook by Tony "Harp Dog" Glover (Music Sales) is a continuation of the above book. It features transcribed solos of some of the great black blues harmonica players and comes with a record with rare recordings of their music so you can hear what they sounded like.

MANDOLIN

Chester Buchanan's Old Kraftsman mandolin
(Country Music Foundation)

The mandolin originated early in the eighteenth century, and the first models looked very much like short-necked lutes. In Italy they were popular as melody instruments, often accompanied by guitar. They were first popular in the United States among Italian-Americans (although Croatian-Americans also played mandolins and various related instruments). The instrument gradually found its way into rural string bands, with one band and then another adding mandolin to the fiddle-banjo-guitar lineup.

In the decades just before and after 1900, mandolin orchestras enjoyed enormous popularity throughout America. These groups, some professional and some amateur, were aided by mandolin manufacturers, particularly the small Kalamazoo, Michigan firm of Orville Gibson. It was Gibson who changed the design of mandolins, which had been generally constructed in the European "potato bug" style, with bulbous backs and flat tops like those of the lute. Gibson applied violin-making principles to come up with arch-top mandolins that had an overall thinner profile than the potato-bug types. As the company grew (Gibson sold the firm to some Kalamazoo-area businessmen in 1902), its marketing became aggressive. The firm published catalogs filled with self-praise, and with photos of mandolin orchestras that endorsed Gibson models. One early model, the Artist,

The mandolin is a descendant of the lute that has undergone a rapid evolution in twentieth-century America, so that it no longer looks very much like a lute at all. It is a fretted instrument with four pairs (courses) of wire strings running from machine tuning heads, over a bridge, to a tailpiece. The strings have a typical scale (vibrating) length of 13⅞ inches. Like a guitar bridge, the full width of the mandolin bridge is in contact with the top of the instrument. The strings of each pair are tuned in unison, while the pairs are tuned at intervals of a fifth from pair to pair, with the lowest pair tuned to the G below middle C—the same tuning as the fiddle. What is probably the most popular style of mandolin for country music has a carved, arched top and back, with violinlike f-holes (other models have oval soundholes, and some models retain the flat top). The arch-top and f-holes in general increase the projection and brilliance of the mandolin's sound.

Although it might seem that the mandolin would compete musically with the fiddle because they share the same range, in fact the instruments complement each other remarkably. In its overtone structure the mandolin retains some of the distinctive mellow woodiness of its lute ancestry. The attack (initiation of the note) produced by a mandolin flat pick striking its tightly strung strings is virtually the sonic opposite of the attack produced by the rosined violin bow drawing against its string. And while both fiddle and mandolin have a unique expressive capacity for controlled sustain of notes, the characteristic tremolo sustain of the mandolin is the complementary opposite of the fiddle's bowed sustain.

featured a basic design that would, in somewhat improved form, become the model most associated with country music.

However, Gibson mandolins aren't often seen in early photos of country string-band players, many of whom played other brands (Gibson prices were higher than the average). Some musicians undoubtedly used the traditional designs, which were still well-represented in the mail-order catalogs from which many rural musicians bought their instruments in the early 1900s.

One of the earliest known country mandolinists was Doc Hopkins, a Kentucky-based mountain balladeer who became known in the World War I years, and later was an influence on other musicians, gaining fame outside of Kentucky once radio barn dances achieved popularity.

Doc Hopkins was only the first of a number of Kentuckians who popularized the mandolin. Even more influential were Lester McFarland and Robert Gardner, known professionally as "Mac and Bob." The two first got together around 1915 when they were both attending the Kentucky School for the Blind. Gardner was a guitarist, McFarland a mandolinist, and they both sang. Their repertoire contained many songs that would become classics in early country music, among them, "When the Roses Bloom Again" and "Twenty-one Years." They began to work professionally on the vaudeville circuit in 1922, and from 1925 to 1931 were regulars on station WNOX in Knoxville, Tennessee. Mac's mandolin licks influenced many other musicians, particularly via the duo's recordings, and his playing was of great importance in spreading the popularity of mandolin in country acts.

In 1931 Mac and Bob joined the WLS "Barn Dance," the popular Chicago-based radio show heard over much of the country. That same year another guitar-mandolin-vocal duo came to the WLS "Barn Dance": Karl (Davis) and Harty (Taylor). They had come to the show from Kentucky as part of the Cumberland Ridge Runners group. Karl had been influenced particularly by the mandolin work of Doc Hopkins. Among his compositions were the classics "I'm Just Here to Get My Baby Out of Jail" and "The Prisoner's Dream."

Another outstanding guitar-mandolin-vocal team, this one from North Carolina, was the Blue Sky Boys. Bill Bolick and his brother Earl became quite popular in the South during the Depression. Bill played mandolin, and he developed a unique ability to incorporate its sound into the duo's vocal harmonies. Their repertoire featured traditional and religious numbers, as well as originals, one of which was Bill Bolick's "Sunny Side of Life," which they recorded for Bluebird, Victor's country and race music label.

The man who took the mandolin's role in country farther than anyone else was another Kentuckian. William Smith Monroe was raised in the hills near Rosine, Kentucky, where he was born in 1911. The area was rich in music, and as he was growing up Monroe listened to the music of black guitarist and fiddler Arnold Schultz, as well as to other fiddle music. The fiddling of his uncle, Pen Vandiver, became an enormous influence on his playing. Monroe learned guitar and fiddle, but never got to play either very much; his older brothers Charlie and Birch had already staked their claims to those two instruments, leaving Bill with the mandolin. He did play guitar behind his Uncle Pen at local square dances (and played it occasionally in later years), but played only mandolin with his brothers. Even that was restricted: they complained that the mandolin's eight strings were too loud, and had Bill remove four of them (one from each note-pair). Bill's brothers eventually left Kentucky. After living for a time with his Uncle Pen (his parents had died), Bill joined them in the Chicago area and went to work at an oil refinery. All three brothers kept their hands in at music, however. With Charlie on guitar, Birch on fiddle, and Bill on mandolin they played at parties, worked with the road show from the WLS "Barn Dance," and performed on smaller local radio stations to publicize their appearances with the "Barn Dance" shows. By 1934, their reputation growing, Bill decided to turn full-time professional. Charlie and Bill began working as the Monroe Brothers; Birch returned to the oil refinery.

For the next two years the Monroe Brothers moved through the Midwest and South, performing over a number of radio stations. Bill Monroe's playing style continued to develop, undoubtedly combining ideas picked up from Karl and Harty, and possibly from Mac and Bob, with the stylistic ideas he'd acquired from Arnold Schultz and his uncle

Pen. Considering their talent and skill, and the audience that developed for the Blue Sky Boys, Karl and Harty, and the others, it was not surprising that the pair became extremely popular. When they recorded for Bluebird in 1936, one of the most outstanding elements of their sound was Bill's sophisticated mandolin playing.

In 1938, Bill and Charlie split up. Bill briefly led a group named the Kentuckians before assembling the original Blue Grass Boys in Atlanta. He auditioned for the Grand Ole Opry in the fall of 1939, playing his driving version of Jimmie Rodgers' "Muleskinner Blues." His bluesy unaccompanied mandolin intro to that song has become a bluegrass cliche, but it remains a fine example of his ability to incorporate blues into his playing. Soon after he was signed to the Opry he made his first recordings with the Blue Grass Boys for Victor, again leading off with "Muleskinner Blues."

During the mid-to-late thirties another very different country mandolin style was evolving in Texas, where musicians were far more eclectic in their musical tastes, listening to jazz, pop, and blues as much as country. That diversity spawned Western swing in the early thirties. Mandolin was not initially popular in early Western swing groups, which at first simply combined Texas fiddle music with elements of blues, pop, and ragtime to create a danceable sound. The year 1936 marks the appearance of the first Western swing mandolinist, Leo Raley. According to prewar Western swing authority Jeff Richardson, Raley began as an acoustic mandolinist with Cliff Bruner's group, the Texas Wanderers. His playing got lost in the sound of the other instruments, particularly when they were playing dance halls. He remedied this by buying an amplifier and having a friend, swing steel guitarist Ted Daffan (composer of "Born to Lose"), rig up an electric pickup for him. Thus amplified, Raley's hot solos cut their way to the ears of the dancers and became an asset to Bruner's band. In 1949 Raley's playing was featured on what became a country classic, his friend Floyd Tillman's recording of "Slippin' Around."

Raley's musical accomplishments have begun to be rediscovered and appreciated only quite recently. More widely known is Western swing player Tiny Moore, who grew up in Port Arthur, Texas, and enjoyed listening not only to the music of Leo Raley but also to that of Benny Goodman. Tiny was initially a fiddler who doubled guitar and some mandolin. After playing in some pop trios around Port Arthur, he played fiddle with Happy Fats and His Rayne-Bo Ramblers, a Louisiana-based band that combined Cajun music and Western swing. He next fiddled with a group called the Port Arthur Jubileers. Around 1943, he began playing a homemade electric mandolin, incorporating ideas from Goodman and his guitarist, jazz pioneer Charlie Christian. Following service in the air force, he connected with Bob Wills and brought his electronic mandolin into the Texas Playboys in 1946, when electric guitars were becoming increasingly important to the group's sound. As a Texas Playboy, Tiny gained an audience of Wills fans all over the country. He was featured on such classic Wills instrumentals as "Punkin' Stomp" and "Fat Boy Rag," where he displayed the articulation and phrasing of a good jazz guitarist.

Johnny Gimble was also a seminal figure in the field. His primary instrument was fiddle, but his abilities on electric mandolin were formidable. When he joined the Texas Playboys in 1949, he and Tiny Moore alternated between fiddling and playing twin mandolins—with particularly outstanding results on "Boot Heel Drag" and "Sallie Goodin."

At times the pair worked out intricate ensemble passages with the steel guitar and lead guitar. Although both men left music temporarily when Western swing's popularity declined in the 1950s, its revival in the 1970s brought them back, playing to younger audiences across the country. Tiny began using a different type of mandolin in the early fifties, the same one he uses now: a custom-built solid-body made by guitar designer Paul Bigsby, with five strings (tuned C-G-D-A-E, bottom to top). Today he markets another electric mandolin styled identically to his Bigsby model.

Western swing and bluegrass were not the only outlets for country mandolin. Another outstanding mandolinist, able to play country or swing with equal finesse, was Kenneth "Jethro" Burns of the comedy duo of Homer and Jethro. Burns and Henry "Homer" Haynes teamed up in the thirties on radio, initially as part of a group known as the String Dusters that played country as well as jazz. Jethro became a follower of French jazz guitar legend Django Reinhardt, and adapted his style to the mandolin. After the pair broke off from the String Dusters they went to Renfro Valley, Kentucky, home of an Opry-style country music show, until the World War II draft caught up with them. Following their discharges, they moved to WLW radio in Cincinnati and began recording for the King label. Though they were best known for their uproarious comedy and their song parodies, Jethro often played vibrant jazz solos on their live appearances, with Haynes playing a driving rhythm guitar behind him. The pair also backed their old friend Chet Atkins (with whom they'd worked off and on over WNOX radio in Knoxville) on many of his early RCA Victor recordings, including his 1949 hit "Galloping on the Guitar." In the sixties the pair recorded two albums of pop and swing instrumentals with Atkins producing. Although Haynes died in 1971, Jethro has continued as a solo performer, combining comedy, country music, and jazz.

Mandolin was also present on other country recordings of the 1940s, though featured less prominently than in either bluegrass or Western swing. Mandolinist Mack McGarr worked on many country recordings of the period, including Ernest Tubb's Decca recording of "Warm Red Wine." In California, the Maddox Brothers and Rose featured raw, bluesy mandolin, played by Cliff Maddox. There were other, more obscure mandolinists like Clyde Baum, who contributed mandolin work to Hank Williams's 1949 recording of "Lovesick Blues." There were also groups that continued in the tradition of the Monroe Brothers and the Blue Sky Boys, groups like the California-based Armstrong Twins, a powerful mandolin-guitar duo who played traditional numbers as well as their own versions of then-contemporary country and Western swing hits, arranged in the old-timey styles of the thirties.

In the postwar years country music of just about all kinds to some extent opened up to the mandolin. There were other duos in the late forties and early fifties, based in the Monroe and Blue Sky sounds, but with a more modern approach. Among these were the Louvin Brothers, who featured Ira Louvin's superb mandolin playing in the group's gospel and country repertoire, and Johnny and Jack, two guitarists and vocalists whose backup group included the superb mandolinist Paul Buskirk (who also played some incredible electric mandolin on singer Eddie Hill's early fifties records, as well as those by Lefty Frizzell).

As rock 'n' roll began to make inroads into the country market, it was the popularity of mandolin, fiddle, and steel guitar that was most affected. Those who played these instruments often found themselves unable to get work as country singers attempted to modernize their sounds. It seemed the mandolin's position was unassailable only in bluegrass music, where a number of other fine mandolinists were developing in Bill Monroe's shadow, among them Pee Wee Lambert of the Stanley Brothers, and Curly Seckler with Flatt and Scruggs. But there were also youthful mandolinists who were taking the instrument beyond Monroe's innovations, just as Monroe had developed a technique beyond that of Karl Davis or Mac McFarland in the thirties. Jesse McReynolds (of Jim and Jesse) developed a complex style of flatpicking the mandolin (known as "crosspicking") that involved picking different combinations of strings to get a rolling syncopation that paralleled what Earl Scruggs was doing with fingerpicks on the five-string banjo. No one had done anything quite like this on mandolin before, and McReynolds became one of the most admired mandolinists of the early fifties.

Others have developed the Monroe style over the years, enriching bluegrass in the process. Among these are John Duffey, who in the fifties broke from the traditional bluegrass mandolin style of reprising a song's melody during an instrumental break, and instead improvised on the melody as a jazz musician would. He began working with the legendary Washington, D.C., Country Gentlemen (one of the first groups to add non-bluegrass material to their repertoire, thus paving the way for the progressive or "newgrass" movement of the early seventies). In 1971 Duffey began working with the Seldom Scene, a progressive group based in the Washington area. Another mandolinist who developed blinding technique on the instrument was Frank Wakefield of the Greenbriar Boys, and yet another was the greatly underrated Buzz Busby (also from the Washington area), who has yet to get the exposure he deserves.

As bluegrass festivals proliferated and the bluegrass audience expanded greatly in the late sixties, more people—especially young people—began playing mandolin, a trend that continued into the seventies. The Western swing revival also helped to generate interest in the mandolin as played by Tiny Moore and Jonnny Gimble, both of whom were featured prominently by Merle Haggard. The appreciation of younger performers with a deep love for traditional music gave the mandolin additional exposure. Emmylou Harris is a notable example. Her love of the music of the Louvins, the Country Gentlemen, and other bluegrass groups prompted her to add a mandolinist to her group (the Hot Band), in the person of Ricky Skaggs. Skaggs, a fiddler, mandolinist, and guitarist who'd played mandolin with Ralph Stanley's group in the early seventies and later fiddled with the Country Gentlemen, joined Harris in 1978 and stayed until 1980. Now a highly successful vocalist as well, he has succeeded in creating a traditional country sound that includes elements of bluegrass and swing in a contemporary package.

In the late 1970s a new type of mandolin music began to emerge, different from anything Bill Monroe, Tiny Moore, Jesse McReynolds, or Jethro Burns probably ever imagined. Its chief exponent was a former bluegrass mandolinist, Dave Grisman, also known by his nickname "Dawg." Grisman began as a straight bluegrass player, working with such bands as Red Allen and His Kentuckians. His idols, along with Monroe, included Wakefield and McReynolds. He became an excellent traditional player, but began in the sixties to experiment with other types of music. One album that inspired him was Homer and Jethro's set of jazz instrumentals, *Playing It Straight* (RCA LPM–245), which showed him that the mandolin could work in non-bluegrass idioms. He began listening to jazz, ethnic, classical, and other musical forms, and by 1966 composed two original instrumentals, "Opus 57" and "Opus 38," that were more melodically complex than anything he'd played before. After a late-sixties stint with ex-Blue Grass Boy Peter Rowan in the Boston rock band Earth Opera, he continued his explorations of various musical forms (though he still plays traditional bluegrass). Grisman often worked with others who had turned to rock and then returned to bluegrass, among them former Blue Grass Boys Richard Greene (known particularly for his fiddling), Peter Rowan (guitar and vocals), Bill Keith (banjo), and guitarist Clarence White of the Kentucky Colonels and the Byrds. For a time Grisman and Greene were part of an eclectic and sophisticated group of acoustic musicians known as the Great American Music Band. The members of this group (which never recorded) played in a variety of styles, as Grisman did. The membership included jazz, rock, country, and folk players, all working on complex fusions of different kinds of music. The group finally dissolved, and in 1976 Grisman formed his own David Grisman Quintet, which featured Mike Marshall on a second mandolin, and progressive bluegrass/jazz guitarist Tony Rice.

Grisman would be the first to admit that the roots of his style spread wide and reach into the past. Aside from his bluegrass background and his admiration of Jethro Burns, he mentions listening to the Western swing of Tiny Moore and Johnny Gimble, and to the work of an obscure mandolinist named Dave Appolon, who, in the thirties and forties, played original music that drew on jazz, pop, and classical sources. Another Grisman influence was Rudy Cipolla, who played complex chords on the instrument (and, like Apollon, was not a country player). Grisman readily acknowledges these influences, and has produced a LP reissue of Apollon's recording, *Mandolin Virtuoso* (Yazoo). An entire school of "Dawg"-style music has developed around Grisman, and another fine bluegrass-rooted mandolinist, Andy Statman, has made his music in a very similar mold.

Today, there are probably more mandolins in music stores than there have been in decades, ranging from beginners' models styled after the Gibson that Monroe and so many others have favored, to an authentic reissue of the original Gibson F-5 itself. As for the F-5 Bill Monroe has used since 1941 (he played an F-7 when he worked with his brother Charlie in the thirties), that model made news not too long ago when Monroe mended relations with the Gibson company. In the fifties he'd sent it back to the factory for repairs, took umbrage at the results, and gouged the Gibson name out of the peghead. Finally in 1980 he and Gibson were reconciled and he permitted them to restore their name to the instrument. Bill Monroe himself is experimenting with different music. In 1981, near his seventieth birthday, he released "My Last Days on Earth," an unusual, non-bluegrass recording with sound effects and a minor-key tonality. Since then, Monroe has mellowed. He played an amplified mandolin—something once unthinkable—on Ricky Skagg's 1984 recording of Monroe's "Uncle Pen."

MANDOLIN RECORDINGS

The Blue Sky Boys

Although they retired early, in part because of their own pride and determination not to conform to changing musical trends, the stark simplicity of the Blue Sky Boys—and Bill Bolick's mandolin work—have not been lost. There are several reissue albums readily available, among them *The Blue Sky Boys: The Sunny Side of Life* (Rounder 1006), which compiles some of their best original recordings from the 1930s and 1940s. Another album, *Presenting the Blue Sky Boys* (JEMF 104) is a reissue of a 1965 Capitol recording they did in the old style. This one is even more worthwhile because of the substantial book accompanying the record that analyzes each of the songs in detail and is filled with discographical data on the group's entire history and biographical information on the group. Another recent album, *The Blue Sky Boys: Bill Bolick and Earl Bolick* (Rounder 0052), recorded in 1974, dips back into their repertoire by including material they'd performed but never recorded in their heyday. All of this features Bill Bolick's playing, and his style of adding the mandolin to the double harmonies.

The Monroe Brothers

Feast Here Tonight (RCA Bluebird AXM–2-5510) features two LPs of the classic material the Monroes recorded in the late thirties, with extensive notes on the pair and on the music. For those who want to hear what happened just before the Blue Grass Boys, this is the album to get. Unfortunately, it is now out of print and has become a collector's item.

Bill Monroe and His Blue Grass Boys

Bill Monroe has recorded an enormous amount of material over many years—too much to even begin to outline here. However it *is* possible to note important albums or those where his mandolin is particularly prominent. Unfortunately, his earliest recordings on Victor are currently out of print, though one album, *The Father of Bluegrass Music* (Camden CAL–719), can still be found with a lot of looking. His classic Columbia sides with Flatt and Scruggs are another story. There are several reissues that contain a fair amount of material from the late forties, the music that defined the bluegrass idiom. Among them are *Bill Monroe with Lester Flatt and Earl Scruggs* (Rounder SS06) and the two volumes of *The Original Bluegrass Band*—(County Country Classics Series 104 and 105). The essential Decca recordings are on *Country Hall of Fame* (British MCA CDL–8505). Many of his other Decca albums are still in print, now on the MCA label. Among those worth checking are *Bluegrass Instrumentals* (MCA 104), which features the classic "Rawhide," *Country Music Hall of Fame* (MCA 140), *Blue Grass Ramble* (MCA 88), *Blue Grass Special* (MCA 97), and *Bill Monroe's Uncle Pen* (MCA 500). *Master of Bluegrass* (MCA 5214) is a 1981 instrumental set. Just about any record store will yield far more albums featuring Monroe's incredibly durable music than could be listed here.

Jim and Jesse (Jesse McReynolds)

Although much of the classic Jim and Jesse work from the early fifties isn't available, the pair are still highly active in the bluegrass world, recording for CMH Records of California. The strongest LP available is the recent double LP *Jim and Jesse Story* (CMH 9022), which features remakes of some of their early classics such as "Border Ride" and "Diesel on My Tail." Another album that does feature four of the Jim and Jesse early 1950s sides on Capitol is the LP *Blue Grass Special* (Capitol, Japan, ECS–50060), from the *Call of the Country* series. Not only are there the four cuts by Jim and Jesse, but also four tracks recorded by Rose Maddox that very possibly include Bill Monroe anonymously picking mandolin. And although they don't fit the album's title, four Blue Sky Boys tracks are also here. This album may be hard to find, but is worth inquiring after.

Leon Morris and Buzz Busby

Honkytonk Bluegrass (Rounder 0031) features the incredible mandolin of Busby teamed with a vocalist. Another, more recent album by Busby is *Traditional Bluegrass* (Webco 0101), which features Busby's mandolin on "Running Away" and most of the other tracks.

The Louvin Brothers

The Louvins' recordings have been regaining popularity. Several of their Capitol albums are now available as reissues. Also notable are *Songs That Tell a Story* (Rounder 1030), compiled from a 1952 show they did at a small Alabama radio station; it concentrates on religious songs. Another excellent reissue is *The Louvin Brothers* (Rounder Special Series SS–07), which features some of the best of their early recordings for MGM back in the early fifties with some of Nashville's best studio musicians.

Leo Raley

Leo Raley, probably the first amplified mandolinist in Western swing, can be heard on several albums. The excellent Texas anthology *Hot As I Am* (Rambler 105) not only features several tracks where Raley is prominently featured, but the superb liner notes include detailed data on Raley's career and details on the early history of amplified Western swing mandolin. The British LPs *Stompin' At the Honky Tonk* (String 805) and *Operators' Specials* (String 807) feature several tracks with Raley.

Tiny Moore

Some of Tiny Moore's finest work with Bob Wills and His Texas Playboys is available on *24 Great Hits by Bob Wills and His Texas Playboys* (MGM 2-5305). He and Johnny Gimble play some awesome twin-mandolin ensembles on "I Ain't Got Nobody" and "Boot Heel Drag." Also well worth digging up are *Billy Jack Wills and His Western Swing Band* (Western 2002) and *Crazy, Man, Crazy* (Western 2004), which chronicle Tiny's work after he left Bob in 1950 to join forces with Bob's younger brother in a Sacramento, California–based band. Tiny was the band's arranger, and aside from writing sophisticated arrangements, he played consistently brilliant mandolin solos and ensembles (with the gifted steel guitarist Vance Terry)—musical work that he still classes as the finest of his career. A recently issued Bob Wills collection that also features Tiny prominently is *The Tiffany Transcriptions, Volume 1* (Kaleidoscope F–16). Although this material is among the most overrated of all the noncommercial records Wills made, Tiny's playing is often the heart and soul of the music. Listen to his excellent interpretation of Benny Goodman's "Mission to Moscow" as part of an amplified string ensemble, as well as "Lone Star Rag" and "I Hear You Talking."

Recent recordings by Tiny include *Tiny Moore Music* (Kaleidoscope F–12), which is built around his clean, if somewhat restrained, interpretations of old swing, pop, and country numbers, and *Back to Back* (Kaleidoscope F–9), produced by David Grisman and featuring both Tiny and Jethro Burns with jazz bassist Ray Brown and drummer Shelley Manne among the backup musicians. Tiny can also be heard on Merle Haggard's later MCA and CBS recordings, as he's now a prominent part of Haggard's band, the Strangers.

Johnny Gimble

Johnny Gimble's mandolin work can be heard not only on *24 Great Hits by Bob Wills and His Texas Playboys* (MGM), but on more recent recordings like *Johnny Gimble and the Texas Swing Pioneers* (CMH 9020), which reunites Gimble with a number of Texas swing musicians like the late J. R. Chatwell. His *Texas Fiddle Collection* (CMH 9027) also features his mandolin work prominently. The Moore-Gimble ensemble was first reunited on Merle Haggard's *A Tribute to the Best Damn Fiddle Player in the World* (Capitol SN–16279), the LP that spawned the Western swing revival, and a classic that's still in print as a budget LP.

Jethro Burns

Unfortunately, all of the RCA Homer and Jethro LPs that seemed omnipresent in the fifties and sixties are now out of print. However, it is possible to hear Jethro's work backing Chet Atkins on *A Legendary Performer* (RCA CPL–1-2503) and *Now . . . and Then*

(RCA VPSX–6079), both culled from Chet's early recordings. Contemporary Jethro recordings include *Back to Back* with Tiny Moore; *S'Wonderful* (Flying Fish FF–035), which features Jethro playing with the late jazz fiddle legend Joe Venuti; *Jethro Burns* (Flying Fish FF–042), his first solo album, which includes country, traditional, and swing numbers; and *Jethro Burns Live!* (Flying Fish FF–072), which concentrates mostly on jazz and swing performances with a small rhythm section.

John Duffey

The Traveler and Other Favorites, a Rebel LP of John Duffey's improvisational bluegrass mandolin stylings from his Country Gentlemen days, is out of print, but albums like *Act Four* (Sugar Hill SH–3709), recorded with the Seldom Scene, are available.

David Grisman

You can get a good grasp of Grisman's magic with only a few albums. *Early Dawg* (Sugar Hill SH–3713) comes from 1966 recordings that are mostly straight bluegrass, but also includes his first forays into his own style. *Muleskinner* (Ridge Runner RR–0016) was recorded with a number of other musicians who had worked first in bluegrass, then in rock, and were rediscovering their bluegrass roots. *The David Grisman Rounder Album* (Rounder 0069) combined some of his newer music with traditional bluegrass, and *The David Grisman Quintet* (Kaleidoscope F–5), now a classic, showed his music clearly for the first time on an entire album. Other albums, all easily available, are *Hot Dawg*, *Quintet '80* (Warner Brothers BSK–3469) and *David Grisman/Stephane Grappelli Live* (Warner Brothers BSK–3550), which features Grisman and group with the legendary French fiddler who recorded so many classic jazz sides with guitarist Django Reinhardt.

MANDOLIN INSTRUCTION

How to Play Mandolin by Jack Tottle (Music Sales) is a fundamental instruction book for the beginning player. The book gets the student playing as quickly as possible, whether the interest is in playing folk or bluegrass mandolin. There are few of the usual exercises in this volume; instead, the lessons use songs. The book includes tips on left and right hand technique, chords, accompanying the voice, as well as a discography and a bibliography for further study. All exercises and the fourteen songs here are in both standard notation and tablature.

Bluegrass Mandolin, also by Jack Tottle (Music Sales), gives solid instruction in the music and styles of Bobby Osborne, Jesse McReynolds, Frank Wakefield, and, of course, the master, Bill Monroe. It includes a record corresponding to the text material.

Jesse McReynolds Mandolin by Andy Statman (Music Sales) takes a look at one of the most skilled mandolinists in bluegrass, best known for his famous crosspicking techniques. Statman analyzes McReynolds's techniques, particularly his crosspicking, from over twenty solos he's recorded throughout the years. Statman also deals with right and left hand exercises needed to get the McReynolds sound. His analysis is minute, providing just about all that's needed to learn the style. The material here is mainly for intermediate or advanced players.

Teach Yourself Bluegrass Mandolin by Andy Statman (Music Sales) deals more with the basics of the genre, with right and left hand techniques and other solo and backup instruction. For someone new to bluegrass mandolin, this is the place to start.

Mel Bay's Deluxe Bluegrass Mandolin Method (Mel Bay) covers a wide variety of techniques, scales, and solos.

Mandolin Songbook (Mel Bay) is a collection of numbers arranged for beginners.

Old Time Mandolin Solos (Mel Bay) is a book of songs designed and arranged to be played solo.

Deluxe Country Mandolin Method by Bud Orr (Mel Bay) provides all the general basics and tips on country mandolin playing.

Bud Orr's Learn to Play Bluegrass Mandolin (Mel Bay) is basic instruction in the bluegrass genre.

Jethro Burns—Mandolin Player by Jethro Burns (Mel Bay) is essential for anyone who wants to tackle country-jazz or Western swing mandolin. This book is an in-depth study of Jethro's techniques, and he deals in detail with his approaches to country, bluegrass, and, of course, jazz.

Jethro Burns Mandolin Picking Solos (Mel Bay) is for the player who got through the first Jethro book. This second volume features more solos and techniques.

Homespun Tapes has an excellent and comprehensive mandolin course for the aspiring bluegrasser taught by Sam Bush, a talented young mandolinist with a grasp of both traditional and more modern styles. *Bluegrass Mandolin* is a six-tape instruction course that gives an introduction to the style, various songs, tips on playing rhythm, and songs in various keys. It also explains in detail the styles of Bill Monroe, Bobby Osborne, and Jesse McReynolds, as well as John Duffey's playing style. There are tips on playing the more modern "newgrass" styles as well. As with all Homespun courses, printed tablature is included.

PIANO

The upright piano, invented in Philadelphia around 1800 (France Menk)

Pianos have been part of country music right from the beginning. The early rural string bands organized in the South almost always included piano to project the sort of strong, pounding rhythms needed for dancers, at a volume the small, unamplified guitars of the time could not achieve. When portability was a problem, small fold-up pump organs—available from Sears, Roebuck for about thirty dollars—were sometimes taken along.

Country musicians who played other instruments learned from and worked with pianists. Uncle Dave Macon, the legendary vocalist, banjoist, and entertainer, learned popular songs of the 1920s and 1930s by listening to piano versions. Sam McGee, the extraordinary Tennessee finger-picking guitar player who worked on the Grand Ole Opry from the 1920s into the 1970s (and played on Nashville radio before the Opry existed) learned many of the ragtime-influenced instrumentals he was known for from a player piano. Dr. Humphrey Bate's Possum Hunters, another Tennessee string band that worked on Nashville radio well before the Opry began, featured Dr. Bate's daughter, Alcyone, as pianist. On the first WSM "Barn Dance" broadcast, octogenarian fiddler Uncle Jimmy Thompson was accompanied by his niece Eva on piano. And in the 1930s fiddler Arthur Smith's niece played piano with Smith's group, the Dixieliners (which also included Sam McGee). Piano also was used on some early country recordings in the 1920s.

It is hard to put down a date when piano was first used as an accompanying instrument for country singers. Charles Wolfe suggests it may have been in August 1927, when an obscure Virginia group known as the Shelor Family String Band was recorded by Ralph Peer in the Virginia-Tennessee border town of Bristol, one day after Peer had recorded

The piano is a member of that sub-class of stringed instruments whose strings are hammered, rather than plucked or bowed (the hammered dulcimer is also a member of this subclass). In the piano's case, the mechanism of levers and linkages that delivers the blow of the hard felt hammer to the string also activates a felt-covered damper that lifts from the string to allow it to sound, and returns to stop the string's vibration when the player's finger lifts from the key. The piano differs notably from the other stringed instruments described in this section in having a separate string for each note, as well as a considerably wider range: from the A three octaves below the A below middle C, to the C four octaves above middle C. The fact that the strings need not be depressed against a neck to produce the desired pitch means that both the player's hands are free to sound the notes, and pianists can produce chords of up to ten notes. The piano is strung with single and paired brass-wound strings for each note in the lower octaves, and with sets of three steel strings per note for the rest of its range. The great tension (as much as twenty tons) produced by the combined pull of these strings requires that they be strung across a cast-iron frame. They pass across a bridge set within this frame that transmits their vibrations to a wooden soundboard that amplifies the sound much like the soundboard of other stringed instruments. The fact that a piano soundboard need not be so nearly enclosed as that of other stringed instruments is due to its large surface area, which has the effect of acting as a self-baffle (much like large, flat electrostatic loudspeakers that need no enclosures).

the Carter Family and the day before he recorded Jimmie Rodgers, all for the first time. On that recording, pianist Clarice Shelor also provided some energetic singing, so it may indeed be the first instance of piano being used to back a country vocalist.

Although there seems to have been little prejudice against pianos from rural musicians, there were some members of the music industry who weren't quite so open-minded, having already formed definite ideas about what rural music should and should not contain. One early string-band legend, banjoist Charlie Poole, was once ejected from a session when he insisted on using a piano on one of his records—the producers felt it "wasn't country enough," and compromised his sound.

After Jimmie Rodgers and Vernon Dalhart made solo country singing fashionable, the string-band tradition began to change. Rodgers, for example, was using a piano on some of his recordings as early as 1929. In 1930 he did a session backed by Louis Armstrong and Armstrong's pianist wife Lillian, resulting in some fine jazz-tinged music. But perhaps the biggest boost to piano as a country music instrument was the development of Western swing in the Southwest in the mid-thirties.

Parts of this article appeared in slightly different form in *Country Music Magazine*, Jan./ Feb. 1981. Copyright 1981 Silver Eagle Publishers, Inc.

Even when Bob Wills was a child fiddle prodigy in Texas, he and his family played dances using a piano. But it was Milton Brown who brought the piano into a Western swing band for the first time, when he hired jazz pianist Fred "Papa" Calhoun in 1932 for his newly formed group, the Musical Brownies. Calhoun brought a new dimension to country music piano. Until then it had been used primarily to accompany other instruments and occasionally vocals, but Calhoun's inventive, freewheeling style soon made him one of the Brownies' top soloists.

When Bob Wills and His Texas Playboys signed their Columbia recording contract in 1935, Wills immediately hired another talented pianist, Al Stricklin, for his band. Stricklin was featured prominently in the Playboys from 1935 until he left in 1941. As long as Wills had the Texas Playboys, he used a number of excellent pianists, including Millard Kelso, Skeeter Elkins, and Doc Lewis.

A Western swing pianist who had a far-reaching effect on country music was Aubrey "Moon" Mullican. A native Texan, Moon grew up listening to black musicians and learning blues and barrelhouse piano techniques on his family's pump organ. As he grew into adulthood he played around Houston, and in the mid-thirties began freelancing with a number of Western swing bands, among them Cliff Bruner's Texas Wanderers, the Sunshine Boys, and the Modern Mountaineers. He added a strong bluesy piano sound to these bands, and also sang some significant vocals, including a memorable one on Bruner's 1939 recording of "Truck Driver's Blues," the first country trucker tune. With boogie-woogie as played by black pianists like Albert Ammons and Meade Lux Lewis becoming a national craze in the forties, Moon's blues and barrelhouse roots allowed him to connect country piano with that style.

The post–World War II years saw increasing activity in the record business in general, and the birth of numerous small independent labels to compete with the majors. Moon Mullican was signed to King Records in Cincinnati, the first country singer-pianist to be given a solo recording contract. He had a big hit in 1947 with a takeoff on the Cajun number "Jole Blon," titled "New Jole Blon." Mullican also became known for his ebullient stage presence. The "pumping piano" style he'd developed on the family pump organ was probably a major influence on Jerry Lee Lewis's famous piano style. Moon was known as one of the pioneers of the "country boogie" idiom that started in the forties. He was a close friend of Hank Williams, who used his clout to get him on the Opry in 1949, not long after Hank himself had joined the show. Some members of the Opry resisted Mullican's presence on the grounds that the piano didn't qualify as a stringed instrument, apparently never having looked under the lid. Dubbed "King of the Hillbilly Piano Players," Moon remained popular until his death in 1967.

Mullican's success cleared the way for other country pianists in the postwar period, such as Roy Hall and Merrill Moore. Iowa-born Moore made his early reputation in the honky-tonks of San Diego, California, and in 1952 began turning out some remarkable country-boogie recordings that influenced Jerry Lee Lewis, then a teenager in Ferriday, Louisiana. Among Merrill Moore's finest performances were "House of Blue Lights" and "Down the Road Apiece," both of which preceded the Jerry Lee sound by several years.

The first successful country piano instrumentalist also appeared in the postwar years: an amiable lady named Del Wood, who had a ragtimey, barrelhouse style best heard on her 1951 country top ten recording of "Down Yonder," which established her on the Opry.

By the mid-fifties, the increased importance of pianos in country music was becoming clear. In 1955 Roy Hall recorded a rhythm-and-blues hit by singer Big Maybelle titled "Whole Lotta Shakin' Going On," in a loping, bluesy style (different from the sound of the million-selling version Jerry Lee Lewis recorded for Sun two years later). But singers with pianos still weren't completely out of the woods when they tried to break in. Jerry Lee Lewis, who was just beginning to test the waters of the music business, was told by one adviser to drop the piano in favor of a guitar. Jerry Lee's reply was characteristically blunt in suggesting what that person could do with a guitar. By 1957 Jerry Lee was creating uninhibited, mad music that drew on Mullican, Moore, Hall, and black pianists like Cecil Gant. Jerry Lee continued with that piano style, adapting it to straight country, through the sixties and seventies, and is still rocking and honky-tonking into the eighties.

When rock 'n' roll sent Nashville reeling in the 1950s, country producers began looking for a way to recover from slipping record sales and radio airplay. A major part of the solution they came up with was the pop-flavored "Nashville Sound," and in the vanguard of that sound was a pianist who would set trends for many years, Floyd Cramer.

Floyd Cramer began his career in 1951, playing piano on the Louisiana Hayride in Shreveport, backing the show's artists. In 1955 he went to Nashville and began working sessions, including Elvis's "Heartbreak Hotel" session in 1956. Cramer's threatening piano riff on the instrumental break is a distinctive feature of the recording. In 1958, Cramer had his first instrumental hit for RCA with "Flip, Flop, and Bop." Then, around 1959, when he was scheduled to do a session with RCA singer Hank Locklin, producer Chet Atkins played him a demo of a song titled "Please Help Me, I'm Falling," sung by the song's coauthor, Don Robertson. Robertson accompanied himself on the piano, and he had developed what became known as the "slipnote" style, using chromatic grace notes to create a sound reminiscent of pedal steel. Atkins suggested that Cramer compose an instrumental in that style: the result was "Last Date," with a sound that became so popular that it's now as ubiquitous as Merle Travis's fingerpicking.

One country singer-pianist who was able to walk the thin line between country and rock in the early sixties, and with even greater success in the mid-seventies, was Charlie Rich. Rich had a background in jazz, gospel, and rhythm and blues, and he parlayed it into early successes with "Lonely Weekend" in 1960 and "Mohair Sam" in 1965. After a period of obscurity he resurfaced, still accompanying himself on piano with a bluesy, jazz-influenced country style that brought him a string of hits, beginning in 1972.

The keyboard was also featured in the acts of more traditional artists. During the World War II years Sally Ann Forrester played accordion in Bill Monroe's Blue Grass Boys, and Roy Acuff used the late Jimmie Riddle on piano for years. Jim Reeves was so insistent on a decent piano for his pianist, Dean Manuel, that he would delay or even cancel shows for lack of a respectable instrument. By the early seventies, more singers than ever played pianos. The late Marty Robbins, who closed the last set of the Grand Ole Opry for years, played piano almost as much as he did guitar. Ray Stevens was solidly established as a country and cross-over artist (and as arranger and producer), and Ronnie Milsap moved from rhythm and blues in Memphis to sign with RCA Nashville in 1973. Billy Swan (former keyboard player with Kris Kristofferson) and Gary Stewart, both of whom played both guitar and piano onstage, became popular. In 1975 Jessi Colter, another piano-playing singer, had a hit with her composition, "I'm Not Lisa." Not all of these players had styles as distinctive as those of Jerry Lee Lewis or Floyd Cramer, but the piano was an important part of the rhythmic structure of their music.

Meantime, the importance of the piano in the recording studios was coming to be appreciated. Hargus "Pig" Robbins joined Local 257 (Nashville) of the musicians' union in 1957, and played the piano behind artists ranging from Porter Wagoner to Bob Dylan on a slew of hits; he won the Country Music Association Entertainer of the Year award in 1976. A number of session pianists have emerged in Robbins's wake, including Randy Goodrum, a successful songwriter as well as a flawless studio pianist, David Briggs, successful producer Larry Butler (who began on the other side of the window), Bill Pursell, Bobby Wood, and Bobby Emmons, to name a few.

PIANO STYLES

An essential country piano style is the "slipnote" style developed by Don Robertson and popularized by Floyd Cramer. It has a distinctively country flavor and seems to work with just about any style of country music except Western swing.

As for the Western swing piano playing of Papa Calhoun and Al Stricklin, both of those players used basic piano jazz styles of the 1920s and 1930s to create their sound, particularly the playing of Teddy Wilson and Earl "Fatha" Hines, two giants of jazz piano. Moon Mullican's style had more blues in it than either Calhoun's or Stricklin's did, and the boogie-woogie elements that emerged in his playing after World War II were very different from the standard Western swing styles.

The Mullican style, improved upon by Merrill Moore, formed the basis of the rockabilly piano styles of Jerry Lee Lewis and Mickey Gilley, but an equally powerful influence (and possibly an influence on Mullican's boogie style as well) was the piano playing of black singer and instrumentalist Cecil Gant, who recorded in Nashville for Bullet Records in the late 1940s.

The Del Wood piano style owes far more to the barrelhouse and ragtime styles of the early parts of this century, but its raucous, uninhibited sound, concentrating on up-tempo stompers, is much like the ragtime of player pianos at times.

PIANO RECORDINGS

Various Artists

Blue Ridge Piano Styles (Blue Ridge Institute Records BRI–005) displays the work of performers from just one area of the upland South, but it covers a wide range of styles and a long span of time—half the cuts were recorded between 1924 and 1929, the others in 1979. Performers include the Shelor Family, Hobart Smith (possibly his only available piano recording), the Highlanders (assembled anonymously by Charlie Poole when Columbia, his label, wouldn't let him record with piano), and present-day performers from the area. There are some blues, ragtime, and old pop numbers on this enjoyable album, but particularly interesting are those that are closely connected with the string band tradition of the Blue Ridge. For anyone learning to play country piano, this album could serve as a most useful primer. You can hear the evolution of a piano style derived from and meant to accompany music played on fiddle and banjo.

Floyd Cramer

Cramer has cut dozens of albums for RCA over the past twenty years or so, but *The Best of Floyd Cramer* (RCA Victor AHL–1-3096) contains all the essentials, including his first hit, "Flip, Flop, and Bop," and the classics that introduced his style, "Last Date" and "On the Rebound," as well as renditions of "Columbus Stockade Blues" and other hits. For a good, solid introduction to the slipnote/pedal-guitar piano style that Don Robertson invented and Cramer popularized, this is the album to get.

Moon Mullican

The Unforgettable Moon Mullican (Starday 398) does not contain the classic Moon Mullican King recordings of the late 1940s and early 1950s, when he was creating not only fine country music, but superb boogie-based piano that still echos today. He was older and less uninhibited when this material was cut in the late fifties. Still, it's possible to hear the basics of his style on the rerecorded versions of "Cherokee Boogie," "Jole Blon," "I'll Sail My Ship Alone," and the rest. A better survey of Mullican, looking at the swinging, rocking music he did for King that inspired so many, is *Seven Nights to Rock* (Western 2001), a collection of stomping up-tempo songs leased from King Records, including some incredible piano passages on "Well, Oh, Well," the classic opening riff on "Cherokee Boogie," and other examples of Moon at his peak.

Merrill Moore

A British import, *20 Golden Pieces of Merrill Moore* (Bulldog BDL–2011) features a pianist whose style was as dynamic (if not more so) as Mullican's, on his classic Capitol recordings from the early 1950s. Backed by peerless L.A. studio pickers like guitarist Jimmy Bryant and steel guitarist Speedy West, Merrill Moore combines an ingratiating vocal style with piano work derived from boogie-woogie and barrelhouse styles. He can rattle your teeth with his fiery version of the old pop/schlock classic "Nola" and anticipate Jerry Lee Lewis with "Cooing to the Wrong Pigeon." Hearing it once will not only make you want to play along if you have a piano but will let you see that rockabilly was around long before anyone really realized what it was. Aspiring Jerry Lees and Gilleys should pay special heed to the music on this one.

Fred Calhoun (with Milton Brown and His Musical Brownies)

Country and Western Dance-O-Rama (Western 1001) is a reissue of a long out-of-print ten-inch Decca LP. Calhoun is performing here with Milton Brown and His Musical Brownies, and his playing is particularly prominent on "St. Louis Blues," "Sweet Jennie Lee," "Texas Hambone Blues," and "Right Or Wrong." He can be heard applying his jazzy style to a traditional country song on the recording of "Washington and Lee Swing." Since these sessions marked some of the earliest infusions of the piano into Western swing (and an early stage of its role as a lead instrument, featured prominently in any sort of country band), it's highly worthwhile.

Al Stricklin (with Bob Wills and His Texas Playboys)

Al Stricklin wasn't the only pianist to work with Wills during the 1935–1946 period when Wills recorded for Columbia, but he was prominent on all Wills recordings up to the beginning of World War II. On *The Bob Wills Anthology* (Columbia PG–32416) his playing stands out on "Steel Guitar Rag," "Corrina, Corrina," and "That's What I Like About the South," and he gets in some bluesy licks on "Honey, What You Gonna Do?" that are unusual in the context of his jazzier playing. He also plays a hot chorus on "Twin Guitar Special" and, probably among his finest work, a memorable break on the Wills classic "Take Me Back to Tulsa."

Jerry Lee Lewis

Just about any Jerry Lee album on any label will provide liberal doses of his piano playing, but *Jerry Lee Lewis—Original Golden Hits Volume 1* (Sun International 102) has all the classics of the fifties, in the same boogie-blues style that he's used ever since he started to play. The piano is everywhere, on "Great Balls of Fire," "Whole Lotta Shakin' Going On," "You Win Again," "Crazy Arms," and "Lewis Boogie." It's easy to hear the echoes of Mullican and Moore in his playing but neither was quite as maniacal about it as the Killer himself. This is the best introduction to the Jerry Lee experience, an album available in just about any good record store. There are countless others to pick from, including his Smash and Mercury albums (often available in budget bins at dirt-cheap prices), and a number of other Sun LPs, not to mention his current work on Elektra.

Those whose appetite for the Killer's music is as heroic as the man himself might want to consider *Jerry Lee Lewis—The Sun Years* (Charly Sun Box 102). This is a twelve-LP boxed set that brings together virtually everything Jerry Lee recorded for Sun from 1956 until he left the label in 1963. The variety turns out to be surprising. Not only are there multiple takes of his greatest hits (permitting one to hear their step-by-step creation), there are also unissued recordings, a surprising number of hard-core country instrumentals, a few oddities, and some weird, occasionally unprintable, studio conversations. You can hear him rocking madly, and then turning around and recording the sort of pure country that revived his career in the late 1960s (the songs are arranged in chronological order). A sumptuously illustrated, informative book chronicles his Sun career and detailed notes on the sleeve of each disc cover every cut. The price is around $75, which seems pretty reasonable.

Charlie Rich

The Original Charlie Rich (Charly CR–30112) is a superb, sixteen-track British anthology that contains some of the finest examples of Rich's piano-based music, long before he had the title of "Silver Fox." His piano is featured prominently on most of the tracks, and on one, "Red Man," it's quite easy to hear the disparate elements in his music: the bluesiness and the subtle but clear traces of his love for jazz. It's also easy to hear how he integrated the piano into his music in a role that continued through his early hits and still does, though he has occasionally used studio pianists in recent years.

PIANO INSTRUCTION

We haven't been able to find a book that actually sets out to teach country piano. That's probably understandable, since there aren't that many clearly identifiable "country" piano styles that can't be incorporated into other kinds of music as well. Perhaps someone will someday write a decent instruction book dealing with the techniques of Cramer, Mullican, Stricklin, and company, but as of this writing there is nothing. However, there are piano books in other areas that should be able to help you get some ideas. Combining that with listening to records, you can probably teach yourself enough to do pretty well.

The Joy of Boogie and Blues (Music Sales) is a book of basic to intermediate piano solos—thirty-one blues and boogie numbers that should be excellent for getting started in boogie-woogie or rockabilly piano.

The Joy of Jazz (Music Sales), in the same series, features basic to intermediate piano solos by players like Fats Waller, Jimmy Dorsey, and some modern jazz solos as well. If you're just getting into piano, and have aspirations to play Western swing, this might be a good start.

How to Play Blues Piano by Eric Kriss (Music Sales) is an excellent instruction book for anyone who's been playing piano for at least a while. Kriss lays out some of the major styles as well as bass lines, chord structure, etc. Each chapter examines a different aspect of blues piano, from boogie-woogie to stride to barrelhouse piano, all valuable.

Barrelhouse and Boogie Piano by Eric Kriss (Music Sales) is probably the perfect companion for the player who's mastered the previous book. This one examines transcribed solos from records by Jelly Roll Morton, Memphis Slim, Meade Lux Lewis, and others. This should get you well on the road to learning any of their styles, combined with listening to your chosen pianist on records.

Introduction to the Blues by Matt Dennis (Mel Bay) examines the basic rhythmic and harmonic concepts of the blues.

Blues Piano Styles by Matt Dennis (Mel Bay) looks at individual blues styles for the intermediate student.

Piano Boogie by Rene Faure (Mel Bay) includes a number of boogie-woogie piano solos.

Preparatory Studies for Jazz Piano (Mel Bay) is a book for the intermediate pianist who's interested in going into jazz improvisation.

How to Play Jazz Piano by Stuart Isacoff (Music Sales) is a good beginning for the newly interested pianist who wants to learn something about jazz improvisation (perfect for would-be Western swingers). It looks at the individual styles of players like George Gershwin (and older players as well), breaking them down so the student can understand what makes each style distinctive.

Floyd Cramer Hits Arranged in Floyd Cramer Style (Acuff-Rose), while not an instruction book, is an invaluable guide to the most famous Nashville Sound piano style. It contains sixteen Floyd Cramer piano solos carefully transcribed by Bill McElhiney, who did the original orchestral arrangements for the recordings of most of the songs included here.

STEEL GUITAR

The steel guitar was developed in Hawaii toward the end of the nineteenth century and soon became popular in America. After Hawaii became a U.S. territory in 1900, a fascination with its culture swept America, and Hawaiian music, complete with the steel guitar, became a part of numerous vaudeville stage shows across the country. For the most part the instruments themselves were not very different from traditional "Spanish" guitars, in some cases distinguished only by a small shim that fit over the instrument's nut to raise the strings for Hawaiian playing.

The sliding, voice-like tones of the steel became extremely popular in America by the 1920s. Door-to-door salesmen peddled steel guitars everywhere, along with home study courses for the instrument. Many young players—a few of whom later became important instrumentalists—got their start this way. Native Hawaiians opened up guitar studios here on the mainland. The major guitar makers, Gibson and Martin among them, built Hawaiian guitars of excellent quality.

By the mid-twenties country musicians were gravitating to the steel. Among the first known to have done so was singer-guitarist Frank Hutchinson, who may have been the first country music performer to feature the instrument. Cliff Carlisle played one while performing with his brother Bill. And a major boost to its popularity in a country context came when Jimmie Rodgers began using it on recordings like "Blue Yodel #2" (played by Ellsworth Cozzens), "Waiting for a Train" (played by John Westbrook), and "My Rough and Rowdy Ways" (played by native Hawaiian Joe Kaipo.)

In 1931 the Rickenbacker Company of California developed the first electric Hawaiian steel. An all-aluminum instrument with a small round body attached to the neck, it was quickly dubbed the "frying pan" for an obvious resemblance. It is doubtful that any country performers used it, given the innate conservatism of most country musicians of the period. It was not until the mid-thirties that any country musicians deigned to go electric. The first man who did was an Oklahoman named Bob Dunn, who had started out as a Hawaiian guitarist and toured with Hawaiian bands. He had a strong interest in jazz and in 1934 he joined the pioneering Western swing band, Milton Brown and His Musical Brownies. Dunn used a hybrid instrument. He took a small Martin O-series acoustic guitar, raised the strings, attached a Volu-Tone pickup to it, and connected it

Merle Travis's Bigsby electric guitar (Country Music Foundation)

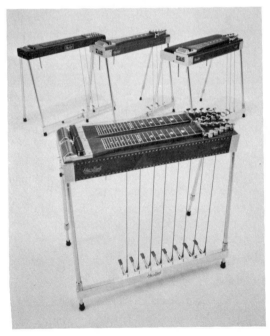

Cousin Jody's Gibson lap steel guitar (Country Music Foundation)

A Sho-Bud doubleneck pedal steel guitar

Instruments in the steel or "slide" guitar family have a similar number and gauge of steel strings as conventional guitars, and similar resonant bodies (in acoustic instruments) or magnetic pickup systems (in electric instruments). However, the method of altering the pitch of the strings is completely different. Steel guitars are played unfretted; in fact, the strings are not stopped against the neck at all. Instead, a metal, ceramic, or glass bar is pressed against the strings from above to effectively change their length and thus the notes they produce. Sliding the bar from position to position produces a much different effect from lifting and moving it; both techniques are used in slide steel playing.

The dobro, covered in an earlier chapter, has evolved as the predominant acoustic form of the slide guitar in country music. As explained in the introduction to the guitar chapter, steel-string guitars began to be electronically amplified in the 1930s. This eventually gave rise to solid-body electric slide instruments, which in turn gave rise to the pedal guitar.

In a pedal steel guitar, the strings are connected to as many as four knee levers and eight foot pedals that can be pushed to change the pitch of a note before or while it is being sounded. Many pedal steel guitars have two necks, each tuned to a different open chord: E9 and C6 are among the most common tunings; in a ten-string pedal steel they begin two octaves below middle C and ascend as follows:

String No.	10	9	8	7	6	5	4	3	2	1
								middle		
C6		C	F	A	C	E	G	A	C	E	G
E9		B	D	E	F#	G#	B	E	G#	D#	F#

(In E9, the D# of string 2 is between the B and E of strings 5 and 4; the F# of string 1 is between the E and G# of strings 4 and 3.)

to an amplifier the size of a cereal box. The solos Dunn played with the Brownies owed far more allegiance to jazz than to the Hawaiian music he'd started out playing. He made an indelible impression on many young Texas musicians. After Milton Brown's death in 1936, the Brownies scattered and Dunn became a popular sideman in a number of Texas Western swing bands.

One of Dunn's biggest admirers was a youngster named Leon McAuliffe. McAuliffe attended dances played by the Brownies specifically to hear Dunn, and was paid the compliment of being permitted to sit in on Dunn's steel while Dunn refreshed himself at the bar. McAuliffe was hired to play acoustic steel with the Light Crust Doughboys, then moved to Tulsa in 1935 to join Bob Wills and His Texas Playboys. Shortly after arriving there, McAuliffe impressed Wills with an instrumental he titled "Steel Guitar

Rag," a mixture of black musician Sylvester Weaver's "Guitar Rag" and part of a Hawaiian tune titled "On the Beach at Waikiki." The song became a favorite, and soon Wills bought McAuliffe a Volu-Tone pickup and amp for *his* steel.

Despite the limitations of early steel guitar technology (McAuliffe recalls using a pickup of unusual design that required having to run a bar magnet up and down the strings to magnetize them before playing), McAuliffe and Dunn became very influential as soloists on the electric steel, though Dunn, with his stronger jazz orientation, initially had much more impact. Gradually McAuliffe gained skill, maturity, and authority and developed a style of his own.

Through the late 1930s evolving steel guitar technology—including the development of doubleneck models—had a dramatic effect on playing styles. Epiphone developed a doubleneck model constructed of aluminum (favored by McAuliffe). Increasing numbers of talented guitarists began applying themselves to the steel. Some, like Emil Hofner of Jimmie Revard's Oklahoma Playboys, fused a Hawaiian style with that of Bob Dunn. Others, Noel Boggs for example, blazed more individualistic trails. An Oklahoman with a strong jazz orientation, Boggs made some excellent recordings in 1939 with Hank Penny and His Radio Cowboys, and later had a massive influence on steel playing. Boggs was also an early convert to the doubleneck steel, obtaining one about the same time McAuliffe did. By then, many steels were no longer held in the lap, but instead were attached to stands similar to those that held sheet music. And the versatility of the instrument was enhanced by the advent of foot-controlled volume pedals that made new and different effects possible (such as a "wah-wah" sound similar to the trumpet effect produced by opening and closing a mute).

Other talented swing steel players of the early 1940s included the innovative but obscure Billy Briggs of the Sons of the West, who played high-register chord solos in a style wholly different from Dunn's, McAuliffe's, or Boggs's. Gradually Dunn's star— though not his talents—began to fade in the world of commercial music. He obtained advanced degrees in music, continued playing steel, and crusaded to give it credibility in the jazz field up until his death in 1969. McAuliffe, on the other hand, gained increasing renown on the instrument.

In mainstream country music in the 1940s the amplified steel, like all electric instruments, had a rough time gaining a foothold. Electric steel guitarists were around: Charlie Mitchell, who co-wrote "You Are My Sunshine" with Jimmie Davis and played in Davis's band, was one. But on the Grand Ole Opry it was another story. Sam McGee, the famous fingerpicker who worked the Opry for decades with his brother Kirk, told historian Charles Wolfe in the early 1970s about his experience playing a National electric lap steel on the Opry in the late 1930s. "I got by with it for two Saturday nights," he reported. "And on the third Saturday night I was ready to play. . . and Judge Hay came out and tapped me on the shoulder, said 'Sam, I'd rather you not play that on the Grand Ole Opry; we want to hold it down to earth.' " McGee complied.

But by the mid-1940s, Pee Wee King and Ernest Tubb, among others, had managed to push this rule to the side. Some skillful musicians were emerging among the tiny cadre of Nashville steel players, including Clyde "Boots" Harris of Curley Williams's

Georgia Peach Pickers, the teenaged Billy Bowman with Paul Howard's Arkansas Cotton Pickers, and Jerry Byrd, who worked with Ernest Tubb briefly in the forties.

In the meantime, other talented steel players were emerging in the Southwest. By 1945 Noel Boggs, then working in California, was one of the premiere steel players in Western swing and a valued member of Bob Wills's Texas Playboys. His brittle, metallic chord solos on Wills tunes like "Roly Poly" and "Texas Playboy Rag" showed a harmonic sophistication that influenced an entire generation of steel guitarists. His use of dynamics revealed an unusual skill for that time. His tone itself could create excitement, even on a relatively simple number like "Steel Guitar Stomp," which he recorded with Hank Penny in 1945. Just his tone and attack, bolstered by Merle Travis's pulsating electric guitar, make the song something to be experienced, even forty years later.

Noel Boggs was not the only steel virtuoso on the West Coast. Another was Earl "Joaquin" Murphey, who was discovered by Spade Cooley's band. Still a teenager, Murphey had initially balked at taking steel guitar lessons, but then developed the talent of a prodigy. His approach to chord melodies and single string soloing was unprecedented for the time. One could hear overtones of Benny Goodman or Django Reinhardt in Murphey's style. Working with Cooley, he contributed outstanding solos to numbers such as "Three Way Boogie" and "Oklahoma Stomp" and would go on to record incredible instrumental solos on tunes like "Honeysuckle Rose" and "Sweet Georgia Brown" as part of the cowboy vocal group Andy Parker and the Plainsmen, where he was a featured and valued soloist. Murphey worked with other performers, among them Merle Travis, T. Texas Tyler, Tex Williams, and again with Cooley. His greatest liability throughout his career was an idiosyncratic moodiness that surfaced when he'd walk offstage if the music being played displeased him. As a result his brilliance never brought him the mass acclaim it should have, and Murphey has spurned interviewers.

The steels themselves were still evolving. A new group of innovative craftsmen—located largely in Southern California—began to make improvements in their design. One of these craftsmen was a radio repairman and veteran tinkerer named Leo Fender, who had built steel guitars and amplifiers in the past. Fender began building multi-neck steel guitars that were happily received by players like Noel Boggs (who rarely, if ever, used any other brand). Bob Wills became an early friend of Leo Fender, and an endorser of the brand. Another of these steel craftsmen was inventor Paul Bigsby, who built some of the earliest solid-body electric guitars (though Fender had built one before him, and Rickenbacker introduced one before Fender); Bigsby made some excellent steels.

One player who road-tested Fender's early multi-neck steels was Herb Remington. An Indiana native, Remington had played Hawaiian music on the steel since he was a boy, and joined Wills's Texas Playboys after leaving the army in 1946. Although Remington was solidly rooted in Hawaiian music, his mastery of the A6 tuning gave him a distinctive harmonic edge in his work with Wills. He was responsible for instrumentals such as "Boot Heel Drag" and "Playboy Chimes" that show off his driving style to good advantage. Remington, who went on to work with Hank Penny (with whom he wrote the steel classic "Remington Ride"), remains one of the handful of Western swing steel innovators still active today.

By the late 1940s Nashville was beginning to boast its own fine group of steel players, some influenced by the sophisticated players on the West Coast. Yet one steel guitarist stood out head and shoulders above any other: Jerry Byrd. Like Herb Remington, Byrd had roots in Hawaiian music. His tone was warm and mellow, his touch and phrasing impeccable. He had become the primary steel guitarist used on recordings in Nashville. For a time he worked with Red Foley's band, the Pleasant Valley Boys. The band later left Foley and went as a unit to Cincinnati, where Byrd played on countless records, including some by Hank Williams.

Byrd's influence was considerable. Countless steel players of all ages wrote him at the Opry to ask about his tuning (he usually obliged with the information). In 1949 he had a hit of his own with "Steelin' the Blues." Other popular Nashville steel players included Don Davis, who worked extensively with Pee Wee King and Joe Talbot; and, in the late 1940s, Don Helms. Helms played the brilliant, high-register, crying steel guitar on Hank Williams's recordings (after 1950), as part of Hank's Drifting Cowboys Band. None of these Nashville players displayed great improvisational skills, as Murphey, Boggs, and Remington did; the very nature of the music they played precluded that. Their strength lay in their ability to color a song and to complement its lyrics in a way that most of the West Coast swing players did not.

In the meantime the innovations in technique continued to appear in California. In the late 1940s, a Missouri-bred steel guitarist named Wesley Webb West, better known as "Speedy," began to be heard. West's strength was not improvisation but a romping musical flamboyance uniquely his. After stints with Spade Cooley and Hank Penny, West joined the "Hometown Jamboree" radio show headed by performer and entrepreneur Cliffie Stone. Speedy's style included swooping, crashing chords that exploded like a volcanic bubble, achieved via manipulation of the tone control, and chords that "skittered" up the neck as he manipulated the steel bar in his left hand. He became a studio musician of enormous productivity, recording with everyone from Tennessee Ernie Ford to Kay Starr and Paul Weston's Orchestra. He also recorded a series of brilliant instrumentals with guitarist Jimmy Bryant (the duo was known as the "Flaming Guitars") for Capitol. Their work featured exciting, daring instrumental interplay that still sounds fresh three decades after it was cut.

Speedy West was also one of the first swing players to use a *pedal* steel guitar. Gibson had introduced the Electraharp pedal steel guitar early in the forties, and an L.A. musician named Dick Roberts had used a pedal instrument in the mid-forties, but West was among the first Californians to take serious advantage of this new development. He was followed by Wayne Burdick, who worked with Tex Williams in the early 1950s, using an Electraharp. The pedal steel principle itself was simple: the individual strings were linked by levers and cables to a set of pedals. Pushing various pedals changed the pitch of their associated strings and created different types of chords. In this way the harmonic limitations imposed by straight steel bar chording of a fixed open tuning were overcome.

Western swing's popularity began to fade in the early fifties, although a few innovators still managed to break through to an audience. Billy Bowman joined Bob Wills's Texas Playboys, where he contributed some outstanding work (including the instrumental classic

"B. Bowman Hop"), and in Sacramento a teenage prodigy named Vance Terry was playing a Bigsby pedal steel and blazing trails with Billy Jack Wills's Western Swing Band. Another fine swing player, Bobby Koefer, also played with Bob Wills for a time. But none of these later swing players achieved the fame of McAuliffe, Boggs, and Murphey. As rock 'n' roll loomed on the horizon, Western swing steel guitarists began fading away. A few fine ones, like Bobby Garrett and Bob White, continued with Hank Thompson's Brazos Valley Boys (one of the few big Western swing bands to survive), but most of the others moved for the time being into obscurity.

At this point the locus of the steel guitar's progress shifted to the Southeast, where a talented group of players continued to expand. Byrd was still at the forefront. Helms was still highly successful (his licks on Hank Williams's recordings are still quoted by today's steel players). Little Roy Wiggins, whose playing remained in the Hawaiian tradition, was highly respected for his restrained work behind Eddy Arnold. But the winds of change were blowing in Nashville, in the form of the pedal steel. A devoted Jerry Byrd follower named Bud Isaacs was attracted to the pedal steel sound and got an Electraharp while he was still a teenager. By the early fifties he had joined Little Jimmy Dickens's raucous, exciting band, the Country Boys, and in 1953 he left to freelance and to record for RCA. One release was "Bud's Bounce," which became a steel guitar standard. In 1953 he began working recording sessions in Nashville, and on "There Stands the Glass" and "Slowly" the Isaacs four-neck Bigsby stood out clearly. "Slowly," which was written to feature the pedal steel, became one of the top country hits of 1954 and started a country music revolution.

Countless non-pedal players were driven to distraction trying to figure out what Bud Isaacs was doing. Some tried pushing the strings down above the nut with their fingers. Others unsuccessfully tried screwball ways of slanting their bars. But a few figured it out and either built their own contraptions to pull the strings of their steels, or else simply invested in a pedal steel, generally the less frustrating approach.

The pedal steel quickly became an accepted part of country music recording in the fifties, and a number of talented musicians came to prominence with it. One was Buddy Emmons, an Indiana native who grew up a fan of Jerry Byrd and Joaquin Murphey, and who had jammed with everyone from country musicians to bebop guitarist Arvin Garrison. Emmons became a major force in the development of the steel. He was already demonstrating considerable talent when he joined Jimmy Dickens's Country Boys in 1955. By 1957 he and dobroist Shot Jackson were producing their own Sho-Bud pedal steels.

The advent of rock 'n' roll temporarily halted the pedal steel's conquest of country music. Many performers felt it and the fiddle were too "country" and replaced their fiddlers and steel players with drummers. Still, this was not a universal view. Singers like Ernest Tubb and Ray Price simply ignored the trends. However, some of the newer generation of country singers—including Johnny Cash—didn't dare to use steel, as they felt it inappropriate to their sound.

For a time in the late 1950s the steel had a certain element of gimmickry, touched off by Santo and Johnny's pop recording of "Sleepwalk." In the meantime Emmons continued his jazz experiments with superb recordings like "Four Wheel Drive," which showed him as the best jazz steel player in the business at the time. It certainly contrasted with the simpler work he was doing as a sideman with Ernest Tubb. In 1963 Emmons scored another first with his Mercury LP *Steel Guitar Jazz* (now available as Steel Guitar Record Club #5 from PSG Products). The first true pedal steel album to explore the jazz idiom, it was recorded in New York City with top talent and remains a milestone steel guitar disc.

But hard-country players were also emerging as major talents. Among them was Pete Drake, who created the "talking guitar," basing it on an old electronic gimmick pop steelman Alvino Rey had used in the 1930s. He used it on sides by Roger Miller and Jim Reeves and had a hit with the sound, titled "Forever." Drake became a formidable country player able to give an artist or record producer any licks or sound he wanted.

Two other capable Nashville steel players were Lloyd Green, who was devoted to the E9 tuning commonly used by country steel players (as opposed to the C6 or A6 tunings favored by swing and jazz players—most two-neck pedal steels have E9 and C6 tunings). Green became known for his recording work on Warner Mack's "The Bridge Washed Out" and on Johnny Paycheck's early hits. Another was Jimmy Day, who began his career in the Louisiana Hayride staff band and worked with both Willie Nelson and Ray Price. His chord-based sound made extensive use of pedals to create rhythmic, swirling chords that came out on the beat.

Curly Chalker was also in a class by himself. An Alabama native and Jerry Byrd devotee who gravitated toward Western swing, Chalker worked with Lefty Frizzell, Hank Thompson, Billy Grey, and Hank Penny (with Penny's 1960s Las Vegas band) before moving to Nashville. His style was his own—although it had clear overtones of Noel Boggs and Joaquin Murphey, he played with a cooler sense of phrasing, and his quaking vibrato added an interesting contrast. Chalker's blunt and plainspoken attitudes kept him from becoming a fixture in the studios as Drake and Green did. However, he quickly became known as a musician's musician.

One artist who brought the pedal steel to a wider audience than ever ironically was Bob Dylan. When Dylan began recording in Nashville about 1965, he came in contact with a variety of talented musicians. In 1967, when he recorded his *John Wesley Harding* LP (Columbia JC–9604), he used Pete Drake on steel guitar. In 1968 the folk-rock band the Byrds, fascinated with country music, recorded their LP *Sweetheart of the Rodeo* (Columbia PC–9670) in Nashville, using Lloyd Green on the sessions. Dylan again used Drake on his *Nashville Skyline* (Columbia JC–9825) in 1969. Suddenly rock writers and fans were listening to the steel guitar with considerable interest, and other rock bands and performers were recording with Pete Drake in Nashville, among them Ringo Starr.

A number of rock musicians, the Grateful Dead's Jerry Garcia for one, began playing pedal steel onstage and on records, which brought the instrument to a wider audience. The Flying Burrito Brothers, founded by the late Gram Parsons, featured the crystal-clear licks of Sneaky Pete Kleinow. Buddy Emmons, who had moved to California, began doing numerous sessions with folk and rock musicians like John Sebastian and Judy Collins.

Another lesser-known school of steel had emerged in California in the 1960s, led by Ralph Mooney, a veteran steel player. Mooney became a pedal player and began working in the Bakersfield honky-tonks. He developed a trebly, high-pitched style that graced many of Buck Owens's early recordings and became a component of the famous "Bakersfield sound" of the 1960s, a modern sound built around electric guitars and steel. Mooney's excellence inspired others like Tom Brumley, who worked in Buck Owens's Buckaroos.

Brumley also jumped on the rock bandwagon when he joined Rick Nelson's group, the Stone Canyon Band, around 1970. The rock influence became most noticeable as steel guitarists, who rarely used any electronic effects other than reverb or a bit of echo, began to avail themselves of the new devices that rock guitarists had inspired: fuzztone, wah-wah, Leslie organ speakers, phasers, and all the rest. Various steel players developed a rock emphasis, Poco's Rusty Young among them. (Young started out playing straightforward country with this country-and-western rock unit; he gradually became an excellent rock steel player.)

Within country music itself a new generation of players who had cut their teeth not on Jerry Byrd or Joaquin Murphy, but on Buddy Emmons and Bud Isaacs, came to the forefront. They included Doug Jernigan, Sonny Garrish, and Paul Franklin, all of whom had their own approaches to the instrument. Meanwhile, some established steel players continued to be involved in instrument design. Maurice Anderson, who has worked in Texas Western swing bands, founded his MSA steel guitar manufacturing concern. Buddy Emmons, having left Sho-Bud, founded his own Emmons company.

And what happened in the middle of all this? Back came Western swing, which everybody had written off in the 1950s. Merle Haggard's 1970 tribute LP to Bob Wills had stirred many. A new generation interested in the music was an inspiration to the players. Two bands, Asleep at the Wheel and Commander Cody and His Lost Planet Airmen, led the way as young people not even born when Bob Wills was in his heyday began to appreciate the music. Two prominent steel guitarists emerged from this new school. One was Reuben "Lucky Oceans" Gosfield, who worked with Asleep at the Wheel and was clearly inspired by Noel Boggs and Joaquin Murphey. The other, Bobby Black, was not really a newcomer; he had worked in San Francisco–area Western swing bands in the 1950s and knew the idiom inside out. But both men became leaders of the renewed interest in Western swing.

The revival also brought Leon McAuliffe, who had largely retired, back to the forefront, playing for an entirely different generation. Speedy West, who had been selling trailers in Tulsa, also came out of retirement as interest in the music grew. A few of the older greats unfortunately missed it. Noel Boggs died in 1974, and Joaquin Murphey had all but quit music (though he recorded again in 1976). As for Jerry Byrd, who inspired so many country players, he drifted from country music back to Hawaiian music. He subsequently moved to the Islands, where he has become a revered part of the Hawaiian music scene, still ignoring the pedal steel.

Today the pedal steel is as strong in Nashville as ever, though Nashville's pop-oriented producers and performers rarely use it because of its "country" overtones. Still, Moe Bandy, Gene Watson, and countless other performers never quit using it on sessions and onstage. Although Pete Drake now does mostly production, Sonny Garrish and Hal Rugg, both fine country pedal players, do extensive session work. Emmons, Franklin, Mooney, Weldon Myrick, and Lloyd Green likewise continue to make major contributions to the advancement of the instrument.

One major area of development in the steel guitar of today is the quality of instruction available. While before most players had to learn the instrument by the seat of their pants, the past decade has brought enormous improvements in the quality of instructional materials. Books and complete courses have become available, and veteran Grand Ole Opry steel guitarists Jeff Newman and Jimmy Crawford have their own steel guitar schools, with both permanent facilities and regular seminars around the country. Today, those who want to play Lloyd Green or Buddy Emmons solos can likely find them transcribed. Those who need instruction in the basics can attend a classroom course, get fine print and tape courses, or find excellent private instruction.

The pedal steel has become a fixture in country music and probably will never lose its popularity. Its unique technology, which developed in time between that of traditional instruments and instruments of the electronic synthesizer age, permits a distinct kind of emotional expressiveness. It voicelike sound has the same haunting effect that attracted people to the earliest Hawaiian guitars. Instruments that can evoke that type of emotion will always be a part of country music.

STEEL GUITAR STYLES

There are a myriad of steel guitar playing styles. Some are primarily accompaniment for a singer, providing fills, brief solo passages, and licks for color. In standard country music, these licks are usually played in the widely accepted E9 tuning. Pop and jazz music is generally played in the C6 (Buddy Emmons's rapid-fire jazz improvisations, for example) or A6 tuning, as is Western swing, since these are more suited to pop and jazz chords and harmonies. There are variations; for example, an increasing number of players use a "universal" tuning, which combines the various harmonies of the E9 and C6 tunings.

STEEL GUITAR RECORDINGS

Various Artists

Steel Guitar Classics (Old Timey LP–113), released in 1973, gives a fascinating look at pre–World War II uses of the steel guitar in country music, with a bit of insight into its Hawaiian roots as well. The Hawaiian background is shown through a rendition of "Farewell Blues" by Sol Hoopii's Trio, and "Tomi, Tomi" by Kanui and Lula. The American country tracks include Jimmie Tarlton, who recorded with the Hawaiian acoustic steel from 1927 to 1932; some early Cliff Carlisle recordings; and some early recordings featuring Jimmie Davis, composer of "You Are My Sunshine," backed by black steel guitarist Oscar Woods. There are also two fine Roy Acuff–Clell Summey performances from 1938: the instrumental "Steel Guitar Chimes," adapted from Hawaiian music, and "Steel Guitar Blues."

Western Swing Volume 1 (Old Timey, LP–105), the first Western swing anthology released, features early sides by Bob Wills, including "Steel Guitar Rag" with Leon McAuliffe, and some Milton Brown material featuring Bob Dunn.

Bob Dunn

The work of Bob Dunn, the first Western swing electric steel guitarist, can best be heard on Milton Brown and His Musical Brownies' *Country and Western Dance-O-Rama* (Western WS–101), a ten-inch LP, and on *Taking Off!* (String STR–804). His work with other Texas bands is well represented on *Stompin' at the Honky-Tonk* (String STR–805), an anthology of tunes by 1930s and early 1940s Texas Western swing bands; several cuts feature Dunn.

Leon McAuliffe

Leon McAuliffe's work with Bob Wills and His Texas Playboys is well represented on record. Some of his best-known tunes, such as "Steel Guitar Rag" and "Twin Guitar Special," are included with many others on *The Bob Wills Anthology* (Columbia PG–32416), *Bob Wills* (Columbia Historical Series FC–37468), *Bob Wills* (Time-Life Country Classics 07), and *Lone Star Rag* (Columbia Encore Series P–14390). Unfortunately, recordings by McAuliffe's own excellent Western band, the Cimarron Boys, which he led from the late 1940s into the 1960s, are all but impossible to come by, save one less than first-rate LP, *Steel Guitar Rag* (Delta 1154), issued in Texas in 1982. It is possible, however, to hear some good McAuliffe work on Bob Wills's *For the Last Time* (United Artists LMBL–216), a 1973 LP that reunited many of Wills's Texas Playboys with their leader for a final collaboration.

Noel Boggs

Some of Noel Boggs's earliest recorded work as part of Hank Penny's Radio Cowboys can be heard on *Tobacco State Swing* (Rambler 103) and on the two-LP *OKeh Western Swing* album (Epic EG–37324), which features a fine Boggs instrumental, "Chill Tonic," never before issued. Some of his work with Bob Wills can be heard on the same Wills anthologies that feature Leon McAuliffe (the Time-Life set includes several Boggs showpieces, including "Texas Playboy Rag"). He can be heard on one track on *Spade Cooley* (Columbia Historic Edition FC–37467) and on several tracks on *The Best of Spade Cooley's Transcribed Shows, Vol. 1* (Club of Spade 101). Later work by Boggs includes *Noel Boggs and Friends—On Stage—Live* (Shasta 531), featuring some outstanding solos culled from cowboy singer Jimmy Wakely's 1950s CBS radio show.

Joaquin Murphey

All of Joaquin Murphey's best work with the early Spade Cooley band, including "Oklahoma Stomp," is available on *Spade Cooley* (Columbia Historical Series). Some truly outstanding work that he did with Tex Williams can be heard on some 1950–1951 Capitol transcriptions assembled on *Tex Williams and The Swingin' Western Caravan* (AFM 711, available from Ken Griffis). A late 1970s LP, *Joaquin Murphey* (Midland MD–12), shows him in excellent form for one who rarely performs. His single-string solo chops have mellowed, but have not diminished in their power.

Jerry Byrd

A reissue of a 1950s Mercury album, *Steel Guitar Favorites (Steel Guitar Vintage Classics No. 2)* (Mercury VC–2), contains some of Byrd's earliest and finest solo material, including his first hit, "Steelin' the Blues" (with cowboy singer Rex Allen, Sr., doing the vocal). It shows Byrd's shimmering, warm tone and exquisite touch at its peak. Hawaiian influences pervade the album, particularly on tracks like "Coconut Grove" and "Steelin' the Chimes." Many of the other tracks, steel guitar standards like "Panhandle Rag" and "Steel Guitar Rag," are equally well handled. Byrd, who now resides in Hawaii and plays Hawaiian styles exclusively, was the man who established the electric steel in Nashville; after listening to this, it's obvious why. (Available from PSG Products.)

Speedy West

Speedy West at one time was one of the most-recorded studio steel guitarists anywhere. Based on the West Coast through his greatest years, he was heavily influenced by players like Joaquin Murphey and Noel Boggs, and spent ample time playing Western swing. His extroverted style, combined with liberal doses of special effects—such as crashing the bar onto the strings to get an explosive sound—gained him considerable fame, but he had the musical talent to back it up. West recorded with everyone from Tennessee Ernie Ford to Paul Weston and His Orchestra in the early fifties. *Speedy* (Steel Guitar Record Club #11), compiled from his Capitol solo releases in the early fifties, features excellent notes by Speedy himself, with sixteen tracks of his style, which here owes nothing to electronic effects. He did it all with his steel and his hands. (Available from PSG Products.)

Herb Remington

Herb Remington emerged as a top steel player with Bob Wills and His Texas Playboys after World War II. *Jean Street Swing* (Steel Guitar Record Club #3) features some of his finest moments with Wills on originals that have since become steel guitar standards, like "Boot Heel Drag." It also looks at his fifties solo recordings, which show a solid combination of swing and Hawaiian influences. Some of Herb Remington's finest work with Bob Wills and His Texas Playboys not included on the *Jean Street Swing* collection is available on *24 Great Hits by Bob Wills and His Texas Playboys* (MGM 2-5305).

Vance Terry

Vance Terry, whose steel drove the Billy Jack Wills band and Jimmie Rivers and the Cherokees, can be heard with Wills on *Billy Jack Wills and His Western Swing Band* (Western 2002) and *Crazy, Man, Crazy* (Western 2004). His work with Jimmie Rivers is prominently featured on *Brisbane Bop* (Western 2003), a live-performance LP taken from tapes recorded in the early 1960s.

Don Helms

Don Helms, who contributed perhaps the most identifiable instrumental trademark to Hank Williams's recordings—the high-register, pealing steel guitar—can be heard on nearly any of the Hank Williams reissues on MGM. The Hank Williams album in Time-Life's Country Classics Series features a booklet, written by Charles Wolfe and Bob Pinson, that provides ample insights into Helms's playing style on Hank's recordings.

Buddy Emmons

Buddy Emmons is one of pedal steel's true innovators. His talents first emerged when he was part of Little Jimmy Dickens's band, and became celebrated through his work with Ernest Tubb's and Ray Price's groups after that. *Four Wheel Drive,* half of a double album (Steel Guitar Record Club #5), includes Emmons's brilliant soloing with all of those groups, taken from old single recordings, along with a few he made on his own, mostly from the fifties. *Steel Guitar Jazz,* the other half of the double album, is Emmons's landmark 1963 jazz LP, the first ever recorded by a pedal steel guitarist. It wears well nearly twenty years later. (Available from PSG Products.)

Emmons has recorded a number of fine solo LPs in recent years. His *Emmons Guitar Co.* (available from PSG Products), a sparkling LP done in the 1960s to be sold through his steel guitar manufacturing operation, features a number of excellent tracks done with a small band. Most of the songs are folk, country, or original tunes performed with good humor and consistent virtuosity. *Buddy Emmons Sings Bob Wills* (Flying Fish FF–017) is one of Emmons's favorite LPs, an engaging group of Bob Wills tunes featuring Emmons as a vocalist. Though he has expressed dissatisfaction with two other Flying Fish sets—*Buddies* (2FF–041) with fiddler Buddy Spicher, and *Minors Aloud* (FF–088) with virtuoso country/jazz guitarist Lenny Breau—both are high-class, sophisticated modern jazz LPs with only minimal bows to Nashville (or even Western swing). To get the excitement of Emmons in person with an all-star band, look for *Buddy Emmons at the International Steel Guitar Convention,* Volumes 1 and 2 (ISGC), recorded in 1977 in St. Louis. (Available from Midland Records.)

Jimmy Day

James Clayton Day is a veteran steel guitarist best known for his work with Ray Price's Cherokee Cowboys and with Willie Nelson in Willie's pre-superstar period. His unique pedal work created a different, more flexible sound that permitted his pedal changes to be used almost as a rhythmic device. One can hear his later work on Nelson LPs like *Shotgun Willie* (Atlantic 72621) or *In the Jailhouse Now* (Columbia PC–38095), recorded with Webb Pierce. In the 1960s Day recorded a fine LP for the Philips label, *Golden Steel Guitar Hits* (Steel Guitar Vintage Classics #18; available from PSG Products). Despite the addition of a superfluous vocal chorus (the "Merry Melody Singers"!), Day attacks twelve numbers, most of them associated with steel, from "Texas Playboy Rag" and "Bud's Bounce" to "Steelin' the Blues" and "Indian Love Call." He manages to keep the choir in the background, making it easy to understand the essence of his style.

Curly Chalker

Curly Chalker is one of the true greats of jazz steel guitar. His approach is a fusion of the 1940s Western swing styles of people like Noel Boggs with the later jazz stylings of Buddy Emmons. Chalker began his professional career working with Lefty Frizzell and later with Western swing bands led by Hank Thompson and Billy Gray. He came to Nashville in the mid-1960s, and gained attention for his cool, swinging accompaniment on Merle Travis's 1962 LP *Travis!* (Capitol ST–1664). After that he found ample work in the studios, yet Chalker never really became a fixture as Pete Drake, Emmons, or Lloyd Green did, largely due to his blunt, uncompromising attitude. Chalker still works as the principal steel player on the "Hee Haw" television show though he makes his home in Las Vegas. *More Ways to Play* (Midland MD–3) is an excellent collection of jazz and pop numbers that show Chalker's gifts to strong advantage.

Lloyd Green

Lloyd Green was one of the preeminent steel players in Nashville in the sixties and seventies, and remains a major innovator today. *The Hit Sounds* (Steel Guitar Record Club #15) is a reissue of an early LP from the old Little Darlin' label that features instrumental versions of some of the country hits Lloyd first distinguished himself on, such as Warner Mack's "The Bridge Washed Out" and Johnny Paycheck's "Heartbreak Tennessee" and "The Lovin' Machine." Green's solo work on the original versions of these songs influenced many steel players; here he has a chance to stretch out more. (Available from PSG Products.)

Various Artists

Steel guitar country-rock music finally fused in the late sixties, and the appearance of new electronic devices made it possible to take the sound of the steel guitar beyond mere twangy licks into dimensions never thought of before. On *Suite Steel* (Steel Guitar Vintage Classics #17), Buddy Emmons, California steelers Jay Dee Maness and Red Rhodes, the Flying Burrito Brothers' Sneaky Pete Kleinow, and Poco's Rusty Young work out incredibly creative and bold arrangements of old rock tunes from the sixties, such as "Sunshine of Your Love," "Something," "Down on the Corner," and country tunes that include "Wichita Lineman" and "Muddy Mississippi Line." This album was one of the most important landmarks in modernizing the steel sound. (Available from PSG Products.)

Corn Pickin' and Slick Slidin', an out-of-print James Burton and Ralph Mooney treasure from Capitol was recently reissued on French EMI (1550751). Mooney was one of the important country steel guitarists to influence the Bakersfield Sound that began with Buck Owens and Merle Haggard in the early sixties. His high-pitched tone and solid command of the instrument is combined with the Telecaster of ex-Rick Nelson guitarist James Burton to make an impressive set of country steel guitar duets.

The Nashville Bar Association (Chimer) is sort of *Suite Steel* revisited, circa 1977. This set goes even further into the future, featuring massed steels playing against massed dobros, and various forms of sophisticated orchestration on some country and pop tunes, including vibrant versions of "Ghost Riders in the Sky" and "The Big Hurt." The players are some of Nashville's best: Buddy Emmons, John Hughey (who works today with Conway Twitty), and Jimmy Crawford are the elders of the tribe heard here; Russ Hicks and Sonny Garrish are the Young Turks. The experiments on this album are musically very fertile and show what the creative use of electronics can do. (Available from PSG Products.)

Bobby Black

Bobby Black's work with Commander Cody and His Lost Planet Airmen can be heard on *Hot Licks, Cold Steel—Truckers Favorites* (MCA 666), *Country Casanova* (MCA 661), and *Live from Deep in the Heart of Texas* (MCA 659), as well as *Lost in the Ozone* (MCA 659) and *We've Got a Live One Here* (Warner Brothers 2939G). He also did an outstanding, underrated solo LP, *California Freedom* (Steel Guitar Record Club #14; available from PSG Products), featuring some excellent interpretations of rock and jazz tunes and a bit of country, with complete data and photos of his early career.

Lucky Oceans

Lucky, who worked with Asleep at the Wheel from the early 1970s to the end of the decade, recorded several LPs with the band including *Comin' Right at You* (United Artists LW–038), *Asleep at the Wheel* (Epic PE–33097), *Texas Gold* (Capitol ST–11441), *Wheelin' and Dealin'* (Capitol ST–11546), *The Wheel* (Capitol ST–11620), *Collision Course* (Capitol SW–11726), and *Served Live* (Capitol ST–11945). In 1982 Lucky recorded a fine solo effort, *Lucky Steels the Wheel* (Blind Pig 1282; available from Rounder) featuring many of his old friends from Asleep at the Wheel as well as Johnny Gimble. The emphasis was on his nonpedal steel abilities as he tackled Western swing classics, blues numbers, and a couple of country and jazz tunes in a fine revival of the Asleep at the Wheel sound.

LAP STEEL INSTRUCTION

Nonpedal, "lap" steel guitar is far less prevalent—and popular—than it once was. Although there are countless lap steel fans and players still around in both Hawaiian and Western swing, many of the classic instruction books, such as Rickenbacker's Jerry Byrd method, are regrettably out of print. One method still available is the *Mel Bay Steel Guitar Method*, Volumes 1 and 2, by Roger Filiberto (Mel Bay). This two-volume course teaches nonpedal, six-string guitar in the E7 tuning. It is not necessarily a country-oriented course, but might work well for the beginner.

PEDAL STEEL INSTRUCTION

Pedal Steel Guitar by Winnie Winston and Bill Keith (Music Sales) is an excellent volume that includes a record and is perfect for beginning to advanced players. It deals with both the E9 and C6 tunings and reveals the special tunings used by some of the top players. It also shows chord theory, picking techniques, and how to read steel guitar tablature.

The New Sho-Bud Pedal Steel Guitar Course (PSG Products) is written by DeWitt Scott, one of the patron saints of steel guitarists. His International Steel Guitar Conventions in St. Louis every year are important to people wanting to hear the greatest steel players in concert. This book-and-record course, published under the auspices of Sho-Bud, deals with the basic E9 tuning used for most country music (but not Western swing). Each pedal is introduced separately to show its capabilities, then all pedals are combined, as in normal playing. Various introductions and endings are explained in different keys, and at the end, some familiar tunes are given in the style that the course teaches. Most of the techniques taught in the book can be heard on the record.

MSA Steel Guitar Course (PSG Products) is a three-volume course, like the one above, that deals with the basic E9 tuning for beginners. It explains tuning the guitar, setting up the pedals, string gauging, positions of the hand, and muting. Four songs diagrammed in the first book are shown again in the subsequent two volumes, each time in arrangements that require the advancing techniques being taught. This is a gradual course that seems quite appropriate for a beginning player.

Anatomy of the Pedal Guitar (PSG Products) is by Tom Bradshaw, proprietor of PSG Products, and one of the most knowledgeable and helpful people involved with the steel guitar. He published this volume to explain how a steel is constructed, to identify the various parts, and to explain what to look for when buying one. It also shows how to troubleshoot any problems you might have with your instrument. In addition, there is a special section on the tunings used by the best-known steel players. For a beginner, it may well be worth buying this *before* hitting the store to buy that first pedal steel.

The Pedal Steel Guitar by DeWitt Scott (Mel Bay) includes not only valuable tips for players at all levels, exercises, standard licks and fills, but also actual numbers transcribed from the records of Buddy Emmons, Jerry Byrd, and other pedal steel stars.

Doug Jernigan's Course for C6 by Doug Jernigan (PSG Products) is a beginner's course for the C6 tuning used in pop, jazz, and Western swing playing. Doug Jernigan is a master of this tuning. The tempo of these numbers is relatively slow and is geared toward pop songs like "Harbor Lights" and "Beautiful Ohio." This might make it appear a waste of time for a country player, but considering the fact that C6 playing is generally sophisticated, and in the more advanced stages is downright difficult (as is all advanced steel playing), this is a worthwhile course to start out with. It includes text and a recording.

Music to Get C6 By by Jeff Newman (PSG Products) is an excellent intermediate course. Newman goes further than Jernigan into swing and jazz here, diagramming and playing tunes like the jazz standard "The Preacher," the Western swing instrumental "B. Bowman Hop" (written by steel guitarist Billy Bowman), the Beatles' "And I Love Her," and seven more. On the accompanying record each is played through straight, then jazzed up and played through again. Some of the single-string solos that Emmons and others excel at are here, giving you a chance to begin developing your abilities. The record is in stereo with Jeff Newman on one channel and the band on the other, so you can shut Jeff off and play with the band.

Music to Back Up By by Jeff Newman (PSG Products) emphasizes the most important responsibilities of the country steel player: filling in behind a singer, playing an introduction to a tune, and playing a turnaround at the end of the closures. Newman shows how to do it in this book and record set by using a singer on all tracks. With every song diagrammed, you can work along on ten country tunes, including "Healing Hands of Time," "Time Changes Everything," "For the Good Times," and "Another Bridge to Burn." Three of the songs are performed in the unique style of the legendary Ralph Mooney, who now works with Waylon Jennings. For advanced players.

10 Diagrammed Tunes by Buddy Emmons (PSG Products) is a book and record set that includes some of the classic songs Emmons recorded with Ray Price's Cherokee Cowboys, here performed as instrumentals and completely diagrammed. The tunes include "Crazy Arms," "Touch My Heart," "Take Back Your Old Love Letters," "The Way to Survive," and six others. There isn't much of the characteristic Emmons improvisation here. Instead, everything is played straight, which makes this set, geared to the moderately advanced player, an excellent way to understand the classic Emmons country and Western playing.

Steelin' Feelin' by Jeff Newman (PSG Products) is made up of an LP and a package of arrangements. The ten songs are all well-known country hits like Mel Street's "Borrowed Angel," "Love Is the Foundation," the Loretta Lynn hit "Friend, Don't Take Her," a Johnny Paycheck classic "Slipping Away," "Tie a Yellow Ribbon," and others. The tuning used is standard E9, with a special pedal change explained in the text. For intermediate to advanced players, not beginners.

Three Diagrammed Tunes by Buddy Emmons (PSG Products) includes no LP; it simply diagrams three of the tunes that are on the classic set *Steel Guitar Jazz/Four Wheel Drive* mentioned in the recommended listening list in this chapter. "Bluemmons" comes from the *Steel Guitar Jazz* LP, "Four Wheel Drive" from an early Emmons solo single, and "Flint Hill Special" from another early single. Definitely not for beginners.

The Pedal Steel Handbook by Rusty Young (PSG Products), written for beginning through advanced players by the pioneering rock steel player best known for his work with the country-rock band Poco, should appeal to anyone interested in playing modern country music. Young deals with many of the songs Poco has recorded, shows how to translate music written in standard notation, how to build chords—even how to cover up mistakes.

Steel Tracks by Newman by Jeff Newman (PSG Products) is a two-record set of prerecorded rhythm tracks for the steel guitarist to play along with. It's extremely important for any steel guitarist planning on performing to get the feel of working with a band. These two albums provide a variety of country and pop/jazz/swing tracks for a player to improvise against. The players on the records are some of Nashville's best, and the student can play whatever he feels will work with the accompaniment. Record 1 features nineteen country tracks; record 2 has sixteen tracks that emphasize blues and swing, including accompaniment for "Ode to Billy Joe" and "The Preacher."

Winnie Winston's *Pedal Steel Guitar: A Manual of Style* (Musym-Tab) is a 134-page book that looks at the styles of four country players in minute detail. The players examined are veteran steel player Jimmie Crawford, longtime Conway Twitty steelman John Hughey, and studio players Weldon Myrick and Terry Bethel. It includes two tunes by each player, diagrams, and a variety of exercises and photographs. All music is in both tablature and standard notation. Two seven-inch extended-play records that correspond with the material in the book are included.

For a truly committed and ambitious steel player at any level, attending Jeff Newman's Jeffran College of Pedal Steel Guitar (Box 293, 3901 Central Pike, Hermitage, TN 37076) can be a highly worthwhile experience. Newman offers beginning, intermediate, and advanced courses for steel players, and even makes available steels for those who don't want to transport their own. He takes the beginner through the basics, helps school intermediate students in more advanced techniques, and puts advanced students in working situations, such as a recording studio atmosphere.

Jimmie Crawford, veteran studio and stage steel guitarist, has recently begun his own instruction course through the Musym-Tab School of Pedal Steel Guitar (Box 87, 112 S. Valley Road, Hendersonville, TN 37075). Like Newman's course, there are beginning, intermediate, and advanced levels. Each course runs five days and is held several times a year.

INSTRUMENT
PUBLICATIONS

GUITAR

Guitar Player, founded in 1967 by steel guitarist Bud Eastman in California, was not the first magazine of its type in America. However, it was the first to succeed and flourish, and it has expanded considerably in the past several years. *GP* runs the gamut of guitar music, including rock, classical, blues, and jazz as well as country. Among the country-oriented features are a monthly column on pedal steel by Jeff Newman, columns on studio guitar, and a short "Pro's Reply" feature built around Q/A interviews with more and less widely-known players. There have been cover stories on Chet Atkins, Roy Clark, and Hank Garland, and features on Joe Maphis, Ray Edenton, Jimmie Crawford, Paul Franklin, Albert Lee, and other players. The interviews are generally quite extensive (particularly the cover stories), with well-researched discographies. However, in recent years country guitarists have received little coverage, a situation one hopes will change in the future. *GP* is published monthly. (*Guitar Player*, 20085 Stevens Creek, Cupertino, CA 95014)

Guitar World, founded in 1980, is a competitor for *Guitar Player*, and it takes a very different editorial approach. Although the bulk of the stories deal with rock or jazz players, *GW*, until recently, did not ignore country. In fact, some of its finest early pieces were written by none other than Merle Travis (including memorable features on Chet Atkins, Joe Maphis, and electric guitar pioneer Paul Bigsby). Other country guitarists covered in *GW* were Dale Sellars, Weldon Myrick, Carl Perkins, Clarence White, Speedy West, Junior Barnard, Buddy Emmons, and Merle Travis. *GW* is published six times a year. (Harris Publications, 1115 Broadway, New York, NY 10010)

FIDDLE, BANJO, MANDOLIN, AND STANDUP BASS

Frets magazine is published by the California–based GPI Corporation, publishers of *Guitar Player* and *Contemporary Keyboard* magazines. It covers a wide scope of instruments, including just about all acoustic string instruments. A fair amount of space is also dedicated to bluegrass and related fields, in part due to the fact that part of the editorial staff of *Frets* comes from the now-defunct *Pickin'*, a bluegrass-oriented magazine that folded in 1979. *Frets* has featured a variety of people: Merle Travis and Grandpa Jones, mandolinists David Grisman, John Duffey, and Tiny Moore, fiddler Richard Greene, and banjoists Tony Trischka, Pete Wernick, and Butch Robins. There are also columns on various aspects of fiddle, dobro, mandolin, and other instruments written by the likes of Mike Auldridge, David Grisman, and Byron Berline. (*Frets*, 20085 Stevens Creek, Cupertino, CA 95014)

MANDOLIN

Mandolin World News, founded by mandolin innovator David Grisman, is a publication dedicated to covering all styles of mandolin playing. It includes interviews and other mandolin-related information. (*Mandolin World News*, Box 2255, San Rafael, CA 94902)

BANJO

International Banjo is a bimonthly magazine dedicated to all styles of banjo, including plectrum (tenor) and five-string banjo. It includes arrangements for various styles of music, and other banjo-related material. (*International Banjo*, Box 328, Kissimmee, FL 32741)

DRUMS

Modern Drummer, whose format is similar to that of *Guitar Player*, covers all styles of drumming. Although its primary focus is on jazz and rock, one issue covered a number of country and country-rock drummers, including session legend Buddy Harman and Willie Nelson's drummer Paul English. The magazine also has tips and information on new products. (*Modern Drummer*, 1000 Clifton Ave., Clifton, NJ 07013)

STEEL GUITAR

One highly ambitious project in the field of steel guitar publications came when Tom Bradshaw, former *Guitar Player* columnist and owner of Pedal Steel Guitar (PSG)

Products decided to start a glossy magazine for the steel player. *Steel Guitarist*, a beautifully designed publication, emerged, but a disappointingly small readership and mounting expenses forced Bradshaw to abandon the project in the spring of 1981. Six issues were published, most of which reflected Bradshaw's whimsical but dedicated style and high standards. All are still available as back issues. (Tom Bradshaw, Box 931, Concord, CA 94522)

Pedal Steel Newsletter is the official publication of the Pedal Steel Guitar Association, a non-profit group of steel players and enthusiasts. (Pedal Steel Guitar Association, Box 248, Floral Park, NY 11001)

PUBLISHERS AND DISTRIBUTORS OF COUNTRY MUSIC INSTRUCTIONAL MATERIALS

ALPHABETICAL DIRECTORY

Acuff-Rose Publications
2510 Franklin Road
Nashville, TN 37204

Alfred Music Co.
75 Chance Drive
Port Washington, NY 11050

ALMO Publications
16333 N.W. 54th Street
Hialeah, FL 33014

Mike Auldridge
Box 745
Silver Springs, MD 20901

Ernie Ball
Box 2117
Newport Beach, CA 92663

Dr. Banjo (Pete Wernick)
7390F Oxford Road
Longmont, CO 80501

Bay (see Mel Bay)

Berklee Press Publications
1265 Boylston
Boston, MA 02115

Emmons Guitar Co.
P.O. Box 1366
1771 E. Webb Avenue
Burlington, NC 27215

Flat Five Press
Box 8127
Roanoke, VA 24014

Thomas Frederick
1748 Joy Avenue
Ashland, OR 97520

Hal Leonard Publishing
8112 W. Bluemound Road
Milwaukee, WI 53213

Harbinger Publications
Box 164
MI-WUK Village, CA 95346

M. Hohner, Inc.
Andrews Road
Hicksville, NY 11802

Niels Hokkanen
Box 211
Astor, FL 32002

Homespun Tapes
Box 694 F
Woodstock, NY 12498

Horton & Tubb Publishing
Levelland Music Center
809 Houston
Levelland, TX 79336

Dan Huckabee
28 Cliffside
Fort Worth, TX 76134

Iowa State University Press
Ames, IA 50010

Kendall-Hunt Publishing Co.
2460 Kerper Boulevard
Dubuque, IA 52001

Leonard (see Hal Leonard)

Le Walt Publishing
783 N. Wheeler Street
St. Paul, MN 58104

Lucky One Music Publishing
% Ernie Ball
(see Ball)

Mel Bay Publications
Pacific, MO 63069

Music Sales Corp.
33 W. 60th Street
New York, NY 10023

Musym-Tab
Box 87
112 S. Valley Road
Nashville, TN 37075

Jeff Newman
Box 293
3901 Central Pike
Hermitage, TN 37076

Oak Publishers
% Music Sales Corp.
(see Music Sales)

Peer-Southern Publications
1740 Broadway
New York, NY 10019

Stacy Phillips Works
157 Monroe Hill Road
Monroe, NY 10950

PSG Products
Box 931
Concord, CA 94522

Ridge Runner Publications
Box 12937
Fort Worth, TX 76116

Sonyatone Records
P.O. Box 567
Santa Barbara, CA 93102

Sound Hole
Box 120355
Nashville, TN 37212

Utah State University
(see Kendall-Hunt)

Pete Wernick
(see Dr. Banjo)

Workshop Records
Box 49507C
Austin, TX 78765

SOURCES OF INSTRUCTIONAL MATERIALS, BY INSTRUMENT

See preceding alphabetical directory for addresses.

Banjo

ALMO Publications
Dr. Banjo
Hal Leonard Publishing
Harbinger Publications
Homespun Tapes
Iowa State University Press
Le Walt Publishing
Mel Bay Publications
Music Sales Corp.
Peer-Southern Publications
Ridge Runner Publications

Bass

Ernie Ball
Mel Bay Publications
Music Sales Corp.

Dobro

Mike Auldridge
Emmons Guitar Co.
Homespun Tapes
Dan Huckabee
Music Sales Corp.

Drums

Thomas Frederick
Music Sales Corp.

Fiddle

Alfred Music Co.
Homespun Tapes
Mel Bay Publications
Music Sales Corp.
Stacy Phillips Works
Sonyatone Records
Workshop Records

Guitar

Ernie Ball
Berklee Press Publications
Emmons Guitar Co.
Homespun Tapes
Horton & Tubb Publishing
Mel Bay Publications
Music Sales Corp.
Sound Hole
Utah State University

Harmonica

M. Hohner, Inc.
Music Sales Corp.

Mandolin

Flat Five Press
Niels Hokkanen
Homespun Tapes

Mel Bay Publications
Music Sales Corp.
Workshop Records

Piano

Acuff-Rose Publications
Mel Bay Publications
Music Sales Corp.

Steel Guitar

Mel Bay Publications
Music Sales Corp.
Musym-Tab
Jeff Newman
PSG Products

The best sources for finding new instruction books are the country, old-timey, bluegrass, and specialized instrument publications listed elsewhere in this book.

part three

THE BUSINESS OF COUNTRY MUSIC

John Lomax III, with Bob Millard

The following pages offer a step-by-step guide to breaking into the country music business as a songwriter, vocalist, or instrumentalist. The focus here is on Nashville, which remains at the center of the industry, though there is also information on the independent labels outside the Nashville region—many long and solidly established—which are increasingly important both in presenting original new talent and in keeping great old recordings available. Some of the advice here is technical: typical contract terms, for example. Some of it is advice on the particular peculiarities of the Nashville music business scene. Some of it is advice that may seem obvious but that gets ignored surprisingly often when people try the mixture of music and big business for the first time.

All the advice that follows must be accompanied by a solemn warning, however: there is no home correspondence course for the music business. If you take a mail-order TV repair course and follow it faithfully all the way through, there's a good chance that you'll be able to fix an old TV set. But you can follow every bit of advice contained here, and in twenty-four other books, and still not have a hope of success in the country music business. There, success is built around three-minute dramas in the form of songs, but the business of music itself is a drama, and one that can easily eat up ten or twenty years of your life. It has been suggested that the only people who belong in the creative end of the music business are people who are literally incapable of doing anything else— or who are so talented and capable that they could succeed at anything they tried.

On the other hand, there are some good things to be said for the music business from the point of view of the would-be performer, songwriter, or instrumentalist. Because of the comparative simplicity of audio technology, record production costs are quite low compared to such other mass entertainment media as movies and television. While $6,000,000 is not a big budget for a 90-minute Hollywood movie, $20,000 can still comfortably produce a 40-minute record album, and a single can be cut for $2,000. The result is that the record business has tended to be a somewhat more fast-gambling, crap-shooting kind of business than other entertainment industries, whose gambles have to be approved by committees of bankers or advertising agencies. And, the record business has generally provided more room for originality.

As the record industry has gotten bigger, as the ownership of labels has become concentrated, as corporate-division bottom-lines have become a major matter to worry about, and as the weight of management has gotten heavier, the pressure to hedge the bets becomes more of a factor. The form this takes is the tendency to try to repackage and resell a proven product or style, or to homogenize everything into one familiar form. Originality seems harder to market, though it is not necessarily harder to sell, and the echo of H. L. Mencken's line, famous long ago in Hollywood, is heard: "Nobody ever went broke underestimating the intelligence of the American public." But those nice, slow-moving, easily-caught audio frequencies seem to keep finding ways around such obstacles, and into the microphones of people like Ralph Peer, Sam Phillips, or maybe somebody with a home four-track recorder, egg-carton sound baffles on the studio wall, and some wonderful three-minute musical dramas to share.

M. M.

WHAT ARE YOU GETTING INTO?

So you want to become a part of the glamorous country music business, sing of infidelity, and star in music videos? Well, before you sell the farm and move to Nashville you ought to give some thought to the prices of failure and success. For every person who does reach the pot of gold at the end of the music business rainbow, literally thousands more fall by the wayside, forced to accept lesser rewards and, in many cases, no reward at all but bitter memories of hundreds of misspent nights in cheap dancehalls playing "Fraulein" to drunken strangers. The sad truth is that thousands of people set out with country fame as their goal, but there are only a few dozen spots at the top. All who seriously try for those spots work hard; all suffer for their dream. As for success, in many cases the price paid is a shattered marriage and an uprooted family, for the spouse in your life will have to get used to the fact that your quest will likely take you away from home more nights than it will keep you under your roof. Before you set out on this perilous road you should ask yourself if you are willing to spend up to 300 nights a year away from your loved ones—part of the price paid by musicians who work the road. Ask yourself if you really want to pass your time in various nightclubs among strangers and folks who are consuming alcohol, many to excess.

If the risks haven't scared you off, and you think you have talent, a capacity for hard work, patience, skill, self-confidence, intelligence, self-critical honesty, personality, luck, and several dozen other attributes—all of which could take you to the heights of any number of professions—then press on as we discuss the nuts and bolts of building a career.

How do you begin working toward a life in professional country music? The first step is to decide exactly what avenue you'd like to pursue. There are three main ways of gaining fame in the popular music arena: as a writer, a singer, or an instrumentalist—or, of course, as some combination of the three. The public, however, will probably only remember you as a vocalist if that is one of the things that you choose to do. Waylon Jennings is a fine songwriter and an excellent guitarist with a distinctive style, but the public is familiar with Waylon as a singer. No doubt many folks are unaware that he wrote "Are You Sure Hank Done It This Way?", "This Time," "I've Always Been Crazy," "Theme from the Dukes of Hazzard," "Bob Wills Is Still the King," and many others. Turn the coin over and you will find that Roy Clark and Billy Grammer are primarily

From its beginnings in a small radio studio, followed by many years in the downtown Ryman Auditorium, the Grand Ole Opry has grown to have its own modern Opry House and Opryland television facility on the outskirts of Nashville. The Opry's growth and success both sparked and was fed by the growth of Music Row, the recording and music publishing area located closer to the city's center. Between them, the Opry and Music Row have transformed a native American musical form into a major entertainment industry and have made Nashville, Tennessee, the country music capital of the world. (Courtesy Opryland USA)

remembered for their instrumental prowess, though both have taken numerous turns before a microphone. The public may only accept you in one role, so you should decide in which area of music you want most to succeed, then concentrate on developing those talents. I'm not saying that writers should forget singing or playing, just that the odds are stacked against your reaching the top of your profession in more than one area.

Even if you know exactly what you want to do—sing, play, or write—don't come to Nashville to start your career. Come here when you have some years of experience under your belt. The level of competition is fierce; an inexperienced writer or musician in Nashville lets himself in for a lot of hurt. The prerequisite for coming to Nashville is to pay some dues before you come to town. They say that some artists are "overnight successes"; ask the artists and they will tell you that night was twenty years long.

Ask yourself if you honestly believe that you have real talent. How objective has the response to your talent been? Have your performances been limited to relatives, polite friends, and folks in your hometown? Or have you played to enthusiastic applause from strangers who have *paid* to get in the door? If you can answer that last question in the affirmative, and if you have done so for some years, not weeks or months, then you *may* just have a chance to get enough from show business to make your time, tears, and sweat worthwhile.

One piece of information that recurs in every book about succeeding in the music business is that talent is important, but not as essential as persistence and patience. Willie Nelson charted his first country record as an artist in 1962, Waylon Jennings in 1965, Conway Twitty in 1966, Dolly Parton in 1967, Kenny Rogers and Barbara Mandrell in 1969, and Crystal Gayle in 1970. In all these cases many years passed before the artist became a country music superstar and all these artists had spent many years honing their talent before they scored that first chart record. If they had lacked the patience, persistence, and confidence in their own talent to persevere they wouldn't have lasted until their time finally did come.

Talent is important—but it is *not* all-important. You have got to be able to write songs people enjoy hearing or have a voice that falls harmoniously on the ears. Country music is full of people with enough talent; the problem is that they also have to have enough confidence in that talent to keep honing their craft while they wait to have a clear shot at a higher rung on the ladder.

PITFALLS FOR
THE NEWCOMER

Warning to anyone getting started in country music: there are sleazy people and shady operators on the fringes of any big business, and music is no exception. In the music business these vultures are known as "song sharks." They prey on people who are unaware of the standard practices of the legitimate music industry. If they hear you sing or listen to your songs they will start foaming at the mouth exclaiming about how much talent you have and promising you the sun, moon, and stars. You can also spot their advertisements, which offer to set your words or poetry to music, write lyrics for your melody, or "examine" your songs. They'll tell you they can get every DJ in the country to play your song or that they can get Kenny Rogers or Dolly Parton or Waylon to cut your songs—*for a fee*. There's your tipoff. No reputable publisher will request any money from you. If someone tells you he can publish your songs if you give him money, he is trying to steal your money. Do not do business with these people, just politely tell them you'll have to think about it, ask for a copy of the contract and the cost, and vamoose. Then phone up each of the performing rights societies (ASCAP, BMI, SESAC) and inquire about the company. It will probably not be affiliated with any one of the rights societies. If it is, the rights societies would like to know about it for they have strict rules prohibiting such activity. Any publisher-member of BMI, ASCAP, or SESAC caught trying to get you to pay them money will be immediately expelled from their membership rolls.

The same type of scheme is frequently used to con hopeful singers. The hustler will tell you that for, say $2,500, he'll produce an album for you "with top Nashville sessionmen," then promote that record for you at every country radio station in the United States. He may even declare that he will be able to get your record played on the radio or on "the national country charts," if you fork over the money. Here's what you most probably will get: One or perhaps two sessions featuring a crew of down-and-out pickers barely able to stay awake. The promotion promised will consist of your album being mailed to country radio stations. Since the programmers at these stations will never play an unknown artist on an obscure label, your record will go straight to the trash bin or the Salvation Army. If you have been "guaranteed" airplay, this sharpie will buy time in the dead of night on the most remote, cheapest low-wattage station he can find, where your record and those of your fellow victims will be played *once*. The "national country charts" will turn out to be a list of similar records also bound for oblivion published in a sloppy Xeroxed tabloid with a circulation of perhaps fifty and an influence in the music business that doesn't extend beyond the hustler's front door.

The only certainty in this scheme is that you will get a very poorly produced album pressed on low-quality vinyl with cover graphics that would make a goat vomit. These operators don't care a whit whether you have any talent—only if you have any cash. No reputable record company will ask you to pay for a record up front. They will bear the expense and hope that they can recoup their costs from sales of that record. If you are uncertain about whether or not someone is trying this gambit on you, take the proffered contract to an attorney.

The following remarks were made in an article in *Music Journal* in February 1971. The writer is Edward M. Cramer, president of BMI.

1) Never pay to have your song published, or to have your lyrics set to music, or music to lyrics. Never pay a fee for examination of your work, or for a promise to promote same.

2) Deal only with a firm whose reliability can be established by intelligent inquiry.

3) Always read and thoroughly understand any contract or agreement *before* signing to make certain the provisions contained therein meet with your approval. If terms of the agreement are not clear to you, seek the advice of a competent attorney *before you sign*. Keep a copy of all contracts for future reference.

4) Remember that any words can be set to music, from the cheapest jingle to the most beautiful poem. A proficient writer can grind out thousands of tunes each year to order, but such music is rarely, if ever, actually published.

5) The offer by a company to *print several* so-called "professional copies" of a song does not mean that the song is being published in the usual sense of the word. The amateur may desire several of them for his own enjoyment, but such copies are generally of no value to music publishers, since they prepare their own copies if they are interested in a song.

6) Although literally thousands of songs are copyrighted each year in Washington, genuine "hits" which are financially successful ventures number only about two hundred songs annually. Of this relatively small number, the overwhelming majority are copyrighted, promoted, recorded and published by music publishing firms who assume all financial responsibility and do not charge the songwriter for their services.

MAKING CONNECTIONS

There are several ways to get your songs, voice, or playing heard and to meet others in your field. A "guitar-pull" is a social occasion in which a fair number of writers and musicians congregate to play songs for one another. This is certainly not a tradition unique to Nashville, though Johnny Cash received lots of attention for his monthly sessions some years back when Bob Dylan, Joni Mitchell, and Steven Stills unveiled new songs at his house. A guitar-pull is a very good way for a newcomer to watch more experienced writers and performers in an informal atmosphere. Stories are told, songs are sung, "licks" are traded, and a camaraderie develops between writers who are technically in competition with one another. Quite often you'll find one writer will pitch another's song merely because he admires the craftsmanship and honestly feels that song would be better suited to a particular artist than one of his own. This sort of get-together is also a good source of information about who is cutting what kind of song and when.

If you do contemplate performing, a guitar-pull is a good place to learn a few songs. You'll want some outside material to fill out your shows, if only to set your own songs off better or to provide a change of pace in your sets. Playing another writer's song or praising his work and asking if you could perform it is a high compliment among writers that won't hurt your chances of making friends.

The sheer exuberance of a guitar-pull is exhilarating. It's a roomful of musicians and writers playing solely for one another and the joy that music brings. There is no pressure to succeed or fail, to gain a cut or secure a record deal. It's a place to trot out your newest material for a good-natured examination by your peers. If they really admire your new songs then you'll hear about it. If they don't respond at all you may assume that your song failed to captivate them. Even if no one says, "Gee, what a rotten song," you can listen between the lines to hear if you are being damned with faint praise.

Many cities, including Nashville, also have public events of this nature, generally held in a local watering-hole and often referred to as a "Writers Night." They are usually very democratic affairs where each writer, whether a CMA winner or just a beginner, is allowed to present a set number of songs or gets a time limit to be on stage. If you are new in town you may have to audition for one of these or at least call ahead of time to reserve a spot. These are remarkable occasions. The cover charge is very low and the audience can see a parade of writers from unknown beginners to, sometimes, those at the top of their profession. Top-rank people *do* turn up from time to time at Nashville writers nights, partly to recapture their scuffling days and partly to try out their own new material for a non-industry audience. It is also not at all unusual to find representatives of major publishing companies in attendance at these writer's showcases. If your town does not have such an affair, perhaps you can find a bar or club willing to host it. Clubs are often willing to schedule such events on their slow nights: Sunday, Monday, or Tuesday.

Another way to accelerate your Nashville songwriting career is to spend a little time selectively hanging out in bars, small clubs, and other oases favored by the music industry. This is not a practice that you'll want to continue indefinitely, but at the dawn of your career it is a good idea to make the rounds of the local spots every once in a while. You can build friendships this way, observe a lot of your fellow writers and singers at work, pick up buckets of street-wise information, and commiserate with those whose careers are also in their early stages.

A word of caution: This is not a good policy to adopt if you're prone to overdrinking, like to get an early start in the morning, or have a slender wallet. It's not a practice you should adopt as a nightly routine. But it is another source of information for you as well as a chance to talk to fellow writers when they may be more relaxed than they would be at their offices.

In this regard it would be wise to listen to Bob Montgomery, vice-president and co-founder of House of Gold Music, one of the very best Nashville publishers: "When a writer comes to town, he usually starts hanging around some place where other writers hang out, and he'll eventually get together with them and sing songs with these other writers. If the guy's got something, generally, the other writers will recognize it and take it to their publishers and say, 'Hey, you ought to listen to this guy, he's got some great tunes.' I think more writers are discovered that way than any other."

WRITING COUNTRY SONGS

If you feel that your talents lie in the writing arena, the most important thing to do is *study the hits*. Take the top country songs apart, phrase by phrase, word by word, to see what makes a hit country song. Naturally you shouldn't *copy* the hits; rather, try to see what makes that song appealing. Is it the lyric or the melody? If it is the lyric, as is the case with most country hits, what is the writer communicating? Study how the writer gets the message across. See if you can figure out a way to say things a little bit differently. Here, as in singing, they key is to set yourself slightly apart from the rest of the crowd. In his book on songwriting, Tom T. Hall relates an incident in a small bar long before he had had a song cut. Faron Young came on the box singing "Hello Walls." Tom T. not only knew instantly who was singing, he also made a bet at the bar that the song was written by a writer new to the Nashville songwriting scene. When the record was done the owner opened up the box and the songwriting credit was to Willie Nelson. It was Willie's first hit, and Tom T. had studied the hit songs and the top writers so thoroughly that he instantly knew he was hearing a new talent.

Most hit country songwriters are voracious readers and keen students of human nature. They also always have an ear open for the short phrase which can lead to a hit song—the "hook." The hook is the key lyric and melodic line that is the song's signature, and it can come from anywhere. Harlan Howard found one of his most famous in a bar when a fellow told a girl to "Pick me up on your way down." Roger Bowling and Hal Bynum got the nucleus of their CMA Award–winning song from overhearing a man tell a woman, "You picked a fine time to leave me, Lucille." Johnny Cash recalled the horror of watching floodwaters creep up on his home and wrote "Five Feet High and Rising." The Bellamy Brothers had a monster record, "If I Said You Had a Beautiful Body (Would You Hold It Against Me?)" that was little more than a hook. In this case the hook was a common line employed as small talk by thousands of men hoping to interest a woman they found attractive—a conversational hook, in fact. Yet, until the Bellamy Brothers came along no one had thought of writing a song around it.

Glenn Sutton and Larry Kingston came up with one of 1980's cleverest hooks for one of George and Tammy's duets: "We're just a pair of old sneakers, stringing each other along." Wayland Holyfield and Bob House took a common dancehall request, "Could I have this dance?", added "for the rest of my life," and watched Anne

Murray rack up a number one single with an idea so simple I'll bet half the writers in Nashville spent part of a day kicking themselves for not coming up with it.

Hooks can be completely silly, as in Roger Miller's "Chug-a-lug, chug-a-lug, makes you wanta holler hi-de-ho." Or they can be dead serious, as in Curly Putman and Bobby Braddock's, "He stopped loving her today," which got George Jones his first number one record in many years.

Songs can be sparked from virtually any source, so be prepared. You could do a whole lot worse things than to practice writing songs based on random phrases you see in the paper, overhear from people's conversations, or pluck from advertising slogans on television.

Your hook line should be *memorable*, melodically catchy, repeated at least once, and instantly recognizable. As for its place in the song's structure, the quicker you get to your hook the better. Publishers listen to dozens of songs every week. They simply don't have time to wade through nine verses to get to your song's selling point. Generally speaking you should get to your hook in the first verse or in the following chorus. When you've had a few hits you can alter that formula. The most common place for the hook is in the chorus because it can then be easily repeated at least once. Not many people will remember all the words to a song but they will remember that hook. If it is a good one they will enjoy singing it as they listen on their car radio or as they toil away at work. If your songs don't have a catchy hook then go back to your pad and pencil and come up with some that do.

Writers differ in their approach. Some write all the time; some strictly from nine to five; some, like Doodle Owens, while they're driving around in the car. Some write late at night; some, like Tom T., set their alarms for three or four A.M. when the rest of the world is asleep. Whatever method suits you best is the one to use; the key is to write a *lot*. Paper is cheap, and at this stage of your career so is your time. There is nothing that will warm a publisher's heart more than a new writer who shows up with a sackful of good songs.

Don't worry about the procedure you use to write a song. Some writers start with a phrase, others get the chorus first. Some writers plot the whole thing out in their heads before they write a word, others let the situation develop as they go along. Some begin with a melody, then the words seem to suggest themselves from the sounds. Some writers work from fragments: bits and pieces of several songs may be assembled into one finished effort. Or they may work on many songs during one session, bouncing from one to the other as the mood strikes. Don Williams notes that, "I'll usually sit down and write a song pretty much in its entirety. I might work on it for a good while after that, polishing it up and everything. But if I don't get it while I'm sitting there, I usually won't fool with it anymore." As long as you come up with a good song no one cares about your working methods. You might try going about it in the various ways I have mentioned, add your own touches, and see which methods work best for you.

Don't worry about the time it takes to write a song, either. Larry Gatlin has been quoted as saying that "All the Gold In California" was written in about six minutes. Don Schlitz labored over "The Gambler" for months, thinking for a long time that it was the worst song he had written—and he didn't even know a thing about playing poker.

Many writers confess to experiencing an eerie, mystical feeling when they write. Bukka White, one of the great blues songwriters, called his songs "sky songs" because he felt like he just reached up in the sky and pulled them out. Townes Van Zandt, a writer whose haunting "Pancho and Lefty" has been recorded by Emmylou Harris and by Willie Nelson and Merle Haggard, told me that when he wrote "Mr. Mudd and Mr. Gold," a long, puzzling tale about a hand of stud poker, "The words were flying at me so fast I could hardly write them down. If my pencil point hadda broke I would have been a goner." In an interview with Mark Rose, Merle Haggard had this to say: "When something hits me, that's when it starts to come, it's kind of like one of those teletype machines. I'm watching one of them and all of a sudden it starts working. That's kind of the way my writing is. I have no idea when that machine's going to start. . . . Somebody hands it to me really. It's really weird. Some songs that I've written, most songs that I've written that are any good, I'm finished with it within an hour."

As one who writes about music I can also state that there are times when I feel that my pen has a mind of its own. It takes me many places undreamed of when I began to write. The important thing for *you* to learn from these examples is that you just never know what may be out there waiting when you do pick up that pen. It may not be quite as important to set out to write as to be ready to write whenever that strange visitor comes.

Here are some songwriting tips you may find useful; I have.

•Most country songs are between two and three minutes long.
•A word count on a half-dozen recent country hits revealed that all of them contained between 117 and 164 words, not counting repeated verses or a repeated chorus.
•You'll double your possibilities if you write songs which can be sung by either sex. "She Thinks I Still Care" was a big hit for George Jones. Anne Murray got a number one single by making it "He Thinks I Still Care."
•If you can come up with a song which can be sung by a man, a woman, or as a duet, then you may really be in high clover. Bob McDill and Dickey Lee's "The Door's Always Open" was released as a single by a male vocal group, then by a male vocalist, then by a female singer, and *then* Dave and Sugar took it to number one as a male-female vocal duet.
•Up-tempo love songs and good duets are always in short supply.
•Women buy far more country records than men.
•Songs that depend on humor, novelty songs, and topical songs rarely have more than one popularity "life," while well-written love songs have more lives than a lucky cat.
•The vast majority of the country audience lives in the South and Midwest.
•Songs and poetry require enormous *compression* to be effective; all other forms of writing require expansion.
•Rhymes help to hold a song together rhythmically and to establish rhythmic accent, but what matters most is the way the words flow together.
•No one cares if you use a rhyming dictionary.
•Nothing rhymes with "orange" or "purple."

GETTING STARTED AS A SONGWRITER

Once you've decided that you are going to try to make it as a country songwriter, you've chosen a semi-honorable calling which attracts a multitude of would-be candidates each year. Despite the odds, some people do make it every year and some of those few make it in a big way.

I would not advise anyone to come to Nashville until he has honed his songwriting craft as much as possible at home. It's a whole lot easier to make some headway back in Freer, Texas, Dothan, Alabama, or Danbury, Connecticut than it is here where you'll be competing with hundreds of people who are a lot more experienced. Every bit of experience you can absorb before you get to Nashville will pay you back because Music City is the capital of the world for songs which rely on lyric expression.

Publishers make their living by finding songs good enough to be recorded. You may have heard that the scene in Nashville is a closed shop. Some failed writer may have come home and told you that only the cronies of the publishers can get in. Balderdash! If you have a good tune a publisher will want it. If your songs aren't good enough then a publisher won't be interested. It's just that simple. In the March 1981 issue of *Country Song Roundup*, Bob Montgomery, writer of "Misty Blue" and a cofounder of House of Gold Music, told writer Bob Allen: "I don't know of any publisher with any sense who will close his door to new writers. A publisher has always got to be building his resources to replace those writers who've retired or stopped writing for one reason or another. And you never know who that next writer who walks in the door is going to be. He may be the next Kristofferson. It may also help you to realize that every writer who is pulling down big bucks today started out with no credentials and somehow built a highly lucrative career."

If you get turned down, and at times you will no matter how good you are, don't tell yourself that "so-and-so don't know beans from buffaloes" and don't blame the company, the person, the system, or the stars. The reason your song was not accepted was simply because that publisher just did not think it was good enough. Now it is certainly possible that the publisher was wrong. But if you've tried a dozen or so and *all* of them pass on your songs, then it would probably be wise to put those tunes on the shelf and try out some new ones, remembering the criticisms the publishers made when they listened to your work.

We're getting a little bit ahead of ourselves. Here you've just decided to try to write country songs for a living and I've already had twelve publishers turn your songs down! There are a few steps that invariably must precede your first appointment—if there is to be a first appointment at all.

You must get to be as good as you can before you come here, but the next cold, hard fact of life is that you will have to move to Nashville if you want to make it as a country songwriter. There just isn't any way around this. If you want to be a *big* movie star you have to go to Hollywood, if you want to be the star of the network TV news you will have to move to Manhattan, and if you want to be a top-level auto executive you'll have to get to Detroit (or Japan). The vast majority of country records are made in Nashville and most of the big writers and performers live there or at least maintain an office there. Don't even think about being an exception to this rule because I don't know of any successful country writers who have become firmly established without taking this key step.

So the question now is not whether you should move here but *when* you should take this step, *how* you can prepare for it, and *what* you should do once you have taken the plunge. The decision will be different for someone who is more a performer than a songwriter, so be sure to check the later chapter for singers if you hope to be a recording artist as well as a writer.

Before you do come here you should make plans to maximize the trip's value. If you don't get some appointments before you come you might well spend two weeks just trying to get in the front door. Face it, the town is not going to stop in its tracks just because you have arrived down at the Greyhound station. Let's assume that you are a singer-songwriter from Florida. In your own humble opinion you're pretty hot stuff. What's more you've been taking home a pretty good amount of money over the past few years. Some of that swag has been put aside for a rainy day. In addition, your bookings are steadily picking up, your little homemade record has done well, and your per night fee has increased 30 percent in the past year. If you are certain that you want to take that step into the unknown and leave this security behind, then schedule two to three weeks off. Call it a working vacation, but avoid coming in the summer: motels are full, costs are high, and music people have been known to take vacations during this span. You should also avoid the last two weeks of December because of the Christmas vacation. You should also dodge Fan Fair Week, usually the second week in June, and the Grand Ole Opry/DJ Week festivities, generally held the second or third week in October. During these two special weeks every place of lodging in town is booked solid and the music industry will be too busy with these pursuits to see you.

Dodging these times still leaves you with some eight months when your visit won't conflict with other situations. Get a professional resume together listing the places you have played, songs you have had recorded, local TV or radio appearances you have made, and any other pertinent data. Basically this should just be a brief summary of your achievements in music. If you have any press clippings be sure to include them, but employ some discretion. Don't send up twenty poorly written, short items from small-town weeklies. Pick out the best features from the better publications and send no more than three or four. This will be enough to show that there are unbiased journalists out there who are excited about your talent. Put these in a package with *one* professionally made black-and-white glossy photograph of yourself (if you are strictly a writer you won't need a picture) and have five to ten copies made of a tape of no more than three of your songs or singing. If you've had some 45s out, that's even better. But don't mail anything yet. What you are doing is assembling your ammunition. There's no point in just shipping these packages off willy-nilly. The most likely end result of such an endeavor would be File 13—the trash can.

Your next step should be to join the Nashville Songwriter's Association, International, 25 Music Square West, Nashville, TN 37203. If you've had a song commercially released you will be eligible for full-fledged membership; otherwise you can join as an associate member. Either way it will cost you $10 a year. The NSAI publishes a newsletter, conducts seminars, has open meetings, holds writers workshops, sponsors a Songwriters Hall of Fame, and holds an annual awards banquet. In 1980 they landed their first TV special, Nashville Songwriter's Night, shown nationally on the Public Broadcasting System. The organization is run by Maggie Cavender, a dedicated woman who at one time or another has aided just about every aspiring songwriter who has come to Nashville in the past eighteen years. When you join up, write her a brief note telling of your hopes, your successes to date, and asking her to recommend some Nashville publishers who will review tapes or make an appointment with you when you come to town. It's likely that if you write a nice letter you will receive a reply listing several publishers to contact. If you are a singer only it still wouldn't hurt to join up as an associate member.

Now write to the people who have been suggested, introduce yourself, mention who referred you, and ask if they would review your songs or see you when you come to town. If they reply in the affirmative then you can send them your package. *Always* include a stamped, self-addressed envelope if you'd like to have your package returned!

If you do strike out you have run head-on into the hardest problem you will have to surmount. Getting at least a *chance* to make your pitch is one tough nut to crack. Sure, it isn't fair for them to say no without even listening to your work. The unfortunate truth of the matter is that many things in life aren't fair. Kicking the dog or muttering obscenities may bring brief relief but that won't solve your problem. If someone will not answer your letter or agree to review your songs, then pick up the phone and see if you can get to someone on the publishing staff at some of the companies you have tried. It is easier for someone to say no or ignore you through the mail than it is over the phone. (Of course it is always easier for them to say no to you over the phone than in person, which is part of the reason that you will eventually have to move here.) If you have been knocking around music for some time you may have made some friends who live in Nashville. Get in touch with them. Perhaps they can assist you in making some appointments.

Don't take it personally if you can't make an appointment through the mail or over

Warner Brothers Records

RCA Records

MCA Records

Elektra/Asylum Records

Music Row occupies an area about two miles square in what was once a residential section of Nashville. The offices of record companies and publishers range from converted residences to modern commercial buildings. (All photos, Bob Millard)

Kenny Rogers Building:
United Artists and
Capitol Records-EMI

Tree International Publishing Co.

The Combine Music Group. Photo by Bob Millard

Acuff-Rose Publishing Co.

the phone. Publishers are busy people and the vast majority of people out there in the hinterlands who think they can write songs really couldn't write a ransom note. Many of them send their songs to publishers, usually prefaced by a note hand-written on notebook or tablet paper. It's a good idea to type your letter on nice paper and do your best to avoid errors in spelling and grammar.

Another possible way to open a wedge in the partially closed door here is through local DJs, music writers, or club owners who are familiar with your talent. People in these occupations often will have made contacts with people in Nashville and might be able to help you get that first appointment. If they can't directly, perhaps they would be willing to write a letter of recommendation. If you have been packing them in at a local night spot which sometimes books nationally known country talent, that club owner probably booked the act through a Nashville agency. Perhaps he can put you in touch with the agent, who may well know of people who are scouting for new writers.

If you have managed to issue several of your songs on a local label, you are eligible for membership in BMI or ASCAP, the two main organizations licensed to collect performance fees for the use of recorded music on radio, TV, and motion pictures. You should write to each requesting membership information. It will cost you something to join one of these groups, but if your songs do get radio play and that play is noted by the performing rights society, then you will be paid for the music's use.

Another advantage to membership in BMI or ASCAP is that as a member you can make an appointment with their staff when you come to town. It is possible that they may know of some publishers who are scouting for new blood. If you really are a good songwriter then the people at BMI or ASCAP will readily notice your skill, and may help get some doors open for you.

These suggestions are far from sure-fire possibilities. There is nothing guaranteed in this business. What I have tried to do is offer ideas for you to try so that your talent can gain a fair hearing. If none of these approaches garner you an appointment you should re-evaluate your priorities. Do you really have to be in such a tough racket? Maybe you would be better off pursuing some other occupation. At this stage of the game you still haven't moved here so no bridges have been burned and no moving and relocation costs have been incurred. You may have to face the same fact George Jones faced in Tom T. Hall's song: "I'm Not Ready Yet."

DEMOING YOUR SONGS

Country writers get a real break when it comes to auditioning their songs. Since country music depends so heavily upon lyrics and the musical basics, an elaborate demonstration tape recording (a demo) is unnecessary. A sophisticated demo of the sort used in pop or rock music may in fact be detrimental; it could draw attention away from your writing. A vocal/guitar or vocal/piano demo will be sufficient in 90 percent of the cases you'll encounter. Publishers and producers in Nashville are concerned with the *song*—the lyric, the melody, and the hook. They don't give a hoot if you can double-track a tuba and xylophone chorus or ornament your demo with seven flavors of Latin percussion. Any extraneous sounds on your tape will divert the listener from the song you are attempting to sell.

There are two ways to prepare demo recordings of your songs: you can pay for them and use someone else's equipment, or you can acquire your own machinery and do your own. (When you get a publisher he will help take this problem away from you.) Commercial recording studios rent two- or four-track studio time at a reasonable rate. For a bit more money they will arrange for a trained singer if you feel your own voice is insufficient. Unless your voice is just awful or you have no idea of the basic principles of key, tone, pitch and timing, you probably would do well to sing on your demos. Vocal clarity and feeling are more important than professional vocalizing at this stage, and you know what you want your song to say better than anyone else.

If you are serious about songwriting as a career, it might make sense for you to invest in your own basic demo recording equipment. Good quality tape recorders and microphones don't depreciate very rapidly, and they are certainly a legitimate tax-deductible expense. The experience with recording will be helpful to you when you come to Nashville—it's one of the basic tools of the music trade.

You don't need to buy anything fancier than a four-channel recorder for home country demos (though there are now some quite inexpensive eight-channel decks, if you think you might want to put together a full-scale personal studio some day). Each channel lets you separately record one or more voices or instruments, and you can balance the volumes of each of those channels when you "mix down" onto a final tape from which you'll dub the demos you give out. The advantage of this system is that you can record without someone else engineering the session, or alternatively without having to constantly replay the tape to check the balances by trial and error: as long as the recording meters on the deck tell you that you're recording each channel at an acceptable level, you can achieve the proper musical blend of levels later, when you don't have an instrument in your hand.

You can also do quite well, using the trial-and-error technique or a friend as an engineer, with a two-channel deck. If you want your demo to have only one vocal and one guitar or piano part, two channels is all you need. All current four-channel and a few current two-channel tape machines are equipped for sync recording. This allows you to record different parts—instrumental and vocal, say—one after another, and to go back and re-record a part if need be. This is definitely a big advantage for most people, and is of course how most studio recording is done these days. Both two- and four-channel machines are now available from at least two manufacturers in cassette as well as reel-to-reel format. Cassette quality isn't as high, and since the price spread (especially for four-channel equipment) isn't that great, it might seem foolish to buy anything but reel-to-reel. But some people find that cassette equipment gets in the way of performance a little less than reel-to-reel does. Since your primary concern is with the creative quality rather than the technical recording quality of what you're doing, that's not to be sneered at.

You can take your original tape—or your "copy master," if you've mixed down from a four-channel original—to a tape copying service to have copies made to distribute. (Many of the tape copying services can now also mix-down a four-channel quarter-inch master for you, or will let you bring in your four-channel deck to mix onto one of their two-channel decks, at an hourly rate.) But if you want to make your own copies at home you'll need a second tape machine. Ideally, you would have both a second two-channel reel-to-reel and a stereo cassette machine, so you can easily make copies in whichever format the publishers or record companies you are pitching to prefer. You can save the expense of one of those two extra machines by carefully making a "copy master" from your reel-to-reel onto your stereo cassette deck (mixing down if the original is four-channel), and then copying back onto your reel-to-reel. You will lose some quality, though. If you master on a four-channel cassette deck you can go the other way (with no further loss of quality). One other point: the reel-to-reel machine in the office your demo is played on will probably have quarter-track heads, thus the deck you make your demo copies on should also have quarter-track heads. If this is to be the deck you are mastering on also, the fact that it will be a little noisier than a comparable two-channel deck with half-track heads is not too serious. You can figure out the permutations of all this with a trustworthy and knowledgeable audio salesman. If you buy from a serious discounter, be sure you understand exactly what equipment you need beforehand.

Your home studio will also need a couple of microphones. This is not a good place to try to go for the bottom-dollar item: the microphone is the essential beginning link of the recording chain, and poor quality will be very apparent. On the other hand, the condenser mikes most popular for studio vocal recording are now selling for roughly $500 to $1,000, and that kind of investment isn't necessary either, particularly since electret microphones are now available that offer many of the virtues of those studio condensers. Choosing a microphone for your own use is really almost as personal a decision as choosing any other instrument. It's useful to remember that mikes can be broadly divided into two categories: those that try to be as "flat," or realistic, as possible; and those designed with built-in "curves" intended to make the voice or instrument they record sound better. The mikes with curves usually add boost at the lower frequencies for warmth, and boost to the vocal or instrumental harmonics for increased "presence." Mikes that enhance a voice often won't do the same thing for a guitar or piano, and vice versa. Very roughly speaking, it can be said that flat mikes are a better bet for instruments, and "curved" mikes a better bet for voices. The other major factor in microphone sound is transient response, how quickly the microphone puts out a signal in response to the sound waves that reach it. The standouts here are the condensers—the studio mikes, the much less expensive electret condensers, and some condenser models that fall in between in price. Dynamic mikes, which is what most stage microphones are, generally have the poorest transient response. Ribbon mikes generally fall somewhere between.

The next step in putting together a home studio would be to buy an external mixing board with equalization, mike panning, and perhaps echo. But as long as your tape recorder has microphone inputs this mixer may not be necessary at first, especially if you choose your microphones carefully. If you want to add echo, it's possible to patch it in ahead of the mix-down machine.

MEETING A PUBLISHER

Your first meeting with a Nashville music publisher will be a memorable event whether you make headway or fall flat. But before you make that visit you should do a little homework. Find out what writers are already signed to that company and what hits the company has recently had. You can obtain this information from the secretary or receptionist if you ask halfway politely, or you can take a gander at the small print next to the entries in the trade listings on the singles charts of the trade publications: *Billboard*, and *Cash Box*. Acquaint yourself with the songs written by the company's writers. You won't get a publishing deal by flattering the publisher's catalog, but it will show him that you're relatively alert, care enough about the company to bone up on their catalog, and have some business sense about you. You can also tell if the company is "hot" or not; if they haven't been in the charts for a while they may be looking just a little bit harder for fresh talent.

When you do go for your appointment, bring your tapes, lyric sheets, and guitars, if that's your instrument. Dress casually and comfortably. For some years now blue jeans and a clean shirt have been perfectly acceptable, so wear that if you like. Walking into a publisher's office in a suit and tie will immediately peg you as an insurance salesman or a revenue agent. You should also be ready to chat a bit. Nashville is a pretty casual place and the publisher may want to break the ice some before getting down to business.

The publisher may not want to hear your songs in person. He may just talk to you a little, then ask you for a tape. You should already have learned whether he prefers a cassette or a reel-to-reel copy and be prepared. You will also have the lyrics *neatly typed* out, perhaps even with the key noted or the chord changes marked. (A professionally done lead sheet may add to your presentation but it costs $25 or more per song. If you have the money it's a pretty good investment, but not an essential one—the typed lyrics are essential, however.) Remember, if a publisher thinks your song is good enough to get recorded he'll be glad to take it on. If so, he'll foot the bill for a professional demo, a proper lead sheet, and the copyright.

You shouldn't bombard a publisher with a tape of two dozen songs. All he wants to hear is whether you can write; he doesn't need a two-hour set to tell. Include no more than three of your *very best* songs. That's sufficient to show whether or not you have writing talent or potential. If he wants to hear more he will ask.

Be sure your name, address and phone number are on both the tape reel or cassette and the tape box, with a list of the songs in their order of appearance on the tape. If you submit your songs on reel-to-reel tape, record them at $7\frac{1}{2}$ i.p.s. and and don't forget to place leader tape before each selection. That leader tape is cheap so it won't hurt to have three to five seconds or so between each tune. Besides sprucing up the look of your tape the leader enables the listener to locate specific selections quickly. Always play the finished tape all the way through before you go to your appointment; you would be amazed at the glitches that can creep onto a tape.

After you've handed over your tape, get out. You could ask the publisher when you could check back but don't be surprised if he tells you, "Don't call me, I'll call you."

He may have a box full of tapes collected which he likes to listen to at his leisure. If you continually call him up to get his opinion you'll merely aggravate him. Take my word, if he does like what he hears you *will* be hearing from him.

If three weeks go by and you've gotten no word you can assume you've drawn a blank there. You can phone up the secretary or receptionist and see if they'll be kind enough to retrieve your tape for you to pick up.

If the publisher asks you to play your tape or take your guitar out of your case, he is paying you a high compliment. It means he believes that you are professional enough to accept his comments about your song in person without argument or insult. It means that you will probably get the benefit of his honest evaluation and his first impression of your song immediately. Pay very close attention to what he says because he is telling you what you need to know if you want to make it as a songwriter. Don't get angry or upset if he takes your song apart and leaves it in bleeding little pieces. You wouldn't take offense at a teacher or coach who criticized your performance. And that's the role the publisher is playing in this high drama. Making effective use of intelligent criticism can mean the difference between success and failure, so learn how to turn this setback to your benefit.

Sometimes the publisher's reaction (in person, or by phone) will be to tell you some good news and some bad news. The good news is that he kind of liked your songs. The bad news is that he doesn't think he can use them. If anyone takes this kind of trouble on your behalf treat them very kindly. Try to find out, in a nice way, as much as you can about his evaluation of your work. Ascertain whether or not he'd like to hear from you again with newer material. If he makes specific suggestions, incorporate them into the next songs you submit. The publisher might even suggest a particular company for you to take your work to. If this is the case, by all means follow up on it, particularly if he says you can use his name. The absolute worst thing you can do is argue with him about his criticism, protest his decision, or be huffy about his refusal to take you on. If he calls back at all, or takes this time in person, he is doing you a favor; pay attention to his suggestions, thank him for this time, find out if the door is open for future submissions, and make arrangements to pick up your original tape.

If he does say you can try him again, write up a couple of new masterpieces, call back in a few weeks and see about dropping off your latest gems. It would not be a good idea to bounce back the very next day with two or three more songs—he will figure he's heard your best efforts on the first go 'round and that you are probably bringing in older songs that aren't as good. Let a little time pass so that it will at least *seem* like you've written some brand new songs, even if you haven't.

This brings me to an interesting point. Some publishers act like an old song is somehow inferior to a spanking new ditty. Maybe they feel that a song has to be as new as tomorrow's dew. Whatever their thinking, I would suggest that you tell them the song or songs you are submitting are *new*. If no one else has recorded them, they are technically new anyway, even if you wrote them three years ago. If that particular song hasn't been pitched too promiscuously all over town, chances are the publisher won't know whether it is new or not but will be glad to hear it when you tell him that it is a fresh effort.

If the worst does happen and you never hear from the publisher again, don't give up! There are several hundred publishing houses in Nashville. If you roll snake eyes at one, try your luck elsewhere. Every successful songwriter alive can tell you a true story about how so-and-so rejected a certain song which later became a monster hit. Remember Don Schlitz's song "The Gambler"? He couldn't get it cut in the beginning so he put it out on a label created solely to expose that song. Then Paul Craft recorded it. Bobby Bare put it on an album. Several other artists took a shot at it before Kenny Rogers's track of it put Don and "The Gambler" on the map. Richard Leigh played a tape of his songs for two of Nashville's top publishers. Both turned him down flat; told him, "I don't hear any hits on here." Undaunted, Leigh played the same tape for Allen Reynolds. Allen immediately agreed to publish one of the songs, "I'll Get Over You," and he cut it with Crystal Gayle. The song became her first number one single. They say that one man's meat is another's poison, so if one publisher turns you down, try another, then another. If *every single publisher* in town turns you down, you should either find a new profession or write some better songs. The songwriting life you have chosen is a tough one—you are going to hear a lot more "no's" than "yes's," no matter who you are or how great your songs are.

One way to determine exactly what publishers are currently "hot" is to get a copy of the issue of the trade magazines which come out during the annual CMA/Grand Ole Opry Birthday Celebration week. This event is held in the second or third week in October. That week's issues of *Billboard*, *Radio 'n' Records*, and *Cash Box* will have a listing of the top publishers for the past year, ranked according to the number of chart records the publisher secured and how high they went in those charts. You can also call or write the Nashville offices of the performance rights societies, BMI, ASCAP, and SESAC, and request a list of their award-winning country songs. These organizations hold their awards banquets during the same week in October. They then honor the most popular songs represented by their organizations as based on radio airplay. Seek out the publishers whose names appear most frequently on those lists. You might as well start at the top.

Let us now assume that you have tried a fair number of publishers and have finally hit paydirt. You've found a publishing company that is very enthusiastic about your writing. So enthusiastic in fact that they feel there is a good chance to get one or more songs of yours recorded. When that lucky day comes they will offer you one of two types of publishing arrangement. They will ask for the right to publish a particular song or songs or they will ask if you would be interested in a staff writing job. I'll tell you how each one works.

If they ask you about a particular song, or several tunes, they may do so for a variety of reasons. They may not think you are quite "there" yet as a writer but feel they can get the particular work they are interested in recorded. They may not have a place for another staff writer at that particular time. Or they just may want to test the water without going to the expense of signing an exclusive deal with you. If you are approached with this sort of offer, ask how long they want to have your songs. I would not want to give a publisher the exclusive right to have a song indefinitely. Six months to a year is ample time for them to secure a recording. If they haven't scored on the song by then they probably aren't going to. Ask if the rights can be returned to you if nothing happens within that time span. (If the answer is no, you ought to have some unusually good reasons for going ahead with the deal.) Ask for an advance on the song. If they think they can get it recorded they should be willing to gamble *at least* $50 to $100 on their judgment. If they agree to pay you this modest amount for the exclusive right to market your song for a fixed period of time then go ahead and let them have a try at it, provided of course that the contract they offer for that song is in order. You can evaluate the contract by checking it against the standard song contract provided in *This Business of Music*, or in several of the books reviewed in the chapter "Business Information Sources" at the end of this part of the book. You can make this same arrangement with as many publishers as you have songs, provided, of course, that you do not give the same song to more than one publisher.

If you do sign up for this sort of arrangement you should make sure exactly what sort of recording would fulfill their part of the bargain and thus give them the right to publish your song from now on. There's a large difference between securing a cut by an artist on a major label or a good independent label and a record on a label no one has heard of by an equally obscure artist. For the most part though, a writer who is trying to get his feet wet should accept any reasonable deal of this nature as long as there is some *payment* for the song and a *time limit* placed upon the publisher. If they do obtain a recording of the song which is commercially released, you should remember that that fact alone entitles you to membership in a performance rights society, with its advantages in contacts and information as well as payment for air play. Your song will be available for purchase and you may have your first leg up on the other arrangement, a staff writing job.

A staff writer offer means that the publisher would like to have the exclusive right to market all your songs for a set period of time. The standard songwriter's agreement will generally be for one year with two to four successive one-year options at the publisher's discretion. This means you and your songs are potentially obligated to that publisher *exclusively* for three to five years, while the publisher is making a commitment to you for one year with a "wait and see" attitude toward the additional years. In other words, the publisher has an out at the end of each year, but you are left hanging until he decides.

As a staff writer you are usually paid by means of a "draw"—advances on expected future earnings. The payments may be labelled "salary" but it is money which the publisher plans to regain. The amount will range from $50 a week on up to a much larger amount if you are an established writer. This "draw" is money to live on so you will have time to write songs for the publisher. If your songs do get recorded, the amount of draw you have received will be deducted from your share of the record(s) earnings in the same way that an advance for recording costs is subtracted from an artist's record royalties. Basically, the draw is an interest-free loan to keep you going until the publisher can get his income from the songs.

A reputable publisher will also provide you with a place to write if you need one, make demo recordings of your songs to pitch to singers, obtain lead sheets, and pay for copyrights when your songs are released for commercial consumption. He'll also give you advice and constructive criticism on your writing. You'll also be provided with a quarterly or semi-annual statement which will tell you what you've earned during that period and how your earnings stack up against your accrued draws.

If you are offered this sort of a deal it means the publisher is *very* serious about your songwriting potential. It means that he is willing to go to considerable time and expense because he believes he can sell your songs and make money from them for his company—and for you. If the company is a good one, if the contract is on the level and the draw is acceptable, I'd say to sign up without delay. As a fledgling writer this kind of deal basically means you will be getting *paid* to do what you've been doing for free.

There's another aspect to a staff writing job. It will put you in close contact with the other writers the company has under contract. You will be able to learn a great deal by closely observing more experienced writers with a few hits under their belts. There's even a possibility that you will be able to establish a co-writing relationship with a veteran writer. Many remarkable writing partnerships have been formed in this manner. If you hang around the office a good bit you'll be drawn into relationships with other writers who will pass along what they have learned to you. You could well have a song with a perfect hook but no first verse. Another writer may have a story waiting for a hook, or a melody that needs to be married to a lyric. You'll be amazed at how easily two people can come up with a song when they write together while neither of them could hack one out writing alone. Of course this means that your share of the income will be cut in half, but half of something is better than all of nothing.

Veteran writers are also good sources for tips on which singer is looking for what type of song, when you should submit a tune to so-and-so's producer, how to get a song to a person who will take it to the artist, or where a particular producer or manager goes to drink beer in the afternoon. In short, a staff writing job will plug you in to a lot of valuable data. If this opportunity comes your way, take the ball and run with it.

Some publishers will put you on the draw and expect a certain minimum number of songs from you each year. Some will expect you to spend some time hanging around the office, working with the other writers or helping with tape copies and whatnot. Other publishers will assign specific duties to writers: pitching songs from the catalog, demoing tunes from the pens of other writers if you sing well, helping out in the demo studio, making deliveries, and other chores. Other publishers may not expect anything from you except a batch of fresh songs every now and then. As a new writer I would spend as much time at the office as you possibly can, short of cutting deeply into song writing time. There's a great opportunity to learn quite a bit about all aspects of publishing: song-pitching, the procedures involved in making demo recordings, administration, matching certain songs to particular artists, and the nitty-gritty of writing hit songs.

Now that you've found a publishing home you may well be thinking that you are closing in on having it made. After all, don't you just have to hand in your masterpieces to the publisher, then sit back and keep track when those song royalties come rolling in? Well, no. It's true that a good publisher will be out there pitching your tunes, but don't think that this gives you carte blanche to lie around in your hammock dreaming of retirement in the Bahamas. The sad truth of the matter is that you *still* have to pitch your own songs. Look at your songwriting as a small business enterprise: just because you have joined up with a salesman doesn't mean that you should hang up your selling shoes. In this case the salesman is paying *you*, so you should have even more incentive to get out and work for your own music.

The person at your publishing house who is pitching your songs may be ineffective, or may not have the right contacts to get in the door to see the people who produce the best-selling acts. He may be working songs from several other writers. He also can't possibly sing a song which you wrote as well or inject as much feeling into it as you can. He also probably can't make as good an on-the-spot change in the melody, lyric, or chord structure if a producer or singer requests a slight modification. And if you are out there pitching your songs and your publisher or his representative is too, then you've got double the effort that you would have if you were laying around with sugarplums dancing in your head.

One of the songwriter's most frequent complaints runs: "I've been with PDQ Music for three years now and the only cuts I've gotten were the ones I pitched myself." Don't let yourself sing that refrain. I'm not defending the publisher's failure to get the job done; it just may be that you are a much better salesman of your own music than they are. You may have developed some contacts which prove more fruitful than their own sources. You live your music twenty-four hours a day, while song publishers actually sleep and visit their families from time to time. With no set hours to report to work you can stay up all night hobnobbing with artists, producers, and other writers, building relationships and working your own music in ways no publisher ever could. As long as the publisher is out there trying and can show you who he pitched which of your songs to, then he is complying with his responsibility to you. Many publishers keep a "pitch log" or some other journal which records what has been sent to whom and when.

If a situation persists for too long without results you might be wise to seek out a new publisher, but walking around griping about what you perceive as your publisher's ineptness isn't exactly the best way to attract a new employer. If you write good songs the industry will know it; moaning about what a rotten company you work for will hurt your own cause. If anyone asks you why you aren't happy with PDQ Music, just say that "things haven't worked out the way I had hoped" and leave it at that. Nashville's music community is actually a very small "town" within a medium-sized city. There aren't many secrets around here that remain secret for very long. You'd be amazed at how quickly derogatory remarks or private treachery becomes public knowledge. As John D. Loudermilk once observed, "Bad news travels like wildfire; good news travels slow." Nashville's music industry is almost entirely located within about a two-square-mile area, so you can well imagine how soon bad news gets around "The Row."

WRITER-PUBLISHER ECONOMICS

For the sake of this exercise, assume that you have signed an exclusive songwriting agreement with Saturn Music. As explained in the previous section, your songs now belong to them for the next five years, provided that they exercise each successive option at the end of each year. As a general rule the publisher will place you on an advance system, or "draw," ranging from $50 to $200 a week so you can eat and pursue your writing. This money will be returned to them when they are compensated for the use of your songs. Since it will take a publisher at least one to two years to begin receiving income from your music, you can see that they are gambling a fair amount of money on their estimation of your talent.

Why does it take a publisher so long to be paid when someone uses your music? Suppose one of your songs sounds like a hit for Merle Haggard. Your publisher makes a tape copy, has a lyric sheet made up and delivers the song to Merle, his producer, or his manager. Say the date at this point is February 15, 1985. This step may take about a week. Merle and his team plow through about nine acres of material over the next three months, eventually selecting a large batch of songs for serious consideration. Their office notifies Saturn Music that they would like an "exclusive hold" on your song. This is a way for the artist to request that the publisher not pitch the song to anyone else until he, his producer, and his manager decide whether they will be recording the song or not. Naturally, the bigger the artist, the more likely the publisher is to honor such a request. This situation arises only with songs that have not yet been recorded. If a recording of the song has already been released for commercial sale, anyone can record it without asking for permission. If a publisher gets wind of a minor artist's intention to cut the same song a major artist has under consideration, he can request that the lesser artist hold off, but that artist may not honor the request. So, the only time a writer and publisher have total control over who cuts a particular song is when the song is a virgin to the vinyl. Once the song gets on a record it's open season, although the label must file a "notice of use" statement to the publisher. This accessibility to recorded material is known as compulsory copyright.

Let's say your song is a virgin. Your man at Saturn Music grants the hold to Merle Haggard. He and his folks winnow the field even further, eventually selecting fourteen songs to take into the studio to try on for size. It's now mid-May. Another month passes while they work in the studio. All fourteen songs are eventually recorded, but most country albums contain ten selections, so four of these tracks will fall by the wayside. Another month passes while the final tracks are selected and an album is mixed, sequenced, mastered, and delivered to the pressing plant for a test pressing before it is finally mass-produced. The four unused tracks are now in that strange limbo known as "in the can"—recorded but not currently scheduled for release. They may be released at some future date or they may languish in that can from then on. But we will asume that your song was one of the chosen ten and is released on the new Merle Haggard LP. It has now been four and a half months since your publisher submitted the tape of your song. For every copy of that album sold, Saturn Music will receive 2¾¢ from the record label for the cut with your song. Saturn receives this money through the Harry Fox Agency, the collection agent licensed by most publishers to receive the money from the record companies. The Fox Agency deducts a sum ranging between 3½ percent to 4½ percent for this service. The net amount is then sent to your publisher, who splits the money with you on a fifty-fifty basis.

The record label pays two times a year for the use of music. Obviously they cannot pay the minute a record is released—they haven't had time to get any money from the retailers and wholesalers, who haven't had time to get the cash from the thousands of people who will buy the new Haggard record or tape. Suppose the album is released on July 1. Haggard's label pays publishers (through Harry Fox) on March 31 and September 30. The September statement which the label sends along with their check to Saturn Music via Harry Fox won't reflect any sales for the new Haggard release, because the month of August is hardly enough time for any money to flow back from the retailers, through the distributors, to Saturn. So you think, "Aha! I'll be seeing a ton of that money on the March statement!" Probably not. The label's books will close some time before March, say on December 31, and they will tally the sales for the period ending then. Your cut on the Haggard LP has been available for purchase from July 1 on but it takes a long time for the record label to collect the money due them from their accounts. There is a good possibility that they will have *collected* on only perhaps 50,000 units despite the fact that the record by now may be in the hands of at least 250,000 eager buyers. So, on March 31 Haggard's label sends a check for all the Saturn Music songs they have used during that pay period. Your song is one of them and the records the label has provided the Harry Fox Agency show that there were 50,000 units sold.

But you won't see your part of that money for a while even now. The publisher is required to provide statements to writers at least twice a year. Few publishers provide statements more frequently because of the amount of paperwork involved. Let's suppose Saturn Music pays on July 1 and January 1. On July 1, 1986, some *16½ months* after your song was pitched, you receive your first income from it.

Let's further suppose that your publisher does not attempt to deduct any of the weekly draw you've been pulling for all that time. (Realistically, a publisher will always want to recoup his advances before making payments, but let's fantasize for the sake of mathematical simplicity.) Your statement will then read something like this:

MCA Records MCA–41073 Merle Haggard 50,000 @ 1.375¢ $687.50
(That one-and-a-fraction cents you get is half the 2¾¢ Saturn receives per disc. We have assumed that Saturn did not deduct one half of the Harry Fox commission from your share. This may not always be the case. The arrangement should be covered in your songwriter's agreement. If you agreed to split the Fox commission, then you would get only from 1.351¢ to 1.344¢ per disc, depending on what the Fox commission is. Those numbers would reduce your check to $675.50 or $672.00.)

(This little example also assumes that the label made an accurate count and paid on time, that the publisher paid on schedule, and that there were no computer breakdowns.)

You're fit to be tied by this time. That Haggard LP has been out on the market for a solid year, it charted very high; in fact it's still on the charts. You know that he sells at least 300,000 copies per LP and here you've had to wait a year to get a check for $687.50! You're calling Haggard's label every name in the book and shouting "lawsuit" and "audit" in between the deleted expletives. Your publisher patiently tries to explain the music payment facts of life to you and he urges you to hang in there—let's see what the next semi-annual statement says.

On January 1, 1987, you get paid on another 150,000 units of the Haggard LP. You start to feel a little better with a check for $2,062.50 looking at you, but you're thinking, "Gosh dawg it, it's been eighteen months now that the LP's been out there, Haggard's already got another one out, and I've still only been paid on 200,000 units sold." You are now becoming aware of the cruel truth in the label-publisher relationship. The record labels have considerably more clout than the publishing companies. As long as they pay your publisher most of what they owe within what, to them, is a relatively reasonable amount of time, then you have no recourse whatsoever. The sad fact of the matter is that the label has used your money and the publisher's money free of charge, and for quite a spell. Not only that, they have probably sold a few copies more than they have reported. That's life in the music business jungle, my friend, and if you can't live with it then I suggest that you seek other employment. Of course you could audit their books. However, unless they have underpaid by a huge amount, the money that you will recover won't even be enough to cover the amount you will be charged by the accountant you engage for the audit. So you can see that the publisher is the tail of a rather big dog, in this case the record company, and you know how often the tail wags the dog. Wasn't it nice of you to give your money—the amount exceeding your draw—to the label? And wasn't it kind of you to float them an interest-free loan for so long? (In our discussion of the Harry Fox Agency, we'll explore a more realistic way that publishers can check up on a label.)

Next July 1 rolls around and your publisher's statement comes with a check for $1,375 on your Haggard cut. By this time you've probably decided you've been slickered out of the money. You certainly will hope that in the *two years* that have intervened you will have landed a few other cuts elsewhere. So that $1,375 will seem like found money to you as will the $343.75 that rolls in six months later from another 25,000 copies sold. Every following six months you'll get smaller and smaller amounts from that LP cut unless you're among the very fortunate few who wind up having a cut recycled as a part of a "Best of" collection or a "Greatest Hits" package. Or the album could go out of print, then be reissued at a later date; or it could remain a catalog item, then enjoy a resurgence of interest if Haggard becomes an artist whose great appeal substantially broadens even further.

When we total all this up we find that you have gotten a grand total of $4,458.75 in the thirty-five-month period that has now elapsed between the time your publisher sent the song to Haggard and the present date, based on a grand total of 325,000 copies sold. It should be clear to you by now that you're going to need a lot of these album cuts to make a good living. It should also be clear to you that if you have been on a $100-per-week draw from Saturn Music for three years and you haven't had any other songs recorded that you'd be in hock to them to the tune of slightly more than $11,000. (52 weeks × 3 years × $100 = $15,600. $15,600 less $4,458.75 = $11,141.25.)

If that was the only song of yours that Saturn Music had gotten recorded, then the chances of their renewing your option at this point would not be good.

What would happen in this case if Saturn Music dropped you after three years? Would you owe Saturn Music that $11,141.25? Yes and no. Your account there is in arrears to that amount, but in reality the publisher knows he can't just hand you a bill and say, "Pay up." Saturn gambled on your talent and lost. The only way he stands a chance to regain his money is by keeping some or all of the songs you have written while you were under contract. Most certainly Saturn Music will insist on keeping the rights to publish the Merle Haggard cut. In all probability they will also insist on keeping some more of your songs in the hope that someday they will be able to secure additional recordings on them. You *might* be able to strike a deal with them and walk away with some of your tunes but Saturn could very well claim that they need to keep all of them because they don't know which one or ones may someday be recorded. It is within the publisher's legal right to do this and it is no doubt stated in your writer's agreement. If he does choose this route you've got little choice other than to thank him for trying to get the tunes cut and head for another publisher, preferably with a batch of new songs you've written since your option lapsed.

If this should happen to you, chalk it up to experience and find yourself a new publisher. You've at least gotten a track record, albeit a slim one, and if you're not a complete fool you will have learned a lot at Saturn Music, made plenty of contacts, and become fairly wise in the ways of the music publishing business. You aren't the first writer to be let go by a publisher and you won't be the last, so buckle down and let your subsequent success come back to haunt them like a bad trade seems to always come back to haunt an athletic team.

You can also pitch the old songs that you have left behind at Saturn Music in an effort to whittle away that deficit account. If you can get something cut, then you could very well move back out of the red and into the black on Saturn's books. If that happens you can let the songs stay over there and cash the checks after you have paid what you owe, or you can approach Saturn about returning the songs now that the account is all squared away. At this point you will find them a lot more amenable to returning your songs, unless of course, one or more of those previously undiscovered treasures has turned into a blockbuster hit. In that case you'll still be getting the same 50 percent from it that you would from any other publisher. See how simple it all is?

Despite the old saying about there being no free lunches, there is an instance where you and your publisher get a free ride. If your song is selected for the flip side of a hit single, your publisher will share in the publishing royalties from record sales. Half of the money collected goes to the publisher of the hit side song; half goes to the publisher of the flip side number. And half of what your publisher collects on the flip side will be yours. This will help balance the disappointment you will feel when your song is bypassed as the side pushed for promotion and airplay.

For you to make really substantial money as a songwriter, you need to have your songs selected for releases as singles so they will rack up that lucrative radio play. We have already talked about how much you would make simply from having a song on a album which sold a substantial number of copies. Country album tracks don't receive much airplay on radio so they don't generate much income in what is known as performance money. Your performance income is separate from the income you receive from record sales. Performance money is distributed by one of three performing rights societies, ASCAP, BMI, and SESAC. These organizations collect money from radio and television stations when they use your music over the airwaves. A record released as a single which makes the country top 100 will generate money for you from its radio exposure. But to really make the big bucks you need to have your song make it to the hallowed ground of the top ten in what are known as the "trade charts" published weekly by *Billboard*, *Radio 'n' Records*, and *Cash Box* magazines.

Since these are weekly publications, there cannot be more than 520 songs which make the top ten in any given year. Now, obviously records don't pop in and out of the top ten like fleas from a dog—a solid hit will stay in this select area from three to six weeks depending on how long it can hold its position in the local radio charts which help determine its ranking in the magazines, and how that record continues to sell at the record stores around the country.

For example, consider *Billboard*'s charts for two consecutive eight-week periods, one in the spring of 1980 and one in the fall of that same year. During those 16 weeks 51 records achieved top ten status. Multiplying this total by 3¼ to extend the sample to a full 52 weeks gives you a rough figure for the number of top-ten records during 1980—166. A significant percentage of this number were songs which were written by the performers; in our sample there were eleven. In addition, some artists like to "recut" or "cover" songs which have been previous hits, a circumstance that was the case for six more top ten songs during the period surveyed. That leaves a potential 149 song slots open for work by independent writers. However, a good many of those songs were provided by the producer, by writers from the producer's or artist's publishing company, by publishing companies controlled by the record label, or by others in a songwriter's own publishing company. Figure that half of the songs were provided by writers with some sort of tie-ins with people involved in the recording projects. Now we are left with about 75 openings in a *full year* of top ten charts. I'll bet that well over 10,000 writers are trying to fill those 75 slots with their songs.

I'd say that your work was really cut out for you! But there's a simple way to beat these forbidding odds: Just write a song with a hook or a message *so good* that it simply cannot be refused. That's not easy, of course. You've got to say an old, familiar thing in a new way in country music. A large majority of the hit songs deal with love—lost, found, hoped for, remembered, forgotten, or gone for good. If we date the country music recording industry's beginnings as 1949, the year that *Billboard* began the "Country and Western" chart, that means that thirty-three years worth of hits have already been released. The most obvious approaches, themes, and hooks have been explored to the *nth* degree. So you're going to have to dig beneath the surface, go beyond the first few ideas that emerge in your mind if you want to get to the top ten these days. Take a look at some of the big hits and see how they handled this challenge. Listen to the lyrics of songs like "The Way I Am," "Good Old Boys like Me," "He Stopped Loving Her Today," "I Believe in You" and "A Lesson in Leavin' " and see how the writers of these songs (Sonny Throckmorton; Bob McDill; Curly Putman and Bobby Braddock; Sam Hogin and Roger Cook; and Randy Goodrum, respectively) handled the problem of coming up with a new approach.

GETTING STARTED AS A SINGER

$\mathbf{M}$uch of the advice to beginning songwriters in the previous chapter applies also to the singer trying to get started in country music. Be sure to read that chapter before proceeding with this and the next chapter, "Recording Deals."

As you can hear from the radio, a classically trained or operatic voice isn't necessary for a career as a vocalist in country music. What you do need to have is a voice with at least a *little* uniqueness to it. You need to sound like someone different, someone new. While it may get you some work in the beginning if you sound like Willie Nelson or Conway Twitty, in the long run it will dent your chances of landing a recording contract. No one will sell records indefinitely; even Elvis Presley endured a serious drought in the sales department during his last decade. In the words of Harlan Howard, "Sooner or later they just get *tired* of hearing your damn voice." If right now you do sound like someone else, don't despair—work on changing your style, phrasing, or approach just enough to set yourself apart from the competition.

While you shouldn't try to sound like the stars of today, you can learn a great deal by studying them. Take note of their onstage manner, the way they move, how they hold the microphone. Listen especially to their between-song remarks; watch the way they "work" the crowd; take notice of the way they pace their shows. See when they insert their big hits and when they sing their new singles. See the eye contact they develop with the audience and how they interact with the band. The top country artists generally have a way of being so at ease onstage that they seem to be back home in their living room. (Kenny Rodgers is the undisputed champion at this.) Some top acts strive for an air of menace, some project an image of wholesomeness. Some favor an image of lawlessness, some aim for vulnerability. The key point here is to note that all of the top acts project an image to those who come to their shows. You'll need to develop your own image if you want to get out of local honky-tonks.

What about being on the scene in Nashville?

If you are a singer in addition to being a writer, I would say that you should move to Nashville *only* when you have gone just about as far as you can go in your particular area. If you're playing almost every night to full or near-full houses, have established good relations with the country DJs in your vicinity, and have possibly released a few singles on a local label to good response, then the time is probably ripe for you to pay a visit to Music City. You'll notice that I said, "pay a visit." Don't move here yet. Your first trip should be a scouting journey to survey the terrain, size up the competition, make some contacts, and check out living costs. Block out at least a few weeks to come here and look over the situation before you make any commitments.

In fact, a singer may be much better off by not moving here at all. If you have a really sweet deal going on your own home turf or you are making big bucks working the road you may be able to come to Nashville occasionally to make records and look into business matters without actually moving here. I notice that Mickey Gilley and Johnny Lee aren't doing too shabbily living near Houston, playing as often as they like, and only visiting Nashville to meet with label people or to tape records or TV shows.

RECORDING DEALS

Your chances of strolling into RCA Records and emerging with a recording contract are about the same as a high school football player's chances of getting signed by the Pittsburgh Steelers. In fact, if you haven't at least some track record on a label people have heard of, your chances of even making it past the receptionist are slender. The people who work in major recording companies are not sitting around with their feet on their desks, hoping that someone will come around to ask them for money. They are in a tough, highly competitive business with a small profit margin as their reward if, and only if, they are extremely careful, yet are willing to take some risks, work hard, release quality recordings, and do so at a time when the public is ready and able to buy them. The number of new artists who are signed to a major label in a given year is very small, perhaps only three to five in a *good* year. If you can show from the beginning that you have a sizeable audience that wants to buy your records, then you may have a fighting chance.

"But I've got talent," you may say. Well, let me clue you in: so does almost everybody else who is trying to make it in the music business. It takes a lot more than talent these days. You've got to have a winning personality, be reasonably attractive, be totally determined to make it, have a good knowledge of the way the business works, have patience in plentitude, possess more self-confidence than a politician, have a distinctive voice, and be blessed with a lot of luck. Things are so tough these days that I often wonder if Hank Williams or Jimmie Rodgers would stand a chance if either were to be reincarnated with a batch of new songs and make the rounds of Nashville label offices, trying to cut a deal.

So how do you land that first recording deal? There are three main avenues you can explore to get there: through a publisher, producer, or manager. Since we've already talked a little about a publisher-contact, let's start there.

Left to right: Tex Ritter, Hank Thompson, Johnny Cash (Country Music Foundation)

Frank Walker with cigar, Hank Williams with pen (Country Music Foundation)

Slim Whitman laying it on the dotted line (Country Music Foundation)

Ink is the glue that cements the bond between art and commerce.

RECORDING DEALS THROUGH YOUR PUBLISHER

First of all you must remember that your publisher *wants* to get you a recording deal if he thinks that you have even the faintest scrap of vocal appeal. Should he snag you a recording arrangement he would automatically find an easy avenue to expose your songs to the public. Thus both of you would be able to collect some money for your songs that appear on the record. Secondly, these songs will then be vinyl advertising for your songwriting expertise and thus liable to be "covered" by other singers, perhaps even by artists who sell records by the boxcar load. If you have a relatively pleasing voice you could wind up selling a fair quantity of records yourself. The fact that the publisher copped a record deal for one of their company's writers is a good lick which will not go unnoticed among local songwriters who are looking for a new home for their tunes. Your publisher may even be able to cut himself in for more of the action by producing the record, placing other songs he publishes on the album, or recording the disc at a studio which his company has an interest in.

Naturally it is to your advantage as well to get a recording deal. You'll stand a lot better chance of obtaining one if you are represented by a reputable publisher. Remember, your publisher has been in town for quite a while and no doubt has a good many more friends than you do in key positions at record labels. If his reputation is good, chances are he'll be able to get in the door to see the folks in town who can make a deal—the same ones who have been giving you the cold shoulder when you've tried by yourself.

In this instance your publisher is actually functioning as your manager. He's carrying the ball for you, helping to broaden your exposure, and working on your behalf to gain entry for you into an extremely competitive field. By all means cooperate with him, even if you don't personally think that you stand much chance of making it as a singer. Tom T. Hall didn't think he had much of a shot either, and you may have noticed that he has sold a substantial number of his own waxings. Whether you think you're a good singer or not has very little bearing on the end result. The final judge in these matters is the public and no one yet knows for sure just what the public will find appealing. There are many, many successful artists in country music who don't have incredible voices. The important thing is to sing with *conviction*, have a bit of distinctiveness and remain reasonably close to the correct key and pitch (an objective outside opinion on this last is usually a good idea). Face it, not everybody can have the sort of vocal tools that Waylon Jennings, George Jones, or Crystal Gayle enjoy.

But before you are able to see if the public wants to buy your singing, you'll have to convince a record label that they will have a fair chance of selling a respectable number of your recordings. If your publisher is willing to take the time to assist you in this endeavor, then do your best to be of some assistance. A writer whose songs are hits for other artists is almost guaranteed a record deal. Don Schlitz was signed by Capitol mainly on the strength of his CMA and Grammy Award winning song, "The Gambler." Richard Leigh's smash hits, "I'll Get Over You" and "Don't It Make My Brown Eyes Blue" opened the door for his record deal at United Artists (now Liberty) Records. Billy Joe Shaver suddenly landed a record deal at Monument after Waylon recorded eight of his tunes for his *Honky Tonk Heroes* album. Sonny Throckmorton's many hits helped him get a recording contract with Mercury Records, Sonny's first effort for a major label after seventeen years on lesser known companies. Tom T. Hall, Kris Kristofferson, Rafe Van Hoy, Randy Goodrum, Bill Anderson, Mel Tillis, Willie Nelson and dozens more artists obtained their first record contracts because the public had shown a willingness to buy their songs when others sang them.

RECORDING DEALS THROUGH A PRODUCER

Perhaps you don't have a publisher. Possibly your publisher is too busy publishing and pitching songs to scout up a record deal for you. In these cases your next best possibility is to seek a record deal through a record producer. He also has a lot to gain by capturing you a deal since he'll be collecting a fee for each track, or "side," he delivers to the label. He'll also be in line for royalties based upon the sale of the record. In addition many producers own or co-own recording studios and/or publishing companies, two circumstances which smack of a conflict-of-interest situation but which are perfectly acceptable industry practices. As in the case of a publisher, a producer has a lot to gain financially from your deal; he generally also has a wider circle of contacts among record people than you, a young writer or a new performer. "Fine," you say, "how do I find a producer and convince him to take me and my talent along?"

Finding a producer in Nashville is about as hard as locating a train at Grand Central Station. You can look at the label or jacket copy on records. You can look at the information next to the top 100 singles listed in the weekly issues of *Billboard* magazine. You can look in any of *Billboard*'s annual directories. You can ask around town among your music acquaintances. Look in the nifty little Nashville music industry directory published by Cedarwood Music. Ask at the local office of the musician's union, or at the local office of the National Academy of Recording Arts & Sciences. Rest assured, producers may be elusive but they aren't invisible.

Convincing a producer to take you on involves many of the same salesmanship principles we discussed when we spoke of finding a publisher. Pick out several producers whose work you admire and write them a note asking if you can submit a tape. Include a description of your professional experience, but make it brief. Tell them you think you've got what it takes, that you are new in town, who is publishing your songs and where you will be performing if you have some live shows lined up. Better yet, if you do have a publisher see if he will help arrange an appointment. If you have a friend in the business who knows a good producer, see if *they* won't help you at least get in the door. In this pursuit it would probably be best to lower your sights to some degree. Everyone would like to have a top producer like Billy Sherrill, Jimmy Bowen, Blake Mevis, or Jerry Crutchfield handle his production. Hit producers like this turn down *established* artists routinely simply because they cannot produce everyone who wants their services. Part of the reason they *are* hit producers is that they exercise a great deal of selectivity in who they choose to take into the studio. What you need to find early in your career is a producer who is hungry, who perhaps hasn't had a big hit in a while, or who may just be starting out in production after previously being involved as an engineer, artist, session player, or publisher. These people will be a lot more accessible and much more likely to take on an unknown if what you do strikes their ears.

Before I go further I should perhaps point out that there are three kinds of producers: staff producers, independent producers, and those who work both sides of the fence. A staff producer works exclusively for a particular record label. He may be doing some minor development projects on his own "on spec" (on a purely speculative basis), but almost all his time is spent on projects for his employer. An independent producer works for several labels, picking and choosing projects as he goes along with considerably more freedom than a staff producer enjoys, because as an independent he is always free to turn down a project. Independent producers also will work on developing artists who have no label at the time, hoping to record tracks so strong that they will be picked up by a recording company when the project is finished or near completion. Some producers have agreements to produce certain artists for a label but are free to take on what other projects they can fit into their schedule. And there are some producers who are contracted directly by the artist to produce their records regardless of the label involved.

For many years country music was recorded only by staff producers. Chet Atkins, Felton Jarvis, Owen Bradley, Jack Kapp, Steve Sholes, Don Law, and a few others were employed directly by the labels; no one else produced discs for their labels. This arrangement began to change in the late sixties when Jack "Cowboy" Clement became the first independent producer to capture major label business by helping bring Charley Pride to the attention of RCA. By 1980 the tide seemed to have turned around. Few of the major labels employed a large staff of producers; most of the work was farmed out either to independents or to the artists themselves. Waylon Jennings and RCA fought many battles in this regard before Waylon finally won the right to produce himself or to select his own producer. At one time an artist had little or no say over producer selection; a producer was assigned and that was it. Nowdays the major artists either produce themselves or they choose their producers. Even minor artists have a great deal of say-so in production matchups now.

I would recommend that you look for either an independent producer or one of the quasi-independents who can take on business from both sources. Your chances of getting in the door to see a label producer aren't much better than they are of buttonholing a label executive. Staff producers are kept very busy by their employers and would most probably tell you to come see them when you get a deal.

By now you may be getting the idea that this is a tough nut to crack. It is. There aren't many openings in this business and the ones that exist certainly aren't found in the classified section of the Sunday paper. If you are good at taking no for an answer you ought to be in an easier racket. Time and again your hopes will be dashed to pieces. Time and again you will think how unfair this business is. The only way to make it is to keep coming back, trying again and again. You will have to adopt the "never quit" philosophy or seek employment in a less rigorous profession.

If you can find a producer who will work with you, bear in mind that he is gambling on your talent and his skill in developing that talent in much the same manner that a publisher gambles on a new writer. A producer won't put you on a salary, but he will be investing his time in your talent. He will be putting you into a studio, which requires time and cash outlays. (One reel of two-inch mastering tape alone costs well over $100). Musicians will be required for your project and they need to be paid. So I would not balk if your producer asks you to sing some songs which he publishes or which he wrote. I wouldn't even be surprised if he asks to publish your songs if he can get you a record deal. It may turn out that a producer can offer you a better arrangement than your present publisher, if you have one. After all, the producer and the artist choose the songs to be recorded while the publisher can only *suggest* candidates and discreetly lobby for them the best way he can. If your new producer asks you to record some of his songs, or a tune which he publishes, or if he asks about publishing your own work, you should be very flattered. Remember, he wouldn't want any old hog-mouth singing tunes he's invested time and money in, and like any other publisher he has no use for a song unless he thinks it can make money for him—and for you.

As a general rule, most independent producers are also publishers. Not all publishers are also producers, however—there are more independent producers who also publish than publishers who also produce. Even so, all good publishers know enough about producing to be able to supervise demo sessions (but not all producers know a great deal about the mechanics of publishing).

Even if you're trying to secure a recording deal through a publisher, it is still a good idea to keep a keen ear open for producers because you will need one if your publisher does bring home a label contract. On top of that, the more producers you know and the closer your relationships with them, the better your chances are when you drop by to pitch them a tune for one of the acts they produce. Getting to know as many producers as you can is just one more avenue you must follow to increase your chances of making it as a songwriter, whether you want to go the recording route or not.

RECORDING DEALS THROUGH A MANAGER

If you're strictly a songwriter you have no more need of a manager than a fish has of wheels. If you're trying to land your *first* recording deal as a performer in the country field you won't be very likely to need one either. Until you achieve some measure of success in country music a manager is just not necessary. The one exception might be your finding a manager who believes in you enough to help by financing your instrument purchases, footing the bill for lead sheets, loaning you money, obtaining a car for you, or providing housing. But be careful about what you agree to do to repay such a person— you could wind up owing him a large percentage of your income when you are a success.

Look at it this way. If you have a publisher, you already have someone who is performing most managerial functions for you. A good publisher will hawk your songs, give you advice on all manner of problems, furnish you a draw against expected future earnings, provide a place for you to write, pay for your lead sheets, demo your songs, collect the money your songs earn, help you find a record deal and call you when you are sick.

If you haven't got a publisher I really don't see how you can be making enough money to go around. The only exception to this is if you are a front man for a band which is continually working long stretches of out-of-town engagements. I don't think that a manager can land a deal for you at a publishing house. It's a nice luxury to have someone out there making the rounds of publishers for you—but the publisher will make his decision based on his assessment of *your* talent, personality, determination, and intelligence. Doing a convincing job of selling yourself is a large point in your favor when it comes to a publisher's evaluation of you and his decision to take you on. You have to sell a publisher on *you* and on *your* songs, so you might as well be the one who is out there pounding the pavement at this stage in your career. The experience you pick up and the contacts you gain will be invaluable to you later.

Once you get a recording deal, have lots of dates booked, hire a band, and have endorsement queries pouring in, you will need a manager to coordinate your personal appearances, help manage your finances, oversee contract negotiations, seek out other areas of remuneration, and perform the thousand-and-one duties you can't possibly have the time to take care of. But until your career has reached the stage where you can't handle all the arrangements by yourself, you simply don't need a fifth wheel on your modest wagon. The final decision in all your major career planning will be up to you anyway, no matter how big you get or what your manager advises.

As a rule of thumb, if you *think* you need a manager you probably don't. When things get going so good that you can't keep up with all the details and be an artist too, *then* would be a good time to start hunting for a manager.

INDEPENDENT DISTRIBUTORS AND RECORD COMPANIES

In the past few years the distribution factor has become one of the most important parts of the record-selling process. The largest labels have now established their own networks for bringing their records to the market. In the past this function was handled by independent distributors who carried the lines of many of the larger labels. When the major companies pulled their lines from these distributors, this combined with skyrocketing fuel, warehousing, and personnel costs to force a number of independents out of the record business. Those that remain generally handle record distribution for a region rather than one city. They'll typically handle a lot of the smaller labels, known as independent record companies.

As the number of independent distributors has decreased so has the number of major recording companies. In the past few years several significant recording companies have given up the battle, either succumbing entirely (Infinity, Stax, Capricorn, Free Flight) or becoming part of a larger concern (A & M with RCA; ABC with MCA; Capitol and United Artists with EMI; Mercury, MGM, and Polydor with Polygram). The number of artists signed to major labels also has declined as the number of major labels has declined. There aren't as many open positions on record company rosters as there once were. For instance, Capitol and United Artists used to be completely separate companies. Capitol has a long and illustrious history in country music, having established the careers of such luminaries as Buck Owens, Faron Young, Sonny James, Ferlin Husky, Hank Thompson, Merle Haggard, Tennessee Ernie Ford, Roy Clark, Glen Campbell, and The Louvin Brothers. United Artists brought us such major acts as Kenny Rogers, Crystal Gayle, Billie Joe Spears and Dottie West. United Artists became Liberty Records (an important label in the 1950s and 1960s but then dormant for many years). Capitol and Liberty are now part of the EMI-America family, a subsidiary of the huge EMI recording and electronics empire which is based in England and is a diversified worldwide concern.

ABC, MCA, and Dot Records were separate companies at one point; ABC absorbed Dot to become the ABC-Dot label. Then MCA bought that company and phased out the ABC-Dot label.

Fewer companies means fewer spots available for the up-and-coming artist. The smaller, independent company now plays a much more vital role in the development of new talent. Though many people in the industry may look down on the indie labels, the reality is that almost every major act of our time began recording for small labels like Zero (Loretta Lynn), Resco (Gene Watson), Tally (Merle Haggard), JMI (Don Williams), Chart (Lynn Anderson), Ken-Lee (Kenny Rogers), and the undisputed king of all the independents: Sun (Elvis Presley, Johnny Cash, Jerry Lee Lewis, and Charlie Rich).

You must face the fact that your chances of landing a major label contract first crack out of the chute are somewhere between slim and none. When you finally do land that major label contract, your past experience on a smaller label will be invaluable.

There are other ways signing with a small label can be a wise move early in a career, even if you make only one release. You will have a record available to take to your shows and sell to fans who inquire. You will have a recorded version of your talent for record stores and radio stations, which will help build name-awareness. If you wrote the song, a released record will enable you to affiliate with one of the performing rights societies (ASCAP, BMI, or SESAC). You will have a demo to present to larger record companies as coin of the realm. (When you approacch a big record label, a disc will make a better impression than a tape. It shows, without your having to say so, that someone believed in your talent enough to go through the considerable expense of mastering your tape, pressing it up, paying for sleeves and affixing a label to the center.)

Smaller companies don't try to get you to sign the sort of long-term contract that the majors do. (The normal industry practice is a "five-year" contract, meaning they are signing you to a one-year contract with four one-year options to be exercised at their discretion. In reality you are signing yourself to them for five years but they are only committing themselves to you for one year.) Smaller companies are willing to make a short-term or one-record deal.

Signing up with a smaller company will increase your exposure and it also shows a larger company, if you eventually merit serious consideration there, that you are no stranger to the recording studio and are acquainted with the problems and inner workings of a record label, at least on a small scale.

You are less likely to get lost in the shuffle at an independent label. The big companies are always working on a minimum of a dozen records at any one time. When the label puts out these records they assign priorities to their field promotion staff. If you're a new artist you can pretty well guess how high your priority will be when you are up against acts who have had previous hits and who are known to the DJs. A smaller label will usually carefully space their releases so that they won't be pushing too many records at any one time.

An independent has a much more informal structure than a major label. If you have a problem, it is generally not too difficult to speak to the label boss about it quickly. At a bigger label it can take you quite a time to catch the ear of a top executive. You're likely to receive more personal attention at an indie label as well. Because they have fewer acts to promote, there's a chance that you can receive a more concerted effort from their press relations department.

Getting your first chart record is a vital step in your progress. Though independent labels rarely make the top ten (since 1977 only L.S., IBC, Scorpion, Republic, Compleat, Sunbird, Noble Vision, and Ovation have managed it), they do place quite a number of records in the top sixty of the trade listings. Once you've at least dented the chart territory you've obtained a very valuable calling card which will increase your future marketability. Getting a top thirty record on Shoe Leather Records is damned impressive, roughly the equivalent of a top-ten record on a big label.

One final thought: independent labels are usually strapped for cash; thus if you launch a good record for an indie they may well be willing to sell your contract to one of the biggies. "Oh, *please* don't throw me into the briar patch, B'rer Fox!"

RECORDING WITH A MAINSTREAM INDEPENDENT LABEL

There are many things that must be done to get a record into the marketplace: recording, record manufacturing, distribution, promotion and all the attendant functions falling under those basic areas. A major label normally has all these services performed in its own facilities by its own staff. Independent labels usually are too small to do business this way. Instead, they buy the services of contractors, using independent record pressing plants, distribution networks, and promoters.

Bob Saporiti, an independent record producer and promoter, is retained by an independent label to produce recording sessions on a flat fee basis for his services. He explained typical costs involved in getting a single into the marketplace.

"It costs as much as $10,000 to put out a record right now," Saporiti said, "and that's really on a mini scale. For that kind of money you are really just aiming at getting radio air play and getting your record in front of wholesalers so they'll know who to order it from if air play generates a demand in stores."

Here is a representative cost and services breakdown for a single record release on an independent record label:

6 union musicians for a 3-hour session (average cost)	$1,400.00
10 hours of 24-track studio rental @ $100 per hour (average cost)	$1,000.00
4 backup vocalists @ $100 each per 3-hour session	$400.00
Recording tape	$160.00
Producer's fee (typical independent's fee of $500 per song)	$1,000.00
Mastering two sides	$75.00
Manufacturing 1,500 copies, mailing 1,000 to DJs, and minimum of 5 weeks telephone follow-up on initial mail-out. (In independent pop-country record production these items are usually handled by the distributor, who also takes a royalty)	$3,000.00
	Total $7,035.00

Some of the best recording facilities in the world are located in Nashville. This is CBS Records Columbia Studio A, as remodeled and expanded in 1979 to handle full orchestras and live dates. Acoustical drapes can be pulled to divide it into smaller recording areas. The glass booths provide acoustic isolation of small groups without sacrificing eye-contact with a leader and accompanists. (CBS Records/Dean D. Dixon)

Tammy Wynette's great hits, produced by Billy Sherrill, were mixed through this 24-track console in the control room of Columbia's Studio B. (Al Atherton)

Every hit recorded by RCA Nashville between 1950 and 1965 was engineered through this simple console, including some of the finest stereo recordings ever captured on tape. It is now in the Country Music Foundation Hall of Fame and Museum. (Country Music Foundation)

"Ring of Fire," "El Paso," "Big Bad John," and "Battle of New Orleans" were only a few of the hits recorded through this console, in continuous service at Columbia Nashville from 1961 to 1969. Before that, it was in the famous quonset hut studio of "Nashville Sound" producer Owen Bradley. It, too, is now in the Country Music Foundation Hall of Fame and Museum. (Country Music Foundation)

(To estimate comparable production costs for an album, figure four three-hour sessions with instrumentalists, including two with vocalists; thirty-five hours of studio time; $400-$500 for mastering ten sides; $600 for tape; negotiable producer's fee; and $3,750 to the distributor for mastering, mailing, and five-week telephone follow-up.)

The rest of the $10,000 estimated necessary for launching a single would go for pressing additional copies and mailing them to music wholesalers and to one-stop stores, and for additional manufacturing and promotion should the record begin to catch the public's fancy. One-stop stores are combination wholesale-retail outlets that stock independent product. They are particularly important to the independents who (unlike the majors) rarely have local sales reps to bring product directly to retail stores.

Once the potential hit has been recorded and manufactured (referred to in the trade as "cut and pressed") the distribution and promotion people take over. The three largest independent country distribution and promotion companies based in Nashville are IRDA/Album Globe, Nationwide Sound Distributors, and Fischer and Lucus Records. These companies accept records from independent labels on a selective basis, according to their own opinion as to the record's potential for chart success. A flat fee is charged for stipulated services.

The independent label normally pays all costs related to production and marketing of a record. There are a number of companies doing business as "custom country" labels, providing what amounts to artist-subsidized production and promotion, and these often fall into the artist rip-off category. This can be a very tricky proposition for the would-be artist. It is always good practice when contemplating affiliation with any independent record label, custom or otherwise, to find out about that label's track record. Do they have a past history of putting out and promoting records which make it onto the charts or not? If making the country charts is your aim, then getting with a label which has proven abilities in this area is a definite plus.

If you are a newcomer country performer looking for a record deal you will find your chances are much greater with an independent, but be sure you know what kind of deal you're making. There are a few common sense rules:

> Be wary of anyone asking you for the capital required to produce your record while promising to make you a "star." The majority of legitimate independent labels are the working entity of one or more investors who are willing to bet on a new artist's potential with their own money.
> Always check around and find out the company's track record before signing a contract.
> Never enter into an unwritten agreement.
> Have any contract read by a competent music business lawyer before signing it.

SPECIALIZED COUNTRY INDEPENDENT LABELS

The independents just discussed deal primarily with mainstream commercial pop-country music. Another segment of the small-label country music industry is dedicated to traditional artists and forms such as bluegrass, newgrass, folk-country, country-blues, and rural country music. Independent labels of this kind cater to the specialized audiences attracted by these musical genres.

It has been said that the major labels in the 1980s are run by corporate accountants, but that by and large the specialized labels are operated by music lovers.

To say that these little labels produce country music of the kind you just don't hear on commercial radio stations anymore is not to say that they are operating without the profit picture in mind. The specialized label is just an independent record company with a distinct market in mind. The successful examples of the breed know the size, tastes, and buying habits of their audience very well. Some great old-time artists, new artists honoring old-time musical styles, and those artists forging new territory in bluegrass, newgrass, blues, Western swing, folk, jazz, and a variety of experimental combinations of these forms have found homes on the labels listed below, all of which include country and country-related products among their releases. (This list is not all-inclusive.)

Rounder Records: Very eclectic roster. Made its reputation with old-time country music, has since branched out into everything from Cajun, rockabilly, and bluegrass to blues. Apparently interested in both traditional presentation and contemporary permutations of the root forms of modern country music.

Flying Fish: Supports an interesting form which could be called "hillbilly jazz," records old-time revivalists and folkies, and records a lot of contemporary bluegrass artists, including Norman Blake.

County Records: Issues old-time revivals and contemporary bluegrass, mostly in a traditional vein.

Yazoo/Arhoolie/Folk Lyric Records: Specialize in blues, both original recordings and reissues; release some new country and country reissues; also cover a variety of ethnic music, such as Tex-Mex and Ukrainian fiddle.

Philo Records: Encourages young singer-songwriters working in the folk and country traditions to take full artistic control of their recorded product, with some interesting results.

Sugar Hill Records: Produces highly commercial country and newgrass records, and has launched such artists as Ricky Skaggs and Buck White and the Down Home Folks.

Rebel Records: Produces basic, straight-ahead bluegrass.

Old Homestead Records: Reissues classic old-time recordings and issues new products by classic old-time musicians.

Takoma Records: Issues mainly acoustic instrumentals but also has produced traditional country artists like Rose Maddox.

Sierra/Briar Records: Leans toward folk singers, folk-country, and country-rock acts.

Ridge Runner Records: Produces bluegrass and contemporary acoustic country music.

Folkways: Records folksingers, and folkies who do old-time country.

Kaleidescope/Vanguard/Mountain Railroad: All basically oriented toward folk, folk-blues, and singer-songwriter artists; each has country-related products in its catalogue.

June Appal: Places emphasis on traditional mountain performers.

CMH: West Coast label that produces new releases by classic country stars such as Grandpa Jones, the late Merle Travis, and Joe Maphis; also bluegrass albums.

GETTING STARTED AS AN INSTRUMENTALIST

SESSION PICKING

One of the most challenging, creative, and financially rewarding things a musician can do is become a session player. For those who do become full-time professional session players there is good pay, the stability of getting off the road, and the glamour of recording with top country music artists.

That's for me, you may be saying. If so, once you decide that you've reached a level of professional competence in your musicianship you should seek out the local chapter of the musicians' union, the American Federation of Musicians (AFM). This national organization operates for the benefit and protection of its member musicians. It is so good at its job that without union membership you simply cannot get major label session work. The Nashville Musicians Association is Local 257 of the AFM. While Nashville is certainly not the only place where country music recording sessions take place, it is still the center of such work, the place where most of the records on the country music charts are produced. Although AFM locals are somewhat autonomous in certain areas of their operation, the Nashville model should serve as a good basic guide to what the union does for musicians.

According to Johnny DeGeorge, president of the Nashville chapter, Local 257 represents approximately 3,000 professional musicians, from oboists to banjoists. Though singer-songwriter John Sebastian once asserted that "There's 1,352 guitar pickers in Nashville," there are in fact about 800 union guitar pickers in Nashville. They became union members by paying an initial new-member fee, which currently is $169.00. This is a one-time fee which includes the normal annual dues of $44. Union locals around the country have various initiation fees and membership requirements. Some require that applicants pass a written exam, though this is not the case in Nashville.

"We've got some pickers in town who are doing well," explained Johnny DeGeorge, "some who make $50,000 or $60,000 a year who can't read [music]. So we're not going to deny them union membership on account of it."

Through national collective bargaining the union establishes pay scales for session work. There are a variety of complex working and use conditions which are taken into account in figuring how much a musician will be paid for different kinds of session work. Every so often the union renegotiates these fees. As of summer 1984 the rate for a three-hour session to record a master tape is $178.15 for the picker. In addition to that amount the record producer pays a 10 percent contribution to the union pension fund and $4.50 to a union health and welfare fund. The Nashville local doesn't maintain an active health and welfare fund, so you would get that money directly in your pay check. A 2 percent working fee is deducted by the union before your check is written. The session musician is paid through the union office. When a session is completed the record producer signs a time card, often referred to as a "ticket," verifying how long the musician played and at what rate the session was booked.

As mentioned above, the master session three-hour rate is $178.15. A demo session pays $29.69 per hour, with a minimum call of two hours. A session to record a commercial jingle for national use pays $70.00 to $75.65 an hour, depending on the number of musicians used. If the commercial is used beyond a thirteen-week period, the musicians receive additional payment. The basic session rate for local-use jingles is $55.00 an hour, also with additional payment after the initial thirteen weeks of usage. Every recording session has one musician designated as the leader. A leader is responsible for getting the sound out of the band that the record producer wants to hear. He may be responsible for writing out chord charts for songs and otherwise coordinating the action in the sound room while the producer coordinates the control room. Session leaders are paid at double the prevailing rate.

Musicians present their time cards at the union pay window to get their money after a session. Depending on the solvency of the record company or producer of a particular session, the musician may have no wait, a short wait, or a long, drawn out ordeal before the session pay comes to the union to be released to the pickers. As a service to its members the union hall keeps a default list posted where pickers can find out who is behind in payments to union musicians for session work.

The union may handle a musician's money and complaints against defaulters but it doesn't handle his bookings. Each musician must find his or her own work. In every major recording center there are musical contractors, people who maintain a reputation among producers for consistantly delivering good string, horn, or rhythm sections. Proving your abilities to one of these contractors can mean steady work for you as a session musician.

A session musician's most important investments are his instruments. The only musician who isn't expected to provide his own instrument for a recording session is a piano player. This can get expensive, as it is wise to own as many instruments as you can play well. A guitarist, for instance, is rarely told what he will be called on to play when he is booked for a session. Many professional guitarists carry steel and nylon string acoustics and at least one electric guitar to a session just to be on the safe side. Utility picker and harmonica ace Charlie McCoy may use only his least expensive Hohner Marine Band C-major harp on a session, but he will carry at least twenty other harmonicas with him. Of course, one need not buy out the music store to get started as a session picker; such acquisitions come with time.

Session work, whether in Nashville, Los Angeles, New York, or any other area with studios, is fast and demanding. A producer may expect to get the music tracks for three or four songs during a three-hour session, a feat that takes a lot of effort and concentration, especially in country sessions. Other kinds of music recorded in other places may feature full notation music charts for the musicians to read and play from, but country music can be very different. According to Johnny DeGeorge, the vast majority of Nashville country music sessions start out with somebody strumming a little rhythm guitar for the other pickers and saying, "It goes something like this." The session leader may then write out a rough chord chart using a unique form of musical shorthand known as the "Nashville Number System."

"Ninety-nine percent of my work is non-reading," a twenty-three-year session picking veteran reported, "and if we do read at all we just read chord charts. When I first came to Nashville in 1960, pickers were just beginning to use the number system. Owen Bradley taught it to me. Before that I guess pickers just had to memorize the songs before sessions because almost nobody read notes."

"I think its really tough to come in now," he began, "more than it was when I came in because there's just more competition, more guys wanting to do it."

A lot of pickers break into session work by doing demos for song publishers. Publishing companies normally pay standard union scale when they go into a studio to cut demos, but there is rarely any formal remuneration for playing on "work tapes." These may be produced on a two-track office tape recorder and serve to get the idea of a song down for future reference. Doing these demos and work tapes is all part of the time-honored tradition of "paying your dues."

There is just no easy way to break into session work. As so many session players will tell you, you have to be willing to starve a little bit. You have to be willing and able to "hang out" until your talents become known to the people who will ultimately pay for the use of them. That's where the human factor comes in, the who-you-know aspect of music which determines who gets a break and who gets stuck among the 80 percent or more of union musicians for whom session work is a secondary source of income if not a near-hobby.

Another truth of the country music business is that a relatively few pickers get the majority of the best work. Because they *are* so good and so well known, they are constantly in demand. But it isn't all just feast or famine in the world of country music session picking. There is an important middle ground of demos, jingles, and the occasional master session, particularly with a new artist signed with a smaller, independent label. This is where the Super Pickers of tomorrow are learning, experimenting, improving their playing, and getting known today. As Johnny DeGeorge explained it, there's always room for a great picker—if that picker can just hang on until people find out about him.

LIVE PICKING

Willie Nelson may have penned the live musician's national anthem in his "On the Road Again," the theme song from the hit movie *Honeysuckle Rose*. However anxious

Willie may have been to travel around the country making music with his friends, there's a lot more to making a living playing live gigs than just loading up your panel truck, Silver Eagle motor coach, or, if you're Kenny Rogers, your private jet airplane, with some guitar picking buddies and going for the gusto.

For the musician willing to perform in front of a live audience there are a great many levels and opportunities for working. These range from the amateur and semi-professional local tavern circuit to the prestige of being a sideman for a top country act. The higher up in the live picking world one gets, the more imperative it is to be working with a band—there are very few solo pickers making the big money in live performance.

As with session picking, live picking on a professional level is a unionized affair. The American Federation of Musicians is also the live musician's friend. The information regarding membership fees and requirements put forth in the preceding section on session picking holds true whether you are a traveling band member or a session player. The pay rates are, of course, not the same. Union scale pay rates vary from one local chapter of the AFM to the next. Rates for union pickers also are determined by the nature of the job. Things like the number of days or nights played per week and the number of hours per day are taken into consideration, as is the size of the job site. For these reasons it is not practical to quote a uniform minimum union live pay rate here. Suffice it to say that the union minimum is greater than the minimum paid for a comparable non-union gig.

Musicians' union halls and most instrument stores frequented by professional pickers tend to feature somewhere in their main area a bulletin board where "Picker Wanted/ Available" notices may be placed. Aside from the occasional Musicians' Trust Fund gigs, which the union books with funds provided by the recording industry to encourage wider public appreciation of live musical performance, that is about all the direct involvement that the union locals have with the musician's search for live work.

Compared to session work, live picking is a great deal more forgiving of an occasional sour note.

"When you are playing with a band . . . there is less chance that an error will be noticed," Johnny DeGeorge says. "Another difference is, of course, you have a lot more time to learn material."

THE ACT

"I played with every band that would let me play with them."

That's how Henry Strezlecki, leader of the session and road band, the Nashville Super Pickers, describes his early days as a freelance live picker. He told of playing seven nights a week, six hours or more a night with various bands around Biloxi, Atlanta, Shreveport, and New Orleans, generally making the Deep South country circuit as it existed in the mid- to late 1950s. That period of "dues paying" and getting a broad street-style music education eventually led him to a seventeen-year gig as Chet Atkins's bass player, both on the road and on record. Charlie McCoy, Monument recording artist, top harmonica player, and touring band leader, tells of similar working conditions when he came to Nashville at the age of seventeen to form the premier country/rhythm-and-blues combo and show band of its time, Charlie McCoy and the Escorts.

Just about any band leader or picker with one of the top country touring acts will tell a similar story. They all started out working with bands doing "cover acts" on one circuit or another which booked country music. These acts play—"cover"—the current country hits, usually mixed with middle of the road pop material and a few disco tunes. Basically formatted for danceable music, the contemporary country music lounge and club act sticks with known popular tunes, occasionally including original numbers if they have any.

There are several circuits that offer opportunities for gigs in the live country picking market. The lounge circuit is about the best circuit for a picker who wants to be exposed to traveling recording artists. Warner Brothers artist John Anderson picked most of his current road band members out of various club acts he saw while touring around through the South one year. The college circuit and the state and county fair circuit are also steady money-makers for country bands.

Kenny Rogers and country-rock star Linda Ronstadt are among the current top country acts which once worked the college circuits heavily. Seen by music business promoters as one of the best avenues to breaking in an act with the youth market, a college campus engagement can pay anywhere from a few hundred dollars per night for a band to a few thousand. College-age audiences like a wide variety of musical styles, from 1950s' nostalgia show bands (Sha Na Na made a good living on this circuit for years) to contemporary country and bluegrass acts. A number of country/folk singer-songwriters such as Steve Young, Townes Van Zandt, and John Prine find this a very receptive circuit, even traveling as solo acts.

The fair circuit tends to be more traditionally oriented. Prior to his death a few years ago, Lester Flatt did a lot of county and state fair work just as he had from his earliest days with Bill Monroe and later with Earl Scruggs. Well-rehearsed acts emphasizing the more rural forms of country music are quite popular on this circuit. State fairs, which tend to be held in capital cities, have the greater crowd potential and urban settings to book the big-name country acts like Waylon Jennings, Loretta Lynn, and Conway Twitty.

The whole idea of building a repertoire or an act for a soloist or a band is to do whatever kind of material a particular market will pay to hear. The best way to find this out is to go to the places where country acts play and listen for yourself. You can bet that an act that gets repeat bookings in a particular market is playing the right kind of music for its audiences.

BOOKINGS

Professional pickers in Nashville refer to gigs as falling into one of two categories: the traveling gig and the sit-down gig. One-night stands and other brief engagements are traveling gigs, known as such because an act can often spend more time getting to the job than it does on stage. The sit-down is the ultimate soft job, at least in the eyes of a traveling band. Acts with long-term engagements, house bands, and the like are said to have a sit-down gig because they will be around long enough to do just that.

In the normal course of business, an act with a sit-down job which is not in the home city is provided with accommodations by the club or lounge in which it is booked. Often these lounges are connected with a hotel or motel, and the traveling act will be put up in that facility. On the average motel lounge circuit a band will be paid between $1,500 and $2,500 per week plus rooms; meals are usually the individual's own responsibility. The pay rates for traveling acts can range from adequate to fabulous depending on who the act is and where the engagement is booked. According to a number of Nashville-based talent booking agencies, $110 per picker is about the minimum pay per night for union players traveling with a headline act, and the pay can be better than that. Naturally, the act's headliner, being the one who draws the audience, gets to take home a bit more.

To take full advantage of their marketability in the large and diverse world of circuits, clubs, and lounges, most professional acts eventually align themselves with a booking agent. It is the agent's job to know where the work is and where his clients are liable to be well received, and to obtain jobs for his clients. In exchange for this the agent will receive between 10 percent and 20 percent of the gross from a booking: in general, 10 percent is the commission for booking a big country act and up to 20 percent for booking a small act (15 percent is the usual rate). The agent pays for his own telephone and office expenses out of his commissions.

Bill Bleckley, of the Nashville-based Joe Taylor Agency, explained that his agency is one of the moderate-sized agencies which book country artists and bands. It is one of 125 Nashville agencies signatory to the musician union's agency agreement. The agreement requires it to book only union acts at union scale or better.

"We booked a fine little old lounge band called 'Wild Country' for several years," Bleckley said. "They would go out and play the Southeast club and Ramada Inn type of circuit and make maybe $1,500 a week tops at that time. They would come back to Nashville and spend their money on recording these songs they'd written over at LSI Studios. When they finally got enough tunes in the can they got a label deal, changed their name to 'Alabama,' and now they make more like $60,000 a night."

Clubs like Gilley's in Houston, Billy Bob's in Fort Worth, and Mama's Country Showcase in Atlanta are the top-paying country night spots in the nation. North Hollywood's Palomino Club and New York City's Lone Star Cafe are examples of well-situated listening rooms that make up for generally smaller pay by being very important showcases where country acts can be seen by an influential audience.

PERFORMANCE RIGHTS AND MECHANICAL RIGHTS

You may often wonder how the writer and publisher of a song get paid when their music is used on radio, TV, at a concert, in a nightclub or restaurant, piped in on a Muzak tape, played through a headset on an airplane, at a ballgame, or at any other time when music is heard. There are three organizations that concern themselves solely with the collection and distribution of this income. They are known as the American Society of Composers and Publishers (ASCAP); Broadcast Music, Incorporated (BMI); and the Society of European Stage Authors and Composers (SESAC). These organizations collect over $200,000,000 annually from the users of music and return most of it to the creators and publishers of that music.

They do this by licensing all music users, from the mighty TV and radio networks to the lowliest cafe, tavern, or club. They have gained the legal right to collect this revenue through a long series of legal battles with every class of music user in existence, beginning with a case instituted in 1915 by Victor Herbert against a New York restaurant named Shanley's. Herbert, a founding member of ASCAP, which was established a year earlier, sued Shanley's for using his music without payment to him. The legal basis for Herbert's claim came from the Copyright Act of 1909, which stated that anyone who used copyrighted material "for profit" could do so only after obtaining a license from the copyright holder. The "for profit" portion of the Act was tacked on to exempt schoolchildren and churchgoers from payment whenever they sang a nursery rhyme or a hymn. Even though the law gave the copyright holder the right to collect, music users had been routinely ignoring it and there was no clear-cut court decision to add backbone to the Copyright Act.

The owner of Shanley's claimed that since he didn't charge people to come to his restaurant, he was not using Herbert's, or any other composer's, music for profit. Herbert and his attorney, another ASCAP founder, Nathan Burkan, took the position that this use violated the written law as stated in the 1909 Copyright Act. Herbert's case was defeated, but he and Burkan doggedly pursued it all the way to the United States Supreme Court. In 1917 the Supreme Court sided with Herbert in a unanimous decision. The court opinion was written by Chief Justice Oliver Wendell Holmes, who stated: "If the music did not pay, it would be given up. If it pays, it pays out of the public's pocket. Whether it pays or not, the purpose of employing it is profit, and that is enough." You won't find the name of Oliver Wendell Holmes and his eight associate justices mentioned in many music books, but that decision has had far-reaching consequences for every songwriter.

From that point on ASCAP, SESAC (formed in 1931), and BMI (founded in 1940), gained the legal teeth they needed to reap the revenue the 1909 Copyright Act said they were entitled to collect. Although every class of music user since has challenged the right of performance rights societies to be reimbursed for the music they represent, all have lost the battle and have been forced to pay up. The last major exemption, to jukeboxes, was erased with the Copyright Act of 1976, the first change in American copyright law in sixty-seven years; owners now pay $50 a year per jukebox. Litigation is currently in progress to collect from cable TV firms for their use of music.

ASCAP and BMI are the two major performance rights organizations. They collect well over 90 percent of the revenues generated from the use of live and recorded music performances in the United States. About 85 percent of that sum is derived from broadcast sources while the rest comes from concert promoters, hotels, airlines, Muzak, nightclubs, theaters, and all other users. Both BMI and ASCAP return about 80 percent of the money collected to the writers and publishers of the music. The 20 percent taken off the top goes to cover the cost of running their operations. Both organizations have reciprocal agreements with the performance rights societies in most other of the countries of the world.

These organizations have different methods of monitoring the users of music to ensure that payments are made according to actual use. Both employ complicated systems to reimburse writers and publishers. Both have offices in the major music centers of the United States. And both employ an administrative staff to locate, collect, and distribute this income. ASCAP is the older organization and it collects more money; BMI has more publisher members and more writer members.

The major difference between the two organizations is that ASCAP is owned by the creators of music—the writers and the publishers—while BMI is owned by the users of music, some 300 broadcasters. As you might expect from such an arrangement, broadcasters pay slightly more to ASCAP for the use of music than they do to BMI. This is partly because the broadcasters own BMI and partly because ASCAP has twenty-six more years of published music in its repertoire. Although the two groups are in direct competition with one another, and despite the fact that they have fought many bitter battles over the past four decades, they now coexist as friendly rivals. They frequently join forces to fight for matters of mutual benefit as they did during the twenty-one years of groundwork which preceded the legislation for the Copyright Act of 1976.

Country Music Association

Country Music Foundation

BMI: Broadcast Music, Incorporated

ASCAP: American Society of Composers, Authors, and Publishers

SESAC: Society of European Stage Authors and Composers

Nashville Association of Musicians: Local No. 257, American Federation of Musicians

Nashville headquarters of some key organizations other than recording companies and publishers in the country music business. (All photos, Bob Millard)

Offices of Billboard *and* Amusement Business *magazines*

Nashville Songwriters Association

United Artists Tower, location of two performers' unions, AFTRA: American Federation of Television and Radio Artists, SAG: Screen Actors Guild

As a country songwriter you will have to make your own decision about which group to join. You cannot join both organizations, although you may resign from one provided proper written notice is given. Your resignation will be routinely accepted and your songs will be returned to you so that you may take them to the other group unless you have taken advances which exceed the income generated. In that case you can still resign but you will have to leave your existing material with the organization you are leaving until your advance payments have been repaid.

I will not make a blanket recommendation for one group over the other, but I will point out that BMI opened its doors to country, rock 'n' roll, blues, folk, jazz, and rhythm and blues music at a time when ASCAP's membership rolls were closed to all but a very tight clique of writers whose music was exclusively found in Broadway shows, movies, or in what was then called "serious" (classical) music. Although ASCAP corrected this error and opened its roster to all writers *many* years ago, BMI still represents more country writers and publishers than ASCAP. In any given week from 55 to 75 percent of the country "Hot 100" are songs from BMI-represented writers and publishers.

As a songwriter you are strongly advised to talk to a representative of each organization, see what sort of advance and rate of payment schedule each can offer, weigh the personal relationships and the feeling you get about each group, and come to your own conclusion. You will not be eligible to join either organization until one of your songs is published and released for commercial sale as a recording. You can, however, make your own record, press it up, offer it for sale and thus meet the requirements for membership. Membership as a writer in BMI is free to those who qualify. Membership in ASCAP will cost you $10 if you qualify. This amount does not have to be paid up front, it will be deducted from earnings.

Songwriters have been cussing and discussing the relative merits of the two groups' payment methods for decades. They are very complicated and very confusing; I will not make any statement regarding which would be more remunerative. In their excellent book, *If They Ask You, You Can Write a Song*, Al Kasha and Joel Hirschhorn, two veteran songwriters with many awards to their credit, have this to say: "I'm an ASCAP writer; Joel belongs to BMI . . . At the beginning people would say, 'Aha, *now* you'll compare checks and see who's getting more.' We did, with some trepidation, but I'm glad to report that we were satisfied and relieved. The specifics may vary from quarter to quarter, but the overall amounts are generally the same, and we feel we've been treated with complete fairness by both organizations."

I should also mention that you receive your performance income directly from BMI or ASCAP. Your publisher receives his payment for the use of his company's music directly from them as well. This income is totally separate from the mechanical rights income derived from the sale of records which contain songs that you wrote.

SESAC is much smaller than ASCAP and BMI and it is a privately owned company. It also collects mechanical rights royalties for its members while BMI and ASCAP are concerned only with performance royalties. In addition, SESAC enters into other activities which are beyond the scope of ASCAP and BMI.

MECHANICAL RIGHTS AGENCIES

The Harry Fox Agency, Inc. has been a subsidiary company of the National Music Publishers' Association since 1969. The NMPA began in 1917, originally as a clearinghouse to handle movie synchronization rights for publishers. In 1938 the NMPA also began collecting revenues owed to publishers by record labels for the use of their music. These fees are called "mechanicals" as contrasted with the "performance" fees collected by the performance rights organizations, ASCAP, BMI, and SESAC.

The Harry Fox Agency handles the collection of about 95 percent of all the mechanical royalties paid annually in the United States. They have agreements with thousands of music publishers in all areas of music. The Fox Agency charges a service fee of 4½ percent of the money collected to publishers whose annual gross revenue from mechanicals is less than $25,000, and 3½ percent to those whose income from this source exceeds $25,000. Once a publisher qualifies for the lower percentage he stays there, even if his income drops below that minimum. The service fee is deducted from the payments record labels make to the agency. The remainder is mailed promptly to the publisher.

This service is of immense aid to all publishers. If there were no similar service available, every publisher would be forced to individually badger each record label for the money due for each song of theirs used on a disc. This process could bankrupt most publishers in a very short time.

In addition, the Harry Fox people retain independent accounting firms that audit the record companies every two years. It goes without saying that this service alone saves publishers bundles of money which otherwise might slip through the cracks.

I don't mean to imply that record labels are robbing the publishers. With the enormous number of songs, composers, and publishers around today honest mistakes are bound to happen. Strict accounting procedures catch those errors which arise from the many songs with the same titles, and the cases where writers share the same last name, and even in some cases the same first name or initial. Computer and human errors are also bound to happen.

The remainder of the mechanical rights income in this country is collected by the American Mechanical Rights Association (AMRA), the Copyright Service Bureau (CSB), and Mietus Copyright Management (MCM). In addition, SESAC collects mechanical rights for its publisher affiliates.

If you are approached by a publisher who is not represented by the Harry Fox Agency or one of the companies mentioned above, *don't sign anything*. If the company has no means for collecting mechanical royalties, they aren't a music publisher and you have nothing to gain from dealing with them.

BUSINESS INFORMATION SOURCES

BOOKS

There is no single source that will provide you with a blueprint for success in country music. The best any book can do is tell you about how specific people have gotten ahead in music, or what the criteria for success are in the music industry. You can learn what the established practices in the industry are and you can learn what your remuneration will be if you do succeed in certain areas. Most of the books discussed here offer general guidelines to follow so that you can avoid being tagged as a rank beginner, or they show you how to prepare a presentation so that you won't be rejected out of hand.

In preparing this portion of the book I decided to review the available publications in reverse chronological order rather than ranking them in order of their usefulness. The books are not all pitched at the same area of the music business and they are aimed at different levels of the success ladder. Some are admittedly for the neophyte; some are for aspiring music careerists further along. Some are very general works while others are more specific. All of them are of some use unless otherwise indicated.

It's a good idea to go to a public library to examine as many of these books as you can before you spend your hard-earned dollars to buy them. If the library doesn't have a particular book you can ask the librarian about the possibility of an interlibrary loan.

1984 Songwriters Market—Where To Sell Your Songs. Barbara Norton Kuroff, ed. Writers Digest Books (9733 Alliance Rd., Cincinnati, OH 45242), 1984.

This book lists music publishers, record companies, record producers, managers, and booking agencies who are potential customers for your songs (as well as advertising agencies and audiovisual firms who use musical material), giving addresses, who to contact, and tips on the kind of material the particular companies are likely to use (often provided by the companies themselves). It also includes fifteen short interviews with producers, publishers, managers, and performers.

Breakin' In to the Music Business. Alan H. Siegel. Cherry Lane Books (Port Chester, New York), 1983.

If you are an aspiring music business professional you will have recovered your investment in this book by the time you get to the end of the nineteen-page "Lexicon Plus" with which it begins. From then on—Chapter 1, "Pennies from Heaven," is an absorbing, up-to-date review of music business economics—you will be turning a profit. The author has been an entertainment lawyer for twenty-five years, and it's rare to have so much inside knowledge presented so intelligently and with real concern for the reader. The book includes informative, to-the-point interviews with major record company and music publishing company executives, producers, and managers.

The Musician's Guide to Independent Record Production. Will Connelly. Contemporary Books, 1981.

You don't need a book to learn how to write a song, and you don't need a book to learn how to sing a song, but you'd be mistaken to try to produce records independently for the first time without reading this book. Connelly obviously has done all of what he talks about, and not just once: he's a guide who marches steadily through the terrain, imparting a fine feeling of security to those behind him. Although the book doesn't attempt to treat the important question of how the independent labels distribute and market in competition with the majors (which could make a second volume), up to that point it is very thorough. It provides detailed, absorbing explanations of most of the technical, financial, and creative processes that go into the creation of a record or cassette and its package, including financing, budgeting, producing, manufacturing, packaging, and the finances of deals with distributors and rack jobbers. The fact that the author's experience has spanned the wide range of recording technologies of the last two decades means that he's objective and informed about the options now available. The book would be useful also for anyone starting to produce studio demos and anyone serious about working in the record industry who would like to understand the mechanics of creating the actual physical product.

How to Become a Successful Nashville Songwriter. Mike Kosser, Porch Swing Press, (Box 15014, Nashville, Tennessee 37215), 1981.

Kosser creates a mythical writer, brings him to town knowing no one, and shows you a very logical way his career might proceed provided he has some talent and not a little intelligence and persistence. The author tells you about "head" sessions, what a "place" or a "hold" on a song means, the strains a songwriter's life places upon a marriage even when successful, and includes mention of how some writers may "sandbag" or "rathole" their songs while they are on their way out of a bad publishing deal, all topics which I did not find in any of the other books. He also talks freely of the dreaded writer's block and how to combat it. If you plan to come to Nashville this book is indispensable because it was written by a person who is intimately familiar with his subject.

Contemporary Music Almanac 1980/1981. Ronald Zalkind. Schirmer Books (Division of MacMillan), 1980.

The *Almanac*'s chief point of interest to you will be a 115-page section titled "Getting Started," which talks about choosing a publicist, picking a lawyer, how to be a record producer or record executive, and how to organize your own business. The sections were all contributed by experts in the field, with a particularly fine contribution on "How to Get Your Song Published" furnished by Walter Wager, formerly publicity director of ASCAP. The rest of the book consists of material of passing interest such as thumbnail bios of the stars, pictures, lists of hit records, and trivia quizzes. There is very little about country music in the volume.

Music Business Handbook & Career Guide. David Baskerville. The Sherwood Co. (Box 21645, Denver, Colorado 80221), 1979.

This is a pretty good piece of work which is very broad in scope. It gives an adequate overview of all areas and provides copies of many types of standard contracts. There isn't very much on country music in particular here but the book is loaded with advice that will stand you in good stead in whichever area of music you choose. Baskerville provides an excellent section on how pop record companies are run, the different production facilities, film scoring, and music-related areas of employment. The wide scope doesn't permit a great deal of development in any one area. The entire Copyright Act of 1976 is included here if you feel you need to plow through every word. This is a useful book and a valuable contribution to the field.

If They Ask You, You Can Write a Song. Al Kasha and Joel Hirschhorn. Simon & Schuster, 1979.

Kasha and Hirschhorn have received two Grammy Awards and written songs which have sold 52,000,000 copies, so they know whereof they speak. The authors' points are profusely illustrated with examples from hit songs from the past. They have included a summary of each chapter, called "Things to Remember," which is an excellent recapitulation for a beginning writer to memorize. This volume also has the most complete list of music industry contacts of any of the books under discussion, save for the publisher listing in 1984 *Songwriter's Market*. Foreign contacts are also included, a valuable list unique to this book. The scope is confined to songwriting and directly related matters but the information, suggestions, and ideas are both thoughtful and well presented. Since the two are writing partners, many of their suggestions relate directly to co-writing, an important point because none of the other books worth buying go into this in detail. You can harvest a lot of solid kernels of wisdom from Kasha and Hirschhorn whether you are a rookie songwriter or a bit further on down the road.

How to Make Money in Music. Herby Harris and Lucien Farrar. Arco, 1978.

Here's another pretty fair overview with a particularly good section on contracts. There is also an excellent breakdown of the costs involved in a recording session, the most realistic and thorough example of this I ran across in the books examined. The authors include many sample contracts, a list of music periodicals, and a fine bibliography. There is nothing here tailored to country music specifically but the advice is good and the facts are correct.

How to Be a Successful Songwriter. Kent McNeel and Mark Luther. St. Martin's Press, 1978. (Originally published in 1976 as *Songwriters with a Touch of Gold*)

McNeel and Luther have taken the interview approach with their book. It could have been a disaster but the authors were very astute: they interviewed hit writers exclusively and did not limit their writers by type of music. There are some extremely big names included here like Henry Mancini, Loggins and Messina, Mark James, Curly Putman, Barry White, Paul Williams, Jeff Barry, Kenny Rogers, Barry Mann and Cynthia Weill, Billy Sherrill, Seals and Crofts, and Mentor Williams. The questions are very well chosen and they elicit a good bit of valuable information.

Most of the writers discuss the way in which they were able to get their foot in the door, as well as which of their songs they feel represents their best work. Unfortunately, the contributions from publishers and record label executives are frequently only attributed to people by their first name, as is the interview with a BMI representative. And the list of publishers is highly selective—only twenty-nine are given for all areas of music. Nevertheless, this book is well worth two or three times its price because of the valuable insights you can get from a group of writers who have collectively sold several hundred *million* records. Highly recommended.

Making it with Music. Kenny Rogers and Len Epand. Harper and Row, 1978.

One of the biggest stars in the business tells his story, adds a fair amount of inside tips, throws in a lot of good pictures, and dispenses some excellent advice, particularly on the realities of fame and how it can be fleeting. Rogers and Epand, a label executive who formerly toiled for *Record World*, have put together a pretty classy book of interest to fans and to those who crave a music career. While it isn't too detailed in any one area and there isn't anything of particular usefulness to a new songwriter, there is a good deal of information aspiring performers can gain from the story of Rogers's career.

The Songwriter's Handbook. Harvey Rachlin. Funk and Wagnalls, 1977.

Rachlin's book is aimed at those a bit further along than folks who are just beginning. Unique features of this volume include a section on producing your own master recordings, a list of advertising agencies with some of the products they handle, exercises in writing lyrics, melody, and jingles, and a test to see if you learned anything from the book. In addition there is a good list of music associations and professional organizations, and the addresses of licensing organizations in the three music capitals. Although Rachlin lists and gives addresses for fifty-five country music publishers, there is no specific chapter addressed to those who want to make it in country music. There are a good many standard contract forms reprinted, but there are no quotes from industry leaders and no specific examples drawn from those who have made it in the business. All in all though this is a fine volume for those who are beyond the neophyte stage.

How I Write Songs (Why You Can). Tom T. Hall. Chappell Music, 1976.

This is as good a lead as you'll get to figuring out why Tom T. Hall is one of Nashville's top songwriters. There's lots of good advice here from Tom, who uses his own career to illustrate points. This isn't too basic and it isn't too advanced; it also has the added benefit of Tom's analysis of some of his own big hits so you can see what he was seeking. In addition to the good tips and the insight into the inner mental workings of a top writer, you'll come away from this book feeling like you know Tom a little. This is a "how-to" book written by a Nashville native; its scope is limited to songwriting. There's concrete advice on how to get ideas, different ways to come at a song, and what to do once you have your teeth into a tune.

The Music/Record Career Handbook. Joe Csida. Billboard, 1975.

Csida is a forty-year veteran of all aspects of showbiz who has drawn from his very spectacular career for many of his examples. The book is a bit out of date and a trifle heavy on the name-dropping. Though slanted towards pop and rock music, the advice Csida gives will serve you well in any musical arena. This isn't for the beginner and it is not particularly thorough in any one area. The value of this volume is that it encompasses areas like educational careers, arranging, agents and personal managers, and disc jockeys, which aren't covered in other books except, in some cases, the book by Baskerville.

How to Write a Hit Song . . . And Sell It. Tommy Boyce. Wilshire Book Company (North Hollywood, California), 1974.

Boyce was a big hit writer in the 1960s who had the financially rewarding but creatively dubious distinction of providing the Monkees with a lot of their big hits. This isn't too bad a book though it is a bit dated for our purposes. There are some interesting anecdotes, Boyce's analysis of a half-dozen of his hits, a section on how to promote your song, a good bit on what makes a hit song, and copies of his mechanical and performance royalty statements for one of his hot years.

This Business of Music (revised and expanded edition). William Krasilovsky and Sidney Shemel. Watson-Guptill, 1977.

More About This Business of Music (revised edition). William Krasilovsky and Sidney Shemel. Watson-Guptill, 1974.

I've saved these two for last because they are absolutely essential if you are indeed serious about a career in the music business. If there is a bible in this racket *This Business of Music* is it. Krasilovsky and Shemel are two of the leading attorneys in the field and their books tell you the way things *should* be done. You can compare their comments with the sort of deals you are offered to see if they are on the up and up. There are literally acres of sample contracts and standard forms which cover every area of the business. This is the standard textbook for the industry and has been since the first edition appeared in 1964. *More About This Business of Music* supplements the first book and covers areas not included there. There is no way you should embark on a music career without these books. If you see one of these in a music industry executive's office you can be assured that he or she at least is acquainted with the legal way to conduct business.

MAGAZINES

Country Song Roundup has many well-written features. Of particular interest to those involved or wishing to be involved with the country music business are the good profiles it sometimes features of a writer or a publisher. Sandwiched between the many articles in each issue are the lyrics to twenty-five to thirty recent country hits. These lyrics represent a truly useful opportunity to study the language, structure, and meaning of songs whose tunes you're probably familiar with, to evaluate just what ingredients it takes for a writer to cook up a hit country song. *CSR* is nationally distributed and can be found at many newsstands.

(CSR, % Charlton Publications Inc., Division Street, Derby, CN 06418.)

NEWSPAPERS

With country music now doing big box office business nationally, we're seeing a lot more interest paid to it by the daily press. Most of the big city dailies now run one or more country music features per week written by staff writers. A partial list would include the *Austin American Statesman*, the *Houston Post*, the *Tulsa World*, the New York *Daily News*, the *San Francisco Herald-Examiner*, the *Charlotte News-Observer*, the *Atlanta Journal-Constitution*, the Nashville *Tennessean*, and the *Memphis Commercial Appeal*.

There are also several fine syndicated writers who cover country music, including Jack Hurst of the *Chicago Tribune* and Boris Weintraub of the *Washington Star*.

TRADE PUBLICATIONS

There are four major weekly trade publications: *Billboard, Radio 'n' Records, Cash Box*, and *The Gavin Report*. They contain news items, features, reviews of new releases, interviews, and other information pertinent to all aspects of all branches of the music industry. In addition, this is where you will find the almighty "charts," the weekly listing of the relative popularity of singles and albums in this country. Records are ranked according to their sales, radio airplay and, to a lesser extent, radio requests. Of the trade papers *Billboard* is the oldest and the most influential. All are high-ticket items, but they are required reading for inhabitants of the industry. They are carried by some large newsstands. Most good large and medium-sized public libraries, and a good many college libraries, subscribe to at least one, usually *Billboard*. You should take the time to get acquainted with these publications if you intend to make a living in music. They are avidly read by those in the business.

COUNTRY MUSIC FOUNDATION LIBRARY
AND MEDIA CENTER

If you're really serious about a career in country music, there is one place where you can find out *anything* you want to know about the field. The Country Music Foundation Library and Media Center is on the bottom floor of the Country Music Hall of Fame, at the corner of Music Square East (16th Avenue South) and Division Street in Nashville. This library is a unique repository which contains more information about country music than any place in the world. It houses over 70,000 country music recordings and hundreds of films, tapes, and video cassettes. It is home to a mammoth Oral History collection which now has over 6,000 pages of transcribed interviews with the men and women who have made country music the vital part of popular music it is today. The library maintains collections of sheet music, fan club publications, songbooks, pamphlets, and catalogs. There are several dozen file cabinets with vertical files of newspaper clippings, photographs, biographies, press releases and magazine articles concerned with every major, and almost every minor, country music person, place, thing or topic in existence. In addition, the CMF Library also includes books and magazines which cover all areas of American popular music. The library has almost 7,000 books, close to 2,000 bound periodical volumes, and maintains subscriptions to more than 300 music magazines, many of them published abroad.

The CMF Library is naturally a noncirculating, closed-stack institution. It requires an advance appointment for admission. However, if you do have a serious interest in country music you will be scheduled in if you call ahead of time (256-1639) and request the type of information you are seeking. It has a reading room stocked with about forty of the latest issues of the most popular music periodicals for your perusal on a self-service basis. All other materials must be retrieved by the staff from the stacks, which are closed to the public.

This institution also answers phone and mail inquiries on specific questions. A bookstore adjoins the excellent museum upstairs and offers several hundred of the most popular consumer-oriented music books and magazines for sale (including most of the publications discussed in the book sections of this volume).

COUNTRY MUSIC AWARDS

There are three annual nationally televised country music awards presentations. In order of importance, they are the Country Music Association (CMA) Awards, the Academy of Country Music (ACM) Awards, and the Music City Awards. In addition the National Academy of Recording Arts and Sciences (NARAS) has an annual televised show in which awards are presented to personalities and writers in country music and all other categories of music. These are the Grammy Awards (named for the first disc phonograph, the Gramophone). Although the Grammies are possibly more prestigious, any country writer or artist would rather get a CMA Award because it indicates selection by his peers, the 7,000-plus members of the Country Music Association. The ACM is a much smaller organization that is headquartered in California. It was founded because the members of the CMA who lived and worked on the West Coast did not feel they were being adequately represented by the membership of the Nashville-based CMA. The ACM has about 2,000 members. The Music City Awards are sponsored by the *Music City News*, a monthly magazine. They select their winners by a poll of their readers. The Music City Awards were first telecast in 1979; the CMA Awards and the ACM Awards have been on the tube for a longer period of time, as have the NARAS Awards.

COUNTRY MUSIC ASSOCIATION AWARD WINNERS
1967–1983

CATEGORY 1—ENTERTAINER OF THE YEAR

1967	Eddy Arnold	1976	Mel Tillis
1968	Glen Campbell	1977	Ronnie Milsap
1969	Johnny Cash	1978	Dolly Parton
1970	Merle Haggard	1979	Willie Nelson
1971	Charley Pride	1980	Barbara Mandrell
1972	Loretta Lynn	1981	Barbara Mandrell
1973	Roy Clark	1982	Alabama
1974	Charlie Rich	1983	Alabama
1975	John Denver	1984	Alabama

CATEGORY 2—SINGLE OF THE YEAR

1967 "There Goes My Everything"/Jack Greene/Decca
1968 "Harper Valley P.T.A."/Jeannie C. Riley/ Plantation
1969 "A Boy Named Sue"/Johnny Cash/Columbia
1970 "Okie From Muskogee"/Merle Haggard/Capitol
1971 "Help Me Make It Through The Night"/Sammi Smith/Mega
1972 "The Happiest Girl In The Whole U.S.A."/Donna Fargo/Dot
1973 "Behind Closed Doors"/Charlie Rich/Epic
1974 "County Bumpkin"/Cal Smith/MCA
1975 "Before The Next Teardrop Falls"/Freddy Fender/ABC-Dot
1976 "Good Hearted Woman"/Waylon Jennings & Willie Nelson/RCA
1977 "Lucille"/Kenny Rogers/United Artists
1978 "Heaven's Just A Sin Away"/The Kendalls/Ovation
1979 "The Devil Went Down To Georgia"/Charlie Daniels Band/Epic
1980 "He Stopped Loving Her Today"/George Jones/Epic
1981 "Elvira"/Oak Ridge Boys/MCA
1982 "Always On My Mind"/Willie Nelson/Columbia
1983 "Swingin' "/John Anderson/Warner
1984 "A Little Good News"/Anne Murray/Capitol

CATEGORY 3—ALBUM OF THE YEAR

1967 "There Goes My Everything"/Jack Greene/Decca
1968 "Johnny Cash At Folsom Prison"/Johnny Cash/Columbia
1969 "Johnny Cash at San Quentin Prison"/Johnny Cash/Columbia
1970 "Okie From Muskogee"/Merle Haggard/Capitol
1971 "I Won't Mention It Again"/Ray Price/Columbia
1972 "Let Me Tell You About A Song"/Merle Haggard/Capitol
1973 "Behind Closed Doors"/Charlie Rich/Epic
1974 "A Very Special Love Song"/Charlie Rich/Epic

1975 "A Legend In My Time"/Ronnie Milsap/RCA
1976 "Wanted—The Outlaws"/Waylon Jennings, Willie Nelson, Tompall, Jessi Colter/RCA
1977 "Ronnie Milsap Live"/Ronnie Milsap/RCA
1978 "It Was Almost Like a Song"/Ronnie Milsap/RCA
1979 "The Gambler"/Kenny Rogers/United Artists
1980 "Coal Miner's Daughter/Original Motion Picture Soundtrack/MCA
1981 "I Believe In You"/Don Williams/MCA
1982 "Always On My Mind"/Willie Nelson/Columbia
1983 "The Closer You Get"/Alabama/RCA
1984 "A Little Good News"/Anne Murray/Capitol

CATEGORY 4—SONG OF THE YEAR

1967 "There Goes My Everything"/Dallas Frazier
1968 "Honey"/Bobby Russell
1969 "Carroll County Accident"/Bob Ferguson
1970 "Sunday Morning Coming Down"/Kris Kristofferson
1971 "Easy Loving"/Freddie Hart
1972 "Easy Loving"/Freddie Hart
1973 "Behind Closed Doors"/Kenny O'Dell
1974 "Country Bumpkin"/Don Wayne
1975 "Back Home Again"/John Denver
1976 "Rhinestone Cowboy"/Larry Weiss
1977 "Lucille"/Roger Bowling & Hal Bynum
1978 "Don't It Make My Brown Eyes Blue"/Richard Leigh
1979 "The Gambler"/Don Schlitz/Writers Night Music
1980 "He Stopped Loving Her Today"/Bobby Braddock & Curly Putman/Tree Publishing
1981 "He Stopped Loving Her Today"/Bobby Braddock & Curly Putman/Tree Publishing
1982 "Always On My Mind"/Johnny Christopher, Wayne Carson, Mark James/Screen Gems, EMI Music, Rose Bridge Music
1983 "Always On My Mind"/Johnny Christopher, Wayne Carson, Mark James/Screen Gems, EMI Music, Rose Bridge Music
1984 "Wind Beneath My Wings"/Larry Henley, Jeff Silbar/Warner House of Music

CATEGORY 5—FEMALE VOCALIST OF THE YEAR

1967	Loretta Lynn	1973	Loretta Lynn
1968	Tammy Wynette	1974	Olivia Newton-John
1969	Tammy Wynette	1975	Dolly Parton
1970	Tammy Wynette	1976	Dolly Parton
1971	Lynn Anderson	1977	Crystal Gayle
1972	Loretta Lynn	1978	Crystal Gayle

1979	Barbara Mandrell	1982	Janie Fricke
1980	Emmylou Harris	1983	Janie Fricke
1981	Barbara Mandrell	1984	Reba McIntire

CATEGORY 6—MALE VOCALIST OF THE YEAR

1967	Jack Greene	1976	Ronnie Milsap
1968	Glen Campbell	1977	Ronnie Milsap
1969	Johnny Cash	1978	Don Williams
1970	Merle Haggard	1979	Kenny Rogers
1971	Charley Pride	1980	George Jones
1972	Charley Pride	1981	George Jones
1973	Charlie Rich	1982	Ricky Skaggs
1974	Ronnie Milsap	1983	Lee Greenwood
1975	Waylon Jennings	1984	Lee Greenwood

CATEGORY 7—VOCAL GROUP OF THE YEAR

1967	The Stoneman Family	1976	The Statler Brothers
1968	Porter Wagoner and Dolly Parton	1977	The Statler Brothers
1969	Johnny Cash and June Carter	1978	The Oak Ridge Boys
1970	The Glaser Brothers	1979	The Statler Brothers
1971	The Osborne Brothers	1980	The Statler Brothers
1972	The Statler Brothers	1981	Alabama
1973	The Statler Brothers	1982	Alabama
1974	The Statler Brothers	1983	Alabama
1975	The Statler Brothers	1984	The Statler Brothers

CATEGORY 8—VOCAL DUO OF THE YEAR
(introduced in 1970)

1970	Porter Wagoner and Dolly Parton
1971	Porter Wagoner and Dolly Parton
1972	Conway Twitty and Loretta Lynn
1973	Conway Twitty and Loretta Lynn
1974	Conway Twitty and Loretta Lynn
1975	Conway Twitty and Loretta Lynn
1976	Waylon Jennings and Willie Nelson
1977	Jim Ed Brown and Helen Cornelius
1978	Kenny Rogers and Dottie West
1979	Kenny Rogers and Dottie West
1980	Moe Bandy and Joe Stampley
1981	David Frizzell and Shelly West
1982	David Frizzell and Shelly West
1983	Merle Haggard and Willie Nelson
1984	Willie Nelson and Julio Iglesias

CATEGORY 9—INSTRUMENTAL GROUP OF THE YEAR

1967   The Buckaroos
1968   The Buckaroos
1969   Danny Davis and the Nashville Brass
1970   Danny Davis and the Nashville Brass
1971   Danny Davis and the Nashville Brass
1972   Danny Davis and the Nashville Brass
1973   Danny Davis and the Nashville Brass
1974   Danny Davis and the Nashville Brass
1975   Roy Clark and Buck Trent
1976   Roy Clark and Buck Trent
1977   The Original Texas Playboys
1978   The Oak Ridge Boys Band
1979   The Charlie Daniels Band
1980   The Charlie Daniels Band
1981   Alabama
1982   Alabama
1983   The Ricky Skaggs Band
1984   The Ricky Skaggs Band

CATEGORY 10—INSTRUMENTALIST OF THE YEAR

1967	Chet Atkins	1976	Hargus "Pig" Robbins
1968	Chet Atkins	1977	Roy Clark
1969	Chet Atkins	1978	Roy Clark
1970	Jerry Reed	1979	Charlie Daniels
1971	Jerry Reed	1980	Roy Clark
1972	Charlie McCoy	1981	Chet Atkins
1973	Charlie McCoy	1982	Chet Atkins
1974	Don Rich	1983	Chet Atkins
1975	Johnny Gimble	1984	Chet Atkins

CATEGORY 11—HORIZON AWARD
(introduced in 1981)

1981	Terri Gibbs	1983	John Anderson
1982	Ricky Skaggs	1984	The Judds

COMEDIAN OF THE YEAR
(discontinued in 1971)

1967   Don Bowman
1968   Ben Colder
1969   Archie Campbell
1970   Roy Clark

MUSIC CITY NEWS AWARD WINNERS
1967–1984

1967

Male Artist	Merle Haggard
Female Artist	Loretta Lynn
Most Promising Male Artist	Tom T. Hall
Most Promising Female Artist	Tammy Wynette
Songwriter	Bill Anderson
Song Of The Year	"There Goes My Everything"
Band	The Buckaroos
Vocal Group	Tompall and The Glaser Brothers
Duet	The Wilburn Brothers

1968

Male Artist	Merle Haggard
Female Artist	Loretta Lynn
Most Promising Male Artist	Cal Smith
Most Promising Female Artist	Dolly Parton
Songwriter	Bill Anderson
Band	The Buckaroos
Vocal Group	Tompall and The Glaser Brothers
Duet	Porter Wagoner and Dolly Parton

1969

Male Artist	Charley Pride
Female Artist	Loretta Lynn
Most Promising Male Artist	Johnny Bush
Most Promising Female Artist	Peggy Sue
Songwriter	Bill Anderson
Song Of The Year	"All I Have To Offer You Is Me"
Band	The Buckaroos
Vocal Group	Tompall and The Glaser Brothers
Duet	Porter Wagoner and Dolly Parton
Instrumentalist	Roy Clark
Country TV Show	"Hee Haw" and "The Johnny Cash Show" (tied)

1970

Male Artist	Charley Pride
Female Artist	Loretta Lynn
Most Promising Male Artist	Tommy Cash
Most Promising Female Artist	Susan Raye

Songwriter	Merle Haggard
Song Of The Year	"Hello Darlin' "
Band	The Buckaroos
Vocal Group	Tompall and The Glasers
Duet	Porter Wagoner and Dolly Parton
Instrumentalist	Roy Clark
Country TV Show	"Hee Haw"

1971

Male Artist	Charley Pride
Female Artist	Loretta Lynn
Most Promising Male Artist	Tommy Overstreet
Most Promising Female Artist	Susan Raye
Songwriter	Kris Kristofferson
Song Of The Year	"Help Me Make It Through The Night"
Band	The Strangers
Vocal Group	The Statler Brothers
Duet	Conway Twitty and Loretta Lynn
Instrumentalist	Roy Clark
Comedy Act	Mel Tillis
Bluegrass Group	The Osborne Brothers
Country TV Show	"Hee Haw"

1972

Male Artist	Charley Pride
Female Artist	Loretta Lynn
Most Promising Male Artist	Billy "Crash" Craddock
Most Promising Female Artist	Donna Fargo
Songwriter	Kris Kristofferson
Song Of The Year	"Kiss An Angel"
Band	The Strangers
Vocal Group	The Statler Brothers
Duet	Conway Twitty and Loretta Lynn
Instrumentalist	Roy Clark
Comedy Act	Archie Campbell
Bluegrass Group	The Osborne Brothers
Country TV Show	"Hee Haw"

1973

Male Artist	Charley Pride
Female Artist	Loretta Lynn
Most Promising Male Artist	Johnny Rodriguez
Most Promising Female Artist	Tanya Tucker

Songwriter	Kris Kristofferson
Song Of The Year	"Why Me"
Band	The Po' Boys
Vocal Group	The Statler Brothers
Duet	Conway Twitty and Loretta Lynn
Instrumentalist	Charlie McCoy
Comedy Act	Mel Tillis
Bluegrass Group	The Osborne Brothers
Country TV Show	"Hee Haw"

1974

Male Artist	Conway Twitty
Female Artist	Loretta Lynn
Most Promising Male Artist	Johnny Rodriguez
Most Promising Female Artist	Olivia Newton-John
Songwriter	Bill Anderson
Song Of The Year	"You've Never Been This Far Before"
Band	The Buckaroos
Vocal Group	The Statler Brothers
Duet	Conway Twitty and Loretta Lynn
Instrumentalist	Roy Clark
Instrumental Entertainer	Charlie McCoy
Comedy Act	Mel Tillis
Bluegrass Group	The Osborne Brothers
Country TV Show	"Hee Haw"
Touring Road Show	Loretta Lynn/Coalminers/Kenny Starr

1975

Male Artist	Conway Twitty
Female Artist	Loretta Lynn
Most Promising Male Artist	Ronnie Milsap
Most Promising Female Artist	Crystal Gayle
Songwriter	Bill Anderson
Song Of The Year	"Country Bumpkin"
Band	The Coalminers
Vocal Group	The Statler Brothers
Duet	Conway Twitty & Loretta Lynn
Instrumentalist	Buck Trent
Instrumental Entertainer	Roy Clark
Comedy Act	Mel Tillis
Bluegrass Group	The Osborne Brothers
Country TV Show	"Hee Haw"

1976

Male Artist	Conway Twitty
Female Artist	Loretta Lynn
Most Promising Male Artist	Mickey Gilley
Most Promising Female Artist	Barbara Mandrell
Songwriter	Bill Anderson
Song Of The Year	"Blue Eyes Crying In The Rain"
Band	The Coalminers
Vocal Group	The Statler Brothers
Duet	Conway Twitty and Loretta Lynn
Instrumentalist	Buck Trent
Instrumental Entertainer	Roy Clark
Comedy Act	Mel Tillis
Bluegrass Group	The Osborne Brothers
Country TV Show	"Hee Haw"
Album	"When The Tingle Becomes A Chill" (Loretta Lynn)
Founders Award	Faron Young

1977

Male Artist	Conway Twitty
Female Artist	Loretta Lynn
Most Promising Male Artist	Larry Gatlin
Most Promising Female Artist	Helen Cornelius
Songwriter	Larry Gatlin
Song Of The Year	"I Don't Want To Have To Marry You"
Band	The Coalminers
Vocal Group	The Statler Brothers
Duet	Conway Twitty and Loretta Lynn
Instrumentalist	Johnny Gimble
Instrumental entertainer	Roy Clark
Comedy Act	Mel Tillis
Bluegrass Act	The Osborne Brothers
Country TV Show	"Hee Haw"
Album	"I Don't Want To Have To Marry You" (Jim Ed Brown and Helen Cornelius)
Founders Award	Ralph Emery

1978

Male Artist	Larry Gatlin
Female Artist	Loretta Lynn
Most Promising Male Artist	Don Williams
Most Promising Female Artist	Debby Boone

Songwriter	Larry Gatlin
Single	"Heaven's Just A Sin Away"
Bluegrass Act	The Osborne Brothers
Instrumentalist	Roy Clark
Comedy Act	Mel Tillis
Vocal Group	The Statler Brothers
Album	"Moody Blue" (Elvis Presley)
Duet	Conway Twitty and Loretta Lynn
Band	Larry Gatlin, Family and Friends
Country TV Show	"50 Years Of Country Music"
Founders Award	Ernest Tubb

1979

Male Artist	Kenny Rogers
Female Artist	Barbara Mandrell
Most Promising Male Artist	Rex Allen, Jr.
Most Promising Female Artist	Janie Fricke
Songwriter	Eddie Rabbitt
Single	"The Gambler"
Bluegrass Group	The Osborne Brothers
Musician	Roy Clark
Comedy Act	Jerry Clower
Vocal Group	The Statler Brothers
Album	"Entertainer On and Off The Road" (The Statler Brothers)
Duet	Kenny Rogers and Dottie West
Band	Oak Ridge Boys Band
Country TV Show	"PBS Live From The Grand Ole Opry"
Gospel Act	Connie Smith
Founders Award	Pee Wee King

1980

Male Artist	Marty Robbins
Female Artist	Loretta Lynn
Most Promising Male Artist	Hank Williams, Jr.
Most Promising Female Artist	Charly McClain
Songwriter	Marty Robbins
Single	"Coward Of The County"
Bluegrass Group	Bill Monroe
Musician	Roy Clark
Comedy Act	The Statler Brothers
Vocal Group	The Statler Brothers
Album	"The Originals" (The Statler Brothers)

Duet	Conway Twitty and Loretta Lynn
Band	Charlie Daniels Band
Country TV Show	"PBS Live From The Grand Ole Opry"
Gospel Act	The Carter Family
Founders Award	Buck Owens

1981

Male Artist	George Jones
Female Artist	Barbara Mandrell
Most Promising Male Artist	Boxcar Willie
Most Promising Female Artist	Louise Mandrell
Songwriter	Curly Putman and Bobby Braddock
Single	"He Stopped Loving Her Today"
Bluegrass Group	Bill Monroe and The Blue Grass Boys
Musician	Barbara Mandrell
Comedy Act	The Mandrell Sisters
Vocal Group	The Statler Brothers
Album	"Tenth Anniversary" (The Statler Brothers)
Duet	Conway Twitty & Loretta Lynn
Band	Marty Robbins Band
Country TV Show	"Barbara Mandrell and The Mandrell Sisters"
Gospel Act	Hee Haw Gospel Quartet
Founders Award	Betty Cox Adler

1982

Male Artist	Marty Robbins
Female Artist	Barbara Mandrell
Most Promising Male Artist	T. G. Sheppard
Most Promising Female Artist	Shelly West
Duet	David Frizzell & Shelly West
Band	Alabama
Vocal Group	The Statler Brothers
Musician	Barbara Mandrell
Country TV Show	"Barbara Mandrell & The Mandrell Sisters"
Single	"Elvira"
Album	"Feels So Right" (Alabama)
Bluegrass Group	Ricky Skaggs
Gospel Act	Hee Haw Gospel Quartet
Comedy Act	The Statler Brothers

1983
Male Artist	Marty Robbins
Female Artist	Janie Fricke
Star Of Tomorrow	Ricky Skaggs
Duet	David Frizzell and Shelly West
Band	Alabama
Vocal Group	Alabama
Living Legend	Roy Acuff
Country TV Show	"Hee Haw"
Country TV Special	"Conway Twitty On The Mississippi"
Single	"Some Memories Just Won't Die"
Album	"Come Back To Me" (Marty Robbins)
Bluegrass Group	Ricky Skaggs
Gospel Act	Hee Haw Gospel Quartet
Comedy Act	The Statler Brothers

1984
Male Artist	Lee Greenwood
Female Artist	Janie Fricke
Star Of Tomorrow	Ronny Robbins
Duet	Kenny Rogers and Dolly Parton
Band	Alabama
Vocal Group	The Statler Brothers
Living Legend	Ernest Tubb
Country TV Show	"Hee Haw"
Country TV Special	"Another Evening With The Statler Brothers: Heroes, Legends and Friends"
Single	"Elizabeth" (The Statler Brothers)
Album	"The Closer You Get" (Alabama)
Bluegrass Group	Ricky Skaggs
Gospel Act	Hee Haw Gospel Quartet
Comedy Act	The Statler Brothers

NATIONAL ACADEMY OF RECORDING ARTS AND SCIENCES GRAMMY AWARD WINNERS, COUNTRY MUSIC FIELD 1980–1983

1980
Best Country Vocal Performance, Female
COULD I HAVE THIS DANCE (Single)
Anne Murray (Capitol)

Best Country Vocal Performance, Male
HE STOPPED LOVING HER TODAY (Single)
George Jones (Epic)

Best Country Performance by a Duo or Group with Vocal
THAT LOVIN' YOU FEELIN' AGAIN (Single)
Roy Orbison and Emmylou Harris (W.B.)

Best Country Instrumental Performance
ORANGE BLOSSOM SPECIAL/HOEDOWN (Track)
Gilley's "Urban Cowboy" Band (Full Moon/Asylum)

Best Country Song
ON THE ROAD AGAIN
Songwriter: Willie Nelson

1981
Best Country Vocal Performance, Female
9 TO 5 (Single)
Dolly Parton (RCA)

Best Country Vocal Performance, Male
(THERE'S) NO GETTIN' OVER ME (Single)
Ronnie Milsap (RCA)

Best Country Performance by a Duo or Group With Vocal
ELVIRA (Single)
Oak Ridge Boys (MCA)

Best Country Instrumental Performance
COUNTRY—AFTER ALL THESE YEARS
Chet Atkins (RCA)

Best Country Song
9 TO 5
Songwriter: Dolly Parton

1982
Best Country Vocal Performance, Female
BREAK IT TO ME GENTLY (Single)
Juice Newton (Capitol)

Best Country Vocal Performance, Male
ALWAYS ON MY MIND (Single)
Willie Nelson (Columbia)

Best Country Performance by a Duo or Group with Vocal
MOUNTAIN MUSIC (Album)
Alabama (RCA)

Best Country Instrumental Performance
ALABAMA JUBILEE (Track)
Roy Clark (Churchill)

Best Country Song
and also Grammy Song of the Year
ALWAYS ON MY MIND
Songwriters: Johnny Christopher, Mark James, and Wayne Carson

1983
Best Country Vocal Performance, Female
A LITTLE GOOD NEWS (Single)
Anne Murray (Capitol)

Best Country Vocal Performance, Male
I.O.U. (Single)
Lee Greenwood (MCA)

Best Country Performance by a Duo or Group With Vocal
THE CLOSER YOU GET (Album)
Alabama (RCA)

Best Country Instrumental Performance
FIREBALL (Track)
The New South (Ricky Skaggs, Jerry Douglas, Tony Rice, J. D. Crowe, Todd Philips)
(Sugar Hill)

Best New Country Song

COUNTRY MUSIC HONORS

The highest honor bestowed on a country music artist, writer, or businessman is induction into the Country Music Hall of Fame. Selection is by the membership of the Country Music Association. From the inception in 1961 of the Hall of Fame—which is administered by the Country Music Foundation (CMF)—to the present writing, only thirty-nine men and women have been inducted. Plaques naming those selected can be found in the Country Music Hall of Fame Museum, Music Square East at Division Street in Nashville.

The Nashville Songwriters Association, International (NSAI) established its own Hall of Fame to honor songwriters in 1970. To date ninety writers have been inducted. Those selected receive a bronzed quill pen called a "Manny." Selections are made by the membership of the NSAI. As with the new inductees into the Country Music Hall of Fame, the selections are announced during the Grand Ole Opry birthday celebration held during the second week in October.

ELECTIONS INTO THE COUNTRY MUSIC HALL OF FAME

1961
Jimmie Rodgers
Fred Rose
Hank Williams

1962
Roy Acuff

1963 (none)

1964
Tex Ritter

1965
Ernest Tubb

1966
Eddy Arnold
James R. Denny
George D. Hay
Uncle Dave Macon

1967
Red Foley
J. L. (Joe) Frank
Jim Reeves
Stephen H. Sholes

1968
Bob Wills

1969
Gene Autry

1970
Bill Monroe
Original Carter Family

1971
Arthur Edward Satherly

1972
Jimmie Davis

1973
Chet Atkins
Patsy Cline

1974
Owen Bradley
Frank "Pee Wee" King

1975
Minnie Pearl

1976
Kitty Wells

1977
Merle Travis

1978
Grandpa Jones

1979
Hubert Long
Hank Snow

1980
Johnny Cash
Original Sons of the Pioneers
Connie B. Gay

1981
Vernon Dalhart
Grant Turner

1982
Lefty Frizzell
Marty Robbins
Roy Horton

1983
Little Jimmy Dickens

1984
Floyd Tillman
Ralph Peer

Nashville Songwriters Association International (NSAI) Hall of Fame

1970
Gene Autry
Johnny Bond
Albert Brumley
A. P. Carter
Ted Daffan
Vernon Dalhart
Rex Griffin
Stuart Hamblen
Pee Wee King
Vic McAlpin
Bob Miller
Leon Payne
Jimmie Rodgers
Fred Rose
Redd Stewart
Floyd Tillman
Merle Travis
Ernest Tubb
Cindy Walker
Hank Williams
Bob Wills

1971
Smiley Burnette
Jenny Lou Carson
Wilf Carter
Zeke Clements
Jimmie Davis
Delmore Brothers (Alton and Rabon)
Al Dexter
Vaughn Horton
Bradley Kincaid
Bill Monroe
Bob Nolan
Tex Owens
Tex Ritter
Carson J. Robison
Tim Spencer
Gene Sullivan
Jimmy Wakely
Wiley Walker
Scotty Wiseman

1972
Boudleaux and Felice Bryant
Lefty Frizzell
Jack Rhodes
Don Robertson

1973
Jack Clement
Don Gibson
Harlan Howard
Roger Miller
Steve Nelson and Ed Nelson, Jr.
Willie Nelson

1974
Hank Cochran

1975
Bill Anderson
Danny Dill
Eddie Miller
Marty Robbins
Wayne Walker
Marijohn Wilkin

1976
Carl Belew
Dallas Frazier
John D. Loudermilk
Moon Mullican
Curly Putnam
Mel Tillis
Stephen Foster (*Special Award*)

1977
Johnny Cash
Woodie Guthrie
Merle Haggard
Kris Kristofferson

1978
Joe Allison
Tom T. Hall
Hank Snow
Don Wayne

1979
The Reverend Thomas A. Dorsey
The Louvin Brothers (Charles and Ira)
Elsie McWilliams
Joe South

1980
Hudie Ledbetter ("Leadbelly")
Ben Peters
Ray Stevens
Mickey Newbury

1981
Bobby Braddock
Ray Whitely

1982
William J. (Billy) Hill
Chuck Berry

1983
W. C. Handy
Loretta Lynn
Beasley Smith

1984
Billy Sherrill
Hal David

part four

COUNTRY MUSIC BOOKS, MAGAZINES, AND MOVIES

Robert K. Oermann

READING ABOUT COUNTRY MUSIC

The books that have been written about country music are an important part of learning about this unique American art form. A good writer can open your mind and ears to the beauty and vigor of this white soul music. There are some that do this by telling you about country music's rich history. Others entertain you with colorful tales of the lives of musicians and fans. Country music books also serve as important reference sources to check for record titles, facts, and details. If you're not already a fan, books can point you to the most interesting sounds to listen for, allowing you to understand and appreciate country's favorites.

Country music book publication is still quite young. Its roots are in the works of Archie Green, D. K. Wilgus, and Norm Cohen, the first real students and serious writers in the field. Their pioneering efforts appeared in 1964–65 in two magazines: *Western Folklore* and *Journal of American Folklore*. These articles are now classics and are available as reprints. Gene Earle, Will Roy Hearne, and Bob Pinson were the groundbreaking record collectors and compilers of record lists. Their works are, by and large, buried in obscure magazines. Amazingly for a recorded music nearly sixty years old, most of the good writing (and nearly all the book-length work) has been done since 1970.

Books on country music fall into several categories. After academic folklorists took notice of country music as a grass roots art form in the mid-1960s, and after country music boomed commercially, several journalists and music lovers began to write down their impressions in book form. These books are listed under the heading "Journalists' Books and General Works." In many ways these are the best writings for the uninitiated to become aware of the pleasures of country.

Because the past is so important to country music, the books listed under "Histories and Discographies" are crucial for making a serious study of almost any aspect of the field. Discographies, which are also included in many of the histories, encyclopedias, and books on individual musicians, are especially valuable because the aural documents are at least as important as the written material in understanding the development of country music.

The various titles in the "Encyclopedias" category are the reference books to consult repeatedly for factual information. The books in "Biographies and Autobiographies" illustrate the social roots and personal meanings of country music; many are so good that they could also serve as introductory books.

Those books marked with an asterisk (*) make up a basic list of highly recommended titles that takes in all the above categories. (Note that recommended instruction books are listed at the end of each instrument chapter in Part 2). Some of the books listed are illustrated with photographs of their covers or dust jackets. Bear in mind that many of these are first editions. Later printings—and especially paperback editions—are quite likely to have different cover designs, so have the title and author accurately in mind when you go looking for them today.

This part of the book concludes with an extensive list of recommended country music periodicals (in addition to periodicals devoted primarily to instruments, listed in Part 2, or to business, listed in Part 3), and a chapter on country music movies. The Appendix lists the names and addresses of record companies, distributors, and specialized dealers.

JOURNALISTS' BOOKS AND GENERAL WORKS

Teddy Bart
Inside Music City, U.S.A.
Aurora, 1970. 164 p.

Nashville hadn't been known as Music City for very long when Bart published this book: it is one of the earliest accounts we have of the country music scene by a Nashville journalist. It deals almost exclusively with the top songwriters of that day: Hank Cochran, John D. Loudermilk, Harlan Howard, Jack Clement, Willie Nelson, Boudleaux Bryant, Bobby Russell, Marijohn Wilkin, and Billy Edd Wheeler.

There are some inaccuracies and distortions in this work, but those interested in the careers of country music's greatest songwriters will find it informative and useful.

Paul Hemphill
The Nashville Sound:
Bright Lights and Country Music *
Ballantine, 1970. 209 p.

After more than a decade, this book is still one of the most lively, readable, and truthful of all country music books. Hemphill had his fingertips on the pulse of Nashville, and he was the first to try to capture the raw, rich life of country music in journalistic terms.

John Grissim
Country Music: White Man's Blues
Paperback Library, 1970. 299 p.

Grissim's book displays insight, understanding, and an almost photographic eye for revealing detail. It is full of great glimpses into the lives of the stars, contains a wealth of wonderful anecdotes, and is an excellent snapshot of Nashville, taken when the country music industry was about to plunge into its most successful decade.

Peter Guralnick
Feel Like Going Home: Portraits in Blues and Rock 'n' Roll
Outerbridge and Dienstfreg, 1971. 222 p.

The only country subjects in this book are Charlie Rich, Sam Phillips, and Jerry Lee Lewis. However, this collection of sensitive and articulate essays laid the groundwork for the author's superb *Lost Highway* of 1979. Guralnick has continued to write consistently and sympathetically about country musicians.

Jan Reid
The Improbable Rise of Redneck Rock
DaCapo, 1974. 342 p.

This attempt to capture the Austin scene covers most of the major country-rock singers. It contains the only in-depth views of such Austin performers as Michael Murphey, Rusty Wier, Bobby Bridger, Willis Alan Ramsey, and Steve Fromholz.

Dorothy Horstman
*Sing Your Heart Out, Country Boy**
Dutton, 1975. (Revised and expanded edition forthcoming from the Country Music Foundation Press.) 393 p.

Horstman's approach to country music is by way of the stories behind 308 of its classic songs, for which the lyrics are included. This is a jewel of a book in which the songwriters and performers, those close to them, and the songs all speak for themselves.

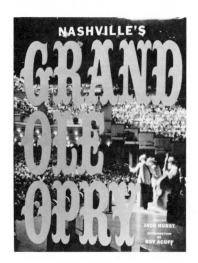

Jack Hurst
*Grand Ole Opry**
Abrams, 1975. 403 p.

This expensive, unsuccessful volume is a very good piece of work. Hurst is a newspaper columnist who has probably written more consistently excellent pieces on country music than any one else alive. He's been writing about country music for years and years with wit, affection, and intelligence. *Grand Ole Opry* should have earned him an even greater reputation.

This book remains the most beautifully, carefully illustrated work in the field. The photos are well chosen and lovingly reproduced. For them, and for Hurst's well-informed writing this is a marvelous book to own. You can now find it on sale in many used book shops at a fraction of its original high price.

Andy Gray
Great Country Music Stars
Hamlyn, 1975. 176 p.

This book is most notable for its photos, almost all of them taken for the book during European tours and not to be seen elsewhere. The text, however, is full of errors and misspellings; it should not be used as a source of accurate facts.

Robert Cornfield, with Marshall Fallwell, Jr.
Just Country
McGraw-Hill, 1976. 176 p.

This book is at once a history, an insider's look, a journalistic appreciation, and a broad overview. It is a solidly professional job with perceptive writing and excellent pictures, and is a fine introductory country book.

Country Music Magazine
The Best of Country Music Volumes I, II, and III
CMM (Country Music Magazine) Press, 1976. approx. 375 p.

This brings together the best writing of a number of major country music writers: the rotating cast of characters who contribute to *Country Music* magazine. Since the book contains articles that span the history of the magazine, there are several interesting views of artists whose situations have changed markedly over the years.

David Graham
He Walks With Me: The Religious Experiences of Country Music Stars
Pocket Books, 1977. 210 p.

These are fairly absorbing accounts of various country stars' feelings about religion—pretty much like any average person's religious thoughts.

Carol Offen, ed.
Country Music: The Poetry
Ballantine, 1977. 120 p.

This is a collection of song lyrics, with the emphasis on well-known modern songs rather than the classics of country music. Offen writes lightly but perceptively in the brief essays that introduce each chapter.

Michael Bane
The Outlaws: Revolution in Country Music
CMM Press/Doubleday/Dalton, 1978. 154 p.

This book tells the story of the Outlaw music movement of the 1970s. Mistakes mar the book, but it effectively captures a time and place that is rapidly becoming part of

Nashville's legendary past—Jack Clement and Tompall Glaser stories have now assumed nearly the status of Hank Williams tales.

Frye Gaillard
Watermelon Wine: The Spirit of Country Music
St. Martins, 1978. 235 p.

This book attempts to describe the appeal, meaning, feeling, and essence of country music. It does this by using country's deepest and finest songs as taking-off points from which to ponder the emotions and stories of country's stars and fans, bringing the world of country to light in an honest, compassionate, pleasant style.

Michael Kosser
Those Bold and Beautiful Country Girls
Mayflower, 1979. 127 p.

This book presents quick sketches of several of today's most prominent women country singers, with lots of nice pictures to look at. The general idea is that country music women have to be both tough and talented to make it, and though light in tone the book is not without insights into the inner workings of the business.

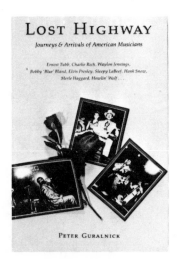

Peter Guralnick
Lost Highway: Journeys and Arrivals of American Musicians*
Godine, 1979. 362 p.

Among those profiled in this superbly written anthology are Hank Williams, DeFord Bailey, Hank Snow, Ernest Tubb, Elvis, Charlie Feathers, Mickey Gilley, Jack Clement,

Charlie Rich, Scotty Moore, Waylon Jennings, Merle Haggard, Hank Williams, Jr., James Talley, Stoney Edwards, and Sleepy LaBeef. They're all brilliant musicians about whom there are fascinating tales to tell, and there's not a writer in all of popular music that can tell them better than Guralnick.

He makes you feel and care for musicians, and always lets his love for music shine through. If you really want to know what these people are all about, buy and read this fine book.

HISTORIES AND DISCOGRAPHIES

More than any other form of American popular music, country music draws on its own traditions, is aware of its historical roots, and respects its past. Until quite recently, however, country music's history was largely in the memories of its musicians, not down on paper.

It is a tremendously difficult job for a writer to recover that history and write it down, and there is still a great deal of work to be done in this area. It was the music of the poor and the working class of America, a music that was scorned and ignored by journalists, scholars, and recording industry historians alike, so there are few previous books on which to draw. Still, some excellent works have emerged in the past few years.

Bill C. Malone
Country Music, U.S.A.: A Fifty Year History*
University of Texas Press, 1968. 422 p.

This is the most accurate, complete, and serious study of country music ever published. It is a treasure of anecdotes, little-known facts, and fascinating stories, as well as a guide to the best musicians and a chronological account of country music's growth from simple, homemade fiddle tunes on scratchy records to an international entertainment industry.

Douglas B. Green
Country Roots: The Origins of Country Music
Hawthorne, 1976. 238 p.

The organization of this book is by music styles: old-time music and string bands, country blues, comedy, singing cowboys, Cajun music, bluegrass, Western swing, gospel, rockabilly, and honky-tonk sounds. The writing is breezy, colorful, and entertaining, and the book has been used successfully as a classroom textbook. It is heavily illustrated with photos of posters, performers, shows, and memorabilia, and is the best popular introductory work.

Charles K. Wolfe
The Grand Ole Opry: The Early Years, 1925–35[*]
Old Time Music (London), 1975. 128 p.

This is not a full history of country music, but rather a fascinating account of the first ten years of the Grand Ole Opry. It is a model of fine scholarship, good writing, and superb storytelling.

Bill C. Malone and Judith McCulloh, eds.
*The Stars of Country Music: Uncle Dave Macon to Johnny Rodriquez**
Avon, 1975. 532 p.

No bookshelf devoted to popular music should be without a copy of this superb collection of essays on the most historically significant personalities, assembled in chronological order. The contributors range from journalists to college professors, from musicians to fans, so the styles of writing vary widely, but all are excellent.

Robert Shelton and Burt Goldblatt
The Country Music Story: A Picture History of Country and Western Music
Castle Books, 1966. 256 p.

This book was the pioneer. Prior to its publication, the only full-length treatment was Linnell Gentry's compilation of historical articles and some academic studies in scholarly journals. In spite of the fact that much more is known today about country's history, it remains a remarkable and important document. It is the finest collection of historical photographs of country artists ever assembled. Highly recommended.

Nick Tosches
Country: Living Legends and Dying Metaphors in America's Biggest Music
Scribners, 1985. 256 p.

This is a selective history consisting of vignettes rather than an all-encompassing chronology. It explores the seamy side of country entertainers' lives in detail. Tosches brings a unique point of view and great writing to this picture of the origins and an aspect of the present reality of country music.

Colin Escott and Martin Hawkins
The Sun Records Story
Quick Fox, 1975. 173 p.

This is the history of Sam Phillips and one of the most important record labels in the history of American music. Fans of rockabilly music will find this essential reading, and no student of country music should fail to consult this research. There's not another book like it.

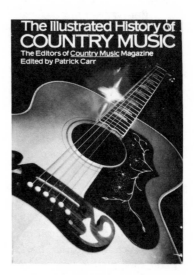

Patrick Carr, editor, and the editors of *Country Music* magazine
*The Illustrated History of Country Music**
Dolphin/Doubleday, 1979. 359 p.

Several of the major writers on country music history collaborated to produce this book; they include Charles K. Wolfe, Douglas B. Green, Bob Pinson, William Ivey, J. R. Young, Roger Williams, and Nick Tosches. Although somewhat loosely tied together, this is one of the best easy-reading introductions to the subject.

Charles K. Wolfe
Tennessee Strings: The Story of Country Music in Tennessee
University of Tennessee Press, 1977. 118 p.

This book is the first to look at country music from a regional perspective. Professor Wolfe brings his usual expertise, graceful writing, and gift for anecdote to this history of

Tennessee's contributions to the form. Once you've read some of the general histories, books like this one are the next place to go.

Tony Russell
Blacks, Whites, and Blues
Stein and Day, 1970. 112 p.

In this book, *Old Time Music* magazine's editor attempts to analyze the relationship between black and white music styles in the South during the first half of this century. He has a fascinating story to tell.

Blues fans who are also country fans—or anyone familiar with the records of Jimmie Rodgers, Charlie Poole, the Carlisle Brothers, the Mississippi Sheiks, the Delmore Brothers, or Bob Wills—will especially enjoy this book.

The John Edwards Memorial Foundation
Folklore and Mythology Center UCLA
Los Angeles, CA 90024

Reprints and pamphlets.
Various dates; various pagination.

The John Edwards Memorial Collection, containing more than 7,500 country recordings, has been relocated from UCLA to The University of North Carolina at Chapel Hill. It was the first archive and study center for country music, and along with the Country Music Foundation in Nashville, it is the leading distributor of historical information on country music. Its periodical, the *JEMF Quarterly* (still available from UCLA; see the later section on magazines), the CMF's *Journal of Country Music*, and Britain's *Old Time Music* are the three leading country music historical periodicals.

Over the years, the JEMF has also issued a series of pamphlets on country music. Some are reprints of significant articles; some are discographies; and some are books on various aspects and personalities of country music. Together, these pamphlets form the single most important historical information source available. A listing of materials available from the JEMF follows.

JEMF SPECIAL SERIES

Pub. No.
  2. *JOHNNY CASH DISCOGRAPHY AND RECORDING HISTORY (1955–1968)*, by John L. Smith. 48pp, photos.

3. *UNCLE DAVE MACON: A BIO-DISCOGRAPHY*, by Ralph Rinzler and Norm Cohen. 54pp, bibliography, photos.
4. *FROM BLUES TO POP: THE AUTOBIOGRAPHY OF LEONARD "BABY DOO" CASTON*, ed. by Jeff Titon. 30pp, musical transcriptions, photos.
5. *'HEAR MY SONG': THE STORY OF THE SONS OF THE PIONEERS*, by Ken Griffis. 148pp, biography, discography, bibliography, photos, filmography, chronology.
6. *GENNETT RECORDS OF OLD TIME TUNES, A CATALOG REPRINT.* Introduction by John K. MacKenzie. 20pp, photos.
7. *MOLLY O'DAY, LYNN DAVIS, AND THE CUMBERLAND MOUNTAIN FOLKS: A BIO-DISCOGRAPHY*, by Ivan M. Tribe and John W. Morris. 36pp, photos, bibliography.
8. *REFLECTIONS: THE AUTOBIOGRAPHY OF JOHNNY BOND.* 79pp, chronology, discography, filmography, photos, sheet music.
9. *FIDDLIN' SID'S MEMOIRS: THE AUTOBIOGRAPHY OF SIDNEY J. HARKREADER*, ed. by Walter D. Haden. 37pp, bibliography, discography.
10. *THE COLUMBIA 33000-F IRISH SERIES.* A numerical listing compiled by Pekka Gronow. 78pp, introduction, release dates, artist and title indexes, illustrations.
11. *THE RECORDINGS OF JIMMIE RODGERS: AN ANNOTATED DISCOGRAPHY*, by Johnny Bond. 76pp, introduction by Norm Cohen, select bibliography, chronology, photos, illustrations.
12. *FOLK FESTIVAL ISSUES: REPORT FROM A SEMINAR*, prepared by David E. Whisnant. 28pp, photos, illustrations.
13. *LORETTA LYNN'S WORLD OF MUSIC*, by Laurence J. Zwisohn. 115pp, annotated discography, complete list of songs she composed, and biographical data.

Linnell Gentry
A History and Encyclopedia of Country, Western, and Gospel Music
Clairmont Corporation, 1969. 598 p.

(See page 366).

Griel Marcus
Mystery Train
Dutton, 1976. 271 p.

This is one of the very best rock 'n' roll histories ever published. It deals extensively with rock's country and rockabilly roots and pays special attention to the story of Sun Records. Many people consider Marcus's pages on Elvis Presley in this book to be the finest piece of writing ever done on him. The book's strengths as a country history lie in its excellent explanation and understanding of the links between country music and the development of rock 'n' roll. Worth reading.

Bill C. Malone
Southern Music, American Music
University Press of Kentucky, 1979. 203 p.

The theme explored here is how various styles of music performed in the South came to interact with and influence our national culture. The book offers a sweeping, readable, historical overview of country music's interconnections with gospel, blues, ragtime, rock 'n' roll, and other folk-based and folk-derived music forms, and country's relationship to our national urban culture. It contains many memorable passages and much useful information.

Archie Green
Only a Miner: Studies in Recorded Coal-Mining Songs
University of Illinois Press, 1972. 504 p.

Green's book is a detailed, meticulous piece of research that examines carefully and at length the subject of coal mining in country songs down through the years. This is academic writing, intended for a specialized audience, but it is invaluable for reconstructing the historical record and offers insights into the lives and the circumstances that country music grows from.

Bob Artis
Bluegrass
Leisure/Nordon, 1975. 182 p.

In style and repertoire, bluegrass music more closely resembles the homemade acoustic music that country music's founding fathers and mothers played than does most of what's heard on country radio stations today. Thus, bluegrass histories properly include the early years of old-time country music as well. This book covers all the important territory and is generally well liked in the bluegrass community.

David Rothel
The Singing Cowboys
Barnes, 1978. 272 p.

The movie singing cowboy once played an extremely important role in country music's rise to national popularity; this book attempts to document that trend. It is primarily about musical cowboy movies and contains very little information about music, songs, or singing. If you are interested in this aspect of country music history, you'll probably want to have it in your library. It contains good filmographies.

Lois Blackwell
The Wings of the Dove: The Story of Gospel Music in America
Donning, 1978. 173 p.

This book is one of the very small number of written histories of gospel music.

Joel Whitburn
Top Country and Western Records
Record Research, Inc. (Menomonee Falls, Wisconsin), yearly. Various pagination.

Published annually, these straight discographies are compilations that list, by artist name and by title, country hit records that have made *Billboard* magazine's country music popularity charts. (The first volume covers 1949–1971). Record label, release number, highest chart position reached, and length of time on the charts during that year are provided for each artist/number listed. Quite expensive, these are the only reasonably up-to-date artist discographies published. A major single-volume update will be available in 1985.

ENCYCLOPEDIAS

Any basic country music library must contain source books. All of these encyclopedias have entries on music, instruments, and business topics as well as on individuals, but they are most useful as collections of brief biographies. If you want to know why Vernon Dalhart ought to be in the Hall of Fame, when Chet Atkins came to Nashville, what Jeanne Pruett's biggest hit is, how Sam McGee died, where Sonny James is from, or how Loretta Lynn broke into the business, these books are the place to look. Each has an area of strength; what one might lack, another will provide. Entertainers exaggerate a lot in providing details to researchers; take these references with a grain of salt and the knowledge that the entries were probably written to show the person in his or her best light. Here they are, in order of accuracy and usefulness.

Fred Deller and Roy Thompson, with Douglas B. Green
*The Illustated Encyclopedia of Country Music**
Harmony/Crown, 1977. 256 p.

If you're going to buy one encyclopedia of country music, this could be the one. It has extensive coverage of historical artists as well as modern stars— almost everyone from Eck Robertson to Emmylou Harris is included. The entries are, by and large, fairly

 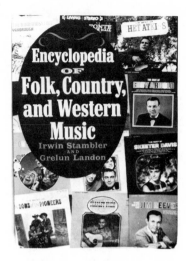

factual; the pictures are many and colorful; representative record albums are listed; and the biographies are pretty complete.

Linnell Gentry
A History and Encyclopedia of Country, Western, and Gospel Music
Clairmont Corporation, 1969. 598 p.

This is really two books in one. The first section reprints seventy-six articles that chronicle country music's coverage by mass-circulation magazines over the period 1908 to 1968. It is thus more a history of the shifts in national media response to country music than it is a history of the music itself, although the authorship of the articles becomes more expert as they get closer to the present.

The second section of the book is the encyclopedia, consisting of over 600 entries written in a tight, facts-only format. This is overall the most factually reliable of the encyclopedias because Gentry got his information by sending out questionnaires to the musicians themselves. Exactly the same questions were asked of each person, so the biographies have a basically consistent format. Although out of print (and in need of updating), it can often be found in public and academic libraries.

Irwin Stambler and Grelun Landon
*The Encyclopedia of Folk, Country, and Western Music**
St. Martins, 1983. 902 p.

This is the long-awaited update of the author's 1969 volume of the same title. At over twice the size of the earlier work, it is actually much more than an update. Many new entries have replaced old ones; most of those that were retained have been completely reworked. Thus, this is a new book, superbly useful by itself or in conjunction with the original volume. Besides being the best available overview of the connections between country music and the folk revival of the 1960s, it is *the* chief research volume in the field of country music today.

Larry Sandberg and Dick Weissman
The Folk Music Source Book
Knopf, 1976. 260 p.

For bluegrass fans, old time string band enthusiasts, country blues players, Cajun devotees, jug band members, ballad collectors, ragtimers, fiddlers, flatpickers, finger-pickers, harmonica, dobro, mandolin, banjo, dulcimer, and piano players, bass slappers, and concertina squeezers, this book offers information ranging from how to play, to who makes the instruments, to where folk music centers are, to the best festivals and events. All of this is in addition to the book's value as an encyclopedia. Here you'll find entries on all the finest traditional country and folk performers, living and dead, as well as lists of their best albums, instruction books, and songbooks. Highly recommended to anyone seriously interested in country music.

Melvin Shestack
The Country Music Encyclopedia
Crowell, 1974. 410 p.

This book's value is less as a country reference book than as a collection of some obscure views of country music stars. Its scant 200 entries include practically no historical ones, and you should beware of errors. However, there are some interesting articles to be found in its pages. Those on Tammy Wynette, Gram Parsons, Dolly Parton, and Johnny Cash, among others, are fascinating interviews and well-written perspectives on these acts, rather than ordinary biographies.

Record World Magazine and Thurston Moore
Country Music Who's Who: 1972
Record World, 1972. Unpaginated.

(Available from Country Music Hall of Fame and Museum, Nashville)

For years Thurston Moore's annual *Who's Who* books were the most important source of information about country music, its stars, its history, and its culture. Though dense and difficult to use, they were invaluable guides, covering a wide range of factual material.

This edition is the last one still available. It is a wonderful picture taken the last time the industry stood still for its complete portrait.

Kristin Baggelaar and Donald Milton
Folk Music: More than a Song
Crowell, 1976. 419 p.

Although neither authoritative nor definitive, this book contains some information on country and folk performers not readily available elsewhere. The emphasis is on East Coast folksong revivalists, although some material on early string bands and contemporary country artists is included. Important country stars like the Nitty Gritty Dirt Band, Don Williams, George Hamilton IV, Hoyt Axton, Emmylou Harris, John Denver, Guy Clark, John Prine, John Hartford, Jerry Jeff Walker, Billy Edd Wheeler, Gram Parsons, and Linda Ronstadt grew out of the folk revival, and that movement supported acts like Doc Watson, Bill Monroe, Mother Maybelle Carter, and Dock Boggs when commercial Nashville didn't seem to have much use for them. This encyclopedia provides a good overview of those interactions.

Jeannie Sakol
The Wonderful World of Country Music
Grosset and Dunlop, 1979. 240 p.

There are only a few rather personally picked entries for inactive performers in this book, and sometimes the selection and style of the entries on active performers seem a little personal, too. On the other hand, there is a good deal of information (including some brief biographies) that isn't compiled anywhere else.

Jesse Burt and Duane Allen
The History of Gospel Music
Silverline Music, 1971. 205 p.

Although it contains a slim 137 entries, this encyclopedia (cowritten by Duane Allen of the Oak Ridge Boys) is the best available on gospel music. There is no other reference book where you can find such things as James W. Blackwood's birth place and date, information about the original members of the LeFevre Family, or a brief biography of the Gospel Music Association's Don Butler.

Robert Anderson and Gail North
Gospel Music Encyclopedia
Sterling, 1979. 320 p.

This shouldn't be called an encyclopedia: The artists covered are not fully described; there are no birthdates, birthplaces, dates of recordings, lists of songs written, or other fundamental facts in the entries; and important artists (including the Chuck Wagon Gang!) are left out. But the photographs are plentiful and well chosen. Since there is no other basic sourcebook that contains pictures of the major gospel acts, the book is worthwhile for these alone. Other extremely valuable elements are found in the book's appendices: lists of Dove Award winners, members of the Gospel Music Hall of Fame, gospel radio stations, the board of directors of the Gospel Music Association, music and lyrics for gospel classics, and representative albums of the encyclopedia's subjects.

BIOGRAPHIES AND AUTOBIOGRAPHIES

These are the biographies of exciting show business personalities. But the subjects were not always stars of the entertainment world and many of them remember well what life outside that world was like. Thus, some of these books are also representative reports of what life is like for millions whose stories rarely get told: the poor; rural people; the working class. Not all of these are good books. In many cases they are simply the only document of a particular performer's life. Some, however, will move you and excite you, and enrich your life tremendously. They are listed alphabetically by stars' names.

ROY ACUFF

Elizabeth Schlappi
Roy Acuff: The Smoky Mountain Boy
Pelican Publishing Co. (Gretna, Louisiana), 1978. 289 p.

Acuff is not an easy man to get to know, so this is probably going to stand as the official biography for many years to come. A straightforward, quite admirably put-together account of what happened when, it is clearly written by a dyed-in-the-wool fan. It has a factual style with very little color or editorializing.

CHET ATKINS

Chet Atkins, with Bill Neely
Chet Atkins: Country Gentleman
Regnery, 1974. 212 p.

Atkins is one of the world's premier guitar players. He was the chief architect of the Nashville Sound, is the youngest member of the Country Music Hall of Fame, and was one of the most powerful men in the recording industry. Like most of the country greats, he comes from plain ol' hillbilly roots.

Guitarists are a funny breed, often seeming to prefer communication via music to any other kind. Chet Atkins still sits down and practices guitar every night, even though he's been playing professionally for years. Maybe that's why this book is not completely satisfying: The man simply isn't used to talking about himself; all his life he's spoken through his instrument. It's either that or the fact that he's too shrewd, powerful, and self-aware to be completely open.

Those wishing a basic biography and an overview of Atkins's accomplishments will be satisfied by this book. Those interested in the inner workings of the Nashville industry establishment, extensive guitar-picking insights, or glimpses of Depression-era poverty will not.

GENE AUTRY

Gene Autry, with Mickey Herskowitz
Back in the Saddle Again
Doubleday, 1978. 252 p.

Now a multimillionaire with a carefully constructed public image, Gene provides no surprising revelations here, few little-known tales, and hardly any insights into his character. This is the story of the good guy in the white hat. The best and most useful part of this book is the appendix, which lists details of all Autry's films.

JOHNNY BOND

Johnny Bond
Reflections: The Autobiography of Johnny Bond
John Edwards Memorial Foundation, 1976. 79 p.

Along with his studies of Tex Ritter and Jimmie Rodgers, Bond found time to write down his own story. He is a composer of great significance ("Cimarron," "I Wonder Where You Are Tonight," "Tomorrow Never Comes," "Ten Little Bottles," etc.), a popular recording artist, and a Western film star. Country fans can be truly grateful that Bond also had such a sense of history. This pamphlet includes lots of interesting pictures, a discography, a list of his movies, scripts for "Town Hall Party" and "Hollywood Barn Dance" radio shows, reprints of newspaper clippings, and lots of fascinating memorabilia.

JUNE CARTER

June Carter Cash
Among My Klediments
Zondervan (Grand Rapids, Michigan), 1979. 156 p.

This short book of text, photos, and poems is short on revelations, too, but does provide glimpses into the personalities of the Carter family; June and Johnny Cash's stories; and nearly as much Christianity as biography. (According to June, a klediment is anything you hold near and dear.)

THE CARTER FAMILY

John Atkins, ed.
The Carter Family
Old Time Music (London), 1973. 62 p.

Sara, Maybelle, and A. P. Carter all died without giving frank, self-revealing accounts of their musical life together. Even the barest outline of the Carter family saga is a fascinating one, however, so this book succeeds remarkably well.

JOHNNY CASH

Christopher S. Wren
Winners Got Scars Too: The Life of Johnny Cash
Ballantine, 1971. 252 p.

Albert Govoni
A Boy Named Cash: The Johnny Cash Story
Lancer, 1970. 190 p.

Johnny Cash
Man in Black
Warner, 1975. 244 p.

George Carpozi, Jr.
The Johnny Cash Story
Pyramid, 1970. 128 p.

Any one of these biographies provides a good introduction to Cash's remarkable life—Wren's is the best—but none goes much beyond that. For the most personal, direct insights, Cash's autobiography should of course be consulted.

JERRY CLOWER

Jerry Clower, with Gerry Wood
Ain't God Good!
Word, 1976. 178 p.

Jerry Clower, with Gerry Wood
Let the Hammer Down!
Word, 1978. 189 p.

These entertaining books reveal a lot about the Mouth of the South, one of the funniest people in America today.

DAVID ALLAN COE

David Allan Coe
Just For the Record
D.A.C. Dream Enterprises (Big Pine Key, Florida), 1978. 200 p.

Coe, easily one of the most colorful country stars who has ever lived, tells his story in his own words and his own style. He spent almost twenty years behind bars, hangs out with motorcycle gangs, has more tattoos than anyone you can think of, and is a master at publicity and self-promotion. Coe is out there on the fringe, and chances are you won't be bored as you travel there with him in this unusual book.

COMMANDER CODY AND THE LOST PLANET AIRMEN

Geoffrey Stokes
Star-Making Machinery: Inside the Business of Rock and Roll
Vintage Books/Random House, 1977. 234 p.

Commander Cody is perhaps most familiar to country fans as the act that revived the country classics "Hot Rod Lincoln" and "Smoke! Smoke! Smoke! (That Cigarette)" in the early 1970s. This book is the story of the band's dealings with record companies, agents, and the music business. It may not be a traditional biography, but it is one of the most interesting and insightful books ever written about being a professional musician in the 1970s.

THE DELMORE BROTHERS

Alton Delmore, with Charles K. Wolfe, ed.
Truth Is Stranger than Publicity: Alton Delmore's Autobiography*
Country Music Foundation Press, 1977. 188 p.

Alton Delmore's effort to make sense of the world and his life—which he firmly and correctly believed was an important story to tell—is true folk literature, written with honesty, directness, informality, and candor. It is completely in Alton's own language, and his sensitivity and eloquence shine through every page. This is one of the finest country music biographies ever written.

DALE EVANS

Dale Evans Rogers
Dale: My Personal Picture Album
Revell, 1971. 127 p.

Dale Evans's evolution from small-town Texas girl, to radio pop music singer, to film star, to singing cowgirl is well documented in pictures in this book. It thus makes a good companion to the prose volumes by and about her, the best of which is Carlton Stowers's *Happy Trails* (see the Roy Rogers listing).

WOODY GUTHRIE

Joe Klein
*Woody Guthrie: A Life**
Knopf, 1980. 476 p.

Woody Guthrie
*Bound For Glory**
NAL/Dutton, 1943. 428 p.

Guthrie is probably the only country musician who has ever lived who could write his own life story (without a helper) as well as any biographer. He was every bit as much a hillbilly as any other country performer, but he had a natural gift for writing and self-expression that was as astounding as it was prolific.

The Klein biography seems to tell the whole story, including the painful, unflattering, and tragic aspects of Woody's life. It is a complex portrait of one of the most unique and baffling figures of American culture.

Don't count Guthrie's own account out, though. It long ago reached the status of a classic of native literature, and deservedly so. It is written in Guthrie's own colorful, cascading style, and reading it is like having him still alive talking to you.

MERLE HAGGARD

Merle Haggard, with Peggy Russell
Sing Me Back Home: My Life
Times Books, 1981. 286 p.

In a powerful, matter-of-fact style this outstanding book chronicles the chain of events that led a wild, fatherless boy to two-and-a-half years in San Quentin, and what happened to him after he got there. It transcends the star autobiography genre, and will particularly affect readers who feel they already know Haggard through his music.

TOM T. HALL

Tom T. Hall
The Storyteller's Nashville
Doubleday, 1979. 221 p.

This is one of the few autobiographies of country stars that actually gives you some insight into the workings of the Nashville music scene. Hall touches on publishing, booking, hanging out, songwriting processes, bands, traveling, and performing. He's a pretty decent prose writer, and open about himself and his own mistakes. This is definitely a book to read before planning to come to Nashville to make it as a musician.

BUDDY HOLLY

John Goldrosen
The Buddy Holly Story
Quick Fox (Music Sales Corp.), 1979. 257 p.

John Tobler
The Buddy Holly Story
Plexus (London), 1979. 96 p.

Dave Laing
Buddy Holly
Collier, 1972. 144 p.

All of these books contain essentially the same information about Holly's short life, and all are satisfactory. The Laing book is less of a biography and more of a musical analysis.

WAYLON JENNINGS

Bob Allen
Waylon Jennings and Willie Nelson
Music Sales, 1979. 186 p.

Although this book is too brief and lacks detail, especially on Willie's early years, it has the basic biographical information and lots of pictures. Allen quotes heavily from interviews published elsewhere, so the book stands as a document of Waylon and Willie's statements to the press, as well as a chronology of their careers. The author's good music criticism provides a useful guide to choosing among Waylon's various albums.

JERRY LEE LEWIS

Nick Tosches
Hellfire: The Jerry Lee Lewis Story
Delacorte, 1982. 276 p.

In 1982, an astonishing four full-length books became available about the wildest piano man ever produced in country music. Ex-wife Myra Lewis's *Great Balls of Fire* (Quill) is lightweight but has some insight. Robert Palmer's *Jerry Lee Lewis Rocks!* (Delilah Books) has some excellent photos; and Robert Cain's *Whole Lotta Shakin' Goin' On* (Dial Press) is chatty and fan-oriented. But it's Nick Tosches's torrential prose that comes closest to capturing the careening character of Jerry Lee Lewis himself.

LORETTA LYNN

Loretta Lynn, with George Vecsey
Loretta Lynn: Coal Miner's Daughter*
Warner Books, 1976. 256 p.

Among the many biographies and autobiographies of country stars, this celebrated work stands out. It preserves Lynn's syntax and world view, and allows her tremendous wit and intelligence to shine through every page.

BARBARA, LOUISE, AND IRLENE MANDRELL

Louise Mandrell and Ace Collins
The Mandrell Family Album
Nelson, 1983. 192 p.

Everything is sweetness-and-light here; don't look for any major ripples in the Mandrell family pond. The family is an American phenomenon, however, and the book is an attractively-mounted showcase for its success story. A true country fan's book.

BILL MONROE

James Rooney
Bossmen: Bill Monroe and Muddy Waters.
Dial Press, 1971. 159 p.

Bill Monroe is the subject of only half this book, but the portrait that is drawn of him is a good, deep one. Rooney alternates his narrative with liberal quotes from Monroe, his musical associates, and people who have observed him for years. This technique works very well in giving insights into the father of bluegrass and into the music he loves so much; no bluegrass fan will want to miss reading it.

WILLIE NELSON

Lana Nelson Fowler
*Willie Nelson Family Album**
H. M. Poirot (Amarillo, Texas),
1980. Unpaginated.

Bob Allen
Waylon Jennings and Willie Nelson
Music Sales, 1979. 186 p.

Willie's daughter, Lana, has produced an affectionate tribute composed of family photos, song lyrics, article reprints, memorabilia, and prose. It's an interesting and often effective approach to biography. See the Waylon Jennings listing for comments about the Allen book.

MOLLY O'DAY

Ivan M. Tribe and John W. Morris
*Molly O'Day, Lynn Davis, and The Cumberland Mountain Folks: A
   Bio-Discography*
John Edwards Memorial Foundation, 1975. 36 p.

This book has helped to keep Molly O'Day's legend alive for country fans who may not have heard her during her classic period of the late 1940s, before she completely dropped out of the music business to become an Appalachian evangelist.

DOLLY PARTON

Lola Scobey
*Dolly: Daughter of the South**
Zebra/Kensington Pub. Corp., 1977. 287 p.

Alanna Nash
Dolly*
Reed/Addison House, 1978. 275 p.

Connie Berman, with Dolly Parton
The Dolly Parton Scrapbook
Target/Grosset and Dunlap, 1978. 80 p.

Scobey never talked to Dolly herself, but interviewed everyone in her family, her hometown, and Nashville who has known her well. In many ways this book provides the fullest and most complex portrait of Dolly.

Parton cooperated with Alanna Nash on her book, and since she's such a great talker it makes interesting reading, too.

The Berman scrapbook is mainly a picture book, with an especially fascinating group of photos of Dolly's childhood.

MINNIE PEARL

Minnie Pearl, with Joan Dew
Minnie Pearl: An Autobiography
Simon and Schuster, 1980. 256 p.

This book is an autobiography of Sarah Ophelia Colley Cannon, the woman who created and played the world-famous country music character, Cousin Minnie Pearl. The book's emphasis is on her upbringing and personal life, rather than on show business and Minnie.

CARL PERKINS

Carl Perkins, with Ron Rendleman
Disciple in Blue Suede Shoes
Zondervan, 1978. 146 p.

Parts of this book are interesting views of life as a musician, parts are reports on the Devil and salvation.

ELVIS PRESLEY

Jerry Hopkins
*Elvis**
Warner Books, 1971. 446 p.

Jerry Hopkins
*Elvis, the Final Years**
St. Martins, 1980. 258 p.

Paul Lichter
The Boy Who Dared to Rock: The Definitive Elvis
Doubleday/Dolphin, 1978. 304 p.

Red West, Sonny West, and Dave Hebler, as told to Steve Dunleavy
Elvis: What Happened?
Ballantine, 1977. 332 p.

Alfred Wertheimer
*Elvis '56: In the Beginning**
Collier, 1979. 160 p.

James Robert Parish
Solid Gold Memories: The Elvis Presley Scrapbook
Ballantine, 1975. 185 p.

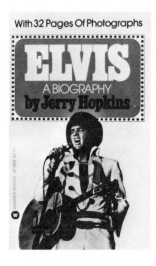 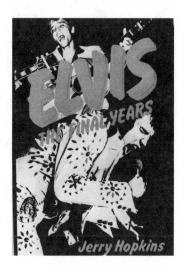 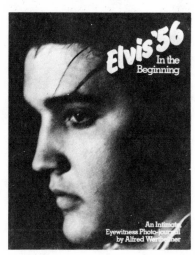

There are dozens of Elvis biographies on the market; this list represents some of the best.

Hopkins's 1971 biography of Presley, taken together with his update published after Elvis died, makes an excellent two-volume biography.

The Lichter book is a short, well-done overview of Elvis and his remarkable career.

Of all the books from the members of Elvis's inner circle, *Elvis: What Happened?*, written by his former bodyguards, is probably as close to the real truth of his strange existence in his last years as will ever be available.

Wertheimer was a photographer assigned to cover Elvis in 1956. His photo book is a superb recreation of the early excitement Elvis had and generated.

Parish's book is the best of the pictorial biographies.

TEX RITTER

Johnny Bond
The Tex Ritter Story
Chappell Music, 1976. 397 p.

Johnny Bond is the unofficial historian of the singing cowboys. He knew them all, and worked with most of them on records or in films. There is probably no one better qualified to write their stories, and his account of Tex Ritter's life is direct and affectionate. Included are lists of the many films and Broadway plays Ritter appeared in, with much information about them; a good discography; the lyrics to nineteen of Ritter's biggest hits; and a list of the films of his wife, Dorothy Faye Ritter.

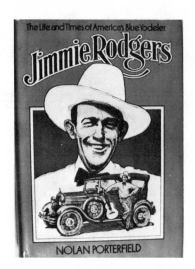

JIMMIE RODGERS

Nolan Porterfield
*Jimmie Rodgers: The Life and Times of America's Blue Yodeler**
University of Illinois Press, 1979. 460 p.

Mike Paris and Chris Comber
Jimmie the Kid: The Life of Jimmie Rodgers
Edison Music Books (London), 1977. 211 p.

Carrie Rodgers
My Husband Jimmie Rodgers
Country Music Foundation, 1975. 264 p.

Nolan Porterfield's book is probably the finest historical biography of a country star ever written. This is an essential book for any good country music home library.

Paris and Comber's work relies heavily on the authors' analysis of Rodgers's records.

Jimmie's wife's book, written in 1935, was the first major biography that ever appeared about a country musician.

KENNY ROGERS

Martha Hume
Kenny Rogers: Gambler, Dreamer, Lover
Delilah/Plume/New American Library, 1980. 159 p.

Kenny Rogers, with Len Epand
Making It with Music
Harper and Row, 1978. 224 p.

Martha Hume's book is the work of a solidly professional journalist. Extensive research into Rogers's early years in Houston has produced a more in-depth portrait than Rogers's own account, although the book is less effective as it draws nearer the present.

Billed as a guide to the music business, Rogers's book is illustrated with examples from his life and career, and serves double duty as an autobiography. It's a down-to-earth tale of climbing the ladder of success, with insights into the music business.

ROY ROGERS

Carlton Stowers, with Roy Rogers and Dale Evans
Happy Trails: The Story of Roy Rogers and Dale Evans
Word, 1979. 213 p.

Roy and Dale's story is told here with simplicity, gentleness, and honesty, though there is little about their music. Dale's songwriting ("Aha, San Antone," "The Bible Tells Me So," "Happy Trails to You," and other classics) is hardly mentioned, and Roy's beautiful voice, superb yodelling skills, and harmony singing aren't discussed much either. But the saga of their show business success and moving personal life together is recorded well. (Also see the Dale Evans listing.)

SONS OF THE PIONEERS

Ken Griffis
Hear My Song: The Story of the Celebrated Sons of the Pioneers
John Edwards Memorial Foundation, 1974. 148 p.

Griffis's work is the definitive study of the Sons of the the Pioneers, country music's premier Western harmony group.

MARIJOHN WILKIN

Darryl E. Hicks
Marijohn: Lord, Let Me Leave a Song
Word, 1978. 159 p.

Marijohn Wilkin wrote such huge hits as "Waterloo," "Long Black Veil," "One Day at a Time," and others, and was also a successful country singer. She has been like a godmother to struggling young songwriters down through the years, and her humanity and kindness are legendary in Nashville. In many ways hers is the most interesting and readable of all the country music inspirational biographies; her music and her faith are treated with equal depth and believability.

HANK WILLIAMS

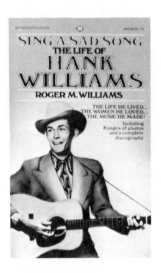

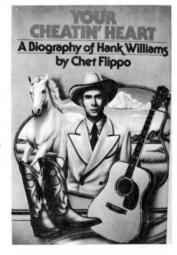

Roger M. Williams
Sing a Sad Song: The Life of Hank Williams*
University of Illinois Press, 1970. 275 p.

Chet Flippo
Your Cheatin' Heart
Simon and Schuster, 1981. 251 p.

Jay Caress
Hank Williams: Country Music's Tragic King
Stein and Day, 1979. 253 p.

The books by Jay Caress and Roger Williams cover similar ground, and each serves as a good introduction to Hank Williams's life. The well-written book by Chet Flippo (a *Rolling Stone* writer) tries to strip away some of the myths and get to the real truth behind the Hank Williams legend.

HANK WILLIAMS, JR.

Hank Williams, Jr., with Michael Bane
*Living Proof**
Putnam, 1979. 222 p.

Unlike most other country music biographies, this one deals extensively with its subject's music, including the writing and recording of Williams's most famous songs and albums. Bane's skills as a listener, editor, and prose stylist are brilliantly combined with Williams's gutbucket emotionalism, sensitivity, and insight.

BOB WILLS

Charles R. Townsend
*San Antonio Rose: The Life and Music of Bob Wills**
University of Illinois Press, 1976. 395 p.

This book will stand as the definitive book on Wills, his life, and his music for many, many years to come. It's a fairly scholarly work (over a decade of research went into the writing), but one even a casual reader will appreciate.

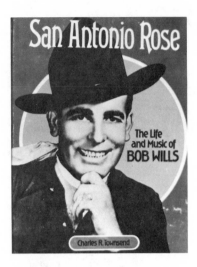

Included is a superb discography by Bob Pinson of the Country Music Foundation, which lists every recording Wills ever made.

TAMMY WYNETTE

Tammy Wynette, with Joan Dew
Stand By Your Man
PB, 1979. 349 p.

Music is scarcely mentioned at all in this book, despite Tammy Wynette's status as one of the finest, most emotionally moving, and most popular singers in country music history. Instead, the reader is treated to an exhaustive, gossipy, interesting chronicle of her marriages and love life.

Country Music Times
P.O. Box 35
North Quay Q4000
Australia

Country Rhythms
475 Park Ave. S.
New York, NY 10016

The Devil's Box
1540 Washington
Emporia, KS 66801

Disc Collector Publications
P.O. Box 169
Cheswold, DE 19936

Dulcimer Player's News
P.O. Box 2164
Winchester, VA 22601

The Folknik
San Francisco Folk Music Club
885 Clayton
San Francisco, CA 94117

Gilley's
4500 Spencer Highway
Pasadena, TX 77504

Gospel News
P.O. Box 1344
San Bernardino, CA 92402

Guitar Player
20605 Lazaneo
Cupertino, CA 95014

Guitar World
1115 Broadway
New York, NY 10010

Hillbilly
E. Reginald Schumann
Im Winkel 7
D-6501 Heidesheim
Germany

International Banjo
P.O. Box 328
Kissimmee, FL 32741

Mandolin World News
Box 2255
San Rafael, CA 94902

Music City Inquirer
38 Music Square East, Suite 216
Nashville, TN 37221

Oak Report
Box 572
Bellvale Road
Chester, NY 10918

Oklahoma Bluegrass Gazette
Box 642
Shawnee, OK 74801

Oldtime Country Music Club of Canada
1421 Gohier Street
St. Laurent, Quebec H4L 3K2
Canada

Renfro Valley Bugle
Renfro Valley, KY 40473

Sing Out!
505 Eighth Avenue
New York, NY 10018

The Singing News
P.O. Box 18010
Pensacola, FL 32523

Strictly Country
Bè Volders
Postbus 22
9590 AA Onstwedde
The Netherlands

Swing 51
41 Bushey Road
Sutton
Surrey SM1 1QR
England

Texas Proud
Route 3, Box 100
Brazoria, TX 77422

Victory Music Folk and Jazz Review
Box 36, Tillicum
Tacoma, WA 98492

SELECTED COUNTRY MUSIC FILMS

One of the major trends of the late 1970s and early 1980s has been Hollywood's attention to country themes and stars. Thanks largely to the support of such major stars as Clint Eastwood and Burt Reynolds, country music has been heard on the soundtracks of several successful motion pictures recently. This trend shows no signs of letting up in the near future, but it's important to recognize that it has a past, too.

Country music was present in the movies almost from the dawn of the talking picture. Jimmie Rodgers was the subject of a short-subject movie as early as 1929.

All through the 1930s and 1940s singing cowboy pictures were quite the rage. Gene Autry starred in at least ninety feature films during his career; Tex Ritter had over sixty starring roles; and Roy Rogers easily equalled Autry's tally as a box office star. Other prominent singings cowboys in films included Eddie Dean (about twenty starring roles), Jimmy Wakely (with nearly thirty starring vehicles), and Rex Allen (around twenty Westerns). Soon, Hollywood drafted other country singers into the singing cowboy films. Bob Wills, for example, was featured in two Charles Starret Westerns, eight Russell Hayden features, a Ken Curtis film, and in *Take Me Back to Oklahoma* (1940) and *Go West, Young Lady* (1941). Bill Boyd was featured in eight motion pictures, including *Texas Manhunt* (1941). Art Davis also made several musical Westerns.

Most of the "B movie" studios recognized the box office potential of country music stars. Republic Studios, for instance, made several series of films built around country personalities. Country comedienne Judy Canova was, in fact, their leading female attraction; she enjoyed a film career of some twenty-three starring features. The Weaver Brothers and Elviry were country music veterans from the days of vaudeville. They starred in eleven Republic films between 1938 and 1943. Grand Ole Opry star Roy Acuff was another who made B musicals. He made five for Republic and three for Columbia Pictures. Monogram, Grand National, and P.R.C. were other studios that recruited country talent. Thanks to Grand National, Dorothy Page became Hollywood's only major singing cowgirl. Country radio greats Lulu Belle and Scotty also had a film career thanks to the B studios. *National Barn Dance* (1944) was one of several screen appearances for them. Honky-tonk pioneer Ernest Tubb made two musical Westerns (*Fighting Buckaroos* and *Ridin' West*) and two country music features (*Jamboree* and *Hollywood Barn Dance*) in the 1940s. Eddy Arnold, too, made a film appearance. His feature was 1949's *Feudin' Rhythm*. A country music movie milestone was reached in 1944 when Jimmie Davis became the first country star to have his life story portrayed on film (in *Louisiana*).

In the early 1950s the trend continued. Foy Willing and Spade Cooley each were in several features. And as country-raised teen stars began to appear on record popularity charts, they too got Hollywood attention. Brenda Lee's appearance in *The Two Little Bears* (1961), Conway Twitty's roles in *Platinum High School, College Confidential*, and *Sex Kittens Go to College* (all 1960), David Houston's minor parts in *The Horse Soldiers* (1959) and *Teenage Kisses*, and Don Gibson in *Lost Lagoon* (1958), are just a few examples of this. *Five Minutes to Live* (1961) was Johnny Cash's thespian screen debut.

The rock 'n' roll movies of the mid-1950s provided vehicles for most of the leading rockabilly performers of the era. The 1956 films *Rock Around the Clock* and *Don't Knock the Rock* ushered in this type of movie; both featured Bill Haley and the Comets. Carl Perkins, Charlie Gracie, and Jerry Lee Lewis were in *Jamboree* (1957); Jerry Lee also sang in *High School Confidential* (1958). Johnny Burnette was in *Rock, Rock, Rock* (1957); both Bob Luman and David Houston were in the cast of *Carnival Rock* (1957); and Ferlin Husky put in an appearance in *Mister Rock and Roll* (1957). Gene Vincent was in *Hot Rod Gang* (1958) and *The Girl Can't Help It* (1957). The latter film also featured Eddie Cochran, who appeared with Richie Valens in *Go Johnny Go* two years later, and in *Untamed Youth* (1957) as well. *Rock, Baby, Rock It* (1957) included rockabilly performances, but despite its title *Rockabilly Baby* (1957) did not.

The modern era of country-oriented moviemaking began in 1958 with the release of the trash exploitation movie *Country Music Holiday*, starring Ferlin Husky, June Carter, Faron Young, and Zsa Zsa Gabor. Since that time Hollywood has continued to produce cheap, badly made country movies. But as the 1970s wore on, such films were supplemented by many fine releases with country themes. The following list is a run-down of twenty years' worth of motion pictures that are about country music, feature country stars, have country music soundtracks, or use country-related plots.

TWENTY-FIVE YEARS OF COUNTRY MUSIC FILMS

1958   *Country Music Holiday*

1959   *Legend of Tom Dooley* (Western based on the folk song, starring Michael Landon)

1962   *Wild Guitar*
        Buffalo Gun (Western starring Marty Robbins, Carl Smith, Webb Pierce)

1963   *Hootenanny Hoot*
        Bye Bye Birdie (parody of an Elvis/Conway-type teen star)

1964 *Your Cheatin' Heart* (Hank Williams biography)
Country Music Caravan
Country Music On Broadway
Moonshine Mountain
Tennessee Jamboree
The College (folkies on campus)
The TAMI Show (rock and folk-rock)

1965 *Second Fiddle to a Steel Guitar*
Forty Acre Feud
Once Upon a Coffee House (campus folk scene)
Kimberly Jim (South African, starring Jim Reeves)

1966 *Nashville Rebel* (starring Waylon Jennings)
Country Boy
The Big T.N.T. Show
The Gold Guitar
John Lair's Renfro Valley Barn Dance
Las Vegas Hillbillys
Music City U.S.A.
Road To Nashville
That Tennessee Beat
Sing a Song, For Heaven's Sake (gospel music)

1967 *Don't Look Back* (Bob Dylan documentary)
Country Western Hoedown
Hillbillys in a Haunted House
What Am I Bid?
Festival (folk music)
C'mon, Let's Live a Little (teen flick with Bobby Vee, Jackie DeShannon)

1968 *A Time to Sing* (starring Hank Williams, Jr.)
Fastest Guitar Alive (starring Roy Orbison)
Monterey Pop (some folk-rock)
Killers Three (Merle Haggard)

1969 *Johnny Cash! The Man, His World, His Music* (Johnny Cash documentary)
From Nashville, With Music
Alice's Restaurant (based on the song by Arlo Guthrie)
True Grit (featuring Glen Campbell)
Paint Your Wagon (Nitty Gritty Dirt Band featured)

1970 *Five Easy Pieces* (Tammy Wynette soundtrack)
Elvis: That's the Way It Is (Elvis Presley documentary)
Woodstock (some folk-rock)
Country Music Jamboree
Carry It On (Joan Baez)
Norwood (starring Glen Campbell)
Little Fauss and Big Halsey (Johnny Cash/Carl Perkins soundtrack)
I Walk the Line

1971 *Pete Seeger . . . A Song and a Stone* (documentary with folk, bluegrass, and country)
Cisco Pike (starring Kris Kristofferson)
Celebration at Big Sur (folk-rock)
Nashville Coyote
A Gunfight (starring Johnny Cash)

1972 *Elvis On Tour* (Elvis Presley documentary)

1973 *Payday*
Deliverance (Eric Weissberg soundtrack)
Pat Garrett and Billy the Kid (Kris Kristofferson and Bob Dylan)
The Gospel Road (starring Johnny Cash and June Carter)

1974 *Nashville*
The Hard Part Begins (Canadian)

1975 *W.W. and the Dixie Dancekings*
Bound for Glory (Woody Guthrie biography)
White Line Fever
MacIntosh & T.J. (starring Roy Rogers; Waylon Jennings soundtrack)

1976 *Ode to Billie Jo* (based on the Bobbie Gentry song)
Gator (starring Jerry Reed)

1977 *Smokey and the Bandit*
Outlaw Blues

1978 *The Buddy Holly Story* (Buddy Holly biography)
Convoy (based on the C. W. McCall song)
Harper Valley P.T.A. (based on the Tom T. Hall song)
The Last Waltz (country-rock with The Band; documentary)

1979 *Every Which Way But Loose* (country soundtrack)
      Atoka (country concert documentary footage)

1980 *Urban Cowboy*
      Coal Miner's Daughter (Loretta Lynn biography)
      Smokey and the Bandit II
      Middle Age Crazy (based on the Sonny Throckmorton song)
      Electric Horseman (with Willie Nelson)
      Roadie (features country and rock performers)
      9 to 5 (starring Dolly Parton)
      The Gambler (made for TV; starring Kenny Rogers)

1981 *Honeysuckle Rose*
      Take This Job and Shove It (based on the David Allan Coe song)
      The Night the Lights Went Out in Georgia
      Any Which Way You Can (country soundtrack)
      This Is Elvis (Elvis Presley documentary)
      Hard Country (based on the Michael Murphey song)
      Heartworn Highways (documentary)
      Bronco Billy
      Stand by Your Man (made for TV; Tammy Wynette biography)
      The Long Riders (Western with Ry Cooder country soundtrack)

1982 *The Best Little Whorehouse in Texas* (starring Dolly Parton)
      Southern Comfort (country and Cajun soundtrack)
      One from the Heart (Crystal Gayle soundtrack)
      Barbarosa (starring Willie Nelson)
      Wasn't That a Time! (the Weavers documentary)
      Six Pack (starring Kenny Rogers)
      Coward of the County (made for TV; starring Kenny Rogers)
      Living Proof (made for TV; Hank Williams, Jr., biography)
      Honkytonk Man
      The Pride of Jesse Hallam (made for TV; starring Johnny Cash)
      Murder in Coweta County (made for TV; starring Johnny Cash)
      Out of the Ice (made for TV; with Willie Nelson)
      Murder in Music City (made for TV)
      Country Gold (made for TV)

1983 *Eddie Macon's Run* (starring John Schneider)
      Tender Mercies
      Smokey and the Bandit III
      The Gambler, Part II (made for TV; starring Kenny Rogers)
      Tough Enough

Hank Williams: The Show He Never Gave (Canadian)

1984   *Rhinestone*
       Songwriter
       Stick (featuring Tammy Wynette)
       Places in the Heart (Doc Watson soundtrack)
       Burning Rage (made for TV, starring Barbara Mandrell)
       Cannonball II
       The Baron (made for TV, starring Johnny Cash)

THE ELVIS PRESLEY MUSICALS

1956   *Love Me Tender*

1957   *Loving You*
       Jailhouse Rock

1958   *King Creole*

1960   *G.I. Blues*
       Flaming Star

1961   *Blue Hawaii*

1962   *Follow That Dream*
       Kid Galahad
       Girls! Girls! Girls!

1963   *It Happened at the World's Fair*
       Fun in Acapulco

1964   *Kissin' Cousins*
       Viva Las Vegas
       Roustabout
       Tickle Me

1965   *Girl Happy*
       Harum Scarum
       Paradise—Hawaiian Style

1966   *Frankie and Johnny*
       Spinout
       Easy Come, Easy Go

1967   *Double Trouble*
       Clambake

1968   *Stay Away, Joe*
       Speedway
       Live a Little, Love a Little

1969   *Charro!*
       Change of Habit
       The Trouble with Girls

APPENDIX: BUYING RECORDS

MAIL-ORDER RECORD SOURCES

Sources marked with an asterisk are those that carry a particularly wide selection of records released by the smaller country specialty labels; the other sources are all well worth checking, however.

Bear Family Records*
2871 Harmenhausen
Hohe Seite
West Germany

Tom Bradshaw
P.O. Box 931
Concord, CA 94522

Cattle Records
Reimar Binge
Moenchstockheim
Rosenstrasse 12
D-8722 Sulzheim, West Germany

Club of Spade Records
Box 1995
Studio City, CA 93065

CMH Records
P.O. Box 39439
Los Angeles, CA 90039

County Sales*
P.O. Box 191
Floyd, VA 24091

Cowboy Carl Records
Box 116
Park Forest, IL 60466

Down Home Music, Inc.*
10341 San Pablo Avenue
El Cerrito, CA 94530

Ken Griffis
4753 Irvine Avenue
North Hollywood, CA 91602

Keith Kolby
6604 Chapel Lane
Fort Worth, TX 76135

Midland Records
9535 Midland
Overland, MO 63114

Mutual Music
254 Scott Street
San Francisco, CA 94117

Uncle Jim O'Neal
Box AK CSR 27
Arcadia, CA 91006

PSG Products
Box 931
Concord, CA 94522

Rambler Records
254 Scott Street
San Francisco, CA 94117

Record Depot
P.O. Box 3057
Roanoke, VA 24015

Ridge Runner Records
Richey Records
P.O. Box 12937
Fort Worth, TX 76121

Roundup Records*
P.O. Box 154
East Cambridge, MA 02140

Shasta Records
Box 655
Simi, CA 93065

Time-Life Records
541 North Fairbanks Court
Chicago, IL 60611

Ernest Tubb Record Shop Mail Orders
P.O. Box 500
Nashville, TN 37203

RECORD COMPANIES

ADELPHI RECORDS
P.O. Box 288
Silver Springs, MD

ARHOOLIE RECORDS
10341 San Pablo Avenue
El Cerrito, CA 94530

ATLANTIC RECORDS
1841 Broadway
New York, NY 10023

BEAR FAMILY RECORDS
2871 Harmenhausen
Hohe Seite
West Germany

CACHET RECORDS
6535 Wilshire Boulevard
Suite 700
Los Angeles, CA 90069

CAPITOL RECORDS
Hollywood & Vine Streets
Hollywood, CA

CMH RECORDS
P.O. Box 39439
Los Angeles, CA 90039

COLUMBIA RECORDS
34 Music Square East
Nashville, TN 37203

COLUMBIA SPECIAL PRODUCTS
51 West 52nd Street
New York, NY 10019

COUNTY RECORDS
P.O. Box 191
Floyd, VA 24091

D RECORDS
% Big Star Distributing Corporation
4830 Lakawanna, Suite 121
Dallas, TX 75247

DAVIS UNLIMITED RECORDS
Route 7 Box 205A
Clarksville, TN 37040

ELEKTRA RECORDS
see WARNER BROS. RECORDS

EPIC RECORDS
see COLUMBIA RECORDS

FLYING FISH RECORDS
1304 W. Schubert
Chicago, IL 60614

FOLKWAYS RECORDS
43 West 61st Street
New York, NY 10023

GLENDALE RECORDS
731 West Wilson
Glendale, CA 91203

HERITAGE RECORDS
Rt. 3, Box 278
Galax, VA 24333

HILLTOP RECORDS
see PICKWICK RECORDS

JEMF RECORDS
John Edwards Memorial Foundation
University of North Carolina
Chapel Hill, NC 27514

JUNE APPAL RECORDINGS
P.O. Box 743-B
Whitesburg, KY 41858

LIBERTY RECORDS
see CAPITOL RECORDS

LIBRARY OF CONGRESS RECORDS
Recorded Sound Section
Music Division
Library of Congress
Washington, DC 20540

MCA RECORDS
27 Music Square East
Nashville, TN 37203

MERCURY RECORDS
Polygram
810 Seventh Avenue
New York, NY 10019

MGM RECORDS
see MERCURY RECORDS

MIDLAND RECORDS
9535 Midland
Overland, MO 63114

MONUMENT RECORDS
21 Music Square East
Nashville, TN 37203

OLD HOMESTEAD RECORDS
Box 100
Brighton, MI 48116

OLD TIMEY RECORDS
see ARHOOLIE RECORDS

PACIFIC ARTS RECORDS
P.O. Box 5547
Carmel, CA 93921

PHILO RECORDS
The Barn
North Ferrisburg, VT 05473

PICKWICK RECORDS
7500 Excelsior Boulevard
Minneapolis, MN 55426

PLANTATION RECORDS
see SUN RECORDS

PLAYBOY RECORDS
see COLUMBIA RECORDS

RCA RECORDS
30 Music Square West
Nashville, TN 37203

REBEL RECORDS
Box 191
Floyd, VA 24091

REPRISE RECORDS
see WARNER BROS. RECORDS

REVONAH RECORDS
Box 217
Ferndale, NY 12734

RIDGE RUNNER RECORDS
P.O. Box 12937
Fort Worth, TX 76116

ROUNDER RECORDS
186 Willow Avenue
Somerville, MA 02144

SIRE RECORDS
see WARNER BROS. RECORDS

SMASH RECORDS
see MERCURY RECORDS

SOLID SMOKE RECORDS
P.O. Box 22372
San Francisco, CA 94122

SONYATONE RECORDS
Department GW
P.O. Box 567
Santa Barbara, CA 93102

STARDAY RECORDS
Gusto Inc.
P.O. Box 60306
Nashville, TN 37206

STRING RECORDS
% TOPIC RECORDS LTD.
27 Nassington Road
London NW3 2TX
England

SUGAR HILL RECORDS
P.O. Box 4040
Duke Station
Durham, NC 27706

SUN RECORDS
3106 Belmont Boulevard
Nashville, TN 37212

UNITED ARTISTS RECORDS
see CAPITOL RECORDS

VANGUARD RECORDS
71 West 23rd Street
New York, NY 10010

VETCO RECORDS
5825 Vine Street
Cincinnati, OH 45216

VOCALION
see MCA RECORDS

VOYAGER RECORDS
424 35th Avenue
Seattle, WA 98122

WARNER BROS. RECORDS
3300 Warner Boulevard
Burbank, CA 91510

WESTERN RECORDS
P.O. Box 16005
San Francisco, CA 94116

The annual special country music issues of *Billboard* and *Cashbox* magazines will prove useful for updating this list, as will the specialized country, bluegrass, and instrument publications listed elsewhere in this book.

SOURCES OF OLD AND OUT-OF-PRINT RECORDS

Allstar Record Shop
2012 24th Avenue
Meridian, MS 39301

Ray Avery, Rare Records
P.O. Box 10518
417 East Broadway
Glendale, CA 91209

BRI Records
Blue Ridge Institute
Ferrum College
Ferrum, VA 24088

Don Cleary
P.O. Box 16265
Fort Lauderdale, FL 33318

Country Music Foundation
Acquisitions Librarian
4 Music Square East
Nashville, TN 37203

Country Turtle Records
Box 417
Cathedral Station
New York, NY 10025

County Records
P.O. Box 191
Floyd, VA 24091

"Disc Collector" Publications
Box 169
Cheswold, DE 19936

DISContinued
444 South Victory
Burbank, CA 91502

L. R. Docks
P.O. Box 13685
San Antonio, TX 78213

Folkways Records
43 West 61st Street
New York, NY 10023

R. E. M. Gottlieb
"Records for Collectors"
2008 Dutton Avenue
Waco, TX 76703

Jim Hadfield
River Road, R.D. 1
Richville, NY 13681

Lawrence Brothers Record Shop
413 Broadway
Nashville, TN 37203

Library of Congress Records
Recorded Sound Section
Music Division
Library of Congress
Washington, DC 20540

Marantha Records
12592 Warwick Boulevard
Newport News, VA 23606

Gerald F. Mills
P.O. Box 1962
San Pedro, CA 90733

Craig Moerer
Box 13247
Portland, OR 97213

Morning Star Records
Dalebrook Park
Ho-Ho-Kus, NJ 07423

Old Homestead Records
Box 100
Brighton, MI 48116

Old Timey Records
Arhoolie Records
10341 San Pablo Avenue
El Cerrito, CA 94530

Uncle Jim O'Neal
Box A5M-CM
Arcadia, CA 91006

Rounder Records
186 Willow Avenue
Somerville, MA 02144

Theo's,
Dept. F
P.O. Box 7511
Van Nuys, CA 91406

Tradition Records
% Everest Records
2020 Avenue of the Stars
Concourse Level
Century City, CA 90867

Ernest Tubb Record Shop Mail Orders
P.O. Box 500
Nashville, TN 37202

Les Zeiger
Andover J253
West Palm Beach, FL 33409

INDEX